Urban Labor Markets in Sub-Saharan Africa

Urban Labor Markets in Sub-Saharan Africa

Philippe De Vreyer and François Roubaud, Editors

A copublication of Agence Française de Développement and the World Bank

ISBN (paper): 978-0-8213-9781-7
ISBN (electronic): 978-0-8213-9782-4
DOI: 10.1596/978-0-8213-9781-7

Cover image: ©Michelle Saint-Léger, IRD, 2013.
Cover design: Debra Naylor, Naylor Design, Inc.

Library of Congress Cataloging-in-Publication Data
Vreyer, Philippe De.
    Urban labor markets in sub-Saharan Africa/Philippe De Vreyer and François Roubaud.
       p. cm.
    Includes bibliographical references and index.
    ISBN 978-0-8213-9781-7 — ISBN 978-0-8213-9782-4 (electronic)
    1. Labor market—Africa, Sub-Saharan. 2. Africa, Sub-Saharan—Economic conditions. 3. City dwellers—Employment—Africa, Sub-Saharan. I. Roubaud, François. II. World Bank. III. Title.
    HD5837.A6V74 2013
    331.120967—dc23

2012050217

The French translation of this book is copublished by Agence Française de Développement and Institut de Recherche pour le Développement (IRD). The IRD, a French public research institute emphasizing interdisciplinarity, has focused its research for more than 65 years on the relationship between man and its environment in Africa, Asia, Latin America, the Mediterranean, and the French tropical overseas territories. Its research, training, and innovation activities are intended to contribute to the social, economic, and cultural development of southern countries. For further information: www.editions.ird.fr.

Africa Development Forum Series

The **Africa Development Forum Series** was created in 2009 to focus on issues of significant relevance to Sub-Saharan Africa's social and economic development. Its aim is both to record the state of the art on a specific topic and to contribute to ongoing local, regional, and global policy debates. It is designed specifically to provide practitioners, scholars, and students with the most up-to-date research results while highlighting the promise, challenges, and opportunities that exist on the continent.

The series is sponsored by the Agence Française de Développement and the World Bank. The manuscripts chosen for publication represent the highest quality in each institution and have been selected for their relevance to the development agenda. Working together with a shared sense of mission and interdisciplinary purpose, the two institutions are committed to a common search for new insights and new ways of analyzing the development realities of the Sub-Saharan Africa region.

Advisory Committee Members

Agence Française de Développement
Rémi Genevey, Director of Strategy
Alain Henry, Director of Research

World Bank
Shantayanan Devarajan, Chief Economist, Africa Region
Santiago Pombo-Bejarano, Editor-in-Chief, Office of the Publisher

Sub-Saharan Africa with featured urban areas

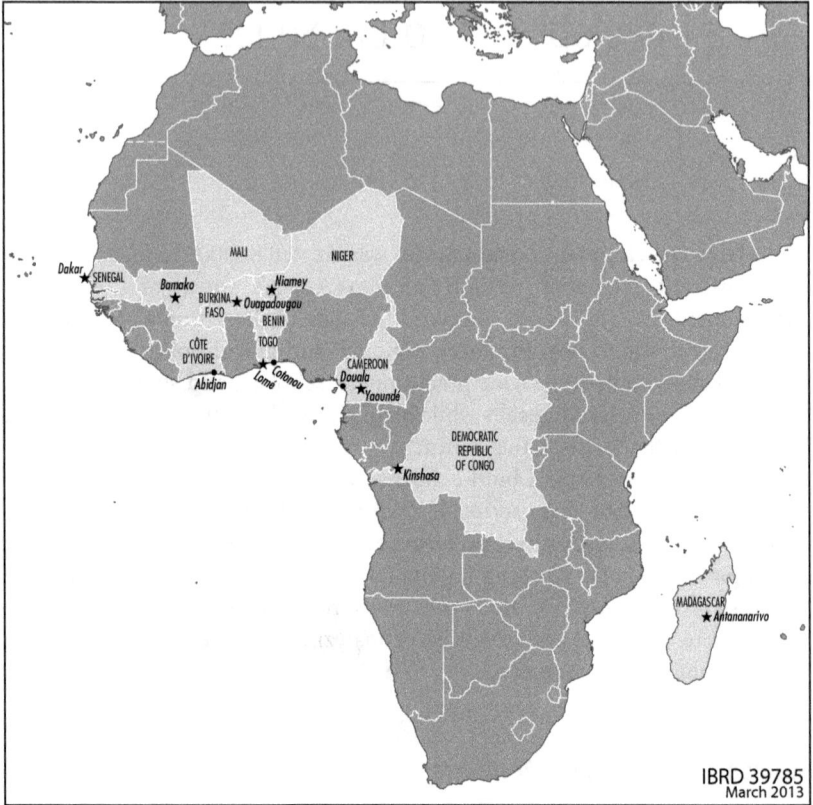

IBRD 39785
March 2013

Titles in the Africa Development Forum Series

Africa's Infrastructure: A Time for Transformation (2010) edited by Vivien Foster and Cecilia Briceño-Garmendia

Gender Disparities in Africa's Labor Market (2010) edited by Jorge Saba Arbache, Alexandre Kolev, and Ewa Filipiak

Challenges for African Agriculture (2010) edited by Jean-Claude Deveze

Contemporary Migration to South Africa: A Regional Development Issue (2011) edited by Aurelia Segatti and Loren Landau

Light Manufacturing in Africa: Targeted Policies to Enhance Private Investment and Create Jobs (2012) by Hinh T. Dinh, Vincent Palmade, Vandana Chandra, and Frances Cossar

Informal Sector in Francophone Africa: Firm Size, Productivity, and Institutions (2012) by Nancy Benjamin and Ahmadou Aly Mbaye

Financing Africa's Cities: The Imperative of Local Investment (2012) by Thierry Paulais

Structural Transformation and Rural Change Revisited: Challenges for Late Developing Countries in a Globalizing World (2012) by Bruno Losch, Sandrine Fréguin-Gresh, and Eric Thomas White

The Political Economy of Decentralization in Sub-Saharan Africa: A New Implementation Model (2013) edited by Bernard Dafflon and Thierry Madiès

Empowering Women: Legal Rights and Economic Opportunities in Africa (2013) by Mary Hallward-Driemeier and Tazeen Hasan

Enterprising Women: Expanding Opportunities in Africa (2013) by Mary Hallward-Driemeier

Securing Africa's Land for Shared Prosperity: A Program to Scale Up Reforms and Investments (2013) by Frank F. K. Byamugisha

Free access to all titles in the Africa Development Forum series is available at
https://openknowledge.worldbank.org/handle/10986/2150

Contents

Foreword

By Martin Rama

Building vibrant cities is critical to the future of Sub-Saharan Africa. With the majority of the population in the continent rural, it will be difficult to make substantive inroads into poverty reduction if agricultural jobs do not become more productive. But without vibrant cities, the surplus labor from rural areas will have no serious prospect for a better life. Rural-urban migration is bound to continue. If cities do not play their part, it will remain a migration of despair rather than a migration of hope. In the absence of poles of economic dynamism, declines in rural poverty will be matched by increases in the number of urban poor.

It is difficult to single out what makes a city thrive. Some point to affordable land, others to infrastructure or the logistics connecting it to the rest of the world. But few would disagree on the importance of well-functioning labor markets. In fact, it can be argued that most of the spillovers and learning associated with economic agglomeration occur through urban labor markets. The importance of these markets is what makes this well-researched book so timely.

A well-functioning labor market is not necessarily the same as a formal labor market. In Sub-Saharan Africa, most economic activity is informal, and the public sector accounts for the lion's share of the rest. With so many people working on their own or in microenterprises, informal is normal. Many workers and economic units choose to stay below the radar of the authorities simply because it would be too costly for them to operate by the rules. And in many cases, forcing them to do so would not lead to substantial efficiency gains, even if they were to pay their share of public goods. When analyzing labor markets in Sub-Saharan Africa, it is important to come to terms with this reality, avoiding a normative view on formality and focusing instead on the way formal and informal activities coexist and interact. Such is the approach taken in this book—yet another reason why it is so welcome.

Methodology is another reason why this book is of value. In industrial countries, we have grown used to looking at labor markets from two sides, mimicking the notion of a place where supply and demand meet. We use household survey data to understand the supply side of the labor market and plant-level data to understand the demand side. Applying this methodology in developing countries, where the informality is the norm, often yields meaningless data. In fact, in places where self-employment and employment in microenterprises are the norm, the very distinction between supply and demand for labor becomes blurred.

Rather than look at plant-level data, this book builds on the pioneering 1-2-3 surveys developed over the years by Développement, Institutions et Mondialisation (DIAL). The great merit of these surveys is that they allow researchers to construct the distribution of economic activities from the household side and, once the universe has been identified, to survey a subset of those activities, regardless of whether or not they are formal. The findings in this book still rely on the household survey side of the 1-2-3 edifice, but the foundation is the right one, and the work bodes well for the continuation of the research program.

The findings themselves are of great interest. One could even argue that they are encouraging. Higher education is associated with higher earnings across all the countries studied. Ethnicity is a less important determinant of earnings than one would have feared. Not all informal activities amount to survivorship: some genuine small-scale entrepreneurs can be found among the pack. Return migrants from industrial countries do better than their peers. In all these ways, labor markets in Sub-Saharan Africa may be more efficient than is usually acknowledged. At the same time, the findings reveal the importance of inherited circumstances and networks in accessing much-coveted formal sector jobs, a hint to an economy of privilege existing alongside more efficient and anonymous markets.

Beyond its specific findings, this book provides a very good analytical model for people working on labor issues in the region. Its rigor in the use and analysis of data, its choice of econometric techniques depending on the topic at hand, and its balanced interpretation of estimation results should serve as guidance for academics and policy advisers in the region.

Despite the importance of the labor market, it is a relatively new area of work in Sub-Saharan Africa. I hope that this book will serve as inspiration to others willing to take this research agenda forward.

Martin Rama
Director of the *World Development Report 2013: Jobs*

Foreword

By Moubarack Lo

Jobs are key to all development processes. Although growth is obviously a driver, it alone cannot ensure the inclusion and sustainability that all nations should seek to guarantee their people. Policy makers therefore need to place this vital task of creating enough quality jobs high on their agenda. Failure to do so will expose their countries to the risk of crumbling social cohesion and, in turn, spiraling political instability. The poverty reduction strategies launched by most of Africa's countries cannot hope to be successful without improving labor earnings, the main (if not the only) resource of the poor.

Regrettably, these basic considerations have been largely overlooked in Africa until very recently; rare are the countries with employment policies worthy of the name. Fortunately, the times are changing. Recognition of the important role played by labor markets can be seen in a number of emblematic publications on the subject. Just two examples are the *World Development Report 2013: Jobs* and the *African Economic Outlook 2012* report on promoting youth employment, public presentation of which sparked an impassioned debate in Dakar in November 2012.

The international development community's interest in employment ties in with national concerns. Senegal has taken a step forward in its political transition with the election of President Macky Sall, whose election has raised high hopes.

It is important to mention the crucial role in this successful election played by young people, who were passed over by the previous authorities. The inability of these people—many of them with skills—to find jobs to match their abilities formed the main driving force for change in Senegal. Leaders in other countries on the continent, such as Tunisia, recognize that the youth employment issue played a key role in the political transition known as the Arab Spring.

African countries now need to define and carry out ambitious programs that promote jobs and income-generating activities. At the same time, they need to improve young people's skills by setting up vocational training centers nationwide; adapting school and university curricula to labor market needs; and assisting project initiators, especially young people and women, with credit facilities (guarantee facilities, in particular).

In view of this continental and national environment, *Urban Labor Markets in Sub-Saharan Africa* comes right on cue. Decision makers need high-quality information and analyses to diagnose problems and take effective action—precisely what this book provides. The authors draw on a series of original, representative, and perfectly comparable surveys of 11 cities in 10 countries in Sub-Saharan Africa to take the reader on a fascinating, multifarious tour of a wide range of labor market topics. The overview discusses the issues, data, and methods and briefly sums up the findings. The first chapter paints a full picture of the main characteristics of labor markets in urban Africa today and the questions raised regarding their functioning. This review, underpinned by sound empirical foundations, shatters many preconceived ideas, such as the weight and role of the informal sector and the particularities of unemployment in Africa, to name but two. The questions it raises pave the way for the following 13 chapters, each of which analyzes a specific area in detail. This far-reaching overview explores and explains an array of issues, including returns to education, segmentation, ethnic and gender discrimination, employment vulnerability and job satisfaction, the role of migration, domestic work, child labor, and social and professional mobility. The analyses in this broad-based and cohesive roundup are commendable for their quality.

The authors—all renowned experts in their fields (many of the chapters have appeared as academic papers in leading international journals)—have done their best to make the reasoning and main conclusions accessible to the lay reader. The comparative approach adopted has two advantages, in that it brings to light the structural regularities found more or less constantly from one country to the next and identifies the particularities of each national environment. There is no one Africa, but many Africas. I naturally followed Senegal's relative position among its peers with particular interest.

To my knowledge, this book is the first undertaking of its kind. As such, it fills a void. There is something in it for all levels of expertise and areas of interest. The book has given me food for thought, both generally and in terms of the huge challenge before me of how to help solve the employment equation in Senegal. I wholly subscribe to the authors' intent to avoid one-size-fits-all thinking and standard, uniform policy recommendations, to be applied across the board. The raw material the authors present forms an invaluable source of inspiration for future employment policies. I therefore suggest this book for African decision makers and the public at large, to build deeper understanding of the employment question with a view to designing suitable policies or enriching the democratic debate in our societies on a key issue that looks set to remain on our agendas for many years to come. I would also suggest that our researchers draw inspiration from this original initiative.

Moubarack Lo
Minister
Deputy Chief of Staff to the President of the Republic of Senegal

Acknowledgments

Little did we know at the start of this project that we were on an odyssey bearing more than a passing resemblance, in time and hazards, to Ulysses' journey home to his beloved Ithaca. We had our own Trojan War to wage—although thankfully not for 10 years—when we conducted the 1-2-3 surveys that served as the raw material for this book. Fortunately, we were not alone. We salute our statistician brothers in arms and unflinching allies in the preparation, promotion, production, and analysis of the first survey findings: experts from the Observatoire économique et statistique d'Afrique Subsaharienne (AFRISTAT), with a special mention for Lamine Diop, Director General when the Programme D'Appui Régional à la Statistique (PARSTAT) was launched in West Africa; managers at national statistics institutes (NSIs); and researchers in the Statistics Division of Développement, Institutions et Mondialisation (DIAL). You all know who you are. At the time, few research centers felt it was worth investing in huge data collection operations. Things have changed somewhat since, mainly as a result of the advent of impact assessment protocols, although alliances with official statistics are still held in low esteem, despite their positive capacity-building outcomes.

The idea for this book germinated in 2004. Who knows whether the chapters' authors, who sailed with us through thick and thin, would have come on board had they known the journey would be so long. We thank them for trusting us to reach our destination. We spare a thought for three crew members (Lisa Chauvet, Jean-Pierre Cling, and Gilles Spielvogel) who, for one reason or another, we failed to steer to harbor. We take our hats off to the revolving DIAL management teams, who never doubted us—or at least never said so in all these years. Others boarded at key ports of call along the way: Robert Peccoud, Director of Research at the French Development Agency (AFD), which provided the project with funding when DIAL was experiencing some serious institutional upheavals; Diane Bertrand, our trusty translator, who braved hell and high water, not only wading through the convoluted language of Molière to fashion a faithful rendition in the language of Shakespeare but also resigning herself to a rehash of her prose by her American cousins tasked with molding it to the World Bank format; our three anonymous reviewers (who shall remain nameless, as they are indeed anonymous, although certainly neither deaf nor blind); our French and English editors (Philippe Cabin, Thomas Mourier, Stephen McGroarty, and Janice Tuten) and their institutions (AFD, the Institut de Recherche pour le Développement [IRD], and the World Bank); Michelle Saint-Léger (IRD) for the cover illustration; our English copyeditor, Barbara Karni, and especially our French copyeditor, Catherine Plasse, whom we managed to talk into work-ing for us despite her visceral aversion to figures; our two foreword writers; our three prestigious endorsers; and, last but not least, Coryne Ajavon-Ecoué, DIAL's secretary, for manning the capstans.

On a more personal level, we pay tribute to our families: to our spouses for not divorcing us—although the prospect of sharing the royalties might have had something to do with that—and to our children, whom we missed grow-ing up. And why not seize the moment for a mutual, albeit modest, pat on the back? Philippe, your proverbial enthusiasm was my driving force; François, your inborn sense of moderation was my guiding light.

We offer up one last word of thanks for the hundreds of survey interviewers and especially the hundreds of thousands of households, men, and women who gave up their valuable time to answer the surveys. And spare a thought for our future readers, slightly fewer in number, but no less courageous.
Thank you all.

François Roubaud   *Philippe De Vreyer*

About the Authors

Philippe Antoine is a researcher at the Centre Population et Développement (CEPED) and the Laboratoire de Recherches sur les Transformations Economiques et Sociales (LARTES) at the Université Cheikh Anta Diop, in Dakar, Senegal. He conducted his research for this book while he was a senior research fellow at the Institut de Recherche pour le Développement (IRD) and a member of Développement, Institutions et Mondialisation (DIAL), a joint research unit of IRD and the Université Paris-Dauphine. He has conducted research on the transformation of the family and intergenerational relations in West Africa for 40 years. He holds an advanced degree in economics from the Université Paris 1 Panthéon-Sorbonne.

Muriel Barlet is an economist and statistician at the Institute of Statistics and Economic Studies in Paris (INSEE). She conducted her research for this book while she was as an associate research fellow at DIAL in Paris. She has extensive experience in applying microsimulation models to labor markets. She holds an engineering degree from the École Polytechnique in Paris.

Philippe Bocquier is a professor of demography at the Université Catholique de Louvain, in Belgium, and an associate research fellow at DIAL in Paris. He conducted his research for this book while he was a fellow at IRD. His research focuses on urban integration, internal migration, and urbanization in developing countries, especially the interrelationship between migration and health in Sub-Saharan Africa. He has extensive experience in longitudinal analysis. He holds a PhD in demography from the Université Paris 5 René Descartes.

Philippe De Vreyer is a professor of economics at the Université Paris-Dauphine and a research economist at DIAL in Paris. His research focuses on the econometric analysis of migration, poverty, and household behavior. He has extensive experience in the design, implementation, and analysis of household surveys. He holds a PhD in economics from the École des Hautes Études en Sciences Sociales in Paris.

Flore Gubert is a research fellow at IRD and a research economist at DIAL in Paris. Her research focuses mainly on migration in Africa and households' strategies for dealing with risk in the context of market imperfections. She is currently coordinating two projects on Senegalese migration. She holds a PhD in economics from the Université d'Auvergne in Clermont-Ferrand, France.

Javier Herrera is a senior research fellow at IRD and a research economist at DIAL in Paris. His research focuses on poverty dynamics, spatial poverty traps, poverty measurement, subjective well-being, labor market transitions, and vulnerability. He is currently coordinating a research project on the impact of Haiti's earthquake on household living conditions. He holds a PhD in economics from the Université Paris Ouest Nanterre.

Mathias Kuépié is a demographer and research fellow at the Centre d'Études de Populations, de Pauvreté et de Politiques Socio-Economiques (CEPS/INSTEAD), in Luxembourg, and an associate research fellow at DIAL in Paris. He works mainly on household behavior, including family dynamics, labor markets, living conditions, and schooling. He has vast experience in survey design and is deeply involved in statistical capacity-building efforts in Africa. He holds a PhD in demography from the Université Paris Ouest Nanterre.

Sébastien Merceron is a statistician at INSEE in Saint-Denis, Réunion, and an associate research fellow at DIAL in Paris. He is a specialist in survey design and management. He holds an advanced degree in statistics from the École Nationale de la Statistique et de l'Analyse de l'Information in Rennes.

Christophe J. Nordman is a research fellow at IRD and a research economist at DIAL in Paris. His research focuses on the functioning of labor markets in developing countries, particularly human capital and social networks formation, gender and earnings inequalities, the informal economy and employment vulnerability, and the labor market consequences of international migration. He holds a PhD in economics from the Université Paris 1 Panthéon-Sorbonne.

Laure Pasquier-Doumer is a research fellow at IRD and a research economist at DIAL in Hanoi. Her research focuses on social mobility and equality of opportunity in education and labor markets. She holds a PhD in economics from the Institut d'Études Politiques in Paris.

Nelly Rakoto-Tiana is an education economist at the World Bank in Madagascar, where she is the field coordinator of a project on education outcomes. She holds a PhD in economics from the Université Paris Nord.

Mireille Razafindrakoto is a senior research fellow at IRD and a research economist at DIAL in Paris. She specializes in development economics, particularly labor market, poverty, inequality, and governance issues. Between 2006 and 2011, she was the scientific coordinator of a DIAL-IRD research program in Vietnam. She holds a PhD in economics from the École des Hautes Études en Sciences Sociales in Paris.

Anne-Sophie Robilliard is a research fellow at IRD and a research economist at DIAL in Paris. She has worked extensively on the development and use of macro-micro tools for analyzing the impact of policies on poverty and income distribution. She is currently leading a research project in Dakar on the links between economic and demographic trends in Africa, with a focus on the demographic dividend and female labor market participation. She holds a PhD in economics from the Université Paris 1 Pantheon-Sorbonne.

François Roubaud is a senior research fellow at IRD and a research economist at DIAL in Paris. He is a pioneer in the implementation of household and enterprise surveys and the use of the 1-2-3 surveys to measure the informal sector in low-income countries. His research focuses on labor markets, the informal economy, governance, and the political economy of development policies. He holds a PhD in economics from the Université Paris Ouest Nanterre.

Constance Torelli is a statistician at INSEE and an associate research fellow at DIAL in Paris. She has extensive experience implementing and monitoring household and enterprise surveys. She has a special interest in employment, the informal sector, and household living conditions. She holds a master's degree in sociology and ethnology from the Université Lille 1, in Villeneuve d'Ascq, France.

Aude Vescovo is the coordinator of research, monitoring, and evaluation at the USAID/PHARE (U.S. Agency for International Development/Programme Harmonisé d'Appui au Renforcement de l'Education) Program—known as "Road to Reading"—and an associate research fellow at IRD-DIAL in Bamako, Mali. She conducted the research for this book while working as a research assistant at IRD. Her research focuses on quality factors of primary education and the improvement of teaching methods, especially in reading and writing. She holds a master's degree in theoretical and applied economics from the Paris School of Economics and an advanced degree in statistics and economics from the École Nationale de la Statistique et de l'Administration Économique in Paris.

Abbreviations

AFRISTAT	Observatoire économique et statistique d'Afrique Subsaharienne
CAP	Certificat d'aptitude professionnelle
CFA	Communauté Financière Africaine
DIAL	Développement, Institutions et Mondialisation
ECOWAS	Economic Community of West African States
FNR	National Pension Fund (Senegal)
IIA	independence of irrelevant alternatives
INSEE	Institut National de la Statistique et des Études Économiques
IPRES	Senegal Pension Insurance Institution
IRD	Institut de Recherche pour le Développement
MLE	maximum likelihood estimation
OECD	Organisation for Economic Co-operation and Development
OLS	ordinary least squares
PARSTAT	Programme d'Appui Régional à la Statistique
WAEMU	West African Economic and Monetary Union

Overview

Philippe De Vreyer and François Roubaud

The population of Sub-Saharan Africa stood at 854 million in 2010 (World Bank 2012a). Annual population growth averaged 2.5 percent, with a relatively high sustained fertility rate, fostered by the fact that two-thirds of the population is under 25. The region has the highest proportion of poor people in the world, with 47.5 percent of its population living on less than $1.25 a day, as measured in terms of purchasing power parity in 2008. It is also the only region in which the number of poor is still rising.

The eradication of extreme poverty and hunger is at the top of the list of the Millennium Development Goals (MDGs) adopted by the member states of the United Nations (UN) in September 2000. This goal comprises three targets:

1. Halve, between 1990 and 2015, the proportion of people whose income is less than $1 a day.
2. Halve, between 1990 and 2015, the proportion of people who suffer from hunger.
3. Achieve full and productive employment and decent work for all, including women and young people.

The three targets are closely linked: monetary poverty is a key factor in malnutrition and is determined in large part by access to employment. In 2007, an estimated 55 percent of working-age women and 79 percent of working-age men in Sub-Saharan African were employed (UN 2008). These rates are slightly higher than the average in developed countries (49 percent of women and 64 percent of men) and developing countries (49 percent of women and 77 percent of men). They thus suggest that lack of access to work is not the main cause of poverty in Africa.

Sub-Saharan Africa has the world's largest proportion of poor workers. In 2007, before the international financial crisis, 51 percent of employed people lived on less than $1 a day, measured in terms of purchasing power parity. The 2007 average for developing countries was 20 percent, representing a sharp drop from 1997, when it stood at 31 percent. Progress in Sub-Saharan Africa was much slower: in 1997, 56 percent of employed people lived on less than $1 a day. These figures suggest that working conditions rather than access to work are behind sustained poverty rates in Sub-Saharan Africa.

Scope and Purpose of the Book

This book contributes to knowledge on the functioning of urban labor markets in Sub-Saharan Africa by investigating a variety of questions. Which individuals lack access to employment or are employed beneath their capacities? Does education improve working conditions? What opportunities does the labor market offer to climb the social ladder? Is the lack of good-quality jobs for adults and the poverty it implies one of the reasons for the prevalence of child labor? Do women and ethnic minorities have the same access to the labor market as everyone else? How does the formal sector live alongside the informal sector? What role does migration play in the functioning of labor markets? Are there traits common to all urban labor markets in Africa, or is each country different?

This book attempts to answer these questions by studying 11 cities in 10 countries (table O.1). Eight are members of the Communauté Financière Africaine (CFA) Franc Zone, and seven belong to the West African Economic and Monetary Union (WAEMU); all 10 are French speaking. They are thus not representative of Sub-Saharan Africa.[1] However, the sample of countries is very close to the continental average, whatever the economic and social indicator considered.

Comparative studies are often based on disparate measurement instruments, which risk marring the validity of the findings.[2] This study differs from earlier studies in that it is based on a set of perfectly comparable surveys (the 1-2-3 surveys, described below).With the notable exception of a report by the International Institute for Labor Studies (Lachaud 1994), no other study presents a detailed overview of the labor market landscape in Sub-Saharan Africa. For 10–15 years, no work of this kind was conducted.[3] The study also covers a number of topics (migration, child labor, job satisfaction, discrimination, and work after retirement) in addition to the topics covered by Lachaud (unemployment, access to employment and mobility, segmentation, labor supply, and poverty). This book also draws on more and better-quality data. The Network for Labor Market Analysis in Africa (RAMTA) surveys contain only a few hundred observations per country, far fewer than the number of observations captured by the 1-2-3 surveys, which survey more than 120,000 people, including 80,000 people of working age and 6,000 unemployed and 50,000 employed workers (table O.2). In addition, the sampling plans adopted by the RAMTA surveys are arguably "quasi-random," with no updated sampling frame available. These

Table 0.1 Geographic, Demographic, and Socioeconomic Characteristics of the 10 Countries Sampled

Country	Land area (1,000 square kilometers)	Population (1,000)	Urbanization (percent)	Per capita GDP (purchasing power parity dollars)	GDP growth in 2010 (percent)	Net primary enrollment (percent)	Life expectancy (years)	Poverty headcount (percent)[a]	Country Policy and Institutional Assessment (CPIA) (1–6)[b]
Benin	111	8,850	42	1,590	3.0	94	56	16	3.5
Burkina Faso	274	16,468	20	1,250	9.2	58	55	45	3.5
Cameroon	473	19,600	58	2,270	3.2	92	51	10	2.5
Congo, Dem. Rep.	2,267	65,965	35	320	7.2	64	48	53	2.0
Côte d'Ivoire	318	19,738	50	1,810	3.0	61	55	24	2.0
Madagascar	582	20,714	30	960	1.6	79	66	81	2.5
Mali	1,220	15,370	33	1,030	4.5	62	51	50	3.5
Niger	1,267	15,512	17	720	8.8	57	54	44	3.0
Senegal	193	12,434	43	1,910	4.1	75	59	11	3.0
Togo	54	6,028	43	890	3.4	92	57	11	2.5
Average	676	20,068	37	1,275	5.0	73	55	35	3.0
Sub-Saharan Africa	491	17,780	37	1,188	5.1	75	54	47	2.7

Source: Based on data from World Bank 2011.
Note: Most data are for 2010. Last available year for net primary enrollment rate and poverty headcount are 2007–10 for most countries. Data on net primary enrollment are from 2003 for Madagascar and 2005 for the Democratic Republic of Congo. Poverty headcount data are for 2003 for Benin, 2005 for the Democratic Republic of Congo, and 2006 for Senegal and Togo.
a. The poverty headcount corresponds to the $1.25 purchasing power parity poverty line.
b. The transparency, accountability, and corruption in the public sector rating (1 = low, 6 = high) was available for 37 out of 48 countries in Sub-Saharan Africa.

Table O.2 Sample Sizes of African Cities Studied

Region/city	Number of households	Number of people	Number of working-age population (10 years and above)	Number in unemployment	Number in employment
West Africa					
Abidjan	2,494	11,352	8,682	769	4,884
Bamako	2,409	13,002	9,061	311	4,435
Cotonou	3,001	11,574	8,967	301	5,276
Dakar	2,479	19,065	14,871	907	6,313
Lomé	2,500	9,907	7,548	428	4,652
Niamey	2,500	14,577	10,141	651	4,231
Ouagadougou	2,458	13,756	10,295	928	4,914
Total	17,841	93,233	69,565	4295	34,705
Central Africa					
Douala	1,399	5,726	4,326	330	2,295
Kinshasa	2,081	12,599	9,054	572	3,251
Yaoundé	1,198	5,159	3,783	304	1,766
Total	4,678	23,484	17,163	1206	7,312
Indian Ocean					
Antananarivo	3,020	12,338	9,459	262	5,499

Sources: Based on Phase 1 of the following 1-2-3 surveys: Cameroon 2005 (Développement, Institutions et Mondialisation [DIAL] and National Statistics Institute [NSI]); Democratic Republic of Congo 2005 (DIAL and NSI); Madagascar 2001 (DIAL and Institut National de la Statistique [INSTAT]); West African Economic and Monetary Union (WAEMU) 2001/02 (Observatoire économique et statistique d'Afrique Subsaharienne [AFRISTAT], DIAL, and NSI).

shortcomings—attributable to the pilot nature of the operation—undermine its analytical potential. Although the 1-2-3 surveys used here focus solely on the main cities, their scope is broader than most other household surveys, which have much smaller sample sizes (generally a few thousand observations for the entire country).

This book makes use of only a small fraction of the data in the 1-2-3 surveys. Although a number of surveys have broad coverage (national coverage in Cameroon and the Democratic Republic of Congo, all major urban centers in Madagascar), coverage here is restricted to the main cities, for several reasons. First, the editors believed that it was preferable to achieve homogeneity across countries by choosing the surveys' highest common denominator (in terms of geographical coverage). Second, rural labor markets were excluded, for theoretical reasons. The questions and analytical instruments used to study peasant farmers in rural Africa are very different from those used in urban settings. Third, the time dimension of existing surveys was not used, either in repeated cross–sections or panel data. Fourth, the study was deliberately restricted to Phase 1 of the 1-2-3 survey, which is most closely associated with the labor market.

Two main factors explain the lack of a comparable study to date. The first is the dearth of data. The second is the change in policy focus by the development community.

The Dearth of Meaningful Data

Although employment is the main source of income for the poor, knowledge of the workings of African labor markets is spotty, giving rise to a number of preconceived—and often mistaken—ideas. Despite the universally recognized role of employment as a driver of macroeconomic growth and poverty reduction, information on African labor markets remains sketchy. Many research projects launched on the subject in the last three decades have run into this wall and been unable to produce significant findings. For example, of the 25 chapters in *Labor Markets and Economic Development* (Kanbur and Svejnar 2009), which presents a good overview of the subject, only three concern Sub-Saharan Africa (excluding South Africa).[4] Moreover, none of the three chapters is based on labor force surveys, the main source of data in this field in the rest of the world. Too often, labor market studies cover a few hundred formal businesses (concentrated mainly in a few English-speaking African countries), which are themselves nonrepresentative. This type of study is unsatisfactory given that the (nonagricultural) informal sector represents 50–80 percent of urban employment, agricultural (and informal sector) employment is the most important type of employment in rural areas, and employment in the formal sector accounts for just a small proportion of total employment in Sub-Saharan Africa.

The Regional Program on Enterprise Development (RPED) project and its avatars are symptomatic of this problem. Launched by the World Bank in a dozen Sub-Saharan African countries in the early 1990s, the project consists of matched (employer/employee) multiround surveys of a few hundred businesses in the formal manufacturing sector (Bigsten and Söderbom 2005). The project has produced some interesting and original results (Fafchamps and Söderbom 2006; Van Biesebroeck 2007; Nordman and Wolff 2009, to cite but a few recent publications). The problem emerges when these findings are used to shed light on the functioning of the labor market as a whole and to determine public policies (Mazumdar and Mazaheri 2002).

The formal manufacturing sector represents just 1–2 percent of total national employment in most Sub-Saharan African countries. Even in the main cities, formal sector industrial employment (including employment in the public sector) accounts for less than 5 percent of total employment (table O.3). In contrast, the informal sector accounts for more than two-thirds of industrial jobs (up to 78 percent in West Africa). Contrary to popular belief, industry in

Table 0.3 Share of Formal Manufacturing Employment in Selected African Cities
(percent)

Region/city	Formal industrial employment in total employment	Informal sector employment in total industrial employment	Wage informal sector employment in total wage employment
West Africa			
Abidjan	6.1	68.7	42.7
Bamako	3.7	81.7	35.1
Cotonou	2.2	87.7	31.2
Dakar	6.2	77.9	43.9
Lomé	2.7	86.9	29.0
Niamey	3.6	86.3	29.0
Ouagadougou	4.8	74.5	32.1
WAEMU countries	4.9	77.6	39.5
Central Africa			
Douala	11.0	50.9	24.2
Kinshasa	4.5	69.7	25.6
Yaoundé	7.6	59.6	25.2
WAEMU countries	6.9	61.0	25.1
Indian Ocean			
Antananarivo	18.4	46.3	22.4

Sources: Based on Phase 1 of the 1-2-3 surveys of selected countries (see table O.1 for details).

Sub-Saharan Africa is essentially an informal sector affair. Even among wage earners, the informal sector accounts for more than a quarter of employment (40 percent in West Africa). The rate of wage employment is therefore not a good indicator for capturing formal sector jobs. Comprehensive coverage of the informal sector is vital for understanding urban labor markets in Sub-Saharan Africa.

The annual report on employment produced by the International Labour Organization (ILO 2010a, b) shows just how poor the statistics on employment in Sub-Saharan Africa are: for the 1991–2008 period, only 11 of 45 countries were able to estimate the national unemployment rate for at least three years, and 16 countries had no employment statistics at all for the period. No other developing region has such a severe lack of data.

Labor force surveys are a key to understanding households' economic activities in most countries, mainly in developed countries but also in the developing countries and emerging economies of Latin America, Asia, and North Africa. Sub-Saharan African countries have not adopted this tool (a notable exception is South Africa), for a variety of reasons (Roubaud 1994; Rakotomanana, Ramilison, and Roubaud 2003; Razafindrakoto and Roubaud 2003; Brilleau, Ouedraogo, and Roubaud 2005; Razafindrakoto, Roubaud, and Torelli 2009).

One is the crowding-out effect triggered by household surveys of living conditions (such as the Living Standards Measurement Study surveys promoted by the World Bank), which occurs when the financial and human resources of national statistics institutes are thin on the ground.

In addition to the dearth of statistical tools, there are conceptual problems caused by the particularities of developing economies' labor markets. Labor markets in poor countries, especially in Sub-Saharan Africa, differ from developed countries' labor markets in terms of their small proportion of wage employment and large proportion of self-employment. These markets are also characterized by apparent segmentation between a formal sector, comprising "modern" businesses known to the public authorities, and an informal sector, comprising "traditional" businesses operating outside of labor law, business law, taxation, and so forth. In addition, worker protection is weak: where unemployment insurance does exist (in a tiny minority of some of the richest countries in Africa), it is reserved for a small proportion of the population working in the formal sector. Few workers pay into a pension or are protected in the event of illness. Public employment agencies are underdeveloped, and the public is largely oblivious to them where they do exist. Job-seekers generally use their families and social networks to find work.

The informal sector's lack of respect for regulations has created some confusion between the informal sector and inactivity, blurring the boundary between being in and out of the labor force and partially invalidating the notion of unemployment as defined by the ILO. Only 35 percent of employed workers in the seven French-speaking countries of WAEMU were wage earners in the early 2000s, according to the 1-2-3 surveys (described below). The other 65 percent were independent workers who had created their own jobs (as employers or self-account workers) or contributing family workers. More often than not, then, finding a job in Africa is a matter of drawing on an informal network to build the information and capital needed to start up a small service or trade without a shop. The strong tendency in Africa to employ family members means that a significant proportion of employed workers are unpaid contributing family workers, who are hard to classify in the usual way. Another complicating factor is that work in rural areas is characterized by large seasonal fluctuations, which means that the seven-day reference period generally used to define work is not relevant.

The measurement of remuneration is also no easy matter. People who work in the informal sector operate in production units that do not keep accounts. Trying to capture their earnings by asking them how much they earned in the past 30 days will therefore probably not yield reliable information, because the notions of value added and intermediate inputs are hard to define and measure in the case of informal production units. In addition, informal production units experience large business fluctuations, making annual extrapolation of income measured over a month risky. For all these reasons, understanding employment in Sub-Saharan Africa calls for the development of a special statistical tool that can home in on the particularities of labor markets on the subcontinent.

Changes in Policy Focus by the Development Community

The lack of data is not the only factor explaining the small number of studies on African labor markets. A second factor is the loss of interest by the development community (researchers and decision makers), which turned to new issues at the beginning of the 2000s.

Beginning in the late 1980s, much was written about structural adjustment. During this period, the catalyst behind the focus on labor issues was the *World Development Report 1995: Workers in an Integrating World*, which examined whether labor markets were too rigid (World Bank 1995). Markets needed to be liberalized, the argument went, by making labor laws (hiring and firing procedures, minimum wages, social security, and so forth) more flexible. The pre-1994 devaluation franc zone countries were viewed as bogeymen (Rama 2000).

Labor markets were liberalized, but the expected effects—upturns in growth in formal employment and wages—did not materialize (Kingdon, Sandefur, and Teal 2006). African labor markets, scholars concluded, were not so rigid after all, and labor regulations were not binding constraints (Teal 2000; AfDB and others 2012). At the time, a few unorthodox economists, in association with the major UN agencies, tried to sound the alarm about the devastating effects of structural adjustment and the need for social adjustment (Rodgers 1989; Standing and Tokman 1991), as a local version applied to labor markets of the "adjustment with a human face" advocated by Cornia, Jolly, and Stewart (1987).

At the end of the 1990s, when the structural adjustment rhetoric fizzled out, the emphasis shifted from the labor market to poverty, and both international and national development policies focused on poverty reduction (Cling, Razafindrakoto, and Roubaud 2003). Rare were the Poverty Reduction Strategy Papers (PRSPs)—the framework in which all national policies (general or specific) were supposed to be embedded—that mentioned specific employment policies.

Only at the end of the 2000s were the virtues of efficient labor markets at reducing poverty rediscovered. National employment policies were put in place in some countries, generally without a suitable system to evaluate their impact.

The international financial crisis of 2008–09, with its disastrous effects on employment in the developed countries, has been a catalyst for putting labor markets back at the top of the development agenda. At the international level, the *World Development Report 2013: Jobs* (World Bank 2012b) and the thematic chapter of the *African Economic Outlook 2012* on youth employment (AfDB and others 2012) are important initiatives. There has not, however, been a massive resurgence of studies on employment in Africa, mainly because of the lack of data.

The 1-2-3 Surveys: A Tool for Understanding Labor Markets in Africa

The contributors to this book use a unique series of identical—thus perfectly comparable—1-2-3 surveys conducted simultaneously in the main cities of seven West African countries and a few other countries (Cameroon, the Democratic Republic of Congo, and Madagascar) in the first half of the 2000s (box O.1). They present original, innovative findings on labor markets using best-practice statistical and econometric methods.

Each chapter begins with a detailed presentation of the descriptive statistics used to elucidate a particular aspect of labor market functioning. Comparisons across locales are conducted. The descriptive sections are followed by in-depth analyses of a broad spectrum of issues, ranging from segmentation to job satisfaction.

Phase 1 is specially designed to measure the informal sector and employment. A series of questions identifies people in the informal sector. The questions cover all the criteria contained in the international definition (the number of people employed in the business, the different types of registration, and the type of accounts for self-employed workers). This information is collected for

BOX 0.1

What Is a 1-2-3 Survey?

The 1-2-3 survey is based on the survey grafting principle. It nests three surveys targeting different statistical populations: individuals, production units, and households. The survey is based on the principle of a mixed (household/business) modular survey.

Phase 1—an augmented labor force survey—is a survey of household and individual employment, unemployment, and working conditions. It documents and analyzes labor market functioning and serves as a filter for Phase 2, in which a representative sample of the heads of the informal production units identified in Phase 1 are interviewed. The Phase 2 survey seeks to measure the main economic and productive characteristics of the production units (production, value added, investment, and financing); the main business development problems encountered; and the kind of support informal sector entrepreneurs want from the public authorities. (Given the characteristics of Phase 2, the survey can also be said to be an employer/employee matched survey.) In Phase 3, a survey on income and expenditure is conducted on a subsample of households selected from Phase 1 to estimate the weight of the formal and informal sectors in household consumption by product and household type. Phase 3 also estimates household standards of living and monetary poverty based on income or expenditure.

both the main job and the second job, making the operational definition of the informal sector extremely flexible, as it can vary depending on the aim of each study (national definition, international comparison, or research). Information can be produced on total employment in the informal sector and on the number of informal production units using the status in employment variable. The number of informal production units is vital for the selection of a representative sample of informal production units for Phase 2.

Use of this survey means that for the first time ever, informal sector employment and its characteristics can be described on a basis that is compatible with the ILO's international recommendations (ILO 1993). Throughout this book, the informal sector is defined as including all unincorporated enterprises (household businesses) that are not registered or do not keep formal accounts. Phase 1 provides all the information required to be disaggregated by the institutional sector.

Phase 1 is also a suitable instrument for measuring informal employment (corresponding to unprotected jobs), as defined by the ILO (2003). In addition to employment in the informal sector, the questionnaire also measures informal employment in the formal sector, using a set of questions on the type of job protection (type of employment contract, payslip, and benefits). The Phase 1 questionnaire allows for a certain amount of flexibility in terms of the informality criteria to be selected in keeping with international recommendations.

Although the focus is on informal employment and the informal sector, Phase 1 also generates classic indicators such as statistics on employment, unemployment, and underemployment. These indicators, especially open unemployment, do not properly measure tensions in African labor markets, however (see chapters 1 and 2).

Phase 1 collects a wide range of information. It is a good instrument for in-depth analysis of earnings and returns to human capital (education and experience); on-the-job training; gender and ethnic discrimination; labor market segmentation; migration; intergenerational mobility; job quality (hours worked, income, bonuses, social security, and so forth); job satisfaction; interaction and neighborhood effects; and other characteristics of the informal markets.

Phase 1 has several limitations, however. First, to keep the length of the questionnaire reasonable, it studies few subjects in detail. For example, only a small set of information can usually be collected on the previous job, parents' job, activities other than the main job and second job, and the income of inactive people. In addition, the choice of a reference period for the questions on employment (generally the previous week, in keeping with international standards) is incompatible with the seasonal nature of certain activities (such as agricultural activities). This information is especially important when households combine informal and agricultural activities.

Second, dependent workers (employees, contributing family workers, and apprentices) may not know precisely what the legal status of the business they are working for is. This problem is serious if the estimation of manpower in the informal sector is based solely on Phase 1. However, the estimate derived from Phase 1 may be corroborated by Phase 2, which directly generates the number of informal workers in each establishment.[5]

Third, measuring earnings in household surveys is a well-known problem: reluctance to declare one's remuneration (especially at the top of the earnings distribution) and unavailability of book accounts or payslips (especially for informal workers) usually generate measurement errors and create downward biases.

Given these shortcomings, special care was taken to capture income in Phase 1. Labor earnings are associated with each remunerated job. For wage workers, the survey captures their current monthly wage as all nonwage components of remuneration (bonuses, public holidays, social benefits, and so forth, in cash or in kind). Unlike usual labor force surveys, Phase 1 captures the earnings of self-employed workers, which correspond to their disposable income (before taxation). National accountants used to call this income *mixed income*, because it includes returns to both capital and labor. For survey respondents who do not want to declare (or do not know) their precise earnings, a complementary question asks for brackets of detailed minimum wage ranges. Measurement errors may remain despite these procedures, but robustness checks can be performed using Phase 2 data.

Like all labor force surveys, Phase 1 authorizes the use of proxy respondents. Many researchers believe that information obtained in this way is less accurate than information obtained by other means (Blair, Menon, and Bickart 2004; Bardasi and others 2010). For this reason, Phase 1 guidelines recommend avoiding proxy respondent answers whenever possible, in order to limit potential bias. In West Africa, 82 percent of individual interviews are self-response; 75 percent of the proxy respondents are either the household head or his or her spouse (Amegashie and others 2005). These indicators are even higher in Madagascar, where 90 percent of individual interviews are self-response and 82 percent are either the household head or his or her spouse (Rakotomanana, Ramilison, and Roubaud 2003).

This book uses, but does not exhaust, the analytical potential of Phase 1 of the 1-2-3 survey. It concentrates on the surveys conducted in the main cities of seven West African countries (Abidjan, Bamako, Cotonou, Dakar, Lomé, Niamey, and Ouagadougou) in 2001/02 (map 0.1). Some chapters also cover surveys of Antananarivo, Madagascar (2001 and 2004); Douala and Yaoundé, Cameroon (2005); and Kinshasa, Democratic Republic of Congo (2005).

Map O.1 Sites of 1-2-3 Surveys Conducted in Africa

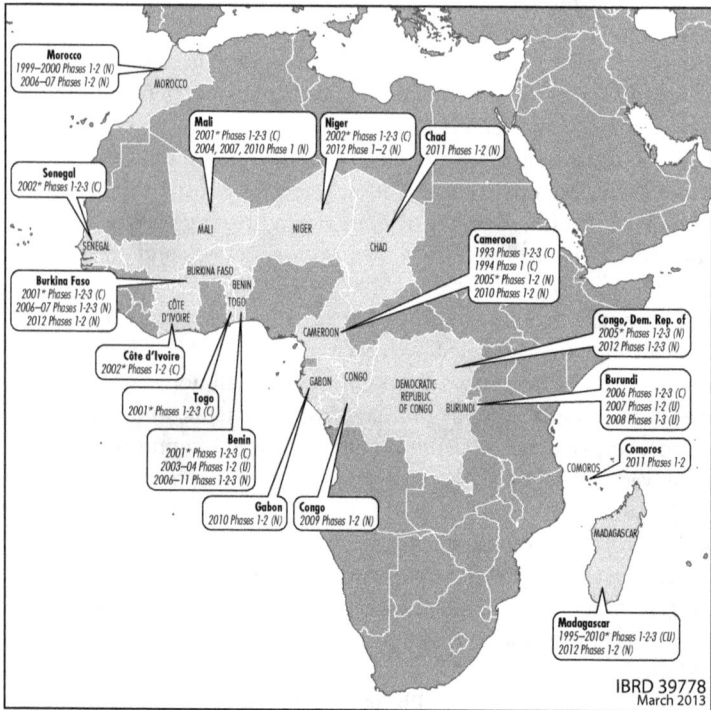

Morocco
1999–2000 Phases 1-2 (N)
2006–07 Phases 1-2 (N)

MOROCCO

Mali
2001* Phases 1-2-3 (C)
2004, 2007, 2010 Phase 1 (N)

Niger
2002* Phases 1-2-3 (C)
2012 Phase 1–2 (N)

Chad
2011 Phases 1-2 (N)

Senegal
2002* Phases 1-2-3 (C)

Cameroon
1993 Phases 1-2-3 (C)
1994 Phase 1 (C)
2005* Phases 1-2 (N)
2010 Phases 1-2 (N)

Burkina Faso
2001* Phases 1-2-3 (C)
2006–07 Phases 1-2-3 (N)
2012 Phases 1-2 (N)

Congo, Dem. Rep. of
2005* Phases 1-2-3 (N)
2012 Phases 1-2-3 (N)

Côte d'Ivoire
2002* Phases 1-2 (C)

Burundi
2006 Phases 1-2-3 (C)
2007 Phases 1-2 (U)
2008 Phases 1-3 (U)

Togo
2001* Phases 1-2-3 (C)

Comoros
2011 Phases 1-2

Benin
2001* Phases 1-2-3 (C)
2003–04 Phases 1-2 (U)
2006–11 Phases 1-2-3 (N)

Gabon
2010 Phases 1-2 (N)

Congo
2009 Phases 1-2 (N)

Madagascar
1995–2010* Phases 1-2-3 (CU)
2012 Phases 1-2 (N)

MALI   NIGER   CHAD   SENEGAL   BURKINA FASO   BENIN   CÔTE D'IVOIRE   TOGO   CAMEROON   GABON   CONGO   DEMOCRATIC REPUBLIC OF CONGO   BURUNDI   COMOROS   MADAGASCAR

IBRD 39778
March 2013

Note: *Surveys used in this book. C = capital city; N = national; U = urban center.

A Brief Survey of Labor Market Theories Applied to Development

This book is about the remuneration, job quality, and allocation of labor across sectors in low-income economies and across economies as a whole—issues that lie at the heart of the earliest models of economic development. The theoretical apparatus of development economics includes a number of key models and assumptions that are concerned with labor market functioning and the movements of labor across sectors. This section briefly reviews these models in order to set up the theoretical framework that is common to all of the chapters and to describe the methodology adopted.

The seminal work of Arthur Lewis (1954) places emphasis on the migration of labor from the agricultural to the industrial sector as a condition for output growth. This model stands as a milestone in the theoretical development economics literature, because it is the first to offer a representation of the functioning of a "dual" economy. Dual economy models are a subclass of two-sector models of economic growth (Kanbur and McIntosh 1987). They are intended to capture the main features of developing economies in order to enable better analysis of development paths and policies. What distinguishes dual economy models from others is not that they are two-sector models but that there exist asymmetries between sectors in their use of factors or in the way in which factor remuneration is established.

In the Lewis model, land is used in agriculture but not in industry, and capital is used in industry but not in agriculture. Land and capital are thus perfectly immobile; equilibrium is reached by the movement of workers between the two sectors.

The second asymmetry lies in the assumption that a surplus of labor exists in agriculture that can be reallocated to industry without decreasing the amount of food produced in the economy, because the marginal productivity of labor in agriculture is zero. Wages in the agricultural sector are set according to "conventional norms" rather than marginal products.

The Lewis model assumes that the urban labor market always clears, making involuntary unemployment impossible. The model predictions are thus at odds with what is observed in urban areas of low-income countries, which are characterized by high levels of visible and disguised unemployment and a large informal sector that includes small unregistered firms and self-employed workers.

Another milestone of development economics, the Harris and Todaro (1970) migration model, explains these features by assuming that agricultural workers' decision to migrate depends on the difference between the prevalent agricultural wage and the expected urban wage, which is positively correlated with the wage level in the modern sector and negatively correlated with the unemployment rate. The model predicts an equilibrium rate of unemployment and is compatible with the existence of a large informal sector with low income levels. Like Lewis's model, the Harris and Todaro model is dual. The wage in the modern sector is assumed to be higher than the market-clearing level, because rigidities can result from labor market legislation (such as minimum wages) or from firm rational behavior (the efficient wage hypothesis [Stiglitz 1974, 1976; Akerlof 1982; Shapiro and Stiglitz 1984] is among the possible explanations). The theory of labor market segmentation was born in the early 1970s to explain the challenge of persistent poverty in the affluent society of the 1960s (Cain 1976). According to this theory, poverty could be best understood in terms of a dual labor market, in which "the poor are confined to the secondary labor market. Eliminating poverty requires that they gain access to primary employment" (Piore 1970, p. 55). Unless segmentation is removed, policies that increase the human capital of the poor are not likely to produce results.

This theory pictures the labor market divided into primary and secondary "segments." Jobs in the primary segment are supposed to be more desirable because they offer higher pay, more promotion possibilities, and better working conditions and are more stable than jobs in the secondary segment. In low-income countries, the secondary segment is often identified with the informal sector, which comprises small unregistered firms and self-employed workers, whereas the primary segment is composed of registered private firms and the public sector. Several explanations have been offered as to why such segmentation persists. Workers in the secondary labor market could be discriminated against because of their race, gender, or social class. It could also be the case that workers confined to the secondary segment develop tastes and attitudes that exacerbate their disadvantaged position (for instance, women preferring to hold part-time jobs in order to dedicate more time to caring and family duties) (Piore 1970; Doeringer and Piore 1971). Segmentation could also result from imperfect capital markets if some occupations require high levels of investment that cannot be supported by people with low initial wealth (Banerjee and Newman 1993). Capital market imperfections may also explain why the informal sector itself is sometimes dual, in the sense that some workers work in the lower tier and others work in the upper tier of the informal sector, into which entry is restricted by human capital and financial capital requirements (Fields 1990, 2010).

These theories challenge the predictions of the human capital theory, which predicts a positive relationship between educational attainment and wages (Becker 1964). The presence of discrimination in the labor market goes against the prediction that better-educated workers should receive higher wages and suggests that gender, race, or ethnicity may play prominent roles.

The job competition theory makes the assumption that the number of jobs in the primary segment is limited and that workers compete to obtain them. In this competition, employers use screening devices to hire workers based on their trainability and adaptability (Thurow 1972, 1975; Thurow and Lucas 1972). Education may be linked to higher wages and better jobs—not because it provides workers with a higher level of human capital but because it helps employers screen people with the desirable characteristics: only people with the capacities desired by firms are able and willing to acquire the signal (in other words, to get educated) (Spence 1973).

The theoretical foundations of development economics were at play in the choice of the topics treated in the 14 chapters of this book. The contributors take an agnostic view, recognizing that although education and working experience remain the principal determinants of individual earnings, disguised unemployment, segmentation, duality, and discrimination are probably key dimensions of labor markets in urban Africa (indeed, several chapters study these phenomena).

Another important assumption implicit throughout the book is the rationality of individuals—the notion that people choose where to live and where to work by maximizing their utility under constraint. Whenever necessary, the contributors account for the self-selection of individuals into activities, sectors, and markets in their econometric estimations.

The development literature is divided over the appropriateness of the "homo economicus" paradigm for studying low-income economies. The "formal" school assumes that the laws of economics apply whatever the society's level of development (Cook 1966; Schneider 1974; see Isaac 2005 for a survey). People everywhere face the same problem of maximizing gains and minimizing losses given their (scarce) resources. The "substantivist" school of Karl Polanyi (Polanyi 1957; Dalton 1967) rejects this assumption for peasant societies and societies with low levels of development, in which, they claim, people do not engage in maximizing behavior. Given that this book assumes that people are driven by some sense of maximizing behavior, it might seem that it stands on the formalist side of the controversy. In fact, it follows Becker (1962), who argues that the most important dimension in explaining individual behavior lies not in the objective function but rather in the constraints under which decisions are made. In other words, it does not really matter whether individuals are rational in the sense that they engage in maximizing behavior. What is important is the fact that it is not possible to use more resources than those that are available at the time decisions are made.

This view is not far from that of Levi-Strauss (2001), who closes the debate between substantivists and formalists by noting that between the two schools of thought

> the difference is relative, not absolute, in that one can compare the explanatory power of economic theory to a piston that moves in a cylinder that is sometimes a bit larger and sometime much larger than it. Even in the best case, the piston never perfectly adheres to the surface and lets a minimum quantity of energy escape or, in the case of economic theory, information that is lacking in order to allow a complete understanding of the society in purely economic terms (authors' translation).

This book testifies to the soundness of Levi-Strauss's view.

Overview of Main Findings

This book is divided into five parts. Part I provides a comparative analysis of urban labor markets in Sub-Saharan Africa. Composed of a single chapter, it provides a descriptive overview and presents the main stylized facts investigated throughout the book. Part II focuses on job quality and labor market conditions (unemployment and underemployment, vulnerability, job satisfaction). Part III explores the many dimensions of labor market inequalities. This multifaceted issue is examined through various lenses, including returns to education, labor market segmentation, intergenerational mobility, time-related inequality, and gender and ethnic discrimination in earnings. Part IV addresses some key coping mechanisms and private responses, with a focus on migration, child labor, and activity in old age. It examines migration from different angles. In particular, it considers for the first time the determinants of subregional migration (within West Africa) and the performance of returning migrants. Part V identifies the way forward. It stresses three promising avenues for the labor market research agenda: employment and the informal sector in relation to poverty, the microeconomic and macroeconomic dynamics of the labor market, and the impact of public policies. It also advocates for urgently addressing the data challenge.

Given the richness and complexity of the chapters, synthesizing the main results is difficult. Two lenses are adopted: a macro perspective, in which country specificities are explored, and a micro perspective, in which the heterogeneity at the level of the individual is taken into account.

The Macro Level: Labor Market Homogeneity and Heterogeneity in Africa

Determining whether labor markets are homogeneous or heterogeneous has important policy implications. If the differences between countries are marginal, policies for improving the way they function will be similar. If the differences are significant, policies will have to be tailored to local situations.

Homogeneity of urban labor markets in Africa. Urban labor markets in Africa are surprisingly homogeneous (the consistency of the results is a good indirect indicator of the quality of the surveys). Despite increases in school enrollment rates, Africa's working-age population is low skilled. The average years of schooling (seven) in the countries studied is more or less the same as the level in France in 1913; in West Africa, the average is comparable to the level in the United Kingdom in 1870 (Maddison 1995).

Unemployment rates (about 10 percent) are similar to the rates observed in developed countries (albeit at the high end of the scale). Unlike in developed countries, however, unemployment rates tend to rise with the level of education (falling off at university level only in certain countries), a feature shared by North African countries (AfDB and others 2012). This finding would appear to bear out the "luxury unemployment" hypothesis that in the absence of unemployment benefits, the very poor cannot afford to be unemployed. Underemployment, rather than unemployment, is the main adjustment variable between labor supply and demand.

One of the main features of urban labor markets in Sub-Saharan Africa is the importance of the informal sector (which employs about 70 percent of all workers) and its corollary, the low rate of wage employment (the correlation coefficient between the two indicators is –0.93, significant at the 1 percent level). Excluding agriculture, nowhere else in the world are wage employment rates as low as in Africa, no matter how far back the historical series go (Marchand and Thélot 1997). In 1851, for example, the wage employment rate was 60 percent in France—well above the less than 40 percent in the African countries covered in this book. Moreover, this gap is hugely underestimated, as the surveys cover only the main cities, where wage employment is highest. Wage employment rates in France (and in developed countries in general) quickly shot up to more than 80 percent. A similar trend has not occurred in Africa, where the particularly rapid urban transition has not been accompanied by a shift to nonagricultural wage employment and workers who enter the informal sector tend to get stuck there (although there is some nonnegligible movement between the formal and informal sectors). Labor market theories and instruments developed by labor economists for the industrial world are thus totally unsuited to analyzing Africa, even its urban areas.

Heterogeneity of urban labor markets in Africa. Urban labor markets in Sub-Saharan Africa also display a great deal of heterogeneity (figure O.1). Differences are at least as great as in the countries of the Organisation for Economic Co-operation and Development (OECD). Labor force participation rates are 43 percent in Kinshasa and 68 percent in Lomé. Observed unemployment rates are 4.4 percent in Antananarivo and 15.4 percent in Ouagadougou. Time-related underemployment rates are 9.9 percent in Yaoundé and 19.6 percent in Kinshasa, and invisible underemployment rates range from 37.1 percent, in Douala to 66.6 percent in Ouagadougou.[6] The informal sector accounts for 53 percent of jobs in Antananarivo and 81 percent in Lomé. Wage employment rates are 24 percent in Lomé and Cotonou and 53 percent in Antananarivo. Even the generally low rate of public employment for all countries (compared with developed countries)—a mark of chronic underadministration—ranges from less than 7 percent in Douala and Abidjan to 17 percent in Kinshasa and Yaoundé, indicating wide differences even within the same country. Multiple jobholding rates range from 4 percent in Dakar to 14 percent in Douala and Yaoundé. Earnings levels range from €20 a month in Kinshasa and €30 in Lomé to €110 in Abidjan and Yaoundé. The formal/informal earnings gap also differs widely across cities, with a ratio in favor of the formal sector of 1.8 times in Antananarivo and Kinshasa and 4.2 in Abidjan and Ouagadougou. Gini coefficients range from 0.53 in Antananarivo to 0.62 in Abidjan, Bamako, Cotonou, and Kinshasa and 0.64 in Ouagadougou. The economic policy implications are clear: even in countries arguably as comparable as the ones examined here, a one-size-fits-all solution is not going to work.

Figure O.1 Key Urban Labor Market Indicators in Sub-Saharan African and OECD Countries

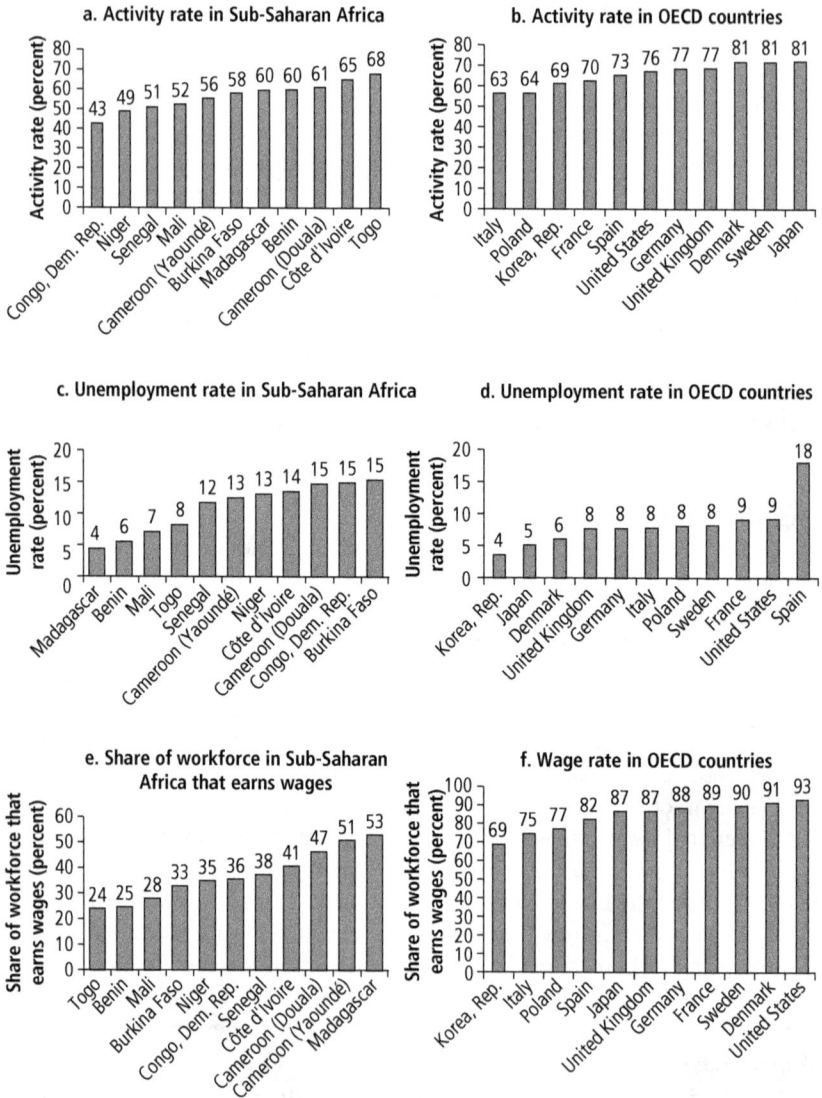

a. Activity rate in Sub-Saharan Africa

b. Activity rate in OECD countries

c. Unemployment rate in Sub-Saharan Africa

d. Unemployment rate in OECD countries

e. Share of workforce in Sub-Saharan Africa that earns wages

f. Wage rate in OECD countries

(continued next page)

Figure 0.1 (continued)

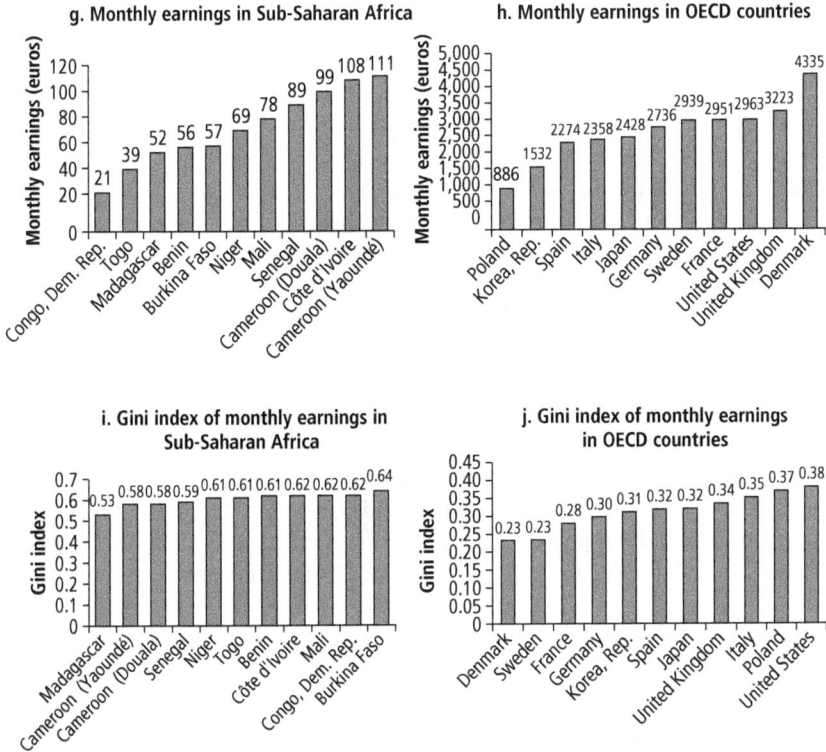

g. Monthly earnings in Sub-Saharan Africa

h. Monthly earnings in OECD countries

i. Gini index of monthly earnings in Sub-Saharan Africa

j. Gini index of monthly earnings in OECD countries

Sources: Panels a, c, e, g, i based on Phase 1 of the 1-2-3 surveys of selected countries (see table O.1 for details); panels b, d, f, h, j, ILO 2012.
Note: OECD = Organisation for Economic Co-operation and Development.

It is difficult to produce a straightforward typology of labor markets; no simple explanatory model seems to withstand examination of the empirical results. A detailed econometric analysis is inappropriate because of the small number of observation points (11, each corresponding to one city). Analysis of the correlation matrix for some key indicators does reveal the diversity and complexity of the configurations, however (see table O.3). The proposed typology of Teal (2000), which includes three archetypes and is based on just three countries (Ethiopia, Ghana, and South Africa), is also much too simplistic. For example, the correlation between unemployment and employment rates in the informal sector is not significantly different from zero (−0.07, not statistically significant), suggesting that there is no easy trade-off between the two, as the mismatch between (formal) labor supply and demand is expressed by either unemployment or the expansion of the informal sector.

A few interesting conclusions can be drawn from table O.4 (although the small number of observations calls for caution, and causal links cannot be established). First, the participation rate is negatively correlated with the unemployment rate (−0.33, not statistically significant) and the extended unemployment rate (−0.63, significant at the 10 percent level). The quantity of labor is thus not constant, and a large labor supply is not associated with higher unemployment—far from it. The quantity of labor is also not associated with employment in the informal sector (the correlation between the two phenomena is not significant). However, as public jobs are rationed, a high labor force participation rate is associated with a low public employment rate (−0.67, significant at the 5 percent level). With respect to unemployment, although the two measures used (the ILO definition and extended unemployment) display huge differences in levels (see chapter 1), they are very closely correlated (0.88, significant at the 1 percent level). However, there are no links between the different forms of underemployment (unemployment and time-related and invisible underemployment). These phenomena are therefore independent manifestations of the mismatch between supply and demand. A high unemployment rate is not associated with a low rate of informal sector employment or a high reservation wage among the unemployed (see chapter 1).

With respect to job structure, the share of informal sector employment is logically inversely proportional to the wage employment share (−0.93, significant at the 1 percent level), even though the informal sector represents a large percentage of wage earners. The relations with the public employment share (−0.36) and the industrial employment share (−0.43) are negative but not statistically significant. However, the multiple jobholding rate falls very significantly with the presence of the informal sector (−0.81, significant at the 1 percent level), highlighting the narrow room for maneuvering (especially in terms of time) freed up by this sector. The higher the share of employment in the informal sector, the lower the earnings (−0.25, not statistically significant); the more widespread invisible underemployment (0.69, significant at the 5 percent level); and the wider the gaps between formal and informal sector earnings (0.49, not statistically significant) and male and female earnings (0.73, significant at the 1 percent level). The relations between these features of the labor markets are reflected by higher levels of inequality in earned income (the correlation with the Gini coefficient of 0.80 is significant at the 1 percent level). The inverse relation is found for the wage employment rate, which is negatively related to the earnings gap by gender and institutional sector and to inequality but is positively related to the multiple jobholding rate. Finally, the higher the invisible underemployment rate, the higher the inequality (0.56, significant at the 10 percent level).

Table 0.4 Correlation Matrix for Main Labor Market Indicators in Sub-Saharan Africa

	PR	UR1	UR2	REG	UTR	IUR	WER	IER	PER	IndER	MJR	Earnings	M/F E	F/I E	Q3/Q1	Gini0	Gini
Participation rate (PR)	1																
Unemployment rate ILO (UR1)	-0.33	1															
Unemployment rate extended (UR2)	-0.63*	0.88***	1														
Reservation earnings gap (REG)[a]	0.58*	-0.21	-0.39	1													
Time-related underemployment rate (UTR)	-0.33	-0.33	-0.06	-0.32	1												
Invisible underemployment rate (IUR)	0.19	-0.06	-0.11	0.36	-0.26	1											
Wage employment rate (WER)	-0.02	0.21	0.44	-0.13	-0.31	-0.64**	1										
Informal sector employment rate (IER)	0.06	-0.07	-0.43	0.19	0.25	0.69**	-0.93***	1									
Public employment rate (PER)	-0.67**	0.44	0.63**	-0.50	-0.12	-0.26	0.21	-0.36	1								
Industrial employment rate (IndER)	0.09	-0.35	0.26	0.34	-0.03	0.04	0.44	-0.43	-0.19	1							
Multiple jobholding rate (MJR)	0.17	-0.29	-0.17	-0.02	-0.15	-0.65**	0.64**	-0.81***	0.09	0.30	1						
Nominal earnings	0.23	0.26	-0.08	0.54*	-0.39	-0.29	0.46	-0.25	-0.23	0.06	0.16	1					
Male/female earnings ratio (M/F E)	0.39	-0.40	-0.73**	0.54*	-0.00	0.48	-0.72*	0.73***	-0.54*	-0.29	-0.37	0.08	1				
Formal/informal sector earnings ratio (F/I E)	0.51	0.35	-0.10	0.64**	-0.52*	0.64**	-0.32	0.49	-0.40	-0.15	-0.52	0.37	0.49	1			
Quartile 3 (high)/Quartile 1 (low)	-0.32	0.19	0.29	-0.04	0.27	0.27	-0.60*	0.50	0.27	-0.28	-0.52	-0.36	0.18	0.38	1		
Gini0 (including earnings = 0)	-0.12	0.38	0.04	0.02	-0.10	0.56*	-0.77***	0.80***	0.05	-0.68***	-0.73***	-0.17	0.57*	0.57*	0.69***	1	
Gini (excluding earnings = 0)	-0.26	0.45	0.25	-0.11	0.08	0.31	-0.63**	0.68**	0.12	-0.67***	-0.73***	-0.12	0.41	0.45	0.78***	0.92***	1

Sources: Based on Phase 1 of the 1-2-3 surveys of selected countries (see table O.1 for details).

a. The reservation earnings gap is the gap between the minimum earnings at which the unemployed would accept a job and the earnings of workers with equivalent characteristics (see the methodology described in chapter 1, table 1.10).

* significant at the 10 percent level, ** significant at the 5 percent level, *** significant at the 1 percent level.

The Micro Level: Heterogeneity across Individuals

Moussa and Fatou are 20-year-olds living in the capital of a French-speaking African country. Both graduated from upper-secondary school. What are their prospects? What benefits can they hope to gain from their qualifications? Were their parents right to invest in their education? Will it increase their chances of entering the world of work and finding a good job? Will they be able to find fulfilling jobs, or will they have to accept jobs for which they are over-qualified? Will they be unemployed, out of the labor force, wage workers, or self-employed? Will they work in the formal or informal sector? What will the outcome depend on? How late in life will they have to keep working to ensure they maintain a decent standard of living?

Moussa, Fatou, and their families have surely asked themselves these questions and many others. They are vitally important. Africa is the youngest continent in the world today, with more than 64 percent of the population under 25 years old. In view of demographic growth, the number of young people arriving on the labor market is expected to grow steadily.

Fatou is an exception. Like Moussa, she graduated from upper-secondary school. She therefore has an above-average education compared with young people in her generation, 27 percent of whom, boys and girls included, did not attend school between the ages of 10 and 14 (chapters 1 and 12). Fatou is even more exceptional than the other young girls, 34 percent of whom (compared with 20 percent of boys) in her generation did not attend school between 10 and 14.

In French-speaking Africa, there continues to be a wide gap between boys' and girls' levels of education, despite substantial narrowing in recent decades as a result of the widespread increase in school attendance rates. At the turn of the 21st century, school enrollment conditions remain difficult. Schooling competes with other activities that potentially bring in income for households. On average, 45 percent of children 10–14 participate in domestic activities and 12 percent engage in an economic activity. These activities do not always prevent them from attending school: nearly 31 percent of children 10–14 both work and attend school. The competition seems to be mainly between economic activity and school, not between domestic activity and school (chapter 12). Children frequently combine domestic activities, sometimes for long hours, with school, whereas economic activity and school attendance tend to be mutually exclusive.

This general finding calls for some qualification. Girls and boys differ. When girls are not in school, their labor is more often used to bring in income for the family or to attend to domestic tasks. Boys are more often employed as apprentices. Although apprenticeships are generally unpaid, they create human capital.

Not surprisingly, differences in time use are evident across cities and social backgrounds. Sons and daughters of educated parents have a higher probability of attending school, as do children from wealthier households. These differences probably reflect the role of the budget constraint in the trade-off between work and education.

What benefits can Fatou and Moussa hope to gain from their qualifications? In most countries, education reduces the risk of unemployment, increases access to good jobs, and raises pay. In West Africa, unemployment increases with education, as shown in chapter 1: 15–18 percent of people with secondary or higher education are unemployed as opposed to just 11 percent of people with primary education and 8 percent of people with no education. The unemployment observed in these countries is therefore often viewed as a voluntary "queuing" phenomenon, in which the unemployed can afford to be unemployed until they find a job in line with their aspirations. In these circumstances, many discouraged job-seekers could be expected to either withdraw from the labor market or accept jobs that are not appropriate given their capabilities.

Chapter 2 examines the extent and impact of this job mismatch. It shows that only 53 percent of workers 25 and over hold jobs that match their skills, with 30 percent underqualified and 16 percent overqualified for their job. Not surprisingly, the incidence of underqualification is higher among workers with low levels of education and overqualification is more common among workers with secondary or higher education. Fifty-nine percent of people with completed lower- secondary school but not upper-secondary school and 69 percent of people with completed secondary education but not completed higher education are overqualified. Higher-education graduates are slightly better off, with "just" 45 percent overqualified for the work they do. Job-seekers' expectations of finding a job that matches their education dwindle with the length of unemployment, bearing out the hypothesis of "queuing" unemployment.

Given these realities, are Fatou and Moussa wrong to have spent time in school? Although their chances of finding a job that matches their qualifications probably fell as a result, they can expect to earn more: each additional year of education implies 10 percent higher pay. And even for overqualified workers, each year of education beyond the minimum required education level to hold their job generates an additional increase in pay of 5–6 percent.

These findings are confirmed in chapter 5, which examines the distribution of workers in different employment sectors (public, formal private, and informal) and evaluates the returns to education in each sector. It shows that although education is no safeguard against unemployment, it does open doors to the highest-paid sectors (public sector and formal private sector) and yields positive returns, including in the informal sector. The returns are convex, contrary to "standard" human capital theory, which posits that they are concave. This finding has important implications for education policy. If returns are convex, the massive investment in primary education may not produce the expected effects if access to secondary education is not also facilitated. Poor households may choose to educate only some of their children to make the most of this convexity—with girls often suffering as a result.

The finding of positive returns to education in the informal sector is important, because this sector employs more than 70 percent of the employed labor force in Sub-Saharan Africa. The large size of the informal sector is often perceived as reflecting segmentation in the employment market. The market is segmented when jobs are rationed by restrictive wage rules (minimum wage, wage-setting based on an efficiency wage principle, and so forth) or other reasons. Because access to this sector is restricted, people who cannot enter it are thrown into a market segment where workers are less protected and less well paid. In developing countries, this issue is usually studied by distinguishing between the formal employment sector (public sector and formal private sector) and the informal sector. This distinction suggests that the informal sector is homogeneous. In fact, it covers a multitude of types of workers, including business heads with employees, employees of these businesses, and own-account workers. Given that people working in the informal sector are able to evade taxation and social security contributions, some people in the sector may have chosen to work in it. This may be the case, in particular, with business heads. In a situation where many workers have only limited access to the capital market, not everyone can become a business head. This means that the informal sector itself could be segmented.

Chapter 6 looks into this issue. It studies the allocation of labor among three sectors: the formal sector (public and private formal), the upper informal sector (entrepreneurs employing at least one person), and the lower informal sector (own-account workers and employees). It finds labor market segmentation between the upper and lower segments of the informal sector in the seven WAEMU cities studied: the proportion of people who, in view of their education and experience, should be working in the formal or upper informal sector appears to be lower than it would be if the market were not segmented. Restriction of access to the upper segment of the informal sector therefore emerges as an explanatory factor for poverty.

The emphasis on remuneration in studying populations exposed to the risk of poverty should not cloud the fact that other aspects of the labor relationship are just as important. Chapters 3 and 4 focus on aspects of employment still rarely addressed in developing countries, especially in Sub-Saharan Africa. Chapter 3 analyzes individual job satisfaction, measured in terms of the absence of desire to change job or status on the labor market. The findings confirm that a high wage increases job satisfaction but that it is not its only determinant. For example, other things equal, satisfaction increases with age (a reflection of youth employment problems) and decreases with the level of education. This inverse relationship with education is consistent with the observation that the risk of being overeducated for one's job increases with one's skills level. In general, working conditions appear to be just as important as earnings in determining satisfaction. For example, satisfaction is increased by working in the public sector; earning a fixed wage; having a steady rather than a casual job; and being a senior executive, employer/proprietor, or even own-account worker. Working in the informal sector does not systematically reduce job satisfaction, a result at odds with conventional wisdom. Chapter 3 also underscores the role of individual aspirations in job satisfaction: other things equal, people whose fathers have more than primary education have lower satisfaction than people with less educated fathers.

Chapter 4 examines some of these employment aspects, addressing the question of vulnerability in employment. This is virgin territory for the literature, at least in Sub-Saharan Africa. The authors build a composite indicator of vulnerability that covers many aspects of the job held: contractual insecurity, working conditions, unstable remuneration, underemployment, and a mismatch between job and individual characteristics. They show that 85 percent of private sector workers in all of the cities considered are vulnerable on the basis of at least one of seven criteria. In a competitive labor market, the theory of compensating wage differentials predicts that everything else equal, people in jobs with undesirable characteristics, in terms of strenuous or hazardous work or the protection offered to workers, should be better paid. Chapter 4 shows that although on average, employment vulnerability is associated with lower pay in the formal private sector, everything else equal, average earnings in the informal sector are higher for high-vulnerability jobs. The assumption that average gains can compensate for a certain level of vulnerability therefore holds in the informal sector.

Fatou may well have the same level of qualifications as Moussa, but does she have the same chances as Moussa of securing the job she wants? Do Fatou and Moussa have the same chances as people of different origins with the same level of qualifications? Chapters 8 and 9 address these questions, each from a different angle. Chapter 8 uses the information on jobs held by respondents and their fathers to analyze inequality of opportunities on the labor market. The findings show that social origin plays a decisive role in labor market position, fostering the intergenerational transmission of inequalities. Transmission channels are both direct and indirect. In some cities, access to the upper segments of the labor market (the public and formal private sectors) is determined by the level of education, itself dependent on the parents' occupational status. In other cities, employment in one sector rather than another depends directly on the parents' socioeconomic status. Ethnic group and migrant status also have significant impacts in some cities.

Chapter 9 addresses discrimination. It decomposes the earnings gap between men and women and between the largest and other ethnic groups. The results show a large earnings gap between men and women, with women earning 21–50 percent of men's earnings. Differences in the average characteristics of male and female workers cannot explain these gaps. The gaps between ethnic groups are much smaller, and the largest group does not appear to systematically enjoy a more favorable position than other groups.

Despite their qualifications, Moussa and Fatou have reason to feel apprehensive about their entry into the world of work. The labor market does not give everyone the same opportunities. Access to the most desirable employment sectors appears to be restricted and to depend as much on parents' social status as on the qualifications individuals hold. Unemployment is high among people with good qualifications, and a sizable proportion of people who are employed are frustrated because they have not found jobs that match their skills, even though they have above-average earnings. The outlook for Fatou is even bleaker, because she is likely to suffer discrimination as a woman.

Fatou might marry quickly and ultimately choose to run the household. She would then specialize in performing domestic tasks and educating the children. Even if she works outside the home, however, she is very likely to shoulder most of the domestic work, as chapter 7 shows. In the 10 countries considered, domestic work represents nearly one-third of the total time worked on average. Despite a lower labor force participation rate, on average, women account for 56 percent of the total time worked in the household, including domestic activities (62 percent in the WAEMU countries). Women in Africa do most of the domestic work whether or not they work a paid job. They account for 43 percent of market working hours but 89 percent of domestic working hours. Working women work a "double day," in that their domestic workload is not lighter than it is for nonworking women.

A number of factors are correlated with inequalities in the gender division of labor. Social norms, measured by various variables, appear to play a decisive role: relative position in the household, age bracket, religion, and, to a lesser extent, education all have a significant impact on the gender distribution of domestic and market work. The type of household and its demographic structure also play an important part in this distribution: large, polygamous households and households with a larger number of adults have a different gender division of labor than households made up of monogamous couples with young children.

Faced with problems finding work, many young people consider migrating. This book addresses the migration question from two novel points of view. Chapter 10 deals with migration within the WAEMU economic area. The simultaneous series of labor force surveys conducted in the same format in the seven French-speaking capitals provides an opportunity to examine the monetary determinants of migration within this zone, in which member countries have signed a free movement agreement.

The chapter paints a picture of migration between Southern countries, a subject still somewhat neglected by the literature; it does not address South-North migration, which requires data of a different type. The chapter documents the magnitude of migration between WAEMU countries. Not surprisingly, Côte d'Ivoire is by far the leading country for immigration in the region. Mali and Burkina Faso supply the largest contingent of emigrants. Togo and Benin post high immigration and emigration figures.

Given that Fatou and Moussa graduated from upper-secondary school, they are unlikely to migrate within WAEMU, as the findings show that migrants who move from one African capital to another are less educated on average than nonmigrants, both in their country of origin and in their destination country.[7] In most countries, they have a higher probability of working in the informal sector and earning lower wages. Therefore, the brain drain phenomenon does not appear to be the main characteristic of migratory flows between French-speaking West African countries. However, other things equal, migrants' choices as to where they live do appear, at least in part, to respond to differences in remuneration: like nonmigrants, migrants choose to live in cities where, given their characteristics, their earnings expectations are highest.

With their qualifications, Fatou and Moussa are more likely to migrate to a developed country than another developing country. Moreover, if they do migrate, they are likely to do so only temporarily: recent analyses of international migration show that a large proportion of migrants ultimately return to their country of origin. The net impact of international migration, skilled or otherwise, on migrants' country of origin is thus still a research question. Migration of educated workers might not be as negative as feared if migrants return in sufficient numbers, bringing with them capital and know-how they manage to use productively in their country of origin.

This subject is analyzed in chapter 11, which uses data from the 1-2-3 surveys conducted in the WAEMU countries to evaluate wage differential between nonmigrant workers and migrant workers who have returned to their country of origin ("return migrants"). The chapter's findings distinguish between migrants based on whether they have returned from a developed country or from another WAEMU capital. Migrants returning from WAEMU member countries and nonmigrants display very similar labor market participation behavior and characteristics. In contrast, migrants returning from OECD countries are much more educated, more likely to be employed, and wealthier than nonmigrants. They also have a greater probability of working in the formal sector. However, this difference vanishes (or turns negative) when migrants' characteristics are taken into account, suggesting that they suffer a loss of social capital that reduces their access to formal sector jobs. In terms of income, the results reveal the existence of a large migration premium for migrants returning from OECD countries. Informal sector businesses run by migrants returning from OECD countries are also more productive than businesses run by nonmigrants or migrants returning from WAEMU or other countries.

One problem is the same for everyone: migrants and nonmigrants, formal sector employees, informal sector entrepreneurs and employees, and even the economically inactive all need to ensure that they have enough disposable income at retirement age to maintain a minimum level of well-being. This question probably has not yet occurred to Fatou and Moussa. Yet they can see around them that many people at retirement age have to keep working because they do not receive enough replacement income. If they foresee finding themselves in this situation when they are old, they might be encouraged to adopt certain precautionary behavior to cope with the situation as best they can when the time comes. For example, they may decide to have more children than they would have had if a public pension scheme had been available, in order to ensure that their children can look after them in their old age. Having people remain in the labor market into old age probably reduces the chances of young people finding work. The question of working at retirement age, addressed in chapter 13, is therefore an important one.

Pensions are available only to the minority of Africans who worked in private firms in the formal sector or the public sector. Moreover, most pensions are paltry, especially in the private sector. Pensions are not a source of wage replacement but more like a minimum subsistence income. Despite the lack of pensions, few seniors in Africa are dependent on their children. In fact, most still have young children to support, forcing them to struggle to make their meager incomes meet family outlays that burden them through a late age. These elderly heads of household also often have to support older children who have not yet entered the labor market. Consequently, a relatively large number of men still work after retirement age. More than 60 percent of people 55–59 and 47 percent of people 60–64 still work. As they age, workers are increasingly confined to the informal sector. The debate on raising the retirement age is therefore high on the agenda in the South, as it is in the North. However, it is not put in the same terms. Whereas workers in the North are calling to keep the retirement age as low as possible, one of the major demands of unions in this Southern subregion is to raise the retirement age.

Many differences can be observed across the cities studied, some of which warrant particular attention. Chapters 2 (job mismatch), 8 (inequality of opportunities), and 9 (discrimination) identify two groups of more or less homogeneous countries. Labor markets in the capitals of the coastal countries (Benin, Côte d'Ivoire, Senegal, and Togo) appear to have greater intergenerational social mobility, less segmentation, and less discrimination against women and ethnic groups than the capitals of the landlocked countries (Burkina Faso, Mali, and Niger). Among the seven WAEMU countries studied, the landlocked countries also have the lowest human development, wealth, and urbanization levels. Without seeking causality, one cannot help but be struck by the link observed between the extent of development and the functioning of the labor market. It may be no coincidence that Burkina Faso, Mali, and Niger are, in that order, the three countries that produce the largest contingents of migrants in the subregion (see chapter 10). The landlocked countries are not behind the coastal countries in all aspects: Mali and Benin post the highest levels of satisfaction (with 50 percent satisfied workers), for example, way ahead of Côte d'Ivoire (37 percent).

Making Data Collection Work for Research

All of this book's contributors are researchers at Développement, Institutions et Mondialisation (DIAL), a joint research unit of the Institut de Recherche pour le Développement (IRD) and the University of Paris Dauphine. (Brief biographies of the contributors appear at the beginning of the book).

This work is based on an original approach taken by DIAL since its establishment (in 1990), which consists of combining statistical production, economic research, and public policy analysis (Cling and Roubaud 2006; Nordman and Roubaud 2010). The involvement of a research center in the production of official statistical data is unusual: economists have long worked "far from the field," using databases produced by others, especially public statistics. (The World Bank's Living Standards Measurement Study program represents a notable exception.) It is only recently, at the instigation of promoters of ex post public policy impact evaluation methods (such as the Abdul Latif Jameel Poverty Action Lab), that academic development economists have started collecting data, albeit generally in the form of ad hoc protocols rather than official surveys. Academic involvement in data collection kills two birds with one stone. It helps fill the hole in statistics in developing countries, particularly in Africa, thereby broadening the scope of applied economics research while ensuring that the analyses produced are compatible with official figures. It also helps build bridges between the statistical and academic communities, which are nowhere as disconnected as in Africa. We hope that readers will see the merits of this approach, which warrants becoming widespread practice.

Target Audience

This book targets the whole development community interested in labor markets and, more broadly, Sub-Saharan African development, including researchers and students, policy makers, donors, and informed ordinary citizens, from the South or the North. Pursuing such a large and heterogeneous audience inevitably creates a trade-off. The book adopts the best econometric practices (for the research-oriented reader) but is accessible to all readers in order to provide food for thought and stimulate democratic debate. Readers interested in more details can consult the full version of the book posted on the book's website (http://www.dial.ird.fr/publications).

Our approach is mainly quantitative, not because we consider it superior to any other approach but because it corresponds to our skills. Therefore, readers who are more prone to qualitative and narrative approaches are invited to put their own in-depth knowledge in the broad picture perspective, in which they are embedded in, and eventually confront, these two complementary lenses.

This book does not provide press-a-button policy recommendations; providing such recommendations is neither our aim nor our area of expertise. Instead, it provides the evidence base on which sound policies should be grounded.

Notes

1. Many characteristics in English-speaking countries are probably quite different, given the lasting imprint of institutions and economic and social structures inherited from colonization (Cogneau 2007; Austin 2010). Sub-Saharan Africa is a mainly rural continent. Focusing only on urban areas, as this book does, ignores a fundamental component of African specificity.
2. The studies by Guha-Khasnobis and Kanbur (2006); Perry and others (2007); Ostrom, Kanbur, and Guha-Khasnobis (2007); Jütting and de Laiglesia (2009); and Bacchetta, Ernst, and Bustamante (2009), for example, contain as many definitions of informal employment as they do chapters.
3. This study, based on the Network for Labor Market Analysis in Africa (RAMTA) network data, draws on a series of pilot employment surveys of households in seven African cities (Abidjan, Antananarivo, Bamako, Conakry, Dakar, Ouagadougou, and Yaoundé) between 1986–87 and 1992. RAMTA collected these data at the initiative of the International Labour Organization's International Institute for Labor Studies. This process closely resembles the Programme d'Appui Régional à la Statistique (PAR-STAT) project system, launched by the WAEMU Commission and funded by the European Commission, from which this book takes its data. The same labor force survey was conducted in several West African cities in a short space of time to allow for comparability.
4. South Africa, with one of the highest unemployment rates in the world and a relatively small informal sector in urban areas, is atypical of the rest of the continent.
5. In most of the countries in which the two phases have been conducted, the Phase 1 and Phase 2 estimates of informal sector size are not significantly different.
6. *Time-related underemployment* is defined as working less than a certain norm (here 35 hours a week) when the individual would prefer to work more. *Invisible underemployment* refers to workers who earn less than a certain amount (here the minimum wage) (see chapters 1 and 2).
7. Not all of the cities examined are administrative capitals. Abidjan and Cotonou are referred to as capitals throughout this book because they are the most important economic centers in their countries (Cotonou is also the seat of government).

References

AfDB (African Development Bank), ECA (Economic Commission for Africa), OECD (Organisation for Economic Co-operation, and Development), and UNDP (United Nations Development Programme). 2012. "Promoting Youth Employment." In *African Economic Outlook 2012*, 99–176. Paris: OECD Publishing.

Akerlof, G. A. 1982. "Labor Contracts as Partial Gift Exchange." *Quarterly Journal of Economics* 97 (4): 543–69.

Amegashie, F., A. Brilleau, S. Coulibaly, O. Koriko, E. Ouedraogo, F. Roubaud, and C. Torelli. 2005. "La conception et la mise en oeuvre des enquêtes 1-2-3 en UEMOA: les enseignements méthodologiques." *Statéco* 99: 21–41.

Austin, G. 2010. "African Economic Development, and Colonial Legacies." *Revue Internationale de Politique de Développement* 1: 11–32.

Bacchetta, M., E. Ernst, and J. P. Bustamante. 2009. *Globalization and Informal Jobs in Developing Countries*. Geneva: International Labour Organization and World Trade Organization.

Banerjee, A. V., and A. F. Newman. 1993. "Occupational Choice and the Process of Development." *Journal of Political Economy* 1011 (2): 274–98.

Bardasi, E., K. Beegle, A. Dillon, and P. Serneels. 2010. "Assessing Labor Statistics in Sub-Saharan Africa: A Survey Experiment in Tanzania." Policy Research Working Paper 5192, World Bank, Washington, DC.

Becker, G. S. 1962. "Irrational Behavior and Economic Theory." *Journal of Political Economy* 70 (1): 1–13.

———. 1964. *Human Capital*. New York: Columbia University Press for the National Bureau of Economic Research.

Bigsten, A., and M. Söderbom. 2005. "What Have We Learned from a Decade of Manufacturing Enterprise Surveys in Africa?" Policy Research Working Paper 3798, World Bank, Washington, DC.

Blair, J., G. Menon, and B. Bickart. 2004. "Measurement Effects in Self- versus Proxy Responses to Survey Questions: An Information Processing Perspective." In *Measurement Errors in Surveys*, ed. P. P. Biemer, R. M. Groves, L. E. Lyberg, N. A. Mathiowetz, and S. Sudman, 145–66. New York: Wiley.

Brilleau, A., E. Ouedraogo, and F. Roubaud. 2005. "L'enquête 1-2-3 dans les pays de l'UEMOA: la consolidation d'une méthode." *Statéco* 99: 15–70.

Cain, G. G. 1976. "The Challenge of Segmented Labor Market Theories to Orthodox Theory: A Survey." *Journal of Economic Literature* 14 (4): 1215–57.

Cling, J.-P., M. Razafindrakoto, and F. Roubaud, eds. 2003. *New International Poverty Reduction Strategies*. London: Routledge.

Cling, J.-P., and F. Roubaud. 2006. "15 ans d'appui à la coopération économique et statistique française avec l'Afrique." *Statéco* 100: 45–62.

Cogneau, D. 2007. *L'Afrique des inégalités: ou conduit l'histoire?* Paris: Éditions Rue d'Ulm/Presses de l'École Normale Supérieure.

Cook, S. 1966. "The Obsolete 'Anti-Market' Mentality: A Critique of the Substantive Approach to Economic Anthropology." *American Anthropologist* 68 (2): 465–70.

Cornia, G. A., R. Jolly, and F. Stewart, eds. 1987. *Adjustment with a Human Face: Protecting the Vulnerable and Promoting Growth.* Oxford: Oxford University Press/UNICEF.

Dalton, G. 1967. "Traditional Production in Primitive African Economies." In *Tribal and Peasant Economies: Readings in Economic Anthropology,* ed. G. Dalton, 61–80. Garden City, NY: Natural History Press.

Doeringer, P. B., and M. J. Piore. 1971. *Internal Labor Markets and Manpower Analysis.* Lexington, MA: Heath.

Fafchamps, M., and M. Söderbom. 2006. "Wages and Labour Management in African Manufacturing." *Journal of Human Resources* 41 (2): 346–79.

Fields, G. S. 1990. "Labour Market Modeling and the Urban Informal Sector: Theory and Evidence." In *The Informal Sector Revisited,* ed. D. Turnham, B. Salomé, and A. Schwarz, 49–69. Paris: OECD Development Centre.

Fields, G. S. 2010. "Labor Market Analysis for Developing Countries." *Labour Economics* 18: S16–S22.

Guha-Khasnobis, B., and R. Kanbur, eds. 2006. *Informal Labour Markets and Development.* London: Palgrave MacMillan.

Harris, J., and M. Todaro. 1970. "Migration, Unemployment, and Development: A Two-Sector Analysis." *American Economic Review* 60 (1): 126–42.

Horton, S., R. Kanbur, and D. Mazumdar, eds. 1994. *Labor Markets in an Era of Adjustment.* EDI Development Studies. Washington, DC: World Bank.

ILO (International Labour Organization). 1993. "Resolution Concerning Statistics of Employment in the Informal Sector." Fifteenth International Conference of Labour Statistics, Geneva, January 19–28.

———. 2003. "General Report." Seventeenth International Conference of Labour Statisticians, Geneva, November 24–December 3.

———. 2010a. *Global Employment Trends.* Geneva: ILO.

———. 2010b. *Global Employment Trends for Youth.* Geneva: ILO.

———. 2012. *Key Indicators of the Labour Market.* Geneva: ILO.

Isaac, B. L. 2005. "Karl Polanyi." In *A Handbook of Economic Anthropology,* ed. J. G. Carrier, 14–25. Cheltenham, U.K. Edward Elgar.

Jütting, J. P., and J. R. de Laiglesia. 2009. *L'emploi informel dans les pays en développement: une normalité indépassable?* Paris: OECD Development Centre.

Kanbur, R., and J. McIntosh. 1987. "Dual Economies." In *The New Palgrave Economic Development,* ed. J. Eatwell, M. Milgate, P. Newman, and W. W. Norton, 114–21. London: Palgrave MacMillan.

Kanbur, R., and J. Svejnar, eds. 2009. *Labor Markets and Economic Development.* London: Routledge.

Kingdon, G., J. Sandefur, and F. Teal. 2006. "Labour Market Flexibility, Wages, and Incomes in Sub-Saharan Africa in the 1990s." *African Development Review* 18 (3): 392–427.

Lachaud, J.-P., ed. 1994. *Pauvreté et marché du travail urbain en Afrique subsaharienne: analyse comparative.* Institut International d'Études Sociales, Geneva.

Levi-Strauss, C. 2001. "Productivité et condition humaine." *Études Rurales*: 159–60.

Lewis, W. A. 1954. "Economic Development with Unlimited Supplies of Labour." *Manchester School of Economics and Social Studies* 22 (May): 139–91.

Maddison, A. 1995. *Monitoring the World Economy: 1820–1992*. Paris: OECD Development Centre.

Marchand, O., and C. Thélot. 1997. *Le travail en France: 1800–2000*. Paris: Nathan, Essais & Recherches.

Mazumdar, D., and A. Mazaheri. 2002. *Wage and Employment in Africa*. Hampshire, U.K. Ashgate.

Nordman, C. J., and F. Roubaud. 2010. "An Original Approach in Development Economics: 20 Years of Work on Measuring, and Analysing the Informal Economy in the Developing Countries." *Dialogue* 31 (November): 2–9.

Nordman, C. J., and F.-C. Wolff. 2009. "Is There a Glass Ceiling in Morocco? Evidence from Matched Worker-Firm Data." *Journal of African Economies* 18 (4): 592–633.

Ostrom, E., R. Kanbur, and B. Guha-Khasnobis, eds. 2007. *Linking the Formal and Informal Economy: Concepts and Policies*. Oxford: Oxford University Press.

Perry, G. E., W. F. Maloney, O. S. Arias, P. Fajnzylber, A. D. Mason, and J. Saavedra-Chanduvi. 2007. *Informality: Exit and Exclusion*. World Bank, Latin American and Caribbean Studies, Washington, DC.

Piore, M. J. 1970. "Jobs and Training." In *The State and the Poor*, ed. S. H. Beer and R. E. Barranger, 53–83. Cambridge, MA: Winthrop Press.

Polanyi, K. 1957. "The Economy as Instituted Process." In *Trade and Market in the Early Empires*, ed. K. Polanyi, C. Arensberg, and H. Pearson, 243–70. Glencoe, IL: Free Press.

Rakotomanana, F., E. Ramilison, and F. Roubaud. 2003. "The Creation of an Annual Employment Survey in Madagascar: An Example for Sub-Saharan Africa." *InterStat* 27: 35–58.

Rama, M. 2000. "Wage Misalignment in CFA Countries: Are Labor Market Policies to Blame?" *Journal of African Economies* 9 (4): 475–511.

Razafindrakoto, M., and F. Roubaud. 2003. "The Existing Systems for Monitoring Poverty: Weaknesses of the Usual Household Surveys." In *New International Poverty Reduction Strategies*, ed. J.-P. Cling, M. Razafindrakoto, and F. Roubaud, 265–94. London: Routledge.

Razafindrakoto, M., F. Roubaud, and C. Torelli. 2009. "Measuring the Informal Sector and Informal Employment: The Experience Drawn from 1-2-3 Surveys in African Countries." *African Statistical Journal* 9 (November): 88–147.

Rodgers, G., ed. 1989. *Urban Poverty and the Labour Market: Access to Jobs and Incomes in Asian and Latin American Cities*. Geneva: International Labour Organization.

Roubaud, F., ed. 1994. "L'enquête 1-2-3 sur l'emploi et le secteur informel à Yaoundé." *Statéco* 78.

Schneider, H. K. 1974. *Economic Man*. New York: Free Press.

Shapiro, C., and J. E. Stiglitz. 1984. "Equilibrium Unemployment as a Worker Discipline Device." *American Economic Review* 74 (3): 433–44.

Spence, M. 1973. "Job Market Signaling." *Quarterly Journal of Economics* 87 (3): 355–74.

Standing, G., and V. Tokman, eds. 1991. *Towards Social Adjustment: Labour Market Issues in Structural Adjustment.* Geneva: International Labour Organization.

Stiglitz, J. E. 1974. "Alternative Theories of Wage Determination, and Unemployment in LDCs: The Labor Turnover Model." *Quarterly Journal of Economics* 88 (2): 194–227.

———. 1976. "The Efficiency Wage Hypothesis, Surplus Labour, and the Distribution of Income in L.D.C.s." *Oxford Economic Papers* 28 (2): 185–207.

Teal, F. 2000. "Employment and Unemployment in Sub-Saharan Africa: An Overview." Document prepared for the project "Employment, and Labour Markets," March, Department for International Development, London.

Thurow, L. 1972. "Education and Economic in Equality." *Public Interest* 28 (Summer): 66–81.

———. 1975. *Generating Inequality: Mechanism of Distribution in the U.S. Economy.* New York: Basic Books.

Thurow, L. C., and R. Lucas. 1972. *The American Distribution of Income: A Structural Problem.* Study for the Joint Economic Committee of the U.S. Congress. Washington, DC: Government Printing Office.

UN (United Nations). 2008. *Millennium Development Goals Report.* New York: UN.

Van Biesebroeck, J. 2007. "Wage and Productivity Premiums in Sub-Saharan Africa." NBER Working Paper 13306, National Bureau of Economic Research, Cambridge, MA.

World Bank. 1995. *World Development Report 1995: Workers in an Integrating World.* Washington, DC.

———. 2011. *World Development Indicators.* Washington, DC.

———. 2012a. *World Development Indicators.* Washington, DC.

———. 2012b. *World Development Report 2013: Jobs.* Washington, DC.

Part I

Comparative Analysis of Urban Labor Markets in Sub-Saharan Africa

Employment, Unemployment, and Working Conditions in the Urban Labor Markets of Sub-Saharan Africa: Main Stylized Facts

François Roubaud and Constance Torelli

This chapter presents an overview of the main characteristics of urban labor markets and the workers employed in them at the turn of the 21st century. The descriptive analysis of a dozen 1-2-3 surveys conducted in Africa over the last decade establishes several robust stylized facts about the particularities of these markets.[1] The chapter examines a broad sweep of indicators, such as the level of education and the training-employment link; unemployment and underemployment; the distribution of jobs and job properties by institutional sector, especially the informal sector; job quality (earnings and social security coverage); and multiple jobholding. These indicators identify the major trends, which are then studied in detail in the subsequent chapters.

This chapter is structured as follows. The first section describes the sociodemographic characteristics of the 11 cities studied. The second section examines labor force participation. The third section looks at unemployment. The fourth and fifth sections examine the structure of employment and labor force characteristics by institutional sector and earned income and working conditions. The last section takes up the question of employment prospects, with a focus on young people. The chapter devotes special attention to unemployment (which other chapters do not specifically address), the informal sector, and earnings. Where possible, indicators are separated by gender.

Sociodemographic Characteristics

The population in the main cities of the 10 countries studied totaled nearly 20 million people in the first half of the 2000s (table 1.1).[2] About 9 million

Table 1.1 Population and Demographic Characteristics of 11 Cities in Sub-Saharan Africa

Item	West Africa								Central Africa			Indian Ocean
	Abidjan	Bamako	Cotonou	Dakar	Lomé	Niamey	Ouagadougou	WAEMU countries	Douala	Kinshasa	Yaoundé	Antananarivo
Population (thousands)	3,046	1,143	809	1,906	784	675	856	9,219a	1,907	5,751	1,817	1,248
Percentage of population	17	11	12	22	16	6	7	13	11	10	10	8
Percentage of urban population	39	37	31	53	43	32	37	39	22	35	21	30
Structure by age												
0–14 (percent)	34.0	44.0	36.5	34.6	35.0	43.0	37.6	36.7	33.2	39.9	36.8	40.5
15–59 (percent)	64.2	52.5	60.0	60.8	62.0	54.0	58.7	60.2	63.8	56.0	61.1	55.7
60 and over (percent)	1.8	3.5	3.5	4.6	3.0	3.0	3.7	3.1	3.0	4.1	2.1	3.8
Average age (years)	22.4	21.1	22.8	23.9	23.0	21.2	22.5	22.5	23.5	23.0	21.3	24.2
Median age (years)	21	17	20	20	21	17	19	20	22	19	20	20
Women (percent)	50.6	50.0	52.0	51.5	51.6	50.7	49.5	50.8	49.1	51.3	49.7	50.3
Migrants (percent)	51.0	36.0	38.0	27.6	48.2	36.5	43.0	41.3	53.6	22.3	51.9	19.9

Sources: Based on Phase 1 of the following 1-2-3 surveys: Cameroon 2005 (Développement, Institutions et Mondialisation [DIAL] and National Statistics Institute [NSI]; Democratic Republic of Congo 2005 (DIAL and NSI); Madagascar 2001 (DIAL and Institut National de la Statistique [INSTAT]; West African Economic and Monetary Union (WAEMU) 2001/02 (Observatoire économique et statistique d'Afrique Subsaharienne [AFRISTAT], DIAL, and NSIs).
Note: Figures for the percentage of the population and the percentage of the urban population should be viewed with caution, as they are based on census figures that can be as much as 10 years old.
a. Total population.

people live in the seven cities in the West African Economic and Monetary Union (WAEMU); 1.3 million live in Antananarivo, Madagascar, the only representative of the Indian Ocean region. The cities range in size from Niamey (675,000 inhabitants) to Kinshasa (5.8 million inhabitants).

The cities in West Africa represent a small percentage of their countries' populations (6–7 percent in Niamey and Ouagadougou, 22 percent in Dakar), reflecting the low rates of urbanization in Sahelian Africa. Together the cities studied represent almost 40 percent of the urban population of West Africa. The underdevelopment of secondary cities is particularly severe in Senegal, where 53 percent of the population lives in Dakar. Cameroon has two similar-sized main cities (Yaoundé and Douala), which together account for more than 40 percent of the urban population of Cameroon. Focusing on capital cities makes sense in Africa not only because secondary cities are relatively underdeveloped but also because the characteristics and functioning of labor markets are more homogeneous than and differ greatly from those of other urban areas.

The age distribution of the population displays the classic characteristics of cities in developing countries, with a massive predominance of young people. Across the 11 cities, the average age is 22.5. The inhabitants of Bamako and Niamey are the youngest (average age 21, median age 17). Gender differences in the age distribution are small. Women account for slightly more than half of the population in the 11 cities.

The proportion of migrants (people who have not always lived in the city) is substantial in all 11 cities (see chapters 10 and 11). The lowest proportions are in Antananarivo (20 percent), Kinshasa (22 percent), and Dakar (28 percent). The highest proportions are in Douala (54 percent), Yaoundé (52 percent), and Abidjan (51 percent). Migration is essentially a domestic phenomenon in all of the cities studied: even within WAEMU, the region that is most open to international migration, for example, just 21 percent of migrants are domestic. Migration from abroad accounts for less than 4 percent of migrants in Antananarivo, Kinshasa, and the Cameroonian cities and about 10 percent in Dakar. The share of foreign migrants is higher in Lomé (28 percent) and Abidjan (25 percent).

Half of migrants—including two-thirds of women migrants—would like to join their families. Thirty percent of all migrants cite the desire to find a job as their main reason for migrating (the figure is even higher among men). Twelve percent cite study as the reason for migrating.

Household Composition

The average household size in the cities sampled is 5.1 people, but national averages cover a wide range, from Lomé (3.9 people) to Dakar (7.4 people). More than a quarter of households in Dakar contain 10 or more people. This proportion is less than 5 percent in Lomé and Cotonou. Dakar aside, household size can be used to define two groups of cities: the Sahelian cities (Bamako,

Niamey, and Ouagadougou), with an average household size of 5.6–6.0 people, and the West African coastal cities (Abidjan, Cotonou, and Lomé) and the cities of Central Africa and Madagascar, with an average household size of 4.6 people.

About one in five heads of household is a woman. In the Sahelian countries, the proportion of female household heads is less than 16 percent (less than 10 percent in Bamako). In contrast, in Cotonou, Dakar, and Lomé, the share reaches 25–30 percent.

Education

In West Africa, 30 percent of people 10 and older never attended primary school. This figure is less than 5 percent in Central Africa and the Indian Ocean, two regions that have long promoted schooling (table 1.2). The percentage of people who never attended school is extremely high in Bamako (41 percent), Niamey (36 percent), and Ouagadougou (34 percent). In contrast, just 16 percent of the population in Lomé and 20 percent in Cotonou never attended school. Abidjan (29 percent) and Dakar (31 percent) are in an intermediate position. In Central Africa and Madagascar, there is a tendency to either educate children beyond primary level or to concentrate on the quality of the education provided.

Few changes in the hierarchy between the coastal and Sahelian cities are evident when the focus switches from stock (all cohorts) to flow (people still in school). However, some changes are worth mentioning. Ouagadougou, with a net primary enrollment rate of 79.7 percent, catches up to Cotonou (81.2 percent) and Lomé (83.2 percent). Ouagadougou's net lower secondary school enrollment rate is second after Cotonou's. In contrast, Abidjan and Dakar leave from one-quarter to one-third of their 6- to 11-year-olds out of the system. With a net primary enrollment rate of 65.9 percent, Dakar performs hardly better than Bamako (70.7 percent). Bamako performs worst across most education indicators, in both stock and flow. In Central Africa and Madagascar, Kinshasa has the highest and longest rates of school attendance. Given the failed nature of the state and years of economic and political crises in the Democratic Republic of Congo, this finding is an indicator of the importance the Congolese attach to education.

In all 11 cities, the rate of school attendance has grown steadily over the generations. Some cities, such as Ouagadougou and especially Niamey, have experienced spectacular growth. In Niamey, for example, 88 percent of adults 60 and older but just 16 percent of children 10–14 never attended school (figure 1.1). In Ouagadougou, these ratios are 84 percent and 12 percent. Both cities have virtually caught up to cities like Cotonou and Lomé. In the cities where high school enrollment is long established, growth in the rate of school attendance is, of course, less spectacular. In Antananarivo, for example, the younger generation has no greater probability of attending school than its elders, with just 6 percent of each cohort never attending school.

Table 1.2 Education of Population in 11 Cities in Sub-Saharan Africa
(percent)

Characteristic	West Africa								Central Africa			Indian Ocean
	Abidjan	Bamako	Cotonou	Dakar	Lomé	Niamey	Ouagadougou	WAEMU countries	Douala	Kinshasa	Yaoundé	Antananarivo
No education (≥10 years old)	28.5	40.8	20.2	31.4	16.1	36.3	33.7	29.7	4.2	4.5	2.7	4.2
Net primary enrollment rate	73.2	70.7	81.2	65.9	83.2	70.5	79.7	73.3	92.6	81.2	90.7	92.3
Net lower secondary enrollment rate	23.0	28.2	33.8	19.9	27.5	28.7	29.4	25.4	63.0	53.9	61.5	39.3
Spoken and written French (≥10 years old)	66.4	49.6	70.9	58.4	72.9	57.4	60.4	62.6	89.2	69.6	91.8	33.0
Postprimary education (≥15 years old)	46.2	38.4	49.2	31.2	47.6	37.2	37.2	41.1	72.6	95.2	75.5	66.3
Higher education (≥20 years old)	13.8	7.1	12.1	7.0	6.8	9.1	6.8	9.9	13.2	16.3	18.6	13.7

Sources: Based on Phase 1 of the 1-2-3 surveys of selected countries (see table 1.1 for details).
Note: Age brackets for calculation of net school enrollment rates are as follows: Abidjan, Antananarivo, Cotonou, Douala, Lomé, Yaoundé: 6–10 (primary), 11–14 (secondary); Bamako, Dakar, Kinshasa, Niamey, Ouagadougou: 7–11 (primary), 12–15 (secondary).

Figure 1.1 Intergenerational Changes in School Enrollment in 11 Cities in Sub-Saharan Africa

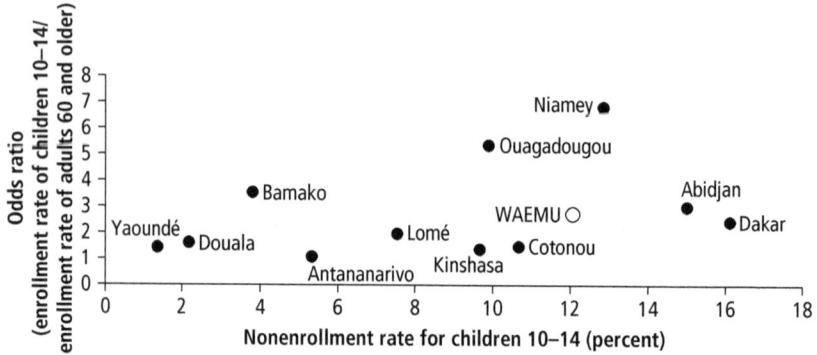

Sources: Based on Phase 1 of the 1-2-3 surveys of selected countries (see table 1.1 for details).
Note: WAEMU = West African Economic and Monetary Union.

Across the board, growth in school enrollment has gone hand in hand with a narrowing in the gender gap. Dakar posts the best performance. Among adults 60 and older, men are four times as likely to have attended school; this difference narrows to 7 percentage points among children 10–14. At the other end of the scale, girls are still highly disadvantaged compared with boys in Cotonou and especially Abidjan. There is room for improvement everywhere: in none of the countries studied are girls' enrollment rates equal to boys'.

School enrollment rates have risen markedly in the countries studied: despite the severe public finance crisis, increasingly large numbers of children are receiving an education. This quantitative performance has probably been secured at the cost of a marked deterioration in the quality of the education provided, however.

Labor Force Participation

There are more than 14 million people of working age (10 and older) across the cities studied: 6.9 million in West Africa, 6.2 million in Central Africa, and 947,000 in Madagascar. On average, nearly 60 percent of them are in the labor force (employed or unemployed). Among people 15 and older, the labor force participation rate is 70 percent. In Abidjan and Lomé, about 70 percent of the population 10 and older is in the workforce. In Niamey, Dakar, Bamako, and especially Kinshasa, labor force participation is lower and averages about 50 percent of the population 10 and older.

Female Employment in the Labor Market
Labor force participation is almost 15 percentage points higher for men than for women (table 1.3). The largest gaps observed are in Niamey (28 points); Dakar

Table 1.3 Labor Force Participation Rates in 11 Cities in Sub-Saharan Africa, by Gender
(percent)

Gender	West Africa							Central Africa			Indian Ocean
	Abidjan	Bamako	Cotonou	Dakar	Lomé	Niamey	Ouagadougou	WAEMU countries	Douala	Kinshasa	Yaoundé	Antananarivo
Men	70.1	59.3	58.8	62.1	68.9	63.5	66.3	65.3	69.7	50.2	63.2	64.0
Women	60.3	45.6	60.9	41.1	66.9	35.2	49.6	52.5	52.4	35.8	47.7	55.5
WAEMU countries	65.1	52.4	59.9	51.1	67.9	48.8	58.0	58.7	61.2	42.8	55.5	59.7

Sources: Based on Phase 1 of the 1-2-3 surveys of selected countries (see table 1.1 for details).
Note: Population 10 and older.

(21 points); Ouagadougou and Douala (17 points); Yaoundé (16 points); and Bamako and Kinshasa (14 points). In Abidjan (10 points) and Lomé (2 points) the gaps are much smaller. In Cotonou, women's participation rates (61 percent) are higher than men's (59 percent).

Variations in labor force participation rates across cities are much more pronounced for women than for men. Less than 20 percentage points separate the highest rate for male workers (70 percent, in Abidjan) from the lowest rate (50 percent, in Kinshasa). In contrast, the differences in female participation rates range from 35 percent (in Kinshasa and Niamey) to 67 percent (in Lomé).

The larger differences for women reflect the social role played by women, who divide their time between domestic activities (including childbearing and rearing) and economic activity in the market. On average, women spend 17 hours (and men 4 hours) a week on domestic activities. The situation is even more unequal in West Africa, where men spend just 2 hours a week on domestic activities and women 17. The least inequitable distribution of domestic chores is in Antananarivo, where men spend 8 hours and women 17. Working women spend more time on domestic activities than women who do not work (18 versus 16 hours), clearly demonstrating the "double day" phenomenon among working women (see chapter 7).

Youth Employment on the Labor Market

Observed labor force participation rates are consistent with the stages of the life cycle. Participation rates rise sharply as people leave the education system and enter the world of work. The peak comes at 30–49, when male participation rates top 85 percent across all cities except Kinshasa. Labor force participation rates start to slide after 50, plummeting after 60.

People 20 and under account for 35 percent of the working-age population (10 and older) in the cities surveyed. Thirty-five percent of these people are active (either working or seeking employment), although the situation varies widely across cities. In Bamako and Niamey, which have the largest percentages of young people, one-quarter of young people work. This proportion is 35 percent in Abidjan and 37 percent in Lomé.

Participation rates are higher for girls than for boys, especially in Abidjan and Cotonou, and more girls than boys are in the labor market. In Cotonou, Abidjan, and Lomé, 35–43 percent of young women work—13–15 percentage points more than their male counterparts. The youth participation rate is lower (less than 25 percent) elsewhere. In Kinshasa, it is just 7 percent, because of the dual effect of higher school enrollment rates and higher inactivity rates (excluding school). The differences between girls and boys are narrower in Kinshasa than elsewhere.

Children in Africa enter the labor market at a very young age. In West Africa, 13 percent of children 10–14 work (table 1.4). The problem is more

Table 1.4 Labor Force Participation Rates in 11 Cities in Sub-Saharan Africa, by Age
(percent)

Age	West Africa								Central Africa			Indian Ocean
	Abidjan	Bamako	Cotonou	Dakar	Lomé	Niamey	Ouagadougou	WAEMU countries	Douala	Kinshasa	Yaoundé	Antananarivo
10–14	16.3	11.2	14.1	9.3	17.2	13.2	9.1	13.0	10.2	1.7	4.5	6.1
15–29	63.0	50.3	56.6	52.1	68.3	42.8	60.6	57.9	57.2	29.3	50.3	58.9
30–49	90.7	81.8	91.1	74.7	93.0	73.6	84.9	85.1	87.1	73.5	88.0	87.7
50+	64.2	53.5	62.6	48.9	60.6	64.1	57.3	57.6	61.8	63.8	62.4	60.3
WAEMU countries	65.1	52.4	59.9	51.1	67.9	48.8	58.0	58.7	61.2	42.8	55.5	59.7

Sources: Based on Phase 1 of the 1-2-3 surveys of selected countries (see table 1.1 for details).

severe among girls than boys, with 16 percent of girls and 10 percent of boys participating in the labor force (see chapter 12). The phenomenon is less severe in Central Africa and Madagascar, where more children are in school. Nevertheless, in Douala 1 in 10 children 10–14 works, most of them combining school and work.

Status within the household also affects labor force participation rates. The highest rates are among heads of household (86 percent for all 11 cities), followed by their spouses (62 percent) and household members other than spouses and children (51 percent). In last place come children, with the lowest labor force participation rates (31 percent). Household survival relies first and foremost on the head of household. Where necessary, the strategy is then to mobilize the spouse and other household members. Children are sent to work as a last resort.

Labor force participation rates also vary a great deal by migrant status, with 66 percent of migrants (and 43 percent of natives) participating. These differences reflect the fact that the prospect of working draws migrants to cities.

The Inactive Population

In West Africa, 41 percent of the potential working population do not have and are not looking for a job. In Bamako, Dakar, and Niamey, about half of the population 10 and older is out of the labor force (table 1.4). The two main inactive groups, school children and students, represent between two-thirds and three-quarters of the inactive population in Cameroon and Madagascar (table 1.5). Housewives are the second most important group of inactive people (20 percent in West Africa and about 15 percent elsewhere). The proportion of retirees is small, averaging less than 4 percent, reflecting both a wide-based age pyramid and the need to work after 60 because of the insufficiency of pensions (see chapter 13).

The share and composition of inactive individuals varies across cities. There are proportionally more pupils and students outside West Africa and more inside West Africa in Cotonou and Lomé, and more housewives in Niamey, Dakar, and Bamako.

Almost all (91 percent) of inactive individuals are looked after by their families. Only about 5 percent rely on pension income (work, disability, and so forth). This finding highlights the underdevelopment of institutional transfers, the major role played by solidarity and informal transfers (within and between households), and the massive predominance of earned income in households' total income.

Nearly 70 percent of all inactive individuals chose this status of their own accord, either because they consider themselves too young to work or because they do not need to work to live. However, for 1.85 million inactive individuals (about 30 percent of the inactive population), the absence of work represents a form of hidden unemployment: they have withdrawn from the labor market, either because they believe that the economic situation is too weak or their skills

Table 1.5 Reasons for Inactivity in 11 Cities in Sub-Saharan Africa

| City | Reason for inactivity (percentage of total) | | | | | Number of inactive individuals |
	In the education system	Housewife	Retiree	Long illness	Other	
West Africa						
Abidjan	58.4	14.1	3.6	4.7	19.2	812,000
Bamako	56.4	21.1	3.2	6.9	12.4	361,000
Cotonou	70.1	9.6	5.5	5.1	9.7	246,000
Dakar	42.8	28.2	4.5	7.1	17.4	712,000
Lomé	65.3	9.0	4.3	7.7	13.7	192,000
Niamey	46.1	36.3	1.8	6.3	9.5	238,000
Ouagadougou	58.1	18.1	3.0	6.9	13.9	267,000
WAEMU countries	54.7	20.0	3.8	6.1	15.4	2,828,000
Central Africa						
Douala	65.5	13.5	3.4	7.0	10.6	515,700
Kinshasa	57.3	15.0	1.8	5.4	20.5	2,300,000
Yaoundé	74.2	14.1	2.2	5.6	3.9	584,700
Madagascar						
Antananarivo	67.9	17.3	6.0	4.4	4.4	381,500

Sources: Based on Phase 1 of the 1-2-3 surveys of selected countries (see table 1.1 for details).

too low to find a job or because they are waiting to hear about a job for which they have applied. On average, people out of the labor force ("discouraged workers") and the unemployed have two more years of education than people who are truly inactive.

The magnitude of unused labor supply is large in Africa. These people join or withdraw from the labor market depending on the incentives they face (increases in the demand for labor, the real wage, and so forth). The number of jobs that need to be created to mop up unemployment is therefore much higher than the number of unemployed.

Unemployment

Based on the ILO definition of unemployment, there are an estimated 963,000 job-seekers in the 11 cities, which corresponds to an average unemployment rate of 12 percent (table 1.6). The rate is slightly higher in Central Africa and much lower in Madagascar, which enjoyed extremely strong growth in 2001, following a trend that began in the mid-1990s. The highest unemployment rates are in Ouagadougou (15.4 percent), Kinshasa (14.9 percent), and Yaoundé (14.7 percent). The lowest rates are in Antananarivo (4.4 percent) and Cotonou (5.5 percent).

Table 1.6 ILO-Defined Unemployment Rates in 11 Cities in Sub-Saharan Africa, by Gender and Age

| | Gender | | Age | | | All | |
City	Men	Women	10–29	30–49	50+	Percentage	Number
West Africa							
Abidjan	13.1	14.0	17.4	10.0	7.3	13.5	205,400
Bamako	7.1	7.0	10.7	4.6	2.9	7.1	28,000
Cotonou	6.3	4.9	7.3	4.2	3.7	5.5	20,400
Dakar	9.9	14.1	14.4	10.0	6.7	11.7	87,000
Lomé	10.9	5.7	10.4	5.8	7.7	8.2	33,300
Niamey	12.1	15.0	18.7	8.7	11.1	13.1	29,900
Ouagadougou	14.6	16.4	22.4	9.2	5.9	15.4	56,500
WAEMU countries	11.2	11.7	15.2	8.3	6.5	11.4	460,500
Central Africa							
Douala	10.6	15.1	17.8	7.8	9.0	12.5	108,900
Kinshasa	17.3	11.8	26.3	11.2	8.5	14.9	259,100
Yaoundé	11.4	19.2	21.1	9.6	5.0	14.7	108,700
Indian Ocean							
Antananarivo	5.0	3.9	7.9	2.5	1.1	4.4	25,300

Sources: Based on Phase 1 of the 1-2-3 surveys of selected countries (see table 1.1 for details).
Note: See text for ILO definition of unemployment.

The ILO definition of unemployment is extremely restrictive. It considers as unemployed only individuals who did not work a job during the reference week, even for an hour; were actively looking for a job; and were available to work it. Expanding this definition to include inactive individuals who may not have looked for a job during the reference month but who are still available to work a job if offered one changes the picture in two important ways. First, the unemployment rates increase from 11 percent to 16 percent in West Africa, from 14 percent to 17 percent in Cameroon, and from 15 percent to 24 percent in the Democratic Republic of Congo, where nearly one in four workers is unemployed under the broader-based definition (data were not available for Antananarivo) (table 1.7). Second, gender gaps widen, as hidden unemployment affects women more than men. The broader unemployment concept includes population groups on the fringes of economic activity—young people, women, and seniors—who have weaker connections to the labor market

The rest of the analysis covers only ILO-defined job-seekers who correspond to the international definition of unemployment.

For the sample as a whole, nearly as many men (11 percent) as women (12 percent) are unemployed. This average conceals some particularities: a

Table 1.7 Broader-Based Unemployment Rates in 11 Cities in Sub-Saharan Africa, by Gender and Age

City	Gender		Age			All	
	Men	Women	10–29	30–49	50+	Percentage	Number
West Africa							
Abidjan	14.2	17.6	20.6	11.2	8.6	15.8	245,000
Bamako	9.2	16.5	17.8	8.5	7.2	12.5	53,000
Cotonou	7.1	6.5	8.6	5.1	5.8	6.8	25,000
Dakar	12.8	26.2	23.0	16.0	10.9	18.9	153,000
Lomé	12.6	9.8	13.9	8.1	10.5	11.2	47,000
Niamey	17.3	32.0	33.4	14.9	16.5	23.3	60,000
Ouagadougou	17.4	28.3	31.0	14.5	8.7	22.4	90,000
WAEMU countries	13.2	18.8	20.9	11.4	9.5	15.9	673,000
Central Africa							
Douala	12.0	21.2	21.4	10.8	13.4	16.0	138,000
Kinshasa	24.2	23.2	38.9	18.2	14.5	23.8	461,000
Yaoundé	12.4	24.8	24.8	12.4	6.2	17.9	131,000

Sources: Based on Phase 1 of the 1-2-3 surveys of selected countries (see table 1.1 for details).
Note: Data on Antananarivo were not available.

higher proportion of women than men are unemployed in Dakar, whereas unemployment rates in Cotonou and Lomé are higher for men than women.

Across the board, the rate of unemployment falls with age. Young people in Ouagadougou are the hardest hit, with an unemployment rate of 22.4 percent among people 10–29. On the whole, young labor force participants find it extremely hard to enter the world of work.

Among older participants, Dakar and Abidjan stand out, with an unemployment rate of 10 percent for the intermediate age bracket (30–49). The oldest age bracket (50+) posts an unemployment rate of more than 11 percent in Niamey.

The unemployment rate also varies by level of education and type of training (table 1.8). Paradoxically, the unemployment rate rises with the level of education across all the West African cities. It is lowest among workers who never attended school, presumably because these workers are the least demanding regarding the jobs they will accept. In four West African cities, Central Africa, and Madagascar, the unemployment rates are bell shaped, falling only after secondary education. Even in these cities, however, unemployment rates among people who attended university are high, indicating that a degree is no guarantee of protection against unemployment (see chapter 5).

Heads of household (the households' main breadwinners) are the least affected by unemployment, with an average rate of 7 percent. "Secondary"

Table 1.8 ILO-Defined Unemployment Rates in 11 Cities in Sub-Saharan Africa, by Level of Education
(percent)

City	All	Uneducated	Primary	Lower-secondary	Upper-secondary	Secondary technical education	Higher education
West Africa							
Abidjan	13.5	8.7	11.4	18.1	19.2	23.3	20.7
Bamako	7.1	5.2	6.9	8.4	10.2	14.0	8.3
Cotonou	5.5	2.4	4.4	6.8	8.9	9.5	12.9
Dakar	11.7	8.9	12.3	15.2	14.6	0.4	12.7
Lomé	8.2	3.5	6.8	9.3	13.4	17.0	19.4
Niamey	13.1	9.1	15.0	21.5	14.1	15.0	8.5
Ouagadougou	15.4	9.5	16.0	23.9	22.7	25.8	14.3
WAEMU countries	11.4	7.6	10.5	15.3	16.1	18.0	16.6
Central Africa							
Douala	12.5	1.5	20.6	25.8	15.7	23.6	12.8
Kinshasa	14.9	7.8	11.8	16.5[a]	16.5[a]	16.5[a]	15.6
Yaoundé	14.7	2.0	18.3	31.0	23.4	12.3	13.0
Indian Ocean							
Antananarivo	4.5	1.4	4.3	5.1	3.6	5.6	4.7

Sources: Based on Phase 1 of the 1-2-3 surveys of selected countries (see table 1.1 for details).
Note: See text for ILO definition of unemployment.
a. Inaccuracies in the Kinshasa survey prevent the disaggregation of the unemployment rate at the secondary level.

members suffer the most from low labor demand, with unemployment averaging 17 percent for "other household members" and 21 percent for children of the head of household.

In all countries, unemployment is higher among natives (15 percent) than migrants (11 percent). This finding reflects not higher wage expectations but rather the fact that natives are more concentrated in the high unemployment risk categories (younger, more educated, and so forth).

Who Are the Unemployed?

Fifty-five percent of the unemployed are men (table 1.9). Men are the majority in all cities except Dakar, where women represent half of the unemployed, and the two Cameroonian cities (women represent 51 percent of the unemployed in Douala and 56 percent in Yaoundé). The average age of the unemployed is 30, but nearly one in four job-seekers (one in two in Ouagadougou) is 15–24. The average level of education of the unemployed is eight years of completed studies.

Table 1.9 Job-Seeker Characteristics in 11 Cities in Sub-Saharan Africa
(percentage of total, except where otherwise indicated)

Characteristic	West Africa								Central Africa			Indian Ocean
	Abidjan	Bamako	Cotonou	Dakar	Lomé	Niamey	Ouagadougou	WAEMU countries	Douala	Kinshasa	Yaoundé	Antananarivo
Men	51.3	56.2	53.3	49.2	64.2	57.7	54.8	53.1	49.3	65.8	44.3	58.7
Women	48.7	43.8	46.7	50.8	35.8	42.4	45.2	46.9	50.7	34.2	55.7	41.3
Average age (years)	28.3	28.7	30.3	29.9	29.6	30.0	26.7	28.7	29.7	33.0	27.9	26.6
Average education (years of completed schooling)	6.9	5.7	8.0	5.6	8.3	5.4	5.9	6.5	9.4	10.2	9.3	7.8
First-time job-seekers	54.0	57.8	40.0	53.8	50.8	61.1	63.2	54.9	39.0	60.9	45.6	42.7
Previously employed	46.0	42.2	60.0	46.2	49.2	38.9	36.8	45.1	61.0	39.1	54.4	58.3
Months of unemployment	36.9	33.3	32.3	46.9	32.1	59.5	48.6	40.7	36.7	66.7	33.0	16.0
Long-term unemployed	69.5	62.1	55.1	64.5	53.9	84.2	70.1	67.4	64.2	62.0	56.4	50.4
Number (thousands)	205.4	28.0	20.4	87.0	33.3	29.9	56.5	460.5[a]	109.7	259.1	108.7	25.3

Sources: Based on Phase 1 of the 1-2-3 surveys of selected countries (see table 1.1 for details).
Note: The long-term unemployed are people who have been looking for a job for more than one year.
a. Total population.

The unemployed are a heterogeneous population that includes two types of job-seekers: first-time job-seekers and previously employed workers. Fifty-three percent of the unemployed are first-time job-seekers, suggesting that the formal sector has adjusted to economic conditions mainly by freezing recruitment and only secondarily by cutting jobs.

Fifty-seven percent of unemployed women are first-time job-seekers. First-time job-seekers represent the majority of unemployed women in all cities; their share is particularly large in Ouagadougou, Niamey, and Kinshasa, where more than 70 percent of unemployed women are first-time job-seekers. First-time job-seekers have more years of education (8.7) than the previously employed (7.6 years), with an even wider gap in West Africa. They also have more years of education than employed women (6.9 years).

Unemployment among the previously employed reflects the weak economic situation in Sub-Saharan Africa: redundancies, contracts coming to an end, business closures, and staff cuts accounted for 57 percent of job losses. Nearly three in 10 job-seekers were made redundant or came to the end of their contract. One-third of job-seekers in Lomé were made redundant and one-quarter in Ouagadougou lost their job at the end of their contract. Abidjan suffered the most from the economic downturn (because of the political crisis), with more than 36 percent of job losses caused by closures and staff cuts.

The unemployment rate for the previously employed is higher among former public enterprise employees, where it affects more than 11 percent of workers (15 percent in Douala and 17 percent in Dakar). Privatization and restructuring have hit redundant employees hard, and a large number of them have not found new jobs.

Across institutional sectors and cities, unemployment hits the bottom of the wage ladder hardest. Whereas less than 6 percent of senior managers are unemployed, 13 percent of unskilled manual and nonmanual employees and 12 percent of laborers are unemployed.

Characteristics and Length of Unemployment

Unemployment averages nearly three and a half years (41 months) in West Africa, 35 months in Cameroon, and more than five years (66 months) in Kinshasa (these figures indicate the period during which the unemployed did not work a "real" job rather than the period during which they did not work at all). Nearly two-thirds of job-seekers have been unemployed for more than a year. On the whole, long-term unemployment hits first-time job-seekers harder than it hits the previously employed. The long average length of unemployment indicates how very hard it is for the unemployed to enter or reenter the labor market.

Two groups of cities can be distinguished. In the first group, made up of Cotonou, Lomé, Bamako, and especially Antananarivo, the labor market appears to be more flexible than elsewhere. The unemployment rate is below 10 percent, and the length of unemployment is shorter than in other cities. The second group, made up of the cities in Central Africa, Dakar, Ouagadougou, and especially Niamey, unemployment rates are higher, and average unemployment lasts four to six years.

Job-Seeking Methods

The preferred job-seeking method among the unemployed is to draw on family solidarity networks. Two-thirds of the unemployed deploy this strategy. One in five job-seekers (55 percent in Antananarivo) directly prospects employers. About 4 percent of job-seekers (8 percent in Cotonou and Bamako and 13 percent in Antananarivo) respond to advertisements for jobs.

Only 7 percent of job-seekers are registered with an employment agency, and just 2 percent have actively tried to find a job through that agency. Registration rates are low because the majority of job-seekers (56 percent) are unaware that employment agencies exist. Another 28 percent are pessimistic about the agency's capacity to help them.

These findings suggest that the authorities need to do a better job of helping job-seekers, especially by providing them with information. Employment agencies should make it easier for job-seekers to look for jobs by matching job vacancies that come in from businesses with the profiles of potential applicants. Placement agencies may need to be restructured if they are to perform effectively.

Type of Job Sought

The majority (59 percent) of job-seekers are looking for a wage-earning job, especially in Central Africa and Madagascar (where this percentage stands at 75 percent). Nearly one-quarter (22 percent) would prefer to be self-employed (8 percent in Antananarivo), and one-fifth have no preference regarding the type of employment found. A large majority (70 percent) would like to find permanent, full-time employment with an average working week of 44 hours. Job-seekers are thus not a pool of manpower on the fringe of economic activity.

The reasons for preferring one type of employment over another are similar across cities. As might be expected, the majority of people seeking wage employment (58 percent) do so for the security it is supposed to provide in terms of employment and wages. Twenty-five percent of job-seekers are prepared to work in any kind of business, and 48 percent will accept any sector or occupation. Only 10 percent are drawn to public administration, which is not the end-all of a trepid workforce, to use an image that is all-too-often evoked. Unemployment therefore is not solely the upshot of dissatisfied manpower with ambitions that are incompatible with market conditions. At least in part, it also reflects the absence of job opportunities.

Earnings Expectations

One possible reason why people are unemployed is that their earnings expectations are unrealistic. Job-seekers in the seven West African cities expect to earn €162 for a 44-hour working week—about twice the average earnings of an employed worker (table 1.10). Only in Ouagadougou and Niamey are expectations closer to reality. Outside West Africa, job-seekers expect to earn €162 a month in Douala (where employed workers earn an average €99 a month), €138 in Yaoundé (where employed workers earn €111), and €67 in Antananarivo (where employed workers earn €58).

However, 75 percent of job-seekers are prepared to revise their earnings demands downward if they remain unemployed too long. The reservation earnings—that is, the minimum earnings a job-seeker would accept—is estimated at an average of €118 across the WAEMU region, about €100 in Cameroon, and €48 in Madagascar. These earnings are higher than average earnings in all cities except Antananarivo.

Table 1.10 Earnings Expectations and Reservation Earnings in 11 Cities in Sub-Saharan Africa

City	Monthly earnings expectations (euros)	Percentage prepared to revise earnings expectations if unemployment lasts too long	Monthly reservation earnings (euros)	Reservation earnings gap (euros)	Ideal working week (hours/week)
West Africa					
Abidjan	206	79.4	151	71.6***	44.5
Bamako	119	68.3	107	85.9***	41.4
Cotonou	115	81.9	90	61.6***	44.7
Dakar	174	78.6	126	85.9***	43.4
Lomé	105	82	71	87.8***	44.6
Niamey	86	77.4	67	80.4***	43.2
Ouagadougou	89	82.3	60	127.0***	45.8
WAEMU countries	162	79.1	118	n.a.	44.1
Central Africa					
Douala	162	86.6	109	53.7***	42.9
Kinshasa[a]	45	57.8	31	89.6***	41.9
Yaoundé	138	87.7	88	37.7***	45.6
Indian Ocean					
Antananarivo	67	86.3	48	2.1[ns]	43.9

Sources: Based on Phase 1 of the 1-2-3 surveys of selected countries (see table 1.1 for details).
Note: The reservation earnings gap corresponds to the percentage of additional earnings targeted by the unemployed (reservation earnings) compared with employed workers. It is calculated from a standard ordinary least squares Mincerian hourly gains equation based on gender, migrant status, status in the household, number of years of education and number of years of education squared, and potential experience. n.a. = not applicable.
a. More than half of the unemployed in Kinshasa did not answer the question.
*** significant at the 1 percent level; ns = not significant.

The explanation for disparities in job-seekers' reservation earnings needs to be developed using such parameters as work experience, skill level, gender, age, and type of employment sought. For example, for identical characteristics (gender, education, potential experience, and migrant status), the minimum wage for which job-seekers would be willing to work is more than 70 percent higher than the earnings of employed workers in their main job in the West African cities and about 40–50 percent higher than in Cameroon. This finding suggests that aspirations are out of line with actual labor market conditions. In Antananarivo, reservation earnings are not significantly different from actual earnings, which probably has something to do with the low unemployment rate. (Results are not reliable for Kinshasa, where more than half of the unemployed did not answer the question about earnings expectations.)

Job Structure and Dynamics

Forty-four percent of the 7 million people employed in the 11 cities studied were women (table 1.11). Women are very much in the minority in Niamey (36 percent of jobholders); in Cotonou and Lomé, they form the majority. Except in Dakar, Kinshasa, and Antananarivo, migrants form the majority of the employed labor force. Average job seniority is seven years. It is higher in Niamey, Bamako, Dakar, and Kinshasa, partly because of a slightly higher average age in these cities.

For the sample as a whole, the rate of wage employment (wage workers as a percentage of all workers), an indicator of the extent of the formalization of labor relations, is 39 percent (35 percent in West Africa). The highest rates of wage employment are in Antananarivo and Cameroon (slightly more than half of all workers) and in Abidjan (41 percent) and Dakar (38 percent), the two most prosperous cities in West Africa.

Multiple jobholding is often considered to be a household and individual strategy for increasing income and offsetting declines in income during recessions. The rate of multiple jobholding is 8 percent for the sample as a whole. In West Africa, the lowest rate of multiple jobholding (less than 5 percent) is in the two largest cities (Dakar and Abidjan). In contrast, 9 percent of workers in Cotonou hold a second job. The highest rate of multiple jobholding is in Antananarivo (14 percent). These figures belie the notion that multiple jobholding is the norm in Africa.

Nearly half of all workers (49 percent) head up their own production unit, either as an employer with Wage-earners or as an own-account worker. The cities in West Africa can be classed into three groups. In Bamako, Lomé, and Cotonou, about 60 percent of workers are self-employed; in Ouagadougou and Niamey, just under 50 percent are self-employed; in Abidjan and Dakar, 45 percent of workers are self-employed. The situation is more disparate in Central Africa and Madagascar, where the proportion is 36 percent in Antananarivo,

Table 1.11 Worker Characteristics in 11 Cities in Sub-Saharan Africa

Characteristic	West Africa								Central Africa			Indian Ocean
	Abidjan	Bamako	Cotonou	Dakar	Lomé	Niamey	Ouagadougou	WAEMU countries	Douala	Kinshasa	Yaoundé	Antananarivo
Number of jobs (thousands)	1,312	369	348	658	371	197	311	3,566[a]	760	1,477	630	540
Men (percent)	53.3	55.9	46.6	59.2	47.1	63.6	58.1	54.4	59.3	55.1	59.5	59.3
Women (percent)	46.7	44.1	53.4	40.8	52.9	36.4	41.9	45.6	40.7	44.9	40.5	40.7
Migrants (percent)	73.3	59.2	56.0	42.7	66.5	61.3	60.5	62.2	75.2	45.3	77.0	28.9
Average age (years)	31.4	33.4	32.7	32.8	31.5	34.2	32.8	32.3	33.4	39.4	33.0	33.4
Education (years)	5.0	4.1	5.4	4.6	5.9	4.7	4.3	4.9	8.8	9.2	9.3	8.8
Seniority (years)	5.4	7.3	6.6	7.4	5.9	8.2	6.0	6.3	4.9	8.1	4.3	4.9
Type of worker (percentage of total)												
Self-employed	44.7	62.5	57.1	44.4	60.2	47.2	49.5	49.9	41.6	60.3	38.2	35.6
Manager	9.0	10.8	8.3	6.7	4.5	13.8	9.1	8.5	9.8	14.9	17.0	8.3
Manual or nonmanual employee	17.3	9.8	11.3	17.9	12.3	11.9	12.8	14.8	25.0	16.0	23.6	32.5
Laborer or similar	29.0	16.9	23.3	31.0	23.0	27.1	28.6	26.8	29.5	8.8	29.2	23.6
Wage employment (percent)	40.8	28.0	24.7	37.5	24.0	35.0	33.0	34.6	46.5	35.7	51.0	53.2
Multiple jobholding (percent)	4.9	7.2	9.2	4.3	6.1	7.7	6.2	5.9	14.0	6.5	11.6	14.0

Sources: Based on Phase 1 of the 1-2-3 surveys of selected countries (see table 1.1 for details).
a. Total number of jobs (thousands).

38 percent in Yaoundé, 42 percent in Douala, and 60 percent in Kinshasa. Skilled manual and nonmanual employees account for just over 18 percent of jobs, largely reflecting the development of wage employment. These figures range from an average of 15 percent in West Africa and Kinshasa to about one-quarter in Cameroon and one-third in Madagascar.

The job structure by sector reveals the predominance of trade and services (the "tertiary" sector). This sector accounts for at least three-quarters of all jobs, except in Antananarivo (60 percent) (table 1.12). Industrial activities account for a little more than one-fifth of jobs. Their weight is heaviest in Dakar (28 percent), Niamey (26 percent), and Antananarivo (35 percent), where a buoyant export processing business sector exists, especially in textiles. Suburban agriculture remains marginal (3 percent), with a maximum of 5 percent in Kinshasa, Niamey, Antananarivo, and Ouagadougou.

The distribution of jobs by institutional sector is a good composite indicator of the structure of the labor market. The largest sector is the informal sector, which employs 70 percent of workers on average and up to 76 percent in West Africa. The formal private sector is in second place, with 17 percent of jobs. Only 11 percent of employed people work in the public sector (8 percent in the administration and 3 percent in public and semipublic enterprises). The very small share of public employment invalidates the idea of a bloated public sector.

The structure by institutional sector reveals some remarkable similarities across cities. In West Africa, Abidjan has the most developed formal private sector (about 18 percent of jobs). Dakar is in second place with 15 percent. Niamey posts the largest concentration of public sector jobs, but they account for just 15 percent of total employment. Cotonou and Lomé are leading cities for the informal sector, which accounts for more than 80 percent of jobs.

Even sharper contrasts are found in Central Africa and Madagascar. At one end of the scale is Kinshasa, where 71 percent of jobs are in the informal sector, the public sectors employs 17 percent of the workforce, and the formal private sector employs just 9 percent of the workforce (the smallest share of the 11 cities). At the other end of the scale are the Cameroonian and Malagasy cities, where a smaller (albeit still high) share (53–62 percent) of jobs are in the informal sector.

Public Sector

Public jobs are naturally concentrated in the nonmarket sectors. However, industrial employment accounts for 25 percent of jobs in semi-public enterprises, a slightly higher share than in the labor market as a whole (21 percent). Women are less well represented in public employment (26 percent) than in the labor market as a whole (45 percent). In all cities, the highest proportion of migrants (70 percent) is found in the public sector (table 1.13).

Table 1.12 Job Structure in 11 Cities in Sub-Saharan Africa, by Institutional and Activity Sector

(percent)

| Sector/industry | West Africa | | | | | | | Central Africa | | | Indian Ocean |
	Abidjan	Bamako	Cotonou	Dakar	Lomé	Niamey	Ouagadougou	WAEMU countries	Douala	Kinshasa	Yaoundé	Antananarivo
Institutional sector												
Public administration	5.5	7.5	6.3	5.7	5.2	13.5	10.4	6.6	4.8	11.9	15.0	8.1
Public enterprise	1.1	2.5	2.2	1.8	2.3	1.8	2.3	1.8	1.8	5.0	2.3	2.6
Formal private sector	17.6	11.4	9.9	15.0	10.5	11.8	11.8	14.2	30.7	8.8	23.8	34.6
Informal sector	74.7	77.5	80.3	76.4	81.0	71.1	73.4	76.2	61.9	70.9	57.2	53.1
Nonprofit organization	1.1	1.1	1.3	1.1	1.0	1.8	2.1	1.2	0.8	3.4	1.7	1.5
Industry												
Primary sector[a]	1.6	2.6	2.1	3.1	2.1	5.4	4.9	2.6	2.7	5.8	2.5	5.0
Industry	19.7	20.0	18.0	28.2	20.5	26.2	23.2	21.9	22.5	14.8	18.8	34.9
Trade	34.1	41.7	37.0	26.6	38.4	26.3	36.4	34.0	27.2	42.3	20.9	23.2
Services	44.6	35.5	42.9	42.1	39.0	42.1	35.5	41.5	47.6	37.1	57.8	36.9

Sources: Based on Phase 1 of the 1-2-3 surveys of selected countries (see table 1.1 for details).

a. The primary sector includes agriculture, forestry, and fishery.

Table 1.13 Job Structure in 11 Cities in Sub-Saharan Africa, by Institutional Sector

(percent, except where otherwise indicated)

Institutional sector	Number	Share of total	Average age (years)	Proportion of women	Proportion of migrants	Completed years of education	Seniority in the job (years)	Proportion of informal employment
Public administration	588,300	8.4	41.7	27.3	69.5	12.3	10.0	8.0
Public enterprise	178,600	2.6	44.0	21.9	72.0	11.4	10.9	11.2
Formal private sector	1,216,700	17.4	34.4	25.8	61.5	9.3	5.3	40.7
Informal sector	4,877,700	69.9	32.8	52.6	58.3	5.4	6.1	97.0
Nonprofit organization	120,200	1.7	36.9	28.8	61.1	9.7	6.6	37.0
All	6,981,500	100	34.2	44.6	60.2	6.9	6.4	76.5

Sources: Based on Phase 1 of the 1-2-3 surveys of selected countries (see table 1.1 for details).

Public sector employees are more skilled than the rest of the labor force. Employees in this sector have by far the highest level of education (12 completed years of education). Public sector employees have more than 10 years seniority on average, compared with just 6 in the other sectors. The longer tenure reflects the job-for-life phenomenon as well as the freeze on recruitment.

Formal Private Sector

The formal private sector has the highest rate of wage employment (86 percent across all the cities) after the public sector. Thirty-five percent of employed workers in the sector work in businesses with fewer than 10 people (21 percent work in businesses with fewer than 6 people); 26 percent work in businesses with more than 100 people. In Bamako, Ouagadougou, Lomé, Niamey, Cotonou, and Yaoundé the majority of formal private sector jobs are in establishments that employ a maximum of 20 people.

The average age (34) is much lower than in the public sector (42). Formal private sector employees have an average of 9.3 years of education, second only to workers in the public sector.

Informal Sector

The informal sector is similar in all cities in terms of age (young), activities, the size of the production unit (small), and rates of wage employment (low). Ninety percent of informal sector jobs are in production units with fewer than six people, and 54 percent are own-account workers. This sector has the lowest wage employment rate of all institutional sectors (17 percent).

Three-quarters of informal sector jobs are in trade and services. Trade accounts for half of all informal sector jobs in Bamako, one-third in Niamey and Dakar, and 56 percent in Kinshasa. However, the industrial sector is not inconsequential; it provides 21 percent of informal sector jobs (25–32 percent in Dakar, Niamey, and Ouagadougou). Sixty-eight percent of industrial jobs (70 percent in WAEMU) are informal. Only in Antananarivo is the formal sector developed enough to provide more than half (54 percent) of industrial jobs.

Across the 11 cities, about 20 percent of informal sector workers work on proper professional premises (more than 25 percent in Abidjan and Dakar, 20 percent in Antananarivo, 9 percent in Niamey). Fourteen percent of informal sector workers work from home without dedicated facilities (20 percent in Kinshasa, 18 percent in Niamey, and 17 percent in Cotonou); 6 percent of informal sector workers work from home in a space specifically set aside for the purpose (13 percent in Antananarivo and 10 percent in Cotonou). Across the 11 cities, 11 percent of workers are itinerant. These percentages are higher in Lomé, Cotonou, and Bamako. Workers in the informal sector are young, with one-third of them under 25. With an average 5.4 years of education, more than

60 percent of informal workers have no more than primary school education (77 percent in the WAEMU countries).

The informal sector is also disproportionately female (53 percent). The percentage of women ranges from 41 percent in Niamey to 60 percent in Cotonou and Lomé. Contrary to a widely held belief that migration is responsible for the development of the informal sector, the sector actually contains the lowest proportion of migrants (about 50 percent).

Informal Employment

The ILO (2003) defines informal employment as employment that does not provide coverage in the institutional social protection scheme. Workers in this sector include the vast majority of the informal labor force and unprotected employees in the formal sector (Herrera and others 2012). We define informal employment as all contributing family workers, all independent workers in the informal sector, and all employees without written contracts and not benefiting from social protection.

Two main conclusions can be drawn from table 1.13 and the detailed results by country (not reported to save space). First, informal employment is dominant: on average, 77 percent of the labor force is informally employed. The largest shares are in Lomé (83 percent), Cotonou and Bamako (82 percent), and Ouagadougou (81 percent); the smallest share is in Antananarivo (62 percent).

Second, informal employment is significant in every institutional sector. As expected, nearly all informal sector jobs (97 percent) are informal. But informal employment represents 41 percent of private formal sector jobs (26 percent in Antananarivo, 33 percent in Abidjan and Dakar, and 36 percent in Kinshasa). Cameroonian cities have both the highest proportion of formal sector jobs and the highest rate of informal jobs in the formal sector (50 percent in Douala and 58 percent in Yaoundé). Informal employment also accounts for 8 percent of public administration jobs and 11 percent of public enterprise jobs.

Composition of Working Labor Force by Age Bracket

Three main groups account for virtually the entire working labor force studied: self-employment in the informal sector (in the form of own-account work or work as an employer) (48 percent); wage employment in the public and private formal sector (27 percent); and dependent employment in the informal sector as an employee, apprentice, or contributing family worker (22 percent) (figure 1.2). The remaining 3 percent are nonwage workers in the formal sector.

Up to the age of about 20, the majority of employed workers work in the informal sector (96 percent among people 10–14, 90 percent among people 15–19, and 80 percent among people 20–24), mainly in dependent employment. The second period sees the emergence of wage employment in the formal sector as a labor market integration mode. This curve rises steadily through age 55.

Figure 1.2 Sectoral Composition of Employed Workforce in 11 Cities in Sub-Saharan Africa, by Age

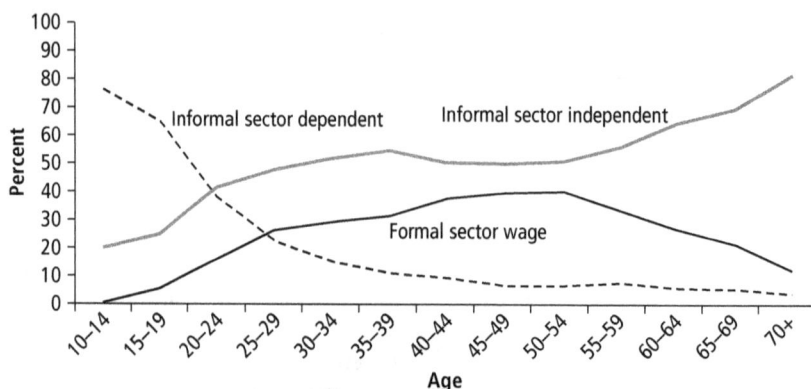

Sources: Based on Phase 1 of the 1-2-3 surveys of selected countries (see table 1.1 for details).

After 55, individuals return to informal sector jobs as self-employed workers. Up to 80 percent of jobs held after age 69 are in self-employment.

It is tempting to interpret this age-based curve in terms of the professional life cycle: workers first acquire informal sector work experience, then integrate into the formal sector as wage earners before setting up in self-employment at the end of the working life with human and financial capital accumulated in the previous stage. In fact, only panel data on the entire life cycle or backward-looking surveys (biographical-type surveys) could bear out this three-phase trajectory at the individual level.

Labor Income and Working Conditions

Labor provides most of the income received by African individuals and households. Analyzing this indicator therefore evaluates the quality of the jobs generated by the different productive sectors and measures the standard of living and extent of poverty in the 11 cities studied. The analysis at this stage concentrates on nominal incomes (further analysis converts these data into real incomes using purchasing power parity). As with all household surveys, capturing incomes is an extremely tricky business (see overview). The following findings should therefore be interpreted with caution. In particular, more attention should be paid to within-city than between-city differences and to the aggregates for the region.

Earnings in Main Job

The average monthly earned income across all 11 cities is estimated at €72 (including contributing family workers' zero earnings). This average conceals large disparities (table 1.14). Average earnings in West Africa are €83. The highest earnings are in Abidjan (€108) and Dakar (€89). By far the lowest earnings are in Lomé (€39). The situation elsewhere ranges from barely €20 in Kinshasa to €52 in Antananarivo and more than €100 in Cameroon.

Public sector workers are better paid than workers in the private sector. An employee in a public enterprise earns €163 and a civil servant in the administration €208, whereas an employee in a formal private business earns just €116 a month. The lowest income is in the informal sector, where monthly earnings average just €52.

The higher earnings of public sector employees partly reflect the characteristics of the manpower employed in the sector, where senior and middle managers account for 59 percent of jobs (as opposed to 20 percent in the formal private sector). The percentage of managers in the public sector ranges from 37 percent in Lomé to 69 percent in Abidjan and 72 percent in Bamako.

Average seniority is also higher in the public sector (10 years versus about 6 in the formal private sector) (table 1.15). Average tenure in the public sector is shorter in Douala (eight years), Ouagadougou (seven years), and Yaoundé (five years).

Distribution of Earnings

Average monthly earnings vary by industry (table 1.16). Civil servants are at the top of the ladder. Civil servants in Dakar earn 10 times more than "small street traders"; civil servants in Cotonou earn 6.8 times more than workers in "clothing." The smallest gap is in Bamako, where civil servants earn 3.8 times more than "small street traders." In general, small traders are paid the least.

The minimum monthly wage ranges from €9 in Kinshasa to €59 in Dakar (table 1.17). Even within WAEMU, the range is wide (€21 in Lomé to €59 in Dakar). About half of workers earn less than the minimum wage in West Africa, ranging from 44 percent in Bamako to 61 percent in Ouagadougou. The proportion is lower elsewhere (about 40 percent in Antananarivo and Kinshasa and 30 percent in Cameroon). This finding reveals clear shortcomings in compliance with the legislation in force. The percentage of workers earning less than the minimum wage is highest in the informal sector. At the other end of the scale, about 10 percent of workers are paid more than four times the minimum wage in all cities except Yaoundé and Douala, where the minimum wage has not been adjusted for many years and the share of workers earning more than four times the minimum wage stands at about 20 percent. All in all, the minimum wage does not seem to be a binding constraint in any institutional sector. The *African Economic Outlook 2012* (African Development Bank and others 2012) confirms this result, concluding that "minimum wage is not an issue."

Table 1.14 Average Monthly Earnings from Main Job in 11 Cities in Sub-Saharan Africa, by Institutional Sector (euros)

Sector	West Africa								Central Africa			Indian Ocean
	Abidjan	Bamako	Cotonou	Dakar	Lomé	Niamey	Ouagadougou	WAEMU countries	Douala	Kinshasa	Yaoundé	Antananarivo
Public administration	337	136	137	228	126	137	144	212	198	18	235	99
Public enterprise	390	214	186	205	106	171	153	226	340	52	400	107
Formal private sector[a]	219	141	100	169	73	121	112	170	149	34	117	59
Informal sector	60	57	40	59	27	44	31	50	58	17	64	38
All	108	77	56	89	39	69	57	83	99	21	111	52

Sources: Based on Phase 1 of the 1-2-3 surveys of selected countries (see table 1.1 for details).
Note: Figures include contributing family workers, whether or not they were paid.
a. Includes formal private businesses and nonprofit organizations.

Table 1.15 Average Seniority in Main Job in 11 Cities in Sub-Saharan Africa, by Institutional Sector (years)

Sector	West Africa								Central Africa			Indian Ocean
	Abidjan	Bamako	Cotonou	Dakar	Lomé	Niamey	Ouagadougou	WAEMU countries	Douala	Kinshasa	Yaoundé	Antananarivo
Public administration	9.8	10.8	9.3	13.3	11.5	10.1	6.9	10.2	8.1	11.4	5.3	10.6
Public enterprise	9.8	11.2	8.4	10.7	10.1	12.7	8.8	10.1	9.0	13.1	7.2	8.2
Formal private sector[a]	5.5	6.7	5.5	7.8	5.9	6.9	5.4	6.1	4.6	6.9	3.3	5.0
Informal sector	5.0	6.9	6.4	6.7	5.5	7.9	5.9	5.9	4.8	7.4	4.4	7.0
All	5.4	7.3	6.6	7.4	5.9	8.2	6.0	6.3	4.9	8.1	4.3	6.6

Sources: Based on Phase 1 of the 1-2-3 surveys of selected countries (see table 1.1 for details).
Note: Figures include contributing family workers, whether or not they were paid.
a. Includes formal private businesses and nonprofit organizations.

Table 1.16 Average Monthly Earnings from Main Job in 11 Cities in Sub-Saharan Africa, by Industry (euros)

Sector	West Africa							WAEMU countries	Central Africa			Indian Ocean
	Abidjan	Bamako	Cotonou	Dakar	Lomé	Niamey	Ouagadougou		Douala	Kinshasa	Yaoundé	Antananarivo
Primary sector[a]	123	87	79	97	30	48	40	79	80	15	42	24
Industry	102	82	46	73	32	47	48	73	120	23	92	49
Trade	63	59	46	70	28	53	32	54	63	18	64	47
Services	145	96	69	110	54	97	90	111	110	23	137	63
All	108	78	56	89	39	69	57	83	99	21	111	52

Sources: Based on Phase 1 of the 1-2-3 surveys of selected countries (see table 1.1 for details).
Note: Figures include contributing family workers, whether or not they were paid.
a. The primary sector includes agriculture, forestry, and fishery.

Table 1.17 Monthly Earnings as Multiple of Minimum Wage in Main Job in 11 Cities in Sub-Saharan Africa

Item	West Africa							WAEMU countries	Central Africa			Indian Ocean
	Abidjan	Bamako	Cotonou	Dakar	Lomé	Ouagadougou	Niamey		Douala	Kinshasa	Yaoundé	Antananarivo
Minimum wage (euros)	55	34	38	59	21	41	34	—	36	9	36	29
Less than the minimum wage (percent)	49.9	43.9	54.9	53.6	49.0	61.3	45.3	51.1	31.1	41.0	29.1	40.1
More than four times the minimum wage (percent)	10.6	12.5	9.0	7.4	10.3	9.1	13.1	10.0	17.8	11.7	22.3	8.1

Sources: Based on Phase 1 of the 1-2-3 surveys of selected countries (see table 1.1 for details).
Note: Figures include contributing family workers, whether or not they were paid.

The distribution of earned income can also be analyzed by comparing quartiles and the interquartile ratio (table 1.18). Median monthly earnings are much lower than average earnings, partly because of the large number of unpaid workers. When unpaid workers are excluded, the gap between median and average earnings narrows, although median earnings still remain much lower. On average, workers in the third quartile of the distribution earn five times more than workers in the first quartile. This ratio is highest in Bamako and Niamey (about 6) and lowest in Cotonou and Dakar (about 4). The gaps are wider in West Africa than in Central Africa and Madagascar.

Taking into account people who work without being paid (zero earnings), especially contributing family workers, the Gini coefficients are similar across cities (table 1.19). In West Africa, they range from 0.59 in Dakar to 0.64 in Ouagadougou. Antananarivo stands out, with a lower albeit still fairly high level of inequality of 0.53. This finding reflects the higher rate of wage employment in Antananarivo, especially in the formal sector.

With no effective labor market regulatory mechanisms, earnings inequalities are very high in all cities. Gini indexes at the household level are of the same order of magnitude, suggesting that no compensating mechanisms are at work within households to mitigate individual inequalities.

Gender Differences

On average, women's earnings are half of men's (table 1.20). Women are even worse off when their incomes are viewed in terms of median earnings: their median remuneration is about one-third of men's. This gap reflects the weight of contributing family workers, who are overwhelmingly female.

These findings are similar across cities, although the ranking depends on the indicator used. Based on average remuneration, comparisons show women to be best off in Central Africa and Madagascar (where the male/female ratio is about 1.6), Dakar (1.87), and Niamey (1.94). They are worst off in Cotonou (2.51) and Bamako (2.59) (see chapter 9).

The second gender-related characteristic of earned income is the higher inequality among women than among men. One of the reasons for this difference is the weight of informal sector jobs, which are less egalitarian than jobs in other sectors. Ouagadougou has both the largest within-gender earnings inequalities and the widest gender gap.

Earnings Ladder

The earnings ladder is evident across all institutional sectors (table 1.21). Managers and employers earn the most. They are better paid in the formal private sector than in the public sector, except in Lomé and Cotonou. Next come manual and nonmanual employees, with laborers and others (apprentices and family workers) earning least.

Table 1.18 Monthly Earnings from Main Job in 11 Cities in Sub-Saharan Africa, by Quartile
(euros)

| | West Africa | | | | | | | | Central Africa | | | Indian Ocean |
Item	Abidjan	Bamako	Cotonou	Dakar	Lomé	Niamey	Ouagadougou	WAEMU countries	Douala	Kinshasa	Yaoundé	Antananarivo
First quartile	23	15	14	22	9	14	11	15	24	3	30	17
Second quartile	55	46	31	46	23	45	23	38	53	10	55	42
Third quartile	112	92	61	92	46	88	61	92	100	19	122	68
Average monthly earnings	108	78	56	89	39	69	57	83	99	21	111	52
Interquartile ratio (third quartile/first quartile)	4.9	6.0	4.4	4.1	5.2	6.1	5.6	6.0	4.2	5.4	4.0	4.0

Sources: Based on Phase 1 of the 1-2-3 surveys of selected countries (see table 1.1 for details).
Note: Figures include contributing family workers, whether or not they were paid.

Table 1.19 Gini Index of Monthly Earnings and Household Income in 11 Cities in Sub-Saharan Africa

| | West Africa | | | | | | | Central Africa | | | Indian Ocean |
Type of earnings	Abidjan	Bamako	Cotonou	Dakar	Lomé	Niamey	Ouagadougou	Douala	Kinshasa	Yaoundé	Antananarivo
Individual earnings from main job, including zero earnings	0.62	0.62	0.62	0.59	0.61	0.61	0.64	0.58	0.62	0.58	0.53
Individual earnings from main job, excluding zero earnings	0.58	0.60	0.54	0.54	0.56	0.56	0.59	0.53	0.59	0.53	0.47
Household labor earnings	0.58	0.58	0.55	0.54	0.57	0.58	0.57	0.55	0.64	0.61	0.47
Total household income	0.59	0.58	0.53	0.51	0.62	0.59	0.56	0.51	0.62	0.55	0.46

Sources: Based on Phase 1 of the 1-2-3 surveys of selected countries (see table 1.1 for details).

Table 1.20 Average and Median Monthly Earnings from Main Job and Gini Index in 11 Cities in Sub-Saharan Africa, by Gender

Item	West Africa								Central Africa			Indian Ocean
	Abidjan	Bamako	Cotonou	Dakar	Lomé	Niamey	Ouagadougou	WAEMU countries	Douala	Kinshasa	Yaoundé	Antananarivo
Average earnings (euros)												
Men	147	106	83	110	55	84	73	111	122	25	132	64
Women	64	41	33	59	25	43	35	49	65	16	81	39
Median earnings (euros)												
Men	83	57	50	79	31	48	46	67	75	15	76	42
Women	29	18	18	28	12	18	13	23	38	7	46	25
Gini coefficient												
Men	0.57	0.58	0.57	0.58	0.57	0.57	0.58	0.59	0.54	0.60	0.55	0.50
Women	0.63	0.59	0.59	0.57	0.60	0.63	0.67	0.63	0.60	0.63	0.60	0.54
All	0.62	0.62	0.62	0.59	0.61	0.61	0.64	0.63	0.58	0.62	0.58	0.53

Sources: Based on Phase 1 of the 1-2-3 surveys of selected countries (see table 1.1 for details).
Note: Figures include contributing family workers, whether or not they were paid.

Table 1.21 Average Monthly Earnings from Main Job in 11 Cities in Sub-Saharan Africa, by Institutional Sector and Socioeconomic Group
(euros)

Sector	West Africa								Central Africa			Indian Ocean
	Abidjan	Bamako	Cotonou	Dakar	Lomé	Niamey	Ouagadougou	WAEMU countries	Douala	Kinshasa	Yaoundé	Antananarivo
Public sector												
Managers	417	182	190	308	177	185	206	281	315	37	311	153
Manual and nonmanual employees	200	96	98	151	80	84	101	131	157	15	152	77
Laborers and others	112	54	39	88	47	48	47	64	73	14	56	45
Formal private sector[a]												
Managers and employers	484	240	149	364	170	248	263	351	370	48	280	152
Manual and nonmanual employees	140	80	76	134	62	74	84	118	108	23	83	50
Laborers and others	84	42	27	61	20	32	30	59	67	20	49	28
Informal sector												
Managers and employers	128	117	87	169	52	156	90	115	155	25	215	94
Own-account	63	61	49	76	30	50	35	56	57	15	64	43
Manual and nonmanual employees	83	60	45	68	34	62	44	69	63	16	55	38
Laborers and others	24	17	6	19	9	14	13	18	23	8	20	9
All	108	78	56	89	39	69	57	83	99	21	111	52

Sources: Based on Phase 1 of the 1-2-3 surveys of selected countries (see table 1.1 for details).
Note: Figures include contributing family workers, whether or not they were paid.
a. Includes formal private businesses and nonprofit organizations.

In the formal sector, internal heterogeneity is greater in the private sector than in the public sector: formal private sector managers earn two to three times more than manual and nonmanual employees. The ratio between managers and laborers ranges from 6 (in Abidjan, Bamako, Cotonou, and Dakar) to more than 8 (in Lomé, Niamey, and Ouagadougou). There is less wage inequality in the public sector, where managers earn no more than twice the wages of manual and nonmanual employees and up to four times more than laborers. On average, the formal private sector pays its managers relatively more and the public sector pays its low-skilled employees relatively more.

The informal sector is the worst-paid sector, both because of the predominance of the least skilled categories of workers and because workers in the informal sector earn less than their counterparts in other sectors (see chapter 5). Own-account workers in the informal sector generally earn less than half the wages of manual and nonmanual employees in the formal sector. However, except in Ouagadougou, they earn more than the monthly minimum wage in all cities.

Working Hours and Underemployment

The average work week is 48 hours for formal private sector workers, 44 hours for workers in public enterprises, and 42 hours in public administration (table 1.22). Informal sector workers also work long hours (more than 47 hours a week). This sector is thus not a source of marginal, part-time jobs; it leaves little time to work a second job. The longest weekly hours are in Lomé and Ouagadougou (about 50 hours a week). The average work week is 45 hours in Dakar and 43 in Antananarivo.

Differences in the work week are very wide in the cities studied: one in five workers works less than 35 hours a week and 41 percent work more than 48 hours. The formal sector (public and private) is the most compliant with legislation on work duration: 70 percent of workers in the sector work 35–48 hours a week. In contrast, just 30 percent of informal sector workers work these hours. The work week is much longer in the informal sector, where 46 percent of workers work more than 48 hours a week (the figure is 29 percent in the formal sector).

Time-related underemployment. The number of hours worked reveals the amount of time-related underemployment. Fifteen percent of employed workers—more than 1 million people—involuntarily work less than 35 hours a week (table 1.23). The rate of time-related underemployment varies across cities (10 percent in Ouagadougou and Yaoundé, 17 percent in Bamako and Lomé, and 20 percent in Kinshasa). It is highest in the informal sector (16 percent).

Invisible underemployment. Time-related underemployment is just one manifestation of underemployment. For example, excessively long working hours

Table 1.22 Average Weekly Hours Worked in Main Job in 11 Cities in Sub-Saharan Africa, by Institutional Sector

Sector	West Africa								Central Africa			Indian Ocean
	Abidjan	Bamako	Cotonou	Dakar	Lomé	Niamey	Ouagadougou	WAEMU countries	Douala	Kinshasa	Yaoundé	Antananarivo
Public administration	43.2	40.8	41.0	41.5	49.9	43.2	41.4	42.7	39.9	42.6	38.0	40.3
Public enterprise	43.5	45.9	44.0	42.7	45.3	43.8	46.6	44.4	41.8	44.7	41.7	43.0
Formal private sector[a]	46.3	50.2	48.0	44.2	51.2	49.7	50.8	47.2	50.0	47.5	50.6	47.7
Informal sector	48.7	45.3	46.8	46.0	49.6	48.0	52.2	48.0	44.3	46.7	49.9	40.9
All	47.9	45.6	46.5	45.4	49.7	47.5	50.7	47.5	45.9	46.2	48.1	43.3

Sources: Based on Phase 1 of the 1-2-3 surveys of selected countries (see table 1.1 for details).
a. Includes formal private businesses and nonprofit organizations.

Table 1.23 Forms of Underemployment in 11 Cities in Sub-Saharan Africa
(percent)

Form of underemployment	West Africa								Central Africa			Indian Ocean
	Abidjan	Bamako	Cotonou	Dakar	Lomé	Niamey	Ouagadougou	WAEMU countries	Douala	Kinshasa	Yaoundé	Antananarivo
Time-related underemployment rate	12.6	17.1	13.4	16.2	17.1	16.0	10.6	14.3	14.4	19.6	9.9	14.0
Invisible underemployment rate (percentage of employed workers earning less than minimum hourly wage)	53.2	45.4	61.1	57.8	55.8	51.1	66.5	55.2	37.1	40.8	38.4	40.9
Total underemployment rate	66.4	58.8	69.2	69.4	68.4	64.4	73.0	67.1	53.7	63.0	53.7	52.7
Not in employment, education, or training (NEET) rate among people 10–24												
All	22.2	21.8	11.3	30.5	11.1	34.3	22.9	22.9	14.1	21.5	14.2	9.8
Women	28.4	28.8	15.0	39.6	14.5	40.3	30.3	29.5	19.3	24.9	18.5	11.6
Men	14.0	14.2	7.2	20.4	7.1	27.1	14.9	15.3	8.6	17.7	9.5	8.1

Sources: Based on Phase 1 of the 1-2-3 surveys of selected countries (see table 1.1 for details).
Note: Time-related and invisible underemployment are based on all employed workers. Total underemployment is based on all workers (employed and unemployed).

can (paradoxically) be a sign of underemployment when they are made necessary by abnormally low labor productivity. This form of underemployment is called *invisible underemployment*.

We have chosen the percentage of employed workers earning less than the minimum hourly wage as our indicator of invisible underemployment. On this basis, we estimate the rate of invisible underemployment at 48 percent across all 11 cities. It is highest in Ouagadougou (66.5 percent). Even in Bamako, it stands at more than 45 percent. Outside West Africa, the rate of invisible underemployment is lower, albeit still high, at about 40 percent.

Intercity comparisons need to be interpreted in relative terms, because the purchasing power of the minimum wage in force is not necessarily the same across cities, and wage policies do not necessarily pursue the same objective. The minimum wage should therefore be seen more as a social standard associated with a national environment than as a universal and absolute benchmark (physiological minimum for subsistence, for example). This manifestation of the mismatch between labor supply and demand is most glaring in the informal sector, where 60 percent of workers are in a situation of invisible underemployment (two-thirds in WAEMU); this share is much lower among formal private sector workers (28 percent), civil servants (14 percent), and public enterprise employees (8 percent).

Another indicator of underemployment is the NEET (not in employment, education, or training) rate, which takes into account discouraged workers. Among people 10–24, the NEET rate is 23 percent in West Africa (31 percent in Dakar and 34 percent in Niamey), 22 percent in Kinshasa, 14 percent in Cameroon, and 10 percent in Madagascar (see table 1.23). The NEET rate for young women is twice as high as for young men, except in Niamey, Kinshasa, and particularly Antananarivo, where both the levels and the gap (3.5 percentage points) are lowest.

When the different components of underemployment (unemployment, time-related underemployment, and invisible underemployment) are aggregated to obtain a composite indicator of underemployment, the total underemployment rate is 62 percent—5 million out of nearly 8 million workers—across all 11 cities. Total underemployment affects almost 60 percent of workers in Bamako and almost 75 percent in Ouagadougou. Women are more affected than men, whatever the type of underemployment (19 percent for women and 12 percent for men for visible underemployment; 61 percent for women and 38 percent for men for invisible underemployment). Underemployment of the labor force therefore seems to be the main problem in the labor market and, more generally, the region's urban economy (see chapter 2).

Working Conditions and Dependent Workers' Benefits

Job quality is conditioned by more than just earnings and working hours. Other factors, such as the steadiness of the job, the provision of an employment contract, the existence of social security coverage and paid holidays, and promotion opportunities and in-house training, are also important. This sub-section focuses on dependent workers (employees, contributing family work-ers, and apprentices), because independent workers are not covered by labor legislations.

Nearly 9 in 10 jobs are permanent across all 11 cities. Niamey leads in the share of casual jobs (19 percent of all jobs). In the informal sector, 85 percent of jobs are permanent jobs. Therefore, job insecurity does not manifest itself in a string of "odd jobs" and short-term jobs.

Job insecurity is expressed in the low level of employment contracts. Nearly two-thirds of employees have no written contract with their employer, and an equivalent proportion do not receive a payslip (table 1.24). Labor relations vary a great deal by institutional sector. In the informal sector, just 9 percent of dependent workers have a written contract, and less than 3 percent receive payslips.

Another indicator of poor job quality is the small share of workers with welfare benefits: 9.1 percent of workers are affiliated with the official social security body, and 3.3 percent have health insurance provided by the busi-ness. Differences are evident across institutional sectors. One-third of public sector employees have social security coverage, and 47 percent are entitled to paid holidays. These figures are much higher than in the formal private sector, where 12 percent of employees have social security coverage and 28 percent are entitled to paid holidays. Dependent workers in the informal sector appear to be totally deprived of these benefits. The gap between the two sectors is widened by the fact that the majority of informal workers are self-employed. Welfare and other benefits (allowances, job security, and so forth) are more common among the highest-paid socioeconomic groups, accentuating the differences in job quality (see chapter 4).

Union membership remains low among dependent workers. It stands at 13 percent in West Africa (ranging from 7 percent in Cotonou to 17 percent in Niamey). It is 15 percent in Kinshasa and less than 10 percent in Cameroon and Antananarivo. Unions are more widespread in the public sector: about one-third of public employees are union members as opposed to from one-tenth (Central Africa) to one-fifth (West Africa) in the formal private sector and less than 2 percent in the informal sector.

Job Mobility and Prospects

Data from Phase 1 of the 1-2-3 surveys can be used to quantify the quality of the match between the jobs people hold and the jobs they aspire to hold. The nature of the mismatches captures potential labor market rigidities, which can affect labor force participation rates, unemployment, and remuneration.

Table 1.24 Working Conditions for Dependent Workers in 11 Cities in Sub-Saharan Africa
(percent)

Feature	West Africa								Central Africa			Indian Ocean
	Abidjan	Bamako	Cotonou	Dakar	Lomé	Niamey	Ouagadougou	WAEMU countries	Douala	Kinshasa	Yaoundé	Antananarivo
Permanent job	92.0	82.6	92.5	84.6	84.7	81.4	87.0	88.2	86.9	87.8	91.8	90.8
Payslip	31.4	39.9	31.5	32.8	25.0	36.1	32.3	32.2	33.8	52.1	37.6	53.8
Contract	34.6	38.3	36.7	32.9	37.0	37.9	33.5	35.0	36.2	65.2	42.6	54.5
Social security	6.5	18.7	7.8	7.7	7.0	15.2	14.9	9.1	8.4	5.8	6.0	44.3
Health insurance	2.9	2.5	3.6	3.7	1.6	5.0	4.6	3.3	4.1	5.2	5.1	41.8
Paid holidays	19.3	22.8	16.1	7.9	11.0	13.1	23.2	16.3	11.7	7.3	17.2	44.7
In-house training	11.9	15.6	11.3	11.1	16.3	21.0	20.4	13.6	22.2	31.0	17.0	17.4
In-house promotion	9.1	3.5	5.7	11.1	13.8	15.5	18.0	10.4	12.1	22.0	13.7	7.2
Union members	15.5	15.0	7.2	10.0	13.2	16.6	7.9	12.8	9.6	14.8	6.9	8.1

Sources: Based on Phase 1 of the 1-2-3 surveys of selected countries (see table 1.1 for details).

The analysis in this section covers only people 15–24, because this generation constitutes the vast majority of people entering the labor market currently or in the near future. Some 4.6 million people 15–24 live in the 11 cities studied: 2.7 million are inactive, 1.5 million have jobs, and 341,000 (18 percent) are unemployed. Among jobholders, 38 percent report being satisfied with the position they hold and do not intend to look for another job in the near future. Fifty-two percent would like to find a new job, either by changing establishment (41 percent) or by being promoted within their current establishment.

The high level of job dissatisfaction decreases with age, falling to 44 percent among people 30–39 and 14 percent among people 60 and older. This phenomenon stems from two factors. The first is the "normal" life-cycle effect, in which work experience and seniority enable young people to secure better-quality jobs. The second is the fact that the depressed labor market is preventing young people from entering jobs that correspond to their skills (see chapter 3).

Young civil servants are more inclined to want to keep their jobs (59 percent) than young people working in the informal sector (37 percent). Surprisingly, this difference virtually disappears in West Africa, where 34 percent of young civil servants and 35 percent of young people in the informal sector are dissatisfied. However, among people who want to change jobs, proportionally more young civil servants would like to remain with their current institution.

The level of dissatisfaction is negatively correlated with remuneration. In West Africa, for example, "satisfied" young people earn an average of €35 a month, whereas people who would like to change jobs earn just €27 a month and people hoping for promotion earn €29. This hierarchy is found irrespective of the institutional sector, socioeconomic group, or city. A similar pattern is found outside West Africa, with the only difference being that people who would like to be promoted earn more than people who want to keep their job. The difference reflects the fact that the prospects for promotion are restricted mainly to the highest-paid jobs.

The mismatch between young people's preferences and real job opportunities is huge. Although the public sector (administration and public enterprises) created virtually no jobs in the two years preceding the survey (less than 4 percent of new jobs), 27 percent of young people still aspire to work in it (table 1.25). The informal sector, the main job provider during the two years before the survey, holds less drawing power for young people. In West Africa, for example, the sector accounted for 82 percent of job creation, but just 48 percent of job-seekers aspired to work in it. These findings are common to all 11 cities, although the extent to which aspirations are unrealistic varies considerably. Young people in Abidjan take the least account of the actual situation. Although fewer than 10,000 civil service jobs were filled in Abidjan in 2001–02, 140,000 young people aspired to secure one. Young people in Niamey have their feet a little more firmly on the ground: the city recruits about 5,000 civil servants from a pool of

Table 1.25 Job Aspirations of People 15–24 in 11 Cities in Sub-Saharan Africa, by Sector
(percent)

Sector	West Africa								Central Africa			Indian Ocean
	Abidjan	Bamako	Cotonou	Dakar	Lomé	Niamey	Ouagadougou	WAEMU countries	Douala	Kinshasa	Yaoundé	Antananarivo
Jobs wanted												
Public administration	22.8	32.7	26.7	13.0	8.7	28.1	32.8	22.4	21.6	10.2	16.7	22.7
Public enterprises	3.5	6.0	7.2	2.9	11.4	4.8	4.6	4.8	7.7	12.7	4.2	6.8
Formal private sector	25.8	15.9	18.3	33.0	23.5	19.8	20.2	24.4	31.3	43.5	23.1	47.8
Informal sector	47.9	45.4	47.8	51.0	56.4	47.5	42.4	48.4	39.4	33.6	56.0	22.7
All	100	100	100	100	100	100	100	100	100	100	100	100
Jobs created												
Public administration	1.8	3.0	3.2	2.8	1.5	11.3	8.1	3.0	2.5	4.9	11.6	3.3
Public enterprises	0.2	1.2	1.9	1.3	1.2	1.0	1.2	0.8	1.2	3.0	1.5	1.4
Formal private sector	15.6	9.7	12.8	17.1	10.5	14.4	15.2	14.5	32.1	14.3	28.8	44.2
Informal sector	82.4	86.1	82.1	78.8	86.8	73.3	75.5	81.7	64.3	77.8	58.1	51.1
All	100	100	100	100	100	100	100	100	100	100	100	100

Sources: Based on Phase 1 of the 1-2-3 surveys of selected countries (see table 1.1 for details).
Note: Findings are for 2000 and 2001 for Antananarivo, Bamako, Cotonou, and Lomé; 2001 and 2002 for Abidjan, Dakar, Niamey, and Ouagadougou; and 2004 and 2005 for Douala, Kinshasa, and Yaoundé. The formal private sector includes formal private businesses and nonprofit organizations.

27,000 young hopefuls. Yaoundé is unique, in that the jobs created are on the whole in line with aspirations.

Analysis of socioeconomic groups confirms that young people's ambitions are unrealistic. In West Africa, for example, nearly 35 percent of young people want to become managers, even though just 5 percent of positions are in management. The situation is similar in Antananarivo, Douala, and Kinshasa. Yaoundé displays similar patterns. Although young people appear to shun the idea of becoming laborers, contributing family workers, or apprentices (only 7 percent aspire to these occupations), these jobs account for 30–40 percent of jobs created.

These findings suggest that young job-seekers are heading for serious disappointment, which, if not corrected, could generate major social tensions. Although problems have not yet emerged and it is not a new issue (Berthelier and Roubaud 1993).

Adjustments need to be made in two directions. First, young people need to be made to understand that wage employment is not the be-all and end-all of a successful career and that the link between a university education and public employment is a thing of the past. Schools should prepare their students to envisage the possibility of setting up their own business by steering the curriculum more toward vocational training. Second, greater fairness and transparency are needed in managing formal sector jobs, particularly in the public sector. A more equitable distribution of these jobs needs to be promoted—by, for example, encouraging voluntary redundancies and early retirement to open the door for more qualified and motivated young people (see ILO 2010).

Notes

1. For a description of 1-2-3 surveys, see box O.1 in the overview.
2. The 10 countries are Benin, Burkina Faso, Cameroon, the Democratic Republic of Congo, Côte d'Ivoire, Madagascar, Mali, Niger, Senegal, and Togo. The 11 cities are Abidjan, Côte d'Ivoire; Bamako, Mali; Cotonou, Benin; Dakar, Senegal; Lomé, Togo; Ouagadougou, Burkina Faso; and Niamey, Niger, in West Africa; Douala and Yaoundé, Cameroon; and Kinshasa, the Democratic Republic of Congo, in Central Africa; and Antananarivo, Madagascar.

References

African Development Bank, Economic Commission for Africa, Organisation for Economic Co-operation and Development, and United Nations Development Programme. 2012. "Promoting Youth Employment." In *African Economic Outlook 2012*. Paris: OECD Publishing.

Berthelier, P., and F. Roubaud. 1993. *Conditions d'activité de la population de Yaoundé: principaux résultats*. Policy Brief, DIAL (Développement des Investigations sur l'Ajustement à Long Terme)/DSCN (Direction de la Statistique et de la Comptabilité Nationale), Paris/Yaoundé.

Herrera, J., C. J. Nordman, X. Oudin, and J.-M. Wachsberger. 2012. "Révision des questionnaires des enquêtes emploi en vue de mieux enregistrer les différentes dimensions du travail décent." An output of the European Commission–funded RECAP project implemented by the International Training Centre of the International Labour Organization, Turin.

ILO (International Labour Organization). 2003. "General Report." Seventeenth International Conference of Labour Statisticians, Geneva November 24–December 3.

———. 2010. *Global Employment Trends for Youth 2012*. Geneva: ILO.

Part II

Job Quality and Labor Market Conditions in Sub-Saharan Africa

Chapter 2

Underemployment and Job Mismatch in Sub-Saharan Africa

Javier Herrera and Sébastien Merceron

Traditional labor market indicators fail to capture the distinctive characteristics of low-income countries and the ways in which markets in those countries adjust. The absence of unemployment insurance, the importance of informal sector employment, and the weakness of state regulations, among other factors, reduce the relevance of quantity adjustments (measured by the unemployment rate) in these countries, where changes in the quality of employment seem to play an important role.

No official indicator captures this dimension. This chapter tries to fill this gap by focusing on the measurement of job mismatch and its consequences on revenues in Sub-Saharan Africa. The chapter posits that a key element of the adjustment of supply and demand is found in changes in the quality of employment. Individuals who are members of households that do not have the necessary resources to withstand extended unemployment are forced either to create their own jobs or to accept wage jobs whose remuneration, skills match, social security, job security, and other features are often inferior to the features of the job they previously held. None of the labor market indicators captures this situation.

The chapter is organized into seven sections. The first section describes the limitations of traditional unemployment and underemployment indicators given the characteristics of the labor markets in developing countries in general and in Sub-Saharan Africa in particular. The second section examines the literature on "overeducation" and discusses the measurement of job mismatch. The third section presents estimates on the extent of job mismatch and identifies its determinants. The fourth section examines the impact of job mismatch on earnings, both in developed countries and in Sub-Saharan Africa. The fifth section examines nonwage compensation for overeducation and undereducation. The sixth section examines wage downgrading as a pathway out of unemployment and economic inactivity. The last section summarizes the main findings and analyzes their implications.

The Inadequacy of Standard Unemployment Indicators in Sub-Saharan Africa

Although work-related issues are central to economic policy debates and to African households' concerns, no regional labor market diagnoses had been conducted until recently (see the overview for a review). The dearth of regional studies mainly reflects gaps in primary data. Very few African countries have employment indicators (the International Labour Organization [ILO] LABORSTA database presents unemployment rates for just 10 African countries). Where these indicators do exist, differences in operational definitions, coverage, period, and type of primary source (surveys, censuses) make the indicators hard to compare across countries. As a result, different sources produce conflicting diagnoses of employment. For example, the *World Development Report 2013: Jobs* (World Bank 2013) sets the youth unemployment rate in Sub-Saharan Africa at less than 10 percent, the second-lowest in the world (after South Asia). The *Economic Report on Africa 2005* paints a totally different picture, estimating youth unemployment at about 18 percent (UNECA 2005). The ILO's regional report (ILO 2006) also paints a bleak picture of youth unemployment.

There is a huge gap between the classic measure of unemployment on the one hand and underemployment and the reality of the situation as perceived by households in developing countries, in Africa in particular, on the other. The forms of labor market imbalances in Sub-Saharan Africa should no longer be assessed solely on the basis of the level of unemployment and the number of hours worked: the specificities of labor markets in Africa call for the use of indicators that address both the quantity and quality of jobs.

The unemployment rate in Sub-Saharan Africa, as in many other developing countries, is relatively low, comparable to the rate in developed countries. In addition, despite wide macroeconomic fluctuations, unemployment rates remain fairly stable. African labor markets thus do not appear to adjust either solely or primarily quantitatively.

Unemployment benefits exist in only a few African countries, and earnings levels are relatively low. As a result, during downturns, households depend on other households—something traditional measures do not capture. The traditional underemployment indicator shows that the employment problem cannot be characterized by the existence of a large contingent of individuals working fewer hours than the statutory working week. In fact, on average, the number of weekly hours actually exceeds the statutory working week.

If the unemployment and underemployment rates in Sub-Saharan Africa are relatively low and stable, why does employment appear to be one of the main challenges perceived by households? How and through what mechanisms do labor markets adjust in Sub-Saharan Africa?

Serious doubts have been raised about the relevance, accuracy, and comparability of the classic indicators of unemployment in Sub-Saharan Africa.[1] The notion of unemployment as defined in the developed countries is not applicable in Sub-Saharan Africa because labor market characteristics there differ. If the ILO definition of unemployment is expanded to include extended unemployment, including discouraged workers (people who are no longer actively seeking a job because they fear they will not find one), the unemployment rate in Sub-Saharan Africa rises by half to some 16 percent (see chapter 1).

Unemployment and time-related underemployment rates (using the ILO definition) are relatively low in urban Sub-Saharan Africa: in the commercial capitals of the countries in the West African Economic and Monetary Union (WAEMU), unemployment averages 11.4 percent and time-related underemployment 14.3 percent (see chapter 1).[2] However, polls of households reveal that lack of work is their main problem, and more than 40 percent of employed workers in West Africa report being dissatisfied with the job they hold (see chapter 3).

Several particularities of the African economies may explain why the standard unemployment indicator is not a useful measure in Sub-Saharan Africa:

- Three-quarters of jobs are concentrated in the informal sector. These jobs typically are highly insecure. They provide no social security coverage and poor working conditions.

- The absence of unemployment benefits and the predominance of family and social networks in job-seeking alters the approach to prospecting. Job-seeking often means getting together enough capital to start up a small informal, own-account business, generally with the help of family and friends.

- The scale of unpaid family and child labor makes it hard to distinguish between work and nonwork.

- Education plays a different role in access to employment. Unlike in developed countries, the level of education and the unemployment rate are inversely related in Sub-Saharan Africa (see chapter 5).

- The seasonal nature of many jobs in Sub-Saharan Africa raises a reference period problem.

These features of African labor markets make the classic labor market evaluation indicators unsuitable. There is a pressing need for better indicators that more fully and accurately cover the reality of African employment problems.

Measures of underemployment do a better job of capturing labor market imbalances. They aim to quantify the number of people who are forced to work fewer hours or take a less skilled job in a less productive economic unit to avoid unemployment and who therefore earn less than they could normally earn (Borgen, Amundson, and Harder 1988; Hecker 1992; ILO 1997).[3]

The 16th International Conference of Labour Statisticians (ILO 1998) decided that underemployment reflects the underutilization of the productive capacity of the employed population. It is to the labor force what the underuse of capital is to business. Time-related underemployment reflects the quantity of work rather than its quality.

On average, time-related underemployment remains low in Sub-Saharan Africa: 14.3 percent of employed workers in the WAEMU capitals spend less than 35 hours a week at their main job when they would prefer to work more.[4] Another 43 percent of employed workers work more than 48 hours a week (48 percent among informal sector workers).

The first limitation of this standard time-related underemployment indicator is that people may work a second job to supplement their main job. Only 5.9 percent of workers across the West African capitals hold a second job in addition to their main job, however. This low rate explains why including hours worked in the second job does very little to change the rate of time-related underemployment, which falls just 0.1 percent on average across WAEMU (0.2 percent in Cotonou, where the rate of multiple jobholding is at the highest, at 9.2 percent).

This notion of time-related underemployment therefore needs to be expanded to include measures of the quality of the work, characterized by such factors as low hourly earnings, the underutilization of professional skills, and low labor productivity resulting from the misallocation of labor resources or a fundamental imbalance between labor and other factors of production.[5] When long hours are made necessary by abnormally low labor productivity or hourly earnings, they may also reflect invisible underemployment.

Minimum wage regulations are generally not relevant in Sub-Saharan Africa. Measuring invisible underemployment in terms of underpayment calls for hourly income norms by type of occupation, rather than just a legal minimum income that is uniform for all individuals.

Invisible underemployment measures the shortfall in productivity, which can be measured at the worker level: individuals may work at jobs that do not require them to use their skills or human capital (Becker 1975). Professional match analysis compares job quality with individuals' expectations and characteristics.

Job Mismatch

Job mismatch is the deviation between a worker's skill level and the level required by the job. It covers two situations. The terms *skill-related underemployment, downgrading,* and *overeducation* refer to workers who are forced to accept jobs for which they are overqualified or that do not match their skills or training. The terms *underqualification* and *undereducation* refer to workers who hold jobs for which they are not qualified enough: in a dysfunctional labor market, applicants may be hired based on their social network rather than their abilities. Both concepts are based on norms that may change over time and space.

The Economic Literature on Overeducation

Job mismatch exists in developed economies, where many people have many years of education. In France, for example, nearly one in five employees reported that their education did not match their job in 1996, a consequence of the flood of graduates (Bodier and Crenner 1997).

Many economists have addressed overeducation. Freeman (1976), one of the earliest, endeavored to explain the downgrading of graduates in the United States by the oversupply of graduates, challenging the principle of an automatic link between qualifications and economic success.

Human capital theory posits that workers are paid commensurate with their level of productivity, which is directly dependent on the level of human capital (education, work experience, training, seniority, skills, and all other unobservable competencies) (Becker 1975). In a flexible labor market, overeducation would be a purely transitional phase of adaptation, during which individuals need to compensate for their lack of other human capital endowments (that is, the lack of experience of young graduate workers) (Groot 1996). Sicherman (1991) finds that overeducated workers change jobs more often, suggesting that overeducation is part of a phase of adaptation to the first stages of a career. Rubb (2003a) posits that overeducation may be a short-run phenomenon for individuals but a long-run phenomenon for the economy. Individuals who take a break in their careers, such as women who have children, are more likely to hold a job for which they are overeducated because of their lack of experience (Groot and Maassen van den Brink 2000). Older workers offset their lack of training with more experience.

The job competition model (Thurow 1975) posits that an individual's employability is inversely proportional to the training costs required after his or her recruitment. He believes that employers' decisions to hire one individual over another are dictated by the training costs they will have to pay to make the individual operational. The more educated individuals are at the point of hiring, the lower these costs will be and the greater their chances of being hired. From this point of view, employers may end up hiring individuals with higher levels of education than strictly required for the position; workers therefore find themselves overeducated for their jobs. Candidates in the queues for each job in an environment of high unemployment have to choose between being unemployed and reducing their reservation wage. Professional downgrading (overeducation) is therefore a defense against unemployment and the decision to remain unemployed a defense against downgrading. The lengthening of education is therefore making education an essentially defensive investment to keep one's place in the queue for the desired job. Overeducation in this model is therefore associated more with macroeconomic circumstances and long-run disequilibria than the human capital life cycle.

Empirical research in developed countries has shown that overeducated individuals earn more than their counterparts with appropriate qualifications doing the same job but less than similarly educated individuals employed in jobs for which they are not overqualified (Sicherman 1991; Cohn and Khan 1995; Verdugo and Verdugo 1989; Groot and Maassen van den Brink 2000). As Rubb (2003b p. 621), notes, "On average, the literature finds that the premium paid for overeducation is about equal to the penalty for undereducation, but lower than the returns associated with an increase in required education."

Very little research has been conducted in developing countries, especially Africa, on job mismatch and overeducation. The only empirical studies are by Simon and Stark (2007) on overqualification as a result of international migration, by Herrera (2005) on Peru, and by Esteves and Martins (2007) on Brazil.

Measuring Job Mismatch

The literature identifies four main ways of measuring the level of education required for a given job (and therefore overeducation and undereducation) (Hartog 2000). "Subjective" methods are based on workers' self-assessment. "Objective" methods are based on experts' job analysis or realized matches.[6] Realized matches measure the difference between the education attained and the dominant level of education observed for the studied worker's occupation. It can be defined in terms of years of education (a method developed by Clogg [1979] and Clogg and Shockey [1984], called the *Clogg indicator*) or education levels (an approach developed by de Grip, Borghans, and Smits [1998], called the *de Grip indicator*). Individuals are overeducated if the number of years (level) of education is greater than or equal to the central value that defines the norm. Individuals have an inadequate match if the observed number of years of education is more than one standard deviation from the mean or two standard deviations from the median number of years of education observed in the occupation for the reference population. In the case of education levels, the norm is defined in terms of the dominant level of education for each occupation.[7]

Each method has advantages and drawbacks. Self-assessment by workers has the advantage of providing education norms directly at the local level. However, individuals tend to subjectively inflate the level required for their job and overestimate the level of their position.

The choice of method is dictated above all by the availability of data. Many authors rely on experts' analysis of job qualifications, which provides an objective, clear, and fairly unbiased measurement of the levels of education required by firms for a given position. No such evaluations exist in developing countries. The method based on realized matches yields the balance between labor supply and demand; it does not measure the level of education required by firms (Hartog 2000). In general, endogenous measurements based on the general trend (such as the modal, median, and mean values) do not reflect each job's required level of education when the economy (or sector) is in a situation of underemployment or overemployment (ILO 1997).

Constructing a Job Mismatch Indicator

The compilation of surveys conducted in the capitals of nine African countries covering more than 100,000 people allows for the first-ever large-scale estimation of empirical educational norms at a detailed (three-digit) occupational classification level and a robust deduction of the job mismatch level and profiles. The data come from the 1-2-3 surveys conducted in seven West African countries (Benin, Burkina Faso, Côte d'Ivoire, Mali, Niger, Senegal, and Togo) between 2001 and 2002; in the administrative capital (Yaoundé) and economic capital (Douala) of Cameroon (2005); and in the capital of Madagascar (Antananarivo 2001–04).[8] The questionnaires used were identical, and the same collection methodology, data processing, and variable coding were used to facilitate their compilation and consolidate the estimates.

The economic and monetary integration of the WAEMU countries studied guarantees strong homogeneousness within the population concerned, worker mobility in the region, and, therefore, the relevance of the norms and indicators developed throughout the region in this study. It allows analysis of questions regarding the impact of the job mismatch on earnings.

The focus in this chapter is on employed workers 15 and older living in urban areas. However, it is useful to restrict the reference population to adults old enough to have finished their schooling (that is, people 25–44). The restricted sample includes 18,000 paid workers, representative of about 3.6 million people after weighting. The occupations are aggregated into 70 categories covering all the jobs on the labor market in the cities concerned.

The realized matches method was used to measure overqualification or underqualification by profession (that is, the distribution of levels of education by occupation was used to estimate an endogenous qualification norm for each of the professions). Doing so entailed first estimating the reference qualification norm for each type of profession. The overqualification indictor is measured by the proportion of workers with a qualification level greater than the normative threshold estimated for the profession concerned.

Estimating the Extent of Job Mismatch

For all professions and all cities together, 14.8 percent of workers 15 and older are undereducated based on Clogg's continuous indicator (25.0 percent based

Table 2.1 Clogg and de Grip Measures of Job Mismatch in 10 Cities in Sub-Saharan Africa
(percent)

Discrete indicator (de Grip)		Continuous indicator (Clogg)				
		Job mismatch				
		Undereducation		Overeducation		
	Job match	Undereducation	Extreme undereducation	Overeducation	Extreme overeducation	All
Job match	47.9	1.6	0.0	4.1	0.1	53.7
Undereducation	11.5	11.9	1.4	0.3	0.0	25.0
Overeducation	5.1	0.0	0.0	13.4	2.7	21.3
All	64.5	13.4	1.4	17.9	2.8	100.0

Sources: Based on Phase 1 of the following 1-2-3 surveys: Cameroon 2005 (Développement, Institutions et Mondialisation [DIAL] and National Statistics Institute [NSI]); Democratic Republic of Congo 2005 (DIAL and NSI); Madagascar 2001 (DIAL and Institut National de la Statistique [INSTAT]); West African Economic and Monetary Union (WAEMU) 2001/02 (Observatoire économique et statistique d'Afrique Subsaharienne [AFRISTAT], DIAL, and NSI).
Note: Figures are for working individuals 15 and older.

on de Grip's discrete indicator) (table 2.1). The share of the labor force that is overeducated is 20.7 percent based on the continuous indicator and 21.3 percent based on the discrete indicator. For developed countries, Groot (1996) estimates undereducation at 21.8 percent and overeducation at 16.0 percent, Cohn and Khan (1995) estimate undereducation at 12 percent and overeducation at 13 percent, and Verdugo and Verdugo (1989) estimate undereducation at 9.9 percent and overeducation at 10.9 percent. A meta-analysis of the literature reveals an average incidence of 14.4 percent for undereducation and 23.3 percent for overeducation in Western Europe and the United States (Groot and Maassen van den Brink 2000). The estimate for Sub-Saharan Africa using the Clogg method is similar.[9]

The Clogg and de Grip measures of overeducation are similar (20.7 percent and 21.3 percent of occupied individuals). A larger discrepancy is evident in undereducation, where the indicators differ by about 10 percentage points (14.8 percent according to Clogg's indicator, 25.0 percent according to de Grip's indicator). The correlation coefficient between the two indicators is 0.77, which means that both indicators capture the phenomenon fairly well.[10]

The Clogg continuous indicator is more restrictive in its job mismatch measurement than the discrete indicator (figure 2.1). It estimates that 64.5 percent of people hold jobs that match their level of education. The de Grip measure estimates this figure at 53.7 percent.

Figure 2.1 Incidence of Job Mismatch (Clogg Indicator) for 10 Countries in Sub-Saharan Africa

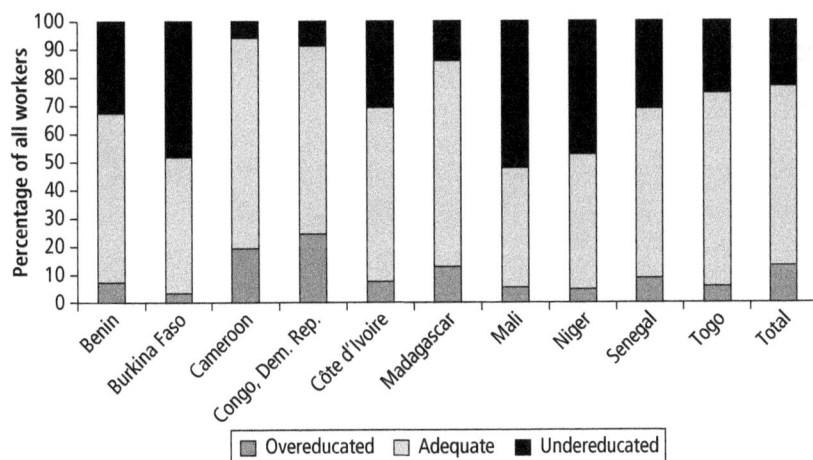

Sources: Based on Phase 1 of the 1-2-3 surveys of selected countries (see table 2.1 for details).

Identifying the Determinants of Job Mismatch

A multivariate nonlinear econometric model is used to identify the effect of each explanatory variable on job mismatch after controlling for bivariate effects caused by the other explanatory variables observed. The specification of a multinomial or ordered logit model seemed most appropriate, because it can simultaneously estimate the probability of overeducation and undereducation. The choice of an ordered or unordered model depends on the type of dependent variable and whether there is a possibility of ranking the variable's categories. As there is no unequivocal order between the dependent variable's categories, an unordered model is used here.[11]

The explanatory variables in the model cover individual characteristics, household characteristics, and characteristics of the business and the job held. The dependent variable is Clogg's continuous indicator. It was chosen in order to reduce the risk of endogeneity in the model introduced by the presence of qualitative education variables as explanatory variables (education dummy variable). This education variable sharply increases the model's explanatory power and reveals that the probability of being overeducated increases with the level of education.[12]

Table 2.2 presents the results of the multinomial model. In most cases, a significant variable for overeducation (such as the size of the business in which the

Table 2.2 Job Mismatch Modeling Results for 10 Cities in Sub-Saharan Africa
(multinomial logit model)

Variable	Undereducated	Overeducated
Type of business (reference = self-employment [1 person])		
Microbusiness (2–5 people)	1.34***	0.81***
Small business (6–20 people)	1.64***	0.43***
Large business (>20 people)	1.64***	0.41***
Migrant status (reference = native)		
Interurban migrant	1.26***	0.99
Rural migrant	1.12**	0.96
Foreigner	1.20***	1.04
Jobholding and time-related underemployment		
Multiple jobholder (reference = one job)	0.80***	1.18**
Time-related underemployment (reference = no time-related underemployment)	0.90***	0.92**
Education (reference = no education or informal education)		
Primary education	0.10***	0.13***
Lower-secondary education	0.01***	39.54***

(continued next page)

Table 2.2 (continued)

Variable	Undereducated	Overeducated
Upper-secondary education	0.01***	346.92***
Higher education	0.01***	726.20***
Position in household (reference = head of household)		
Head of household's spouse	1.01	1.04
Secondary household member	0.88***	1.06
Marital status and gender		
Couple (married or unmarried) (reference = single)	0.70***	1.04
Male (reference = female)	1.38***	1.21***
Sector (reference = secondary sector)		
Tertiary sector	1.80***	0.93
Primary sector	1.89***	1.28***
Sector (reference = public sector)		
Informal sector	0.86	1.48***
Formal private sector	0.83*	1.23***
Age		
Age	0.97***	1.07***
Age squared	1.001***	0.999***
Cohort (reference = 50+)		
Young cohort (10–29)	0.81**	1.01
Medium cohort (30–49)	0.98	1.03
Religion (reference = other)		
Christian	0.41***	2.33***
Muslim	0.43***	2.67***
Seniority in the business		
Seniority in the business	1.00	0.99***
City (reference = aggregate of Douala and Yaoundé)		
Abidjan	1.61***	0.53***
Antananarivo	7.19***	0.41***
Bamako	1.54***	0.38***
Cotonou	1.94***	0.47***
Lomé	0.87	0.93
Niamey	1.47***	0.33***
Ouagadougou	1.16	0.49***
Constant	1.60	0.001
Number of observations	61,984	61,984

Sources: Based on Phase 1 of the 1-2-3 surveys of selected countries (see table 2.1 for details).
Note: Figures are for working individuals 10 and older. Dakar was dropped because of collinearity.
* significant at the 10 percent level, ** significant at the 5 percent level, *** significant at the 1 percent level.

individual works) is also significant for undereducation. A "confusion matrix" is used to evaluate the quality of the model by comparing the predicted values with the true values of the indicator. The correct classification rate—the ratio of the number of correct predictions to the sample size—is 74 percent.[13]
Several findings emerge from the data in table 2.2:

- The probability of being overeducated (undereducated) increases (decreases) as the level of education increases (decreases). The higher a worker's qualifications, the greater his or her risk of being overqualified for the job he or she holds.

- Internal migrants have a greater probability than nonmigrants of holding a job that requires more education than they have. The fact that on average they are less educated than the native population probably reflects their lower access to the education system, despite recent decentralization and deconcentration efforts in most African countries.

- Foreign migrants also have a higher probability of being undereducated: the role of social capital (social and community networks of migrants living in the country's main city) appears to come into play here. Moreover, a selection bias exists for migrants: other unobservable characteristics explain the fact that for a given level of education, migrants are more likely to occupy jobs that require education levels higher than those they have attained. We find no statistically significant support to the stylized fact posited by Simon and Stark (2007) that overeducation in developing countries is the result of international migration.

- Members of the oldest cohort are more likely to be undereducated than members of younger cohorts, because the qualification norms (level of education) for a given occupation were lower when they entered the labor market.

- After controlling for cohort effects (and therefore differential access to education by generation), age increases the chances of being overeducated, in a nonlinear manner (both age and age squared are significant). As age is closely related to potential experience, it may be individuals' potential experience (and not age) that positively influences the probability of being overeducated. This paradoxical result would tend to invalidate the stylized fact noted by Sicherman (1991) and Freeman (1976) that individuals become overeducated in order to compensate for the lack of human capital endowments, such as experience and training. What is being measured here is the age effect within a cohort (age bracket); the cohort effect is wholly in line with human capital theory.

- Working in the informal sector increases the chances of being overeducated. This finding can be explained by the fact that the informal sector does not offer sufficiently skilled work because of lack of access to technology and capital.

- Men have a higher probability than women of being undereducated or overeducated.
- Overeducation is positively correlated with job dissatisfaction. This finding comes not from the estimation of the multinomial model but from the simple study of the coefficient for the correlation between the dichotomous overeducation variable and the variable covering job satisfaction as reported by the individual. The correlation (0.18) is positive. The job satisfaction variable is not introduced into the model as an explanatory variable because of the high risk of endogeneity: although overqualification can clearly generate job dissatisfaction, job dissatisfaction (measured by the desire to change a job) can influence the probability of a job mismatch.

Having a high level of education, being a man, and belonging to a young cohort are correlated with overeducation; having a low level of education, being a migrant, being a woman, and working in a very small business are correlated with undereducation.

Impacts of Job Mismatch: Premium or Penalty?

Does wage or nonwage compensation exist for job mismatch? Are overeducated individuals paid more or less than matched individuals, after controlling for the effects of other individual characteristics? Do they have more stable jobs?

Impact of Job Mismatch on Earnings in Developed Countries

Human capital is defined as the stock of productive capacities an individual acquires (through the accumulation of general and specific knowledge, know-how, and so forth) (Becker 1975). Investment in human capital is an individual choice resulting from the cost-benefit trade-off between the costs (out-of-pocket cost of education and opportunity cost of going to school rather than working) and the future discounted earnings that can be generated by additional education. Individuals may choose to invest in order to raise their future productivity and therefore their earnings. Human capital theory assumes that individuals are paid in accordance with their productivity level at work and that this marginal productivity is determined more by the components of human capital (education, training, experience, skills, and so forth) than by the characteristics of the job (Mincer 1974; Becker 1975).

Becker posits that wage growth over a career more or less reflects the accumulation of human capital. He believes it to be concave: gross investment tends to decline with age, because any wage increase raises the opportunity cost and the return diminishes with age, because there are fewer years available in which to make the investment pay off. Thus, from a human capital point of view, the rates of return on investment in education are expected to be positive: the more an individual has studied, the higher his or her earnings.

The results of 11 studies on different countries reviewed by Card (2001) suggest that the marginal returns to education estimated by the instrumental variables method were 6–10 percent. As with any investment, the returns to education diminish: the more an individual studies, the smaller the margin gain in earnings for each additional year of studies. Kuépié, Nordman, and Roubaud (2009; see also chapter 5 of this book) invalidate this assumption for Sub-Saharan Africa, finding that private returns to education are convex for workers in the West African capitals. Spence (1973) notes that, as human capital is hard for others to perceive, qualifications form a credible signal of the worker's level of productivity for an employer in a situation of information asymmetry. Wages in this case are essentially contingent upon the level of qualifications.

Impact of Job Mismatch on Earnings in Sub-Saharan Africa

Individual earnings are modeled to identify the effect of overeducation and undereducation on the level of earnings, controlling for the classic explanatory effects. For this purpose, Mincer's model can be extended as follows:

$$\ln Ys = c + rS + aE + bE^2 + \Sigma d_i X_i + f_1. \ UNDER + f_2 \ OVER + u \qquad (2.1)$$

where the X_i cover observable demographic characteristics (gender, ethnic group, religion, migratory status, father's socioeconomic group); $OVER$ is a dummy variable taking the value 1 if the individual is overeducated for the job he or she holds and 0 if not; and $UNDER$ is a dummy variable taking the value 1 if the individual is undereducated for the job he or she holds and 0 if not.

The estimations of $\ln Y$ based solely on observed earnings therefore need to take selection bias into account (Heckman 1979). After estimating a selection model (on the probability of working a paid job), we incorporate the Mills ratio into the earnings models to correct for selection bias.

Use of the standard ordinary least squares method is potentially problematic when estimating returns to education (and therefore returns to overeducation), because of the endogenous nature of education (that is, its correlation with the earnings equation residuals because of unobservable individual characteristics). In principle, this endogeneity can be overcome using the instrumental variable procedure, which consists of finding variables that are assumed to be correlated with education but not earnings. In practice, no convincing instrument (that had not already been used as an explanatory variable in the model) was found.

Earnings Model 1 proposes inserting job mismatch (undereducation and overeducation) dummy variables into Mincer's equation. This log-linear regression model of hourly earnings is initially tested on all adults 25–44. Two additional estimations are made, for men and for women (table 2.3). The model yields the following results:

- A (small) penalty for overeducation and a premium for undereducation is evident after controlling for the level of education and selection biases. Overeducated individuals earn more than individuals in the same occupation with an appropriate level of education for the job, but they earn less than individuals with the same level of education working in better jobs. The penalty or premium associated with the job mismatch is smaller among women than men.

Table 2.3 Heckman-Corrected Mincerian Earnings Equation with Overeducation and Undereducation Variables for Men and Women in 10 Cities in Sub-Saharan Africa
(log of hourly earnings)

Variable	All	Men	Women
Job mismatch (reference = job match)			
Undereducated (discrete indicator)	0.179***	0.187***	0.159***
Overeducated (discrete indicator)	−0.0901***	−0.0945***	−0.0547
Years of education	0.0820***	0.0799***	0.0770***
Size of business (reference = self-employment [1 person])			
Microbusiness (2–5 people)	0.1510***	0.0645***	0.2000***
Small business (6–20 people)	0.263***	0.138***	0.516***
Large business (>20 people)	0.418***	0.281***	0.740***
Migrant status (reference = native)			
Interurban migrant	−0.0378**	−0.0319	−0.0387
Migrant from the rural exodus	−0.0615**	−0.0493	−0.0756*
Foreign migrant	0.01250	0.00355	0.02180
Jobholding and time-related underemployment			
Multiple jobholder (reference = one job)	−0.0291	−0.0377	−0.0219
Time-related underemployment (reference = no time-related underemployment)	0.640***	0.666***	0.635***
Position in household (reference = head of household)			
Head of household's spouse	−0.208***	−0.262	−0.146***
Secondary household member	−0.200***	−0.204***	−0.179***
Marital status and gender			
Couple (married or unmarried) (reference = single)	0.0602***	0.0565**	0.0432
Male (reference = female)	0.320***	—	—
Sector (reference = secondary sector)			
Tertiary sector	0.0942**	0.1280**	0.0440
Primary sector	−0.00367	0.0247	−0.0231

(continued next page)

Table 2.3 (continued)

Variable	All	Men	Women
Sector (reference = public sector)			
Informal sector	−0.352***	−0.308***	−0.454***
Formal private sector	−0.181***	−0.155***	−0.227**
Age			
Age	0.0328	0.0341	0.0215
Age squared	−0.000348	−0.000310	−0.000244
Religion (reference = other)			
Christian	0.0129	−0.0145	0.0278
Muslim	0.0553*	0.0444	0.0491
Seniority in the business			
Seniority in the business	0.0199***	0.0182***	0.0202***
Selection model: Probability of participation			
Cohabiting couple (married or unmarried) (reference = single)	0.313***	0.349***	0.207***
Age	0.0281***	0.0267***	0.0266***
Male (reference = female)	−0.109***	—	—
Number of earners in household	0.571***	0.540***	0.651***
Number of children in household	0.0514***	0.0323**	0.0860***
Total number of people in household (excluding visitors)	−0.166***	−0.157***	−0.183***
Constant	−3.324***	−0.173	−0.157

Sources: Based on Phase 1 of the 1-2-3 surveys of selected countries (see table 2.1 for details).
Note: Figures are for working individuals 25–44.
* significant at the 10 percent level, ** significant at the 5 percent level, *** significant at the 1 percent level.

- The penalty for overeducation and the premium for undereducation do not offset each other: undereducation is much more profitable than overeducation is costly (in the log-linear model, the parameter corresponding to overeducation is twice as high in absolute value as the parameter corresponding to the undereducation dummy variable). This finding is different from what Groot and Maassen van den Brink (2000) report for developed countries

- The penalty (premium) for overeducation (undereducation) is smaller than the returns to high levels of education. The returns to education are positive and high (8 percent), for both women and men.

The model was also estimated using the number of surplus (deficit) years of education the individual has above (below) the norm for the years of education required for the occupation (Model 2 [not shown]). This model allows estimation of the returns to years of overeducation. The results confirm that the returns to required education are positive and large: one additional year of required education (which enables the worker to hold a job demanding one more year of schooling) generates a 10.1 percent increase in the hourly earnings logarithm, for both men and women. Each year of education beyond the required schooling norm for the occupation generates additional earnings (by 6.2 percent in the hourly earnings logarithm); each year of education short of the normal length of schooling for the occupation decreases earnings (by 5.1 percent in the hourly earnings logarithm). The return to years of overeducation is thus positive but lower than the return to years of required education. As in Model 1, undereducated individuals earn a premium over their colleagues in the same occupation with the level of education required for the job. Model 2 erases the asymmetry revealed in Model 1 between the overeducation penalty and the undereducation premium: the results for the two components are similar in Model 2. By way of comparison, the meta-analysis conducted by Groot and Maassen van den Brink (2000) estimates the average returns to one year of overeducation in developed countries at 3 percent.

The results of the two models bear out the results of Verdugo and Verdugo (1989), Groot (1996), and Hartog (2000) for developed countries: overeducation generates a penalty and undereducation a premium once the effects of required education, selection biases, and other sociodemographic variables are controlled for.

Underemployment and Nonwage Compensation

In developed countries, nonwage benefits often compensate individuals who are overeducated for the position they hold (for a discussion of compensating differential theory, see chapter 4). This section examines whether nonwage compensation exists in Sub-Saharan Africa in the form of increased job security.

Insecurity (the risk of losing one's job) can be measured across an array of variables reflecting the extent of formality linking employee to employer: the existence or absence of a written contract that protects the employee; the existence of a payslip; social security coverage; the steady or unsteady nature of the work done (casual, temporary, or steady); access to a union; and so forth. The choice of components for this indicator was determined by the availability of data.

Workers are classified as dependent (wage-earners) or independent (own account, managers, and employers). The insecurity score for dependent workers is the arithmetic sum of the values of three variables: contract (long-term written contract, short-term written contract, oral contract, no contract); payslip; and steadiness (steady, casual, or temporary). For independent workers, the presence of written accounts captures the extent of the business's formality (and therefore its sustainability). Apprentices were excluded from the analysis.

The job mismatch indicators (Clogg's continuous indicator covering three to five categories and de Grip's discrete indicator covering three categories) and the insecurity score are negatively correlated.[14] This correlation suggests that overeducated workers are indeed compensated with greater job security (table 2.4).

To analyze the net effects of job mismatch on insecurity (by controlling for other influential variables), it would be preferable to conduct an ordered multinomial logistic regression (because the score values are discrete, whole, and ordered). However, the number of categories in this score (six) makes the analysis and interpretation tricky and the conclusions hazy. For this reason, a simple linear regression of the insecurity score on the classic explanatory variables (from the corrected Mincer equation) and the overeducation and undereducation dummy variables (measured by the Clogg continuous indicator, for example) using the ordinary least squares (OLS) method is presented (table 2.5). It would have been desirable to address the possible endogeneity of the job mismatch in the explanation of the level of insecurity using an instrumental variable procedure, but no instrument was found to be conclusive.

Given the construction of the insecurity indicator, it appears preferable to concentrate on a split (dependent/independent) interpretation of the results. The results of the regression model show that for dependent workers, other things equal, the insecurity score (and hence the level of job insecurity) increases with overeducation and decreases with undereducation. This result means that after controlling for the level of completed education (in particular), the level of job security of overeducated workers is actually higher. For independent workers, the explanatory variables associated with job mismatch are not significant. This phenomenon is therefore of concern to employees, not employers or self-account workers.

Table 2.4 Correlation Matrix between Job Mismatch and Insecurity Indicators in 10 Cities in Sub-Saharan Africa

Variable	Continuous job mismatch indicator (Clogg indicator)		Discrete job mismatch indicator (de Grip indicator)
	Five categories	Three categories	Three categories
Insecurity of dependent workers	−0.09	−0.17	−0.12
Insecurity of independent workers	−0.07	−0.15	−0.15
Insecurity score	−0.08	−0.22	−0.18

Sources: Based on Phase 1 of the 1-2-3 surveys of selected countries (see table 2.1 for details).
Note: Figures are for working individuals 15 and older.

Table 2.5 Insecurity Score Equation with Overeducation and Undereducation Variables for Dependent and Independent Workers in 10 Cities in Sub-Saharan Africa
(ordinary least squares)

Variable	All	Dependent workers	Independent workers
Job mismatch (reference = job match)			
Undereducated (continuous indicator)	−0.0807***	−0.2000***	0.0322
Overeducated (continuous indicator)	0.2210***	0.1980***	0.0716
Size of business (reference = self-employment [1 person])			
Microbusiness (2–5 people)	−0.3090***	−0.2220***	−0.0775***
Medium-size business (6–20 people)	−0.815***	−0.559***	−0.297***
Large business (>20 people)	−1.426***	−1.152***	−1.599***
Migrant status (reference = native)			
Interurban migrant	−0.0318	−0.0547*	0.0302
Migrant from the rural exodus	0.00259	−0.02680	0.06090**
Foreigner	0.0385	0.0536	0.0594**
Jobholding and time-related underemployment			
Multiple jobholder	0.0867**	0.0800	0.0331
Time-related underemployment	0.332***	0.478***	0.227***
Education (reference = no education or informal education)			
Primary	−0.1060***	−0.2570***	0.0111
Lower-secondary	−0.27900***	−0.49000***	−0.00262
Upper-secondary	−0.673***	−0.892***	−0.212***
Higher	−0.977***	−1.247***	−0.408***
Standing in household (reference = head of household)			
Head of household's spouse	0.0979***	0.1190**	0.0533*
Secondary household member	0.06940**	0.15500***	−0.00527
Marital status and gender			
Couple (married or unmarried) *(reference = single)*	−0.0880***	−0.1040***	−0.0882***
Male (reference = female)	0.1320***	0.1790***	0.0416*
Sector (reference = secondary sector)			
Tertiary sector	−0.348***	−0.445***	−0.346***
Primary sector	−0.240***	−0.449***	−0.312***
Sector (reference = public sector)			
Informal sector	1.363***	0.894***	1.752***
Formal private sector	0.371***	0.258***	0.513***

(continued next page)

Table 2.5 (continued)

Variable	All	Dependent workers	Independent workers
Age			
Age	−0.01530***	−0.03220***	−0.00571
Age squared	0.000166***	0.000318***	0.0000532
Religion (reference = other)			
Christian	−0.0112	−0.0645	0.0318
Muslim	0.0214	−0.0104	0.0792*
Seniority in the business			
Seniority in the business	−0.00750***	−0.01940***	−0.00262**
R^2	0.59	0.50	0.61

Sources: Based on Phase 1 of the 1-2-3 surveys of selected countries (see table 2.1 for details).
Note: Figures are for working individuals 15 and older.
* significant at the 10 percent level, ** significant at the 5 percent level, *** significant at the 1 percent level.

Wage Downgrading as a Pathway Out of Unemployment or Economic Inactivity

The decision to remain unemployed can be interpreted as resistance to downgrading and skill-related underemployment. Conversely, overeducation can be interpreted as resistance to unemployment. Examination of an overeducated jobholder's previous situation (similar job or unemployment) was used to evaluate the likelihood of this hypothesis. Table 2.6 presents the results.

A Chi-squared test rejects (at the 5 percent level) the hypothesis of independence between the mobility variable change between the employed worker's previous situation and current employment and the job mismatch indicator (Clogg indicator).

Relative to individuals in a job match situation, proportionally more overeducated individuals were upwardly mobile (that is, moved up socioeconomically since their previous job or completion of studies). This finding could reflect the theory of the human capital life cycle, which states that individuals temporarily hold a series of jobs below their level in order to accumulate experience and know-how that prepare them to apply for positions more in keeping with their qualifications.

A slightly smaller than average proportion of overeducated workers is unemployed or out of the labor force just before holding their current job. This finding contradicts the economic intuition that overeducation often follows a period of unemployment. This question calls for further examination of the determinants of professional mobility.

Table 2.6 Labor Market Status before Current Employment in 10 Cities in Sub-Saharan Africa
(percent)

Situation before current employment	Situation in current employment			
	Undereducated	Job match	Overeducated	All
Unemployed/inactive	61.8	64.2	61.8	63.2
Previous employment				
Held better job	3.4	8.2	22.0	7.3
Held worse job	3.8	4.9	3.9	4.4
Held similar job	31.0	22.7	12.3	25.1

Sources: Based on Phase 1 of the 1-2-3 surveys of selected countries (see table 2.1 for details).
Note: Figures are for working individuals 25–44.

Table 2.7 Type of Job Sought by the Unemployed in 10 Cities in Sub-Saharan Africa, by Length of Unemployment
(percent)

Job sought	Long-term unemployed	Short-term unemployed	Total unemployed
Job corresponding to trade or training	29.4	36.6	31.0
Job in another trade or sector	16.1	15.7	16.0
Indifferent	54.5	47.7	53.0
Total	100.0	100.0	100.0

Sources: Based on Phase 1 of the 1-2-3 surveys of selected countries (see table 2.1 for details).
Note: Figures are for working individuals 25–44.

The long-term unemployed (people unemployed for more than a year) appear to be less particular than the short-term unemployed about the match between the job and their qualifications: just 29 percent of the long-term unemployed seek a job that corresponds to their training or their trade, as opposed to 37 percent of the short-term unemployed (table 2.7). This simple empirical result validates the theory that a mismatch occurs in the event of a strong risk of unemployment and a long period of unemployment: the longer the period of unemployment, the more the unemployed reduce their reservation wage and the skill level of the job they will apply for.

Conclusion

The special features of its labor markets—the lack of unemployment benefits, the predominance of the informal sector, the prevalence of personal networks to obtain jobs, the low unemployment rate, and so forth—make the classic indicators of unemployment and time-related underemployment inappropriate, if not misleading, for understanding labor markets in Sub-Saharan Africa. The harmonized job mismatch measurement captures these as yet unmeasured aspects by concentrating on underutilization of productive capacities. Job mismatch should be considered an extension of the underemployment notion.

Overeducation—measured as the gap between individual qualifications and the qualifications usually required for the job held—is not confined to developed countries: it affects 21 percent of workers in Sub-Saharan Africa. Men, older people, migrants, workers in the informal sector, the uneducated, and the highly educated are more likely than other workers to find their job mismatched with their education.

Job mismatch affects both earnings and job insecurity: other things equal, workers who are overeducated for the work they do have less job security than workers whose qualifications match their job and workers who are undereducated for their jobs. The job mismatch evolves over the course of a career, with overqualification following economic inactivity, unemployment, or more extreme overeducation.

The analysis makes a case for the widespread harmonization of job quality indicators and the extension of the inadequate employment measurement. The empirical methods used here need to be compared with other measurement methods, such as the expert job analysis method, which is more focused on business demand for qualifications and workers' own declarations, which are more subjective but easier to set up.

Notes

1. In its 2006 evaluation of African labor markets, the World Bank identified four problems: the dearth of data, lack of comparability, measurement problems, and low relevance for low-income countries.
2. The ILO definition of unemployment (1997) corresponds to workers who did not work (even one hour) in the seven days preceding the survey, who sought work during the previous month, and who are available to work. Time-related underemployment covers gainfully employed workers whose working week is shorter than the statutory working week and who would like to work more.
3. This type of situation used to be called *disguised unemployment* (Robinson 1937).
4. Although Abidjan and Cotonou are not administrative capitals, we refer to them as capitals because they are the most important economic centers in their countries (Cotonou is also the seat of government).
5. This extension used to be called *invisible underemployment*, which the ILO described as "primarily an analytical concept reflecting a misallocation of labour resources or a fundamental imbalance between labour and other factors of production. Characteristic symptoms might be low income, underutilization of skill, and low productivity. Analytical studies of invisible underemployment should be directed to the examination and analysis of a wide variety of data, including income and skill

levels (disguised underemployment) and productivity measures (potential under-employment)" (ILO 1982, pp. 52–53).

6. Thurow and Lucas (1972), Hartog (1980), and others use the *Dictionary of Occupational Titles* (U.S. Department of Labor) to measure overeducation.

7. De Grip developed an algorithm to identify the dominant (qualitative) level of education for each type of occupation. Depending on the distribution of the types of education within the given occupation, the dominant type of education is either the most commonly occurring or a combination of two or three levels grouped together. The algorithm had some flaws, which are corrected for here (de Grip, Borghans, and Smits 1998).

8. For a description of 1-2-3 surveys, see box O.1 in the overview. Cameroon and Madagascar were included because their labor markets are very similar to labor markets in West Africa (see chapter 1).

9. The fact that the share of overeducated people in Europe and the United States is similar to the share in Sub-Saharan Africa does not mean that the levels of education are similar. The level of education in Africa is still much lower than in the developed countries.

10. If we use the mean instead of the median to estimate the norms when building the continuous indicator, the correlation factor rises to 86 percent.

11. Stata's test of independence on the logit procedure returns a positive and significant result.

12. The final model estimated aims to be as sparing as possible. The explanatory variables ultimately chosen for the model are selected by a procedure of gradual elimination of the variables or categories with the least explanatory power.

13. In the absence of an additional test sample, this confusion matrix was constructed from the data used to build the model. This evaluation could therefore be criticized for being overly optimistic.

14. Clogg's five ordered categories are –2 (extreme undereducation), –1 (undereducation), 0 (match), 1 (overeducation), 2 (extreme overeducation). De Grip's three categories are undereducation, job match, and overeducation.

References

Becker, G. S. 1975. *Human Capital: A Theoretical and Empirical Analysis, with Special Reference to Education,* 2nd ed. Cambridge, MA: National Bureau of Economic Research.

Bodier, M., and E. Crenner. 1997. "Adéquation entre formation et emploi: ce qu'en pensent les salariés." *INSEE Première* 525 (June): 1–4.

Borgen, W. A., N. E. Amundson, and H. G. Harder. 1988. "The Experience of Underemployment." *Journal of Employment Counseling* 25: 149–59.

Card, D. 2001. "Estimating the Return to Schooling: Progress on Some Persistent Econometric Problems." *Econometrica* 69 (5): 1127–60.

Clogg, C. 1979. *Measuring Underemployment: Demographic Indicators for the United States.* New York: Academic Press.

Clogg, C., and J. Shockey. 1984: "Mismatch Between Occupational, and Schooling: A Prevalence Measure, Recent Trends, and Demographic Analysis." *Demography* 21 (2): 235–57.

Cohn, E., and S. P. Khan. 1995. "The Wage Effects of Overschooling Revisited." *Labour Economics* 2 (1): 67–76.

de Grip, A., L. L. Borghans, and W. Smits. 1998. "Future Developments in the Job Level, and Domain of High–Skilled Workers." In *Towards a Transparent Labor Market for Educational Decisions*, ed. J. Heijke and L. Borghans, 21–57. Aldershot, U.K.: Ashgate.

Esteves, L., and P. Martins. 2007. "Job-Schooling Mismatches and Wages in Brazil." Queen Mary College, University of London.

Freeman, R. B. 1976. *The Overeducated Americans*. New York: Academic Press.

Groot, W. 1996. "The Incidence of and Returns to Overeducation in the UK." *Applied Economics* 28: 1345–50.

Groot, W., and H. Maassen van den Brink. 2000. "Overeducation in the Labor Market: A Meta-Analysis." *Economics of Education Review* 19 (2): 149–58.

Hartog, J. 1980. "Earnings and Capability Requirements." *Review of Economics and Statistics* 62 (2): 230–40.

———. 2000. "Over-Education and Earnings: Where Are We, Where Should We Go?" *Economics of Education Review* 19 (2): 131–47.

Hecker, D. E. 1992. "Reconciling Conflicting Data on Jobs for College Graduates." *Monthly Labour Review* 115 (7): 3–12.

Heckman, J. J. 1979. "Sample Selection Bias as a Specification Error." *Econometrica* 47: 153–61.

Herrera, J. 2005. "Sobre y subeducacion en el Peru urbano." In *Cambios globales y el mercado laboral peruano: comercio, legislación, capital humano y empleo*, ed. G. Yamada and M. Jaramillo, 181–227. Lima: Universidad del Pacifico.

ILO (International Labour Organization). 1982. "General Report." 13th International Conference of Labour Statisticians, Geneva, October.

———. 1993. "Resolution Concerning Statistics of Employment in the Informal Sector." 15th International Conference of Labour Statistics, Geneva, January.

———. 1997. "Underemployment: Concept and Measurement." Report I, Meeting of Experts on Labour Statistics, Geneva, October 14–23.

———. 1998. "Report of the Conference." 16th International Conference of Labour Statisticians, Geneva, October 6–15.

———. 2006. "Regional Labour Market Trends for Youth: Africa." ILO Youth Employment Programme, Geneva, September.

Kuépié M., C. Nordman, and F. Roubaud. 2009. "Education and Earnings in West Africa." *Journal of Comparative Economics* 37: 491–515.

Mincer, J. 1974. *Schooling, Experience, and Earnings*. New York: National Bureau of Economic Research.

Robinson, J. 1937. *Essays in the Theory of Employment*. London: Macmillan.

Rubb, S. 2003a. "Overeducation: A Short or Long Run Phenomenon for Individuals?" *Economics of Education Review* 22 (4): 389–94.

———. 2003b. "Overeducation in the Labor Market:" A Comment and Re-analysis of a Meta-analysis." *Economic of Education Review* 22 (6): 6121–29.

Sicherman, N. 1991. "Overeducation in the Labor Market." *Journal of Labor Economics* 9 (2): 101–22.

Simon, C., and O. Stark. 2007. "The Brain Drain, 'Educated Unemployment,' Human Capital Formation, and Economic Betterment." *Economics of Transition* 15 (4): 629–60.

Spence, M. 1973. "Job Market Signaling." *Quarterly Journal of Economics* 87 (3): 355–74.

Thurow, L. 1975. *Generating in Equality: Mechanism of Distribution in the U.S. Economy.* New York: Basic Books.

Thurow, L. C., and R. Lucas. 1972. *The American Distribution of Income: A Structural Problem.* Study for the Joint Economic Committee, U.S. Congress. Washington, DC: Government Printing Office.

UNECA (UN Economic Commission for Africa). 2005. *Economic Report on Africa 2005: Meeting the Challenges of Unemployment and Poverty in Africa.* Addis Ababa: UNECA.

U.S. Department of Labor. Various years. *Dictionary of Occupational Titles.* Washington, DC: U.S. Department of Labor.

Verdugo, R., and N. Verdugo. 1989. "The Impact of Surplus Schooling on Earnings." *Journal of Human Resources* 24 (4): 629–43.

World Bank. 2006. "Labor Diagnostics for Sub-Saharan Africa: Indicators, Problems, and Data Available." Technical Note, World Bank, Washington, DC.

———. 2012. *World Development Report 2013: Jobs.* Washington, DC: World Bank.

Chapter 3

Job Satisfaction in Eight African Cities

Mireille Razafindrakoto and François Roubaud

Researchers from various disciplines have examined job satisfaction. Psychologists and sociologists have explored the role of job satisfaction in individuals' mental balance; other researchers have also studied individual well-being taking a broader, multidisciplinary approach. Economists have studied job satisfaction with a view to improving the understanding of the match between the supply and demand of labor.[1]

Most work has focused on developed countries. Recent interest in this issue in developing countries stems largely from concerns about the quality of working conditions, as seen from discussions at the International Labour Organization (ILO) and elsewhere on the concept of "decent work."

The analysis in this chapter seeks to improve the understanding of labor market conditions in Sub-Saharan Africa. To the authors' knowledge, only two studies (Falco, Maloney, and Rijkers 2011; Rakotomanana 2011) examine the broad determinants of job satisfaction in Africa.[2]

Empirical analyses confirm the existence of negative links between job satisfaction and objective facts such as the decision to quit a job (Freeman 1978; Lévy-Garboua, Montmarquette, and Simonnet 1999; Clark 2001). Studies also show that job satisfaction is correlated with on-the-job behavior, including absenteeism and productivity (Judge and others 2001). These findings challenge the idea that individuals' assessments of their satisfaction are purely idiosyncratic and economically irrelevant (pure "noise").

Job satisfaction came to the fore with the rise in analyses of subjective well-being, especially research by Easterlin (2001, 2003) and Frey and Stutzer (2002). The importance of work in an individual's life, for both the income it provides and its intrinsic value, makes job satisfaction a key component of well-being. Judge and Watanabe (1993) show that the causal link between job satisfaction and subjective well-being can run in both directions. Most empirical results, however, find that job satisfaction affects well-being (Warr 1999).

Interest in job satisfaction is growing in the developed countries, and research on the issue is on the rise in transition economies. Studies on this theme are still rare, if not nonexistent, in developing countries, however, especially in Africa. The lack of research is surprising given that employment is the main source of income in these countries, and working conditions are often harsh; work is therefore particularly important in an individual's life. Understanding how individuals assess their work—their earnings, working conditions, and intrinsic value placed on different types of employment (fulfillment, social recognition, participation/exclusion, and so forth)—is vital for evaluating labor markets.

This chapter is organized as follows. The first section reviews the economic literature on this subject. The second section presents the data used and describes the approach adopted. The third section provides a preliminary descriptive analysis of job satisfaction in the eight African capitals studied.[3] The fourth section presents and analyzes the results of the econometric estimations. The last section summarizes the main findings and proposes avenues for further research.

Review of the Literature

Warr (1999) distinguishes between intrinsic and extrinsic job satisfaction. Intrinsic components include the opportunity to manage and supervise, the degree of autonomy, the use of capacities and skills, the variety of tasks, the absence of physical danger, the clarity of information on the professional environment, work relations, and social position. Extrinsic components include remuneration, working conditions, and job security.

Sousa-Poza and Sousa-Poza (2000) adopt the classification used by Judge and Watanabe (1993) to compare job satisfaction in some 20 countries. They adopt a bottom-up approach, assuming that various external factors affect job satisfaction. Job satisfaction is determined by the balance between work-role inputs (hours worked, effort, education) and work-role outputs (remuneration, nonwage benefits, status, opportunities for advancement, independence and self-direction, job security, job interest, social recognition, and relations with colleagues). This approach explains differences across countries in terms of the weight and relative importance of the two types of factors.

D'Addio, Eriksson, and Frijters (2003) look at the many criteria that come into play when assessing the quality of a job. They identify another way of understanding satisfaction by distinguishing between the economic contract (in which the focus is on the relationship between effort and reward) and the psychological contract (in which the focus is on working conditions).

Much of the debate in the literature concerns how to interpret several key findings. The first is the relationship between income level and satisfaction, which is not obvious (Clark and Oswald 1996; Lévy-Garboua and Montmarquette 1984). A second issue is the relationship between objective job characteristics (working hours and work pace, leave, job security, job type) and job satisfaction levels.

The literature finds a weak correlation between these variables and job satisfaction (D'Addio, Eriksson, and Frijters 2003; Llorente and Macías 2005). Some findings are counterintuitive: although women and the least educated generally have poorer-quality jobs, they are more inclined than other workers to report job satisfaction (Clark and Oswald 1996; Clark 1997; D'Addio, Eriksson, and Frijters 2003). Age also plays a role, with job satisfaction declining until about age 40 and then rising (Lévy-Garboua and Montmarquette 1984; Clark, Oswald, and Warr 1996).

Two factors may help explain these results. First, classic economic variables (such as wages and working hours) do not capture job quality. A wide range of other job characteristics, which surveys rarely measure, also affect satisfaction (see chapters 1, 4, and 5). Second, the level of self-reported satisfaction depends on the individual's aspirations, which are determined by various factors, including social background and reference group. The closeness of the match between expectations and outcomes plays a decisive role in individual satisfaction levels. Based on an analysis of 19 countries in the Organisation for Economic Co-operation and Development (OECD), Clark (2004) observes that workers report that wages and working time are among the least important characteristics in rankings of what matters in a job. Factors such as promotion opportunities are considered very important. Job type, content, and interest and work relations are also important (Sousa-Poza and Sousa-Poza 2000; D'Addio, Eriksson, and Frijters 2003). Idson (1990) and Garcia-Serrano (2008) stress the importance of the work environment. They find less flexibility and autonomy in large businesses and posit that this characteristic explains the lower level of satisfaction at large companies.

The many factors involved in evaluating job quality are also behind the differences in satisfaction by socioeconomic group, industrial sector, and institutional sector in some studies (Clark and Oswald 1996; D'Addio, Eriksson, and Frijters 2003; Beuran and Kalugina 2005). Beuran and Kalugina (2005) observe that in the Russian Federation, working in the informal sector increases well-being, despite lower average earnings, poor working conditions, job insecurity, and exclusion from the social security system. Razafindrakoto and Roubaud (2006) draw the same conclusion for African countries. In Madagascar, Rakotomanana (2011) shows that, everything else equal, levels of job satisfaction in the informal sector and private formal sector are not significantly different; public sector employees are systematically the most satisfied. Using Ghanaian panel data, Falco, Maloney, and Rijkers (2011) find that the informal sector and the formal sector (both private and public) provide similar levels of job satisfaction. Razafindrakoto, Roubaud, and Wachsberger (2012) find the same result in Vietnam. Own-account workers—who may be more exposed to income instability—are more satisfied than wage earners (Blanchflower and Oswald 2004). Falco, Maloney, and Rijkers (2011) confirm this pattern in urban Ghana. These findings confirm the importance of factors such as self-direction and independence, flexibility, employment status, and the quality of work relations.

Some analyses find that union members express less satisfaction than other workers (Freeman 1978; Clark 2004). This seemingly paradoxical result may be explained by the finding by Bryson, Cappelari, and Lucifora (2005) that people who join unions have the highest expectations of working conditions and are therefore harder to satisfy. Their expectations may stem from better knowledge of their rights (labor law) or from higher levels of individual aspirations.

Women, the least educated, and the youngest and oldest workers have lower (or downward revised) aspirations and are therefore more inclined to say they are satisfied with their job. Individual, especially psychological, characteristics, also affect overall subjective well-being and job satisfaction, with causality running in both directions (Judge and Watanabe 1993; Warr 1999).

Different interpretations have been posited to explain the weak correlation between income and job satisfaction. Cross-sectional analyses of subjective well-being show that once vital needs have been satisfied, the link between well-being and income is not strong (Easterlin 2001; Frey and Stutzer 2002). A large number of sociologists and psychologists have also looked at the role of culture, including both collective and individual values regarding work in general and certain types of work (Malka and Chatman 2003; Gelade, Dobson, and Auer 2008).

Various authors emphasize the importance of social interaction effects ("social comparison"). Clark and Oswald (1996) show the negative effect of the income of the reference group (estimated from the predicted income value based on the characteristics of the job and the individual). Relative income (the subjective perception of one's income level compared with the income of one's peers) has a greater effect on satisfaction than actual income amount (Clark 2004). Pichler and Wallace (2009) reach the same conclusion in an analysis of 27 European countries. They show that, job and individual characteristics aside, the average level of earnings in a country influences the level of satisfaction.

A broader view is that not only the immediate environment but also the past and present context affect the formation of individual aspirations. Hamermesh (2001) points to the influence of changes in the socioeconomic context. Llorente and Macías (2005) draw on an analysis of some 20 countries to suggest that the fact that aspirations adjust with time and actual conditions indicates the weak correlation between objective variables and the level of satisfaction. Aspirations are revised downward or upward depending on the how the situation in a country develops.

Many analyses study the weight of the past as a determinant of satisfaction (Lévy-Garboua and Montmarquette 1984; Clark and Oswald 1996; Hamermesh 2001). Employment history (mobility and experience) influences the formation of individuals' aspirations. Longitudinal analyses study the relationship between individuals' employment trajectories and their level of satisfaction. Lack of satisfaction is found to be a good predictor of professional mobility, in particular of quitting or changing jobs (Freeman 1978; Lévy-Garboua, Montmarquette, and Simonnet 1999; Clark 2001; Kristensen and Westergård-Nielsen 2004).

As with the majority of analyses of perceptions (especially subjective well-being), uncertainty remains regarding the direction of causality. It is hard to deal with problems of endogeneity, especially when psychological factors simultaneously affect the variables studied. For instance, optimistic people could feel intrinsically more satisfied and earn more because they are more dynamic or better appreciated by their boss or clients. Earning a good salary may be a source of satisfaction, but feeling satisfied may be a way to increase one's wage (through promotions, for example). The nature of the data does not allow the causality path to be identified.

Self-selection biases, linked to nonrandom labor market participation or sectoral allocation, are also at play. Indeed, it could be said that people who work are people who can potentially derive the highest level of satisfaction from their job. Such a bias could prove important in explaining why women report satisfaction more often than men. Given these problems, the results in this chapter should be interpreted as statistical correlations, not causal impacts.

Data Used and Approach Taken

The Data

The data for the analysis come from Phase 1 of the Programme d'Appui Régional à la Statistique (PARSTAT) regional program's 1-2-3 surveys of seven West African economic capitals (Abidjan, Bamako, Cotonou, Dakar, Lomé, Niamey, and Ouagadougou) and Antananarivo (Madagascar).[4] These surveys were conducted in 2001/02 using exactly the same methodology (Brilleau, Ouedraogo, and Roubaud 2005). The data are thus perfectly comparable. (For a description of the 1-2-3 surveys, see box O.1 in the overview.)

The surveys, which provide information on both individual characteristics (including trajectory elements) and objective characteristics of the jobs held, provide an extremely rich database for studying job satisfaction. The question used to capture satisfaction differs from the one usually put to address this subject, which is generally "How satisfied are you with your main job?" The question in the 1-2-3 surveys, put to all respondents 15 and older, was "What are your employment plans for the future?" The answer categories were as follows: 1. Find a first job, 2. Find a new job in the same firm (job promotion), 3. Find a new job in another firm, and 4. Keep the job you currently have or continue not to work. Given the difficulty of ranking the categories using an ordinal scale,

respondents were divided into two groups: people who want to keep their job/
employment status (category 4; that is, people who are presumably satisfied)
and people who want to change their job (categories 1, 2, and 3; that is, people
who are dissatisfied).[5]

The drawback to using a different question than usual is that the results
are not entirely comparable with the findings presented in the literature. In
addition, some workers may declare not wishing to change their position not
because they are satisfied but because they have revised their aspirations downward. This criticism is not unique to the question included in this analysis; it
applies to all subjective approaches (including the standard job satisfaction
question). It should be kept in mind when interpreting the results, however.

The approach used here links satisfaction and aspirations. It also allows for
the inclusion of job-seekers and inactive (in particular, discouraged) workers and hence assessment of the extent to which inactivity is voluntary or
involuntary.

Methodological Approach and Model Tested

We identify the determinants of job satisfaction by combining the approaches
focusing on the importance of aspirations and of (generally unobserved) intrinsic work value factors (the possibility of promotion, training, autonomy, work
relations) on the one hand and the classic objective working conditions variables (remuneration, working hours), which procure extrinsic satisfaction, on
the other. We use the classification used by Warr (1999) to capture job quality
(figure 3.1). Our hypothesis is that satisfaction exists when a job's characteristics
are well matched to the jobholder's aspirations.

Figure 3.1 Model of Job Satisfaction

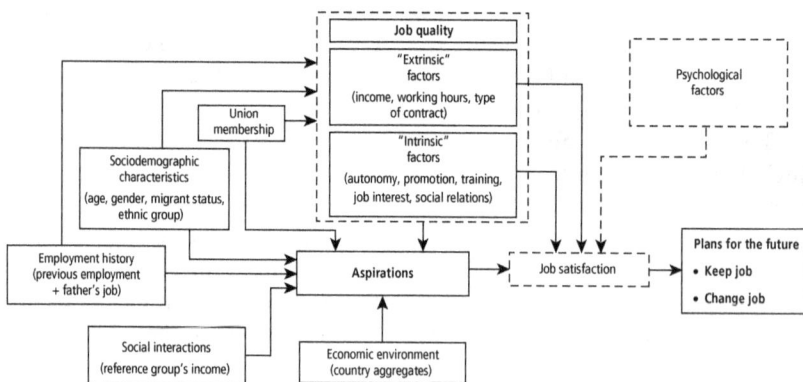

The model we test is $S_{ik} = f(\mathbf{X1}_{ik}, \mathbf{X2}_{ik}, \mathbf{A}_i)$, where S_{ik} is the satisfaction of individual i with job k; $\mathbf{X1}_{ik}$ is the job's extrinsic characteristics vector; $\mathbf{X2}_{ik}$ is the job's intrinsic characteristics vector; and $\mathbf{A}_i$ is the individual's aspirations vector. $\mathbf{X1}_{ik}$ captures earnings, fringe benefits, hours worked, and job security variables such as a written contract, status as a wage-earner, and steady work. Given the absence of accurate information on the majority of the factors relating to the intrinsic value of the job, we use the following proxies for $\mathbf{X2}_{ik}$: variables on socioeconomic group (which typifies job content); institutional sector (public, formal private, and informal sector); firm size; and presence of a union.

Taking the results obtained in the literature as a starting point, we assume that aspirations ($\mathbf{A}_i$) are determined by the individual characteristics of individual i (gender, age, level of education, marital status, migrant status, and social background, including father's level of education and employment) as well as by the characteristics of the individual's reference group (reference group earnings = y^*) and the socioeconomic context in the country (country dummy). Aspirations are not perfectly controlled for: if sociodemographic variables do capture some sociological patterns, they are at best rough proxies of individual expectations.

Individual factors also influence the quality of the job held. For equal job characteristics, however, the significance of individual factors in determining the level of satisfaction essentially reflects the effect of aspirations. More generally, we relax part of the endogeneity biases by introducing fixed effects (countries and households).

Because income relative to the reference group has a stronger effect than absolute income, rather than introduce individuals' earnings levels, we use a variable that ranks individuals by the income centile to which they belong in their country (y/y^* [earnings/average earnings in the country]). This option, adopted to overcome the problem of earnings comparability across countries, directly incorporates the comparative income effect and therefore one of the channels through which aspirations are determined. The two measurements are equivalent for the country models.

This approach provides a way to identify the nature and influence of the "intrinsic" job value factors, the more classic objective ("extrinsic") variables, and the factors likely to influence aspirations. We do not seek to isolate the effect of psychological factors (which affect aspirations in particular), about which we have no information. However, if psychological factors are correlated with individual sociodemographic variables, they can at least partially be taken into account. At the same time, we can check the extent to which the stylized facts obtained in developed countries apply to the African cities considered here.

Descriptive Findings on Satisfaction Levels

Level of Satisfaction by Labor Force Status

Analysis of the perceptions of the entire working-age population (15 and older) finds relatively similar satisfaction rates across cities (table 3.1). Overall, no more than half of the population report satisfaction with their situation. Abidjan and Antananarivo differ from the other capitals for the very low percentage of satisfied individuals who are inactive. As labor force participation rates are not particularly low in the two cities (Abidjan has a higher than average rate), this finding reflects labor market entry constraints that conceal the fact that many inactive individuals would actually like to work.

Not surprisingly, job-seekers are the least satisfied with their status, with a satisfaction rate of close to zero (the difference from zero may reflect measurement errors). This finding may appear to be a truism, as job-seekers are by definition looking for jobs. However, it contradicts the theories about the voluntary nature of unemployment. It bears out the conclusions of recent studies on the monetary and social integration deficit and the psychological costs of unemployment (Frey and Stutzer 2002; Alesina and Glaeser 2004).

More than 90 percent of discouraged workers are also dissatisfied. This finding points to the huge growth that could be expected in labor force participation rates in the event of an economic upturn.

When the analysis is narrowed to employed workers, the inhabitants of Dakar, Lomé, and Abidjan are the most dissatisfied (with rates of about 45 percent); a larger number of residents of Antananarivo (61 percent) and Cotonou (57 percent) report being satisfied with their work. It is hard to compare these figures with findings in other countries, because the question was not put the same way. Nonetheless, satisfaction rates appear to be much lower than in the developed countries and similar to those found in transition economies.[6]

Level of Satisfaction by Sociodemographic Characteristics

The rest of the analysis focuses on the employed working-age population. In keeping with the findings in the literature, women are more often satisfied with their job than are men (table 3.2). However, additional analysis is required to determine the extent to which this phenomenon persists after controlling for other factors and handling any selection bias problems. Household heads and their spouses express job satisfaction much more often than other household members. Single people report job satisfaction less often than married people. This observation is surprising given that single people would seem to face fewer constraints (especially financial constraints) and have greater leeway when looking for a job. Age may partially explain these results, as the job satisfaction rate increases with age. Job satisfaction among young people is very low (less than one-quarter of people under 20 are satisfied), mainly because of the entry

Table 3.1 Level of Job Satisfaction in Eight Cities in Sub-Sub-Saharan Africa, by Labor Force Status, 2001/02
(percent)

Status	Abidjan	Bamako	Cotonou	Dakar	Lomé	Niamey	Ouagadougou	Antananarivo
				West Africa				**Indian Ocean**
Employed	46.9***	54.9***	56.7***	45.0***	46.8***	49.1***	53.1***	61.1***
	(1.2)	(1.8)	(2.0)	(1.1)	(1.8)	(1.6)	(2.2)	(2.0)
Unemployed	2.3***	6.7***	4.0***	5.5***	3.8***	2.6***	1.0***	0.4***
	(0.7)	(1.9)	(1.5)	(1.0)	(1.2)	(0.7)	(0.3)	(0.3)
Discouraged	2.6***	10.1***	8.2***	7.8***	13.2***	3.4***	3.7***	16.5***
	(1.3)	(2.5)	(4.2)	(1.3)	(3.6)	(0.7)	(1.2)	(2.5)
Inactive	28.5***	50.1	44.9**	50.7***	45.6	50.6***	54.5***	28.4***
	(1.8)	(2.7)	(3.6)	(1.6)	(3.0)	(1.7)	(2.1)	(2.3)
All	36.8***	49.2***	50.4***	41.7	42.9	42.4	44.8*	42.6
	(1.1)	(1.7)	(2.0)	(1.0)	(1.7)	(1.2)	(1.6)	(1.1)

Sources: Based on Phase 1 of the following 1-2-3 surveys: West African Economic and Monetary Union (WAEMU) 2001/02 (Observatoire économique et statistique d'Afrique Subsaharienne [AFRISTAT], Développement, Institutions et Mondialisation [DIAL]; and national statistics institutes); Madagascar 2001 (DIAL and Institut National de la Statistique [INSTAT]).

Note: Figures are for individuals 15 and older. The mean was modified to allow for the sampling design; the mean test shows the difference between each category and the rest of the sample. Figures in parentheses are standard errors.

* significant at the 10 percent level,** significant at the 5 percent level,*** significant at the 1 percent level.

117

Table 3.2 Level of Job Satisfaction in Eight Cities in Sub-Saharan Africa, by Individual Characteristics, 2001/02
(percent)

Characteristic	West Africa							Indian Ocean	All
	Abidjan	Bamako	Cotonou	Dakar	Lomé	Niamey	Ouagadougou	Antananarivo	
Gender									
Male	43.9*** (1.2)	52.2* (1.8)	54.5 (2.0)	36.8*** (1.0)	44.4*** (1.8)	45.6*** (1.6)	50.1*** (2.0)	60.9 (2.2)	47.3*** (0.7)
Female	57.2*** (2.8)	61.1* (4.7)	60.1 (6.6)	63.6*** (5.3)	60.3*** (4.6)	57.5*** (4.0)	62.9*** (2.8)	63.6 (4.7)	60.3*** (1.7)
Position in household									
Household head	54.1*** (1.6)	62.4*** (2.0)	63.0*** (2.0)	49.2*** (1.6)	52.8*** (1.9)	54.1*** (1.8)	57.8*** (2.7)	68.9*** (2.1)	57.4*** (0.9)
Spouse	53.3*** (1.9)	57.3*** (2.7)	67.4*** (2.5)	46.5*** (2.1)	55.3*** (2.5)	55.0*** (2.3)	59.5*** (2.5)	69.3*** (1.7)	58.2*** (0.9)
Other	31.2*** (1.5)	34.8*** (2.2)	34.5*** (2.8)	33.1*** (1.1)	28.0*** (1.9)	31.9*** (1.9)	39.5*** (2.7)	41.3*** (3.9)	33.5*** (0.8)
Marital status									
Married	55.2*** (1.4)	60.7*** (2.1)	65.1*** (2.0)	47.6*** (1.2)	55.1*** (2.0)	55.2*** (1.8)	59.4*** (2.4)	60.6* (2.1)	57.1*** (0.7)
Single	32.1*** (1.6)	34.3*** (2.0)	33.0*** (2.7)	29.5*** (1.3)	27.7*** (1.8)	29.0*** (1.9)	36.1*** (2.8)	53.9* (3.4)	31.9*** (0.8)
Separated, divorced, or widowed	56.5*** (3.3)	61.1* (5.1)	64.3** (4.5)	46.0** (3.1)	52.4*** (3.1)	59.6*** (3.2)	69.6*** (4.3)	80.5*** (2.7)	58.6*** (1.5)
Age									
<20	22.3*** (1.9)	23.3*** (2.3)	24.3*** (3.3)	25.8*** (1.9)	20.0*** (2.1)	22.6*** (2.2)	30.3*** (2.4)	26.6*** (6.6)	24.1*** (1.0)
20–29	37.3*** (1.6)	45.3*** (2.6)	44.6*** (2.6)	32.0*** (1.5)	39.3*** (2.2)	37.1*** (2.3)	41.9*** (3.2)	43.4*** (2.3)	38.9*** (0.8)

30–39	47.9** (1.7)	52.0 (2.5)	59.6*** (2.4)	37.5 (1.9)	47.1 (2.3)	45.4 (1.9)	52.2 (2.4)	62.7 (3.0)	49.9*** (0.9)
40–49	61.4*** (2.1)	67.3*** (2.6)	68.6*** (2.8)	48.4*** (1.8)	59.7*** (2.5)	60.7*** (2.3)	63.9*** (2.6)	73.0*** (2.6)	62.4*** (1.1)
50+	72.2*** (2.2)	76.4*** (2.6)	82.1*** (2.2)	60.4*** (1.9)	73.0*** (2.7)	69.3*** (2.2)	81.9*** (3.1)	84.9*** (2.0)	74.4*** (1.0)
Education									
None	54.0*** (1.8)	57.3*** (2.2)	61.2*** (3.2)	42.6*** (1.4)	55.3*** (2.3)	54.8*** (1.9)	58.0*** (2.8)	65.2 (7.5)	53.3*** (0.9)
Primary	38.1*** (1.5)	46.0*** (2.7)	49.6*** (2.3)	31.7*** (1.5)	39.9*** (2.3)	34.8*** (2.1)	43.0*** (2.2)	55.9** (3.1)	41.9*** (0.9)
Lower-secondary	39.0*** (2.1)	44.2*** (2.7)	53.0 (2.8)	38.6 (1.8)	43.1 (2.1)	43.1* (2.5)	44.5*** (2.8)	58.4 (2.7)	45.5*** (1.0)
Upper-secondary	49.8* (2.8)	43.5*** (3.5)	53.2 (3.6)	37.7 (2.4)	44.2 (2.5)	41.8 (3.1)	52.7 (3.8)	67.5*** (2.3)	51.5*** (1.4)
Higher	40.7 (3.5)	60.4*** (3.2)	59.0 (3.9)	48.5*** (3.1)	45.8 (3.3)	45.3 (3.2)	53.0 (3.5)	71.3*** (2.2)	51.8** (1.6)
Migrant status									
Native	39.6*** (1.8)	46.7*** (2.1)	50.2*** (2.3)	37.5** (1.2)	43.0* (1.9)	37.5*** (1.7)	48.1*** (2.6)	60.3** (1.9)	46.2*** (0.9)
Migrant	47.6*** (1.3)	57.5*** (2.3)	58.6*** (2.1)	41.4** (1.5)	46.4* (2.0)	52.6*** (1.7)	53.8*** (2.4)	65.1** (2.6)	50.1*** (0.8)

Sources: Based on Phase 1 of the 1-2-3 surveys of selected countries (see table 3.1 for details).
Note: Figures are for all employed workers. The mean was modified to allow for the sampling design; the mean test shows the difference between each category and the rest of the sample. Figures in parentheses are standard errors.
* significant at the 10 percent level, ** significant at the 5 percent level, *** significant at the 1 percent level.

problems they encounter and the fact that labor market conditions often fail to satisfy their aspirations.

The link between job satisfaction and education reveals a *U*-shaped curve: people at the two tails of the distribution (the least educated and the most educated) post high rates of satisfaction. The fact that people with the least education—and therefore the fewest opportunities to find good jobs—have high job satisfaction probably reflects the fact that the least educated limit their aspirations. Labor market conditions are more positive for the few graduates there are.

Migrants report satisfaction with their jobs more often than nonmigrants. Either a selection effect is at work or migrants adapt their aspirations, or they are driven by an integration goal and actually manage to find better jobs than native residents.

These results do not establish direct links between satisfaction and individual characteristics (particularly position in the household and marital status), given the endogeneity issues. The variables do reflect some psychological unobservables that influence both satisfaction and employment.

Level of Satisfaction by Job Characteristics

Public sector workers are more likely than workers in other sectors to want to keep their job—an unsurprising result given the better benefits these workers enjoy (table 3.3). Workers in the informal private sector are more satisfied with their jobs than workers in the formal private sector (except in Antananarivo and Dakar). Additional checks are needed to determine whether this result holds after controlling for other variables and aspirations.

The results by industry vary a great deal across countries, but they appear to reflect the ranking of the sectors by their level of development and prosperity. Satisfaction is highest in trade in Cotonou and Lomé (and, to a lesser extent, in Niamey and Dakar). In Abidjan, satisfaction is higher in the primary sector (the country's most buoyant sector). Wage-earner status does not guarantee greater job satisfaction in the countries studied. Although wage-earners are more satisfied than non-wage-earners in Antananarivo, Dakar, and Bamako, in the other cities, at least as many non-wage-earners as wage earners report being satisfied with their job.

The level of satisfaction tends to grow as employees climb the socioeconomic ladder, with the highest rates found among managers (except in Niamey, where managers have a very low rate of satisfaction). Among non-wage-earners, employers and proprietors are more likely to be satisfied than workers who are self-employed. The ranking of contributing family workers and apprentices is not clear-cut, but both categories exhibit low levels of satisfaction (about 20 percent on average; Antananarivo is once again an exception, with 44 percent of family workers reporting being satisfied).

Table 3.3 Level of Job Satisfaction in Eight Cities in Sub-Saharan Africa, by Job Characteristics, 2001/02

				West Africa				Indian Ocean	
Sector	Abidjan	Bamako	Cotonou	Dakar	Lomé	Niamey	Ouagadougou	Antananarivo	All
Institutional sector									
Public sector	58.3*** (3.6)	67.4*** (3.0)	64.4** (5.0)	58.1*** (2.7)	61.5*** (3.3)	48.7 (2.4)	59.7*** (2.9)	79.5*** (2.1)	62.9*** (1.4)
Formal private sector	44.1 (2.3)	48.6 (2.8)	53.0 (3.3)	38.9 (1.9)	37.4*** (2.4)	42.1* (2.5)	47.3* (2.6)	62.9 (2.8)	47.9 (1.3)
Informal sector	44.3 (1.3)	51.1** (2.0)	53.9 (2.2)	37.1*** (1.1)	44.5 (1.9)	46.8 (1.8)	50.8 (2.5)	56.7*** (2.0)	46.6*** (0.7)
Industrial sector									
Primary	56.6** (4.8)	55.7 (5.0)	59.3 (8.1)	40.3 (3.6)	46.3 (4.6)	43.4 (3.6)	50.9 (4.1)	64.5 (5.1)	53.5*** (2.0)
Manufacturing	42.5* (2.0)	47.2*** (2.7)	46.1*** (3.0)	33.7*** (1.6)	42.3* (2.3)	43.7** (2.2)	52.4 (2.8)	60.8 (2.8)	45.2*** (1.1)
Trade	51.0*** (1.5)	54.3* (2.0)	61.8*** (2.3)	43.0*** (1.5)	47.9*** (2.2)	51.1*** (2.1)	52.8 (2.6)	62.3 (1.8)	52.3*** (0.8)
Services	41.3*** (1.5)	53.1 (2.0)	51.8*** (2.1)	39.9 (1.3)	43.4 (2.0)	45.9 (1.9)	49.3* (2.3)	60.2 (2.1)	46.3*** (0.8)
Wage-earner status									
Non-wage-earner	46.7** (1.4)	51.1** (2.0)	55.0 (2.2)	37.5** (1.1)	46.1** (1.9)	46.3 (1.8)	52.1 (2.3)	59.6** (1.9)	48.3 (0.7)
Wage-earner	42.9** (1.6)	56.4** (2.3)	53.8 (2.8)	41.6** (1.5)	41.2** (2.2)	46.6 (2.0)	49.9 (2.5)	62.9** (2.3)	48.3 (1.0)
Socioeconomic group									
Wage-earner									
Senior manager, engineer, or similar	55.2*	71.3***	62.8	65.5***	58.3*	45.3	59.2	81.9***	61.4***
	(5.6)	(4.7)	(5.3)	(5.1)	(8.1)	(4.3)	(4.7)	(3.9)	(2.1)

(continued next page)

Table 3.3 (continued)

Sector	West Africa							Indian Ocean	All
	Abidjan	Bamako	Cotonou	Dakar	Lomé	Niamey	Ouagadougou	Antananarivo	
Middle manager, supervisor	53.5**	54.9	59.6	52.9***	53.6*	50.0	57.8	67.7*	55.6***
	(3.3)	(3.7)	(5.2)	(2.9)	(5.0)	(3.1)	(4.2)	(3.9)	(1.6)
Skilled manual/nonmanual	44.2	60.8**	55.5	48.6***	49.7*	54.7**	58.6**	69.1***	56.0***
	(3.5)	(4.1)	(3.0)	(2.2)	(3.0)	(3.9)	(3.6)	(2.2)	(1.5)
Semi-skilled manual/ nonmanufacturing	44.7	51.1	51.4	35.1	34.2***	40.4*	51.4	59.1	45.0**
	(2.5)	(4.6)	(4.1)	(2.9)	(3.3)	(3.5)	(7.1)	(4.0)	(1.5)
Unskilled	32.2***	47.1	36.2***	30.3***	26.6***	44.0	35.9***	48.9***	35.9***
	(2.8)	(4.6)	(5.2)	(2.7)	(3.5)	(3.4)	(2.7)	(3.7)	(1.5)
Non-wage-earner									
Employer	65.3***	65.8***	72.5***	50.0*	55.5***	69.3***	66.0***	84.5***	66.4***
	(2.5)	(4.3)	(3.9)	(6.1)	(3.9)	(4.5)	(4.5)	(4.6)	(1.6)
Self-account worker	52.9***	54.4**	63.0***	43.4***	52.0***	54.7***	61.0***	61.3	54.2***
	(1.6)	(2.1)	(2.2)	(1.4)	(2.1)	(2.0)	(3.3)	(2.5)	(0.8)
Apprentice	18.6***	22.7***	23.7***	23.1***	21.6***	15.1***	16.6***	11.2***	20.6***
	(2.4)	(4.2)	(3.9)	(1.9)	(3.5)	(2.0)	(2.7)	(7.9)	(1.2)
Contributing family worker	22.1***	20.1***	27.1***	19.5***	20.9***	28.2***	35.3***	43.8***	28.4***
	(3.1)	(3.7)	(4.1)	(2.6)	(3.1)	(2.9)	(3.7)	(4.0)	(1.5)

Sources: Based on Phase 1 of the 1-2-3 surveys of selected countries (see table 3.1 for details).

Note: Figures are for all employed workers. The mean was modified to allow for the sampling design; the mean test shows the difference between each category and the rest of the sample. Figures in parentheses are standard errors.

* significant at the 10 percent level, ** significant at the 5 percent level, *** significant at the 1 percent level.

Econometric Analyses

Results at the Aggregate Level

The aim of the analysis was to identify the influence of three types of factors on job satisfaction:

- Variables affecting the formation of aspirations (individual, country, and household characteristics)
- Classic objective job variables that generate "extrinsic" satisfaction (remuneration, working conditions, and job security)
- Variables that reflect a job's intrinsic value (socioeconomic group, institutional sector, firm size, and existence of a union). These variables capture the opportunity to manage and supervise, work on one's own initiative, use one's capacities and skills, perform a variety of tasks, maintain good work relations, hold a suitable social position, and so forth.

Controlling for the effect of aspirations clarifies the nature of the effects of various job characteristics on job satisfaction.

Several approaches were considered to at least partially allow for endogeneity effects. First, country dummy variable controls were introduced for the unobserved factors relating to the national context, which influence the individuals' satisfaction levels; access to good-quality jobs (employment contract, steady work, wages, and so forth); and even the number of hours worked. Second, given that in the vast majority of households individual data were available on several members, we were able to conduct estimates purged of household fixed effects. This approach controls for unobserved factors related to household characteristics (family background, potential common traits), which influence the individuals' type of labor market integration as much as satisfaction does.

Several stylized facts have been observed in developed countries and transition economies. Women; the least educated; people from modest social backgrounds (people whose father had no more than primary education, people who are self-employed in a small family business); and, to a certain extent, the oldest individuals are more inclined than other workers to express job satisfaction (table 3.4). These stylized facts can be interpreted as evidence of the downward revision of aspirations.

The level of education has a convex effect on job satisfaction, with the least educated and university graduates more inclined to be satisfied with their jobs (the coefficient corresponding to the square of the number of years of education is positive). The negative correlation with the level of satisfaction for widowed and divorced workers and migrants may reflect the effect of psychological factors on general well-being. The fact that the coefficients are no longer significant

Table 3.4 Logit Model of Determinants of Job Satisfaction in Eight Cities in Sub-Saharan Africa, 2001/02

Variable	(1)	(2)	(3) Household fixed effect	(4)	(5)	(6) Household fixed effect
Sociodemographic characteristics						
Female	0.366***	0.365***	0.495***		0.291***	0.406***
Age	0.030**	0.024**	0.036*		0.017*	0.022
Age squared	0.000	0.000*	0.000		0.000***	0.000
Number of years of education	−0.046***	−0.047***	−0.057***		−0.042***	−0.054***
Number of years of education squared	0.000***	0.001***	0.000***		0.000***	0.000***
Father self-employed	0.090***	0.099**	0.098*		0.080**	0.092*
Father's education > primary	−0.220***	−0.220***	−0.430***		−0.222***	−0.436***
Migrant		−0.121***	−0.101		−0.125***	−0.076
Single		−0.131*	−0.093		−0.065	−0.017
Widowed or divorced		−0.219**	−0.003		−0.207**	−0.004
Job characteristics						
Relative income	0.015***	0.015***	0.018***	0.012***	0.012***	0.014***
Number of hours worked				0.004***	0.004***	0.005***
Wage-earner				0.146	−0.241***	−0.097
Written contract				0.153***	0.125***	0.022
Steady work				0.401***	0.316***	0.292***
Wages and benefits (reference = not fixed, no benefits)						
Fixed wage				0.245***	0.213***	0.235***
Benefits				0.222**	0.171*	0.142
Sector (reference = formal private)						
Public sector				0.284***	0.188**	0.326**
Informal sector				0.053	0.016	−0.077
Type of worker (reference = unskilled/apprentice)						
Senior manager				0.081	0.329**	0.563**
Middle manager				−0.022	0.140*	0.216
Skilled/semi-skilled				0.161***	0.230***	0.203*
Proprietor/employer				1.207***	0.704***	0.851***
Self-employed				1.085***	0.481***	0.595**
Family worker				0.480**	0.299*	0.097
Number of workers (reference = >50)						
Own account (1)				−0.275**	−0.236*	−0.165
2–5				−0.169**	−0.129*	−0.037
6–50				−0.164***	−0.099	−0.093

(continued next page)

Table 3.4 (continued)

Variable	(1)	(2)	(3) Household fixed effect	(4)	(5)	(6) Household fixed effect
Union						
Union in the firm				−0.016	0,017	−0,038
Union member				0.071	−0,031	−0,053
Country dummy (reference = Togo)						
Benin	0.399***	0.383***		0.474***	0.399***	
Burkina Faso	0.110***	0.101***		0.308***	0.145***	
Côte d'Ivoire	−0.029*	−0.014		0.129***	0.036*	
Madagascar	0.724***	0.629***		0.867***	0.718***	
Mali	0.202***	0.174***		0.317***	0.187***	
Niger	−0.077***	−0.083***		0.204***	0.002	
Senegal	−0.282***	−0.298***		−0.072***	−0.197***	
Constant	−1.981***	−1.736***		−2.184***	−2.264***	
Number of observations	38,532	38,532	17,029	38,270	38,264	16,841
Pseudo R^2	0.105	0.106	0.237	0.08	0.117	0.254
Log (pseudo-likelihood)	−2,3895.7	−2,3868.9	−4,941.6	−2,4369.2	−2,3409.4	−4,776.1

Sources: Based on Phase 1 of the 1-2-3 surveys of selected countries (see table 3.1 for details).
Note: Relative income refers to the classification of each individual based on income centile. Categories of income centile are calculated for each country: the first centile category includes the 1 percent of the population with the lowest income.
* significant at the 10 percent level,** significant at the 5 percent level,*** significant at the 1 percent level.

when we consider household fixed effects confirms that the link between these two variables and job satisfaction is not direct.

The classic objective variables used to describe working conditions are all significantly correlated with job satisfaction:

- The link with income (relative income here) is significant and has the expected sign. The higher the income (compared with standard earnings in the country studied), the greater the tendency to express job satisfaction. Income far from determines the level of satisfaction, however, as the variance explained by the univariate models of earned income only is no greater than a few percentage points (models not reported).

- Steady work, a fixed wage, and fringe benefits have a positive effect on satisfaction.

- The positive value for the number of hours worked reflects the specific circumstances in the countries studied, where the risk of underemployment is high (and the fear of working too hard limited).

- Being a wage-earner does not appear to significantly influence the level of satisfaction, other things equal.[7] In countries where wage labor is not the rule, employees probably perceive employer-employee relations as a form of dependence, prompting a feeling of subordination and vulnerability (as the employer can decide to terminate employment at any time).

- Most of the variables used to capture the intrinsic value of the job also influence satisfaction in the expected direction, although middle managers express less job satisfaction than would be expected. This finding could be explained by the ambiguous situation in which middle managers—who have some autonomy but may be burdened by pressure from senior managers— find themselves.

- The public sector (administration and public corporations) is the most highly valued: given identical job characteristics, employed workers prefer to work in this sector. Job security elements are not captured by the models; prestige probably plays a decisive role in the preference for public sector employment.

- The formal private sector does not appear to be more desirable than the informal sector. This finding challenges the queuing theory put forward by many economic studies, which see it as a refuge sector.

- People who work in large firms (more than 50 people) are more likely to be satisfied with their job. Advantages in terms of community and social networks (events, a company canteen, the firm's reputation) may well win out over the benefits associated with smaller firms (autonomy, flexibility, more family-type relations). However, as the link between firm size and satisfaction is no longer significant when household fixed effects are taken into account, it probably reflects endogeneity.

The existence of or membership in a union has no effect on satisfaction, possibly because of the weak bargaining power of unions in the countries studied.

Analysis of the country dummy variables shows that people in Benin and Madagascar are more inclined to report being satisfied with their job; people in Côte d'Ivoire and Senegal tend to be more critical. These findings reflect differences in labor market conditions (not captured by the variables in our models). The sociopolitical contexts allow optimistic views in Antananarivo and Cotonou; it is less satisfactory in Dakar and Abidjan.[8]

Results by Country

The signs of the coefficients are the same in all capitals for most of the factors that have a significant influence on satisfaction, and their magnitudes are extremely similar, suggesting the overall robustness of the approach and the results (table 3.5). However, the correlations are not systematically significant

Table 3.5 Logit and Household Fixed-Effect Models of Determinants of Job Satisfaction in Eight Cities in Sub-Saharan Africa, 2001/02

Variable	Abidjan	Antananarivo	Bamako	Cotonou	Dakar	Lomé	Niamey	Ouagadougou
Sociodemographic characteristics								
Female	0.283*	0.649***	0.517***	0.693***	0.041	0.294**	0.496***	0.780***
Age	0.078**	0.082**	0.041*	0.044	−0.027	0.034	0.012	−0.027
Age squared	0.000	0.000	0.000	0.000	0.001***	0.000	0.000	0.001**
Number of years of education	0.000	−0.102	−0.120***	−0.001	−0.051*	−0.085**	−0.090*	−0.087**
Number of years of education squared	−0.006*	0.000	0.005	−0.002	0.001	0.002	0.003	0.001
Father self-employed	0.046	−0.006	0.061	−0.071	0.225**	0.027	−0.025	0.063
Father's education > primary	−0.605***	−0.123	−0.547***	−0.528***	−0.176*	−0.317*	−0.868***	−0.678***
Migrant	−0.108	−0.049	0.231	−0.288*	0.049	−0.183	−0.095	−0.016
Job characteristics								
Relative income	0.021***	0.021***	0.008**	0.013***	0.016***	0.019***	0.009**	0.018***
Number of hours worked	0.001	0.010**	0.007*	0.004	0.007***	−0.002	0.002	0.010***
Wage-earner	−0.584*	−0.371	0.312	0.341	0.050	−0.544	0.150	0.069
Written contract	0.112	−0.001	−0.502*	0.128	0.133	0.099	0.475*	−0.185
Steady work	0.345	0.772***	0.141	0.262	0.337***	0.076	0.257	0.215
Fixed wage (reference = not fixed)	0.174	−0.059	0.893**	0.278	0.061	0.098	0.369	0.243
Sector (reference = formal private)								
Public	0.598**	0.110	0.428	0.641**	0.672***	0.770**	−0.349	0.227
Informal	0.156	−0.356	−0.302	0.028	0.159	−0.300	0.003	−0.484**

(continued next page)

Table 3.5 (continued)

Variable	Abidjan	Antananarivo	Bamako	Cotonou	Dakar	Lomé	Niamey	Ouagadougou
Type of worker (reference = middle manager/skilled or semi-skilled)								
Senior manager	1.129**	0.486	0.647	−0.165	0.552	−0.382	0.031	0.822**
Proprietor/employer	0.766**	1.037**	1.211***	1.337***	0.091	0.688**	1.109**	1.146***
Self-employed	0.485*	0.009	0.798***	1.220***	0.217	0.731***	0.616**	0.981***
Union								
Union in the firm	−0.200	0.250	−0.183	0.170	−0.423**	0.280	−0.327	0.192
Union member	0.294	−0.362	0.395	−0.015	−0.094	−0.181	−0.023	−0.155
Number of observations	2,035	1,789	1,715	2,086	3,536	1,867	1,639	2,171
Pseudo R^2	0.339	0.388	0.264	0.366	0.150	0.289	0.267	0.304
Log (likelihood)	−503.2	−401.3	−472.9	−504.7	−1194.8	−486.8	−462.2	−573.3

Sources: Based on Phase 1 of the 1-2-3 surveys of selected countries (see table 3.1 for details).

Note: Relative income refers to the classification of each individual based on income centile. Categories of income centile are calculated for each country: the first centile category includes the 1 percent of the population with the lowest income.

* significant at the 10 percent level, ** significant at the 5 percent level, *** significant at the 1 percent level.

for each country. The level of education has no effect on aspirations in Anta-nanarivo and Cotonou. The influence of father's education is significant in all cities except Antananarivo. In Dakar the relationship between satisfaction and father's self-employment is stronger than elsewhere.

Some working conditions are associated with the level of satisfaction only in certain cities. For example, the written contract is highly valued only in Niamey. Having a fixed wage is seen as positive, other things being equal, only in Bamako. Wage labor is perceived negatively in Abidjan (where wage-earning appears to imply adverse working conditions).

Working in the public sector is likely to generate satisfaction in Abidjan, Cotonou, Dakar, and Lomé; it has no significant effect on satisfaction in Antananarivo, Bamako, Niamey, or Ouagadougou. The correlation between job satisfaction and informal sector employment is positive in Dakar but negative in Ouagadougou. Self-employment is associated with job satisfac-tion except in Antananarivo and Dakar, where the link is not significant. Having a union in the firm is not associated with higher job satisfaction; the link is actually negative in Dakar, where workers are more inclined to express dissatisfaction in firms with a union. An endogeneity effect is probably at work here (the union may have been set up in the firm because of poor work-ing conditions).

Conclusion

Analysis of job satisfaction in eight Sub-Saharan Africa capitals finds signifi-cant links between objective job characteristics and the satisfaction individuals express with their jobs. For some job characteristics, these links appear more clearly after controlling for individual aspirations. The effect of aspirations is identified through the influence of individual characteristics and the circum-stances in the country.

The results validate the idea that job satisfaction is a suitable indicator of job quality, for three reasons. First, satisfaction provides a gauge of the match between jobs and individual aspirations. Given that a mismatch between expec-tations and outcomes could create economic and social tensions, this match needs to be measured. Second, after controlling for the effect of aspirations, the correlations between satisfaction and objective job characteristics indicate that individuals take these characteristics into consideration in evaluating their working conditions. Third, labor market conditions (and the characteristics that capture those conditions) vary across countries. Different values can be placed on a given job or status depending on the circumstances in a country. The findings hence reflect the intrinsic quality of a category of employment in the country studied.

The analysis shows that the explanatory power of the factors chosen is limited. The controls used for endogeneity and selection biases are imperfect; the use of panel data or attitudinal questions would be a useful avenue for future research that would allow further exploration of causality, by explicitly controlling for unobservables and psychological factors that shape behaviors and opinions. Closer attention should also be paid to the factors associated with employment history (to take account of upward and downward trajectories), in particular the characteristics of individuals' previous job. Analysis of the impact of national socioeconomic circumstances could be honed by introducing macroeconomic variables (growth, stagnation, or crisis spells) or by building indicators to typify individuals' reference groups and capturing comparison peer effects.

Notes

1. Economists long overlooked job satisfaction—although pioneering work was done by Hamermesh (1977), Freeman (1978), and, more recently, Clark and Oswald (1996)—out of scepticism about drawing economic conclusions from data on feelings and personal perceptions. Their interest in job satisfaction increased when the link was identified between job satisfaction and work performance.
2. The other studies related to this topic are ad hoc analyses of specific professions (nurses, surveyors, and teachers, for example).
3. The cities are Abidjan, Côte d'Ivoire; Bamako, Mali; Cotonou, Benin; Dakar, Senegal; Lomé, Togo; Niamey, Niger; and Ouagadougou, Burkina Faso, in West Africa and Antananarivo, in Madagascar. Although Abidjan and Cotonou are not administrative capitals, we refer to them as capitals because they are the most important economic centers in their countries (Cotonou is also the seat of government).
4. The 1-2-3 surveys have been conducted since 1996 in Antananarivo, where the methodology was strengthened before the surveys were implemented in West Africa in the framework of the PARSTAT program.
5. For unemployed and inactive individuals in category 1 (find a first job), satisfaction concerns their situation on the labor market (rather than job satisfaction). These categories are not included in the econometric analyses on job satisfaction, which examine only the employed labor force.
6. We refer here in particular to the figures provided by Sousa-Poza and Sousa-Poza (2000). The satisfaction rate in their study includes everyone who indicated being more or less satisfied.
7. Other variables (steady work, full-time work, fixed wage) take into account some of the advantages of being a wage-earner.
8. In 2002, Madagascar had just emerged from a major political crisis whose positive outcome raised high hopes. Benin is one of the rare African countries to have seen real democratic progress (with changeovers of political power made possible by transparent elections) following a long period of instability and dictatorship until the late 1990s. The hope inspired by the directions these two

countries have taken may have had a psychological effect on job satisfaction. The less stable sociopolitical situation in Côte d'Ivoire and Senegal at the time of the survey probably had a negative impact on individuals' perceptions of working conditions.

References

Alesina A. and E. Glaeser. 2004. *Fighting Poverty in the U.S. and Europe: A World of Difference.* New York: Oxford University Press.

Beuran M., and E. Kalugina. 2005. "Subjective Welfare and the Informal Sector: The Case of Russia." Working Paper, Centre d'Economie de la Sorbonne, Université Paris 1, Centre National de la Recherche Scientifique (CNRS), Paris.

Blanchflower, D., and A. Oswald. 2004. "Well-Being over Time in Britain and the USA." *Journal of Public Economics* 88 (7–8): 1359–86.

Brilleau, A., E. Ouedraogo, and F. Roubaud. 2005. "L'enquête 1-2-3 dans les pays de l'UEMOA: la consolidation d'une méthode." *Statéco* 99: 15–170.

Bryson, A., L. Cappellari, and C. Lucifora. 2005. "Why So Unhappy? The Effects of Unionization on Job Satisfaction." IZA Discussion Paper 1498, Institute for the Study of Labor, Bonn, Germany.

Clark, A. 1997. "Job Satisfaction and Gender: Why Are Women So Happy at Work?" *Labour Economics* 4 (4): 341–72.

———. 2001. "What Really Matters in a Job? Hedonic Measurement Using Quit Data." *Labour Economics* 8 (2): 223–42.

Clark, A. 2004. "What Makes a Good Job? Evidence from OECD Countries." DELTA Working Paper 2004–28, Département et Laboratoire d'Economie Théorique et Appliquée, École Normale Supérieure, École des Hautes Études en Sciences Sociales, Paris.

Clark, A., and A. J. Oswald. 1996. "Satisfaction and Comparison Income." *Journal of Public Economics* 61: 359–81.

Clark, A., A. J. Oswald, and P. Warr. 1996. "Is Job Satisfaction U-Shaped in Age?" *Journal of Occupational and Organizational Psychology* 69 (1): 57–81.

D'Addio, A. C., T. Eriksson, and P. Frijters. 2003. "An Analysis of the Determinants of Job Satisfaction When Individuals' Baseline Satisfaction Levels May Differ." DT 2003-16 CAM, Centre for Applied Microeconometrics, Institute of Economics, University of Copenhagen.

Easterlin, R. A. 2001. "Income and Happiness: Towards a Unified Theory." *Economic Journal* 111 (2): 465–84.

———. 2003. "Building a Better Theory of Well-Being." IZA Discussion Paper 742, Institute for the Study of Labor, Bonn, Germany.

Falco, P., W. F. Maloney, and B. Rijkers. 2011. "Self Employment and Informality in Africa: Panel Evidence from Satisfaction Data." March, Centre for the Study of African Economies (CSAE), Department of Economics, Oxford University.

Freeman, R. B. 1978. "Job Satisfaction as an Economic Variable." *American Economic Review* 68 (2): 135–41.

Frey, B., and A. Stutzer. 2002. *Happiness and Economics. How the Economy and Institutions Affect Human Well-Being*. Princeton, NJ: Princeton University Press.

Garcia-Serrano, C. 2008. "Does Size Matter? The Influence of Firm Size on Working Conditions and Job Satisfaction." Working Paper 2008-30, Institute for Social & Economic Research (ISER), Columbia University, New York.

Gelade, G. A., P. Dobson, and K. Auer. 2008. "Individualism, Masculinity, and the Sources of Organizational Commitment." *Journal of Cross-Cultural Psychology* 39 (5): 599–617.

Hamermesh, D. 1977. "Economic Aspects of Job Satisfaction." In *Essays in Labor Market and Population Analysis,* ed. O. Ashenfelter and W. Oates, 53–72. New York: Wiley.

Hamermesh, D. 2001. "The Changing Distribution of Job Satisfaction." *Journal of Human Resources* 36: 1–30.

Idson, T. L. 1990. "Establishment Size, Job Satisfaction, and the Structure of Work." *Applied Economics* 22: 1007–18.

Judge, T. A., C. J. Thoresen, J. E. Bono, and G. K. Patton. 2001. "The Job Satisfaction–Job Performance Relationship: A Qualitative and Quantitative Review." *Psychological Bulletin* 127 (3): 376–407.

Judge, T.A., and S. Watanabe. 1993. "Another Look at the Job Satisfaction–Life Satisfaction Relationship." *Journal of Applied Psychology* 6: 939–48.

Kristensen, N., and N. Westergård-Nielsen. 2004. "Does Low Job Satisfaction Lead to Job Mobility?" IZA Discussion Paper 1026, Institute for the Study of Labor, Bonn, Germany.

Lévy-Garboua, L. and C. Montmarquette. 1984. "Reported Job Satisfaction: What Does It Mean?" *Journal of Socio-Economics* 33 (2): 135–51.

Lévy-Garboua, L., C. Montmarquette, and V. Simonnet. 1999. *"Job Satisfaction and Quits: Theory and Evidence from the German Socio-Economic Panel."* Théorie et Applications en Microéconomie et Macroéconomie (TEAM), Centre d'Economie de la Sorbonne, Université Paris 1.

Llorente, R. M., and E. F. Macías. 2005. "Job Satisfaction as an Indicator of the Quality of Work." *Journal of Socio-Economics* 34 (5): 656–73.

Malka, A., and J. A. Chatman. 2003. "Work Orientation and the Contingency of Job Satisfaction and Subjective Well-Being on Annual Income: A Longitudinal Assessment." *Personality and Social Psychology Bulletin* 29: 737–46.

Pichler, F., and C. Wallace. 2009. "What Are the Reasons for Differences in Job Satisfaction across Europe? Individual, Compositional, and Institutional Explanations." *European Sociological Review* 25 (5): 535–49.

Rakotomanana, F. 2011. "Secteur informel urbain, marché du travail et pauvreté: essais d'analyse sur le cas de Madagascar." PhD diss., École Doctorale Entreprise, Économie, Société, Université Montesquieu, Bordeaux IV.

Razafindrakoto, M., and F. Roubaud. 2006. "Les déterminants du bien-être individuel en Afrique francophone: le poids des institutions." *Afrique Contemporaine* 220: 191–223.

Razafindrakoto, M., F. Roubaud, and J. M. Wachsberger. 2012. "Travailler dans le secteur informel: choix ou contrainte? Une analyse de la satisfaction dans l'emploi au Vietnam." In *L'économie informelle dans les pays en développement,* ed. J.-P. Cling, S. Lagrée, M. Razafindrakoto, and F. Roubaud, 47–66. Paris: Edition de l'AFD.

Sousa-Poza, A., and A. A. Sousa-Poza. 2000. "Well-Being at Work: A Cross-National Analysis of the Levels and Determinants of Job Satisfaction." *Journal of Socio-Economics* 29 (6): 517–38.

Warr, P. 1999. "Well-Being and the Workplace." In *Well-Being: The Foundations of Hedonic Psychology,* ed. D. Kahneman, E. Diener, and N. Schwartz, 392–412. New York: Russell Sage Foundation.

Chapter **4**

Are Workers Compensated for Accepting Vulnerable Jobs? Evidence from West Africa

Philippe Bocquier, Christophe J. Nordman, and Aude Vescovo

One of the main focuses of studies on labor markets in Sub-Saharan Africa is the institutional segmentation between formal and informal sectors (Maloney 2004; see also chapter 6). Informal work is defined from the point of view of the firm, worker, or line of business, depending on the policy aim. The 1993 System of National Accounts (SNA93)—a set of international standards designed to establish a framework for the production of statistics on national accounts—classifies firms based on statistical or tax registration criteria and whether they keep written accounts. This distinction serves no purpose when it comes to capturing individuals' working conditions, especially employment vulnerability.

The concept of vulnerability refers to how difficult it is for individuals to manage the risks or cope with the losses and costs associated with the occurrence of risky events or situations.[1] The vulnerability of workers can be seen, for example, in contract insecurity (unstable remuneration and no written contract); adverse working conditions; and, more generally, a high level of exposure to job risks. Firm or business vulnerability criteria (industry, business size, and institutional sector) are not used here, because they reflect interfirm rather than interindividual dualism.

Vulnerable workers can be found in all formal and informal private firms; they work in public and semi-public corporations as well. This chapter focuses solely on the private sector (formal and informal businesses), based on the assumption that vulnerability is driven by different mechanisms in the public and private sectors.

The theory of compensating differentials—as formalized by Brown (1980), Rosen (1986), and Murphy and Topel (1987)—posits that workers may receive pecuniary compensation commensurate with the danger or strenuousness of their tasks or the adverse nature of their working conditions.[2] In developed countries, for instance, everything else equal, hazardous and highly strenuous jobs are often better paid than jobs without these attributes.[3] Our interpretation of the link between vulnerability and income draws on developments in the theory of compensating differentials, which we apply to both working conditions and employment vulnerability for the first time in African countries. Our working assumption is that, other things equal, workers classified as vulnerable earn more than more stable, steady workers classified as less vulnerable. If this is the case, some individuals will be willing to hold vulnerable jobs, especially if the immediate need to earn income outweighs the medium- or long-run advantage associated with stable jobs.

The questions of what determines vulnerability and how vulnerability and remuneration are linked raise several methodological problems, which this chapter tries to solve. First, entry selection occurs in the labor market. Second, sample selection concerns the individual's sector allocation (public, formal private, or informal). Observable individual characteristics (such as human capital in general) as well as unobservable individual characteristics influence both the decision to participate in a particular labor market segment and the level of individual earnings in Africa. Third, vulnerability is likely to be endogenous in the earnings equations. It is endogenous if individuals' unobservable characteristics are correlated with both their level of vulnerability and their level of earnings. It is important to take these effects into account, because they can produce biases, such as overestimation of the impact of vulnerability on individual earnings if, for example, unobservable characteristics such as low worker motivation or ability (or conversely, worker perseverance) are positively correlated with the probability of obtaining a vulnerable job and negatively correlated with earnings.

Our analysis takes a distributional approach.[4] It assumes that the worker's relative position on the remuneration scale influences how vulnerability affects income. Whereas workers with vulnerable jobs at the low end of the pay scale receive less in compensation than workers with identical characteristics who do not hold vulnerable jobs, workers in vulnerable jobs at the high end of the pay scale are paid premiums. These different mechanisms could reflect differences in bargaining power and labor market imbalances. Their greater bargaining would enable workers at the upper tail of the earnings distribution to secure higher pay for greater vulnerability. Conversely, workers at the bottom of the earnings distribution may be more forceful in negotiating for premium pay if they are seeking to secure a living wage. Compensation for vulnerability therefore would decrease the further the worker moves from a minimum subsistence income. In the case of labor market imbalances, employers' capacity to provide financial compensation for adverse working conditions may also depend on the demand for and supply of labor. Where, for example, labor supply outstrips demand, employers do not need to compensate workers for adverse working conditions.

All these hypotheses, which assume that the effect of vulnerability on earnings differs depending on the position in the earnings distribution, are tested by quantile regressions.

The chapter is organized as follows. The first section briefly examines the theoretical arguments underlying the existence of compensating differentials and highlights the theory's implications for the case study. The second section presents the data from the 1-2-3 surveys of the West African economic capitals and shows how key variables were constructed.[5] The third section presents the econometric models. The fourth section discusses the results. The last section draws conclusions.

The Theory of Compensating Differentials

There is a long history of economic research into the forces that narrow or widen wage differentials between individuals. The first models focused on competitive markets. They found wage premiums compensating nonpecuniary job attributes, such as working conditions, and differences in job stability across industries (Brown 1980; Rosen 1986; Murphy and Topel 1987). Most authors acknowledge that when job characteristics other than wages enter into the labor market decisions of firms and workers, market balance is achieved by the equalization of workers' utilities rather than their wages.

Rosen (1986) posits that the reasoning behind compensating mechanisms is a simple supply-and-demand structure. Labor supply decisions have to balance the trade-off between earned income (wages) and the cost of performing a job (stress, repetition, production deadlines, and so forth) such that, at the optimum, wage differences correspond to the marginal rate of substitution between consumption and working conditions. Labor demand decisions by firms are based on a trade-off between the need to provide compensation commensurate with the strenuous or hazardous nature of a task and the need to improve the working conditions offered.

Under the assumption of homogeneous individuals and heterogeneous work environments, wages across workers differ such that all workers obtain the same utility. To encourage workers to accept worse working conditions, firms have to offer higher wages. Lifting the assumption of homogeneous individuals necessarily introduces a great deal of uncertainty as to the existence of compensation for working conditions when it is observed at the midpoint of the worker distribution. It could prove necessary to divide the population into more homogeneous groups—by, for example, using a conditional wage quantile derived from quantile regressions, in order to reduce the noise created by the presence of individual heterogeneity in the estimation of the compensating differential.

Noncompetitive theories argue that wage deviations between apparently identical individuals tend to reflect noncompensating differentials, such as workers' relative bargaining power (Daniel and Sofer 1998; Manning 2003) and the existence of efficiency wages.[6] Other hypotheses point to the existence of information asymmetries, which may increase friction in the match between the supply of and demand for labor (Hwang, Mortensen, and Reed 1998), and interfirm differences in factor productivity (Burdett and Mortensen 1998; Pissarides 2000; Mortensen 2003).

There is a dearth of research on the link between compensating differentials and observed job attributes, especially when it comes to distributional approaches.[7] Fernández and Nordman (2009) show that the compensating differential probably depends on the worker's relative position in the earnings distribution. For example, pecuniary compensation for adverse working conditions could well be overestimated if the most capable (or resistant) workers are selected for employment where these attributes are more common. Moreover, given the assumption that the most capable individuals are also the most likely to receive efficiency wages, or to have a certain amount of bargaining power, working conditions could well have less to do with the wage-setting process for these individuals than for workers without these characteristics. More generally, workers could find it easier to ask for premiums for adverse working conditions when the demand for labor exceeds the supply, creating a labor market imbalance that probably varies along the earnings distribution.

Data and Definition of Vulnerability

The data come from Phase 1 of the 1-2-3 surveys conducted in the following economic capitals in 2001/02: Abidjan (Côte d'Ivoire), Bamako (Mali), Cotonou (Benin), Dakar (Senegal), Lomé (Togo), Niamey (Niger), and Ouagadougou (Burkina Faso) (for a description of the surveys, see box O.1 in the overview). The sample was restricted to all working-age individuals as defined by International Labour Organization (ILO)—that is, people 15 and older. It was then reduced to include only people with at least five years of potential labor market experience, in order to take account of workers' employment histories and thereby understand the longitudinal aspects of vulnerability. Potential experience is defined as the individual's age minus the number of years of education and the six years theoretically preceding the start of school. The five-year potential experience span is broad enough to circumvent the problem of date measurement errors (end of education and end of previous job) and narrow enough to prevent the samples from being too small.

The sample was reduced from 58,385 individuals 15 and older to 50,772 individuals 15 and older with five years or more of potential experience, from 33,390 employed workers 15 and older to 32,314 employed workers 15 and older with five years or more of potential experience. Among the employed workers, we are interested only in formal and informal private sector workers with some income. Informal work is defined from the point of view of the firm, worker, or line of business, depending on the policy aim. The 1993 System of National Accounts—a set of international standards designed to establish a framework for the production of statistics on national accounts—defines informality based on statistical or tax registration criteria and the keeping of written accounts.

The formal private sector regression samples include 302–950 workers (depending on the country), with a small minority of self-employed workers (table 4.1). The informal private sector regression samples range from 2,230 to 3,492 workers, with a majority of self-employed workers. Individuals with no income are people with five years of potential experience who are not working (as wage or self-employed workers). Unpaid (contributing) family workers are included among the self-employed, because they share profits with the leading independent worker in the family. Earnings for dependent workers include wages and benefits (bonuses, paid holidays, housing, benefits in kind, and so forth). Nonmonetary benefits are converted into wages. Profits of independent workers were reconstituted by recapping income and expenses (including intermediary spending, employee's wages, taxes, investment) over a reference period to which the respondent could relate. For both dependent and independent workers, monthly net income was estimated and divided by the number of hours worked per month to obtain hourly earnings.

Construction of the Vulnerability Variables

We used a number of individual employment status indicators, which we believe best capture the multifaceted nature of vulnerability in the main job. Business or production unit criteria (industry, business size, and institutional sector) were not used, because they reflect interfirm rather than interworker differences.

Worker vulnerability is defined by nine dichotomous variables, corresponding to different aspects of vulnerability (table 4.2). The variables distinguish independent workers (employers and own-account workers) from dependent workers (employees, contributing family workers, and apprentices).

The first variable, contractual insecurity, concerns the informal nature of the contract. This variable equals 1 if the individual has no written contract or does not receive a payslip and 0 otherwise. (It is not defined for self-employed workers, to whom it does not apply.) No distinction is made between workers with fixed-term contracts and workers with open-ended contracts.

Table 4.1 Descriptive Statistics of Study Sample in Seven Cities in West Africa

Statistic	Abidjan	Bamako	Cotonou	Dakar	Lomé	Niamey	Ouagadougou
Sample total	11,343	13,002	11,574	19,054	9,906	14,524	13,733
Working-age population	7,503	7,529	7,639	12,487	6,418	8,284	8,525
Working-age population with five or more years potential experience	6,537	6,561	6,517	11,014	6,546	7,269	7,328
Working-age population with zero income	2,568	2,746	2,374	6,074	2,081	4,053	3,663
Public sector (positive earnings)	302	457	398	498	306	577	584
Regression samples							
Formal private sector (positive earnings)	825	452	509	950	302	409	336
Dependent	782	365	423	868	261	373	307
Independent	43	87	86	82	41	36	29
Informal sector (positive earnings)	2,842	2,906	3,236	3,492	2,857	2,230	2,745
Dependent	894	528	460	1,123	508	562	724
Independent	1,948	2,378	2,776	2,369	2,349	1,668	2,021

Sources: Based on Phase 1 of the 1-2-3 surveys of selected countries in the West African Economic and Monetary Union (WAEMU) conducted in 2001/02 by the Observatoire économique et statistique d'Afrique Subsaharienne (AFRISTAT); Développement, Institutions et Mondialisation (DIAL); and national statistics institutes.

Table 4.2 Distribution of Vulnerability Criteria by Sector and Job Status in Seven Cities in West Africa

Criterion	Criterion/job status		
	Formal private sector	Informal sector	All private sector
Contractual insecurity (no contract or no payslip)			
Independent	n.a.	n.a.	n.a.
Dependent	0.49	0.97	0.76
All	n.a.	n.a.	n.a.
Independent with no employees (wage-earning or otherwise)			
Independent	0.11	0.68	0.66
Dependent	n.a.	n.a.	n.a.
All	n.a.	n.a.	n.a.
Adverse working conditions (premises not dedicated to the job)			
Independent	0.17	0.60	0.59
Dependent	0.05	0.22	0.15
All	0.06	0.50	0.42
Casual labor (piece-rate, day, or seasonal work)			
Independent	0.13	0.20	0.20
Dependent	0.10	0.15	0.13
All	0.10	0.19	0.17
Unstable remuneration (paid in form other than fixed wage or, for independent workers, profits)			
Independent	0.06	0.05	0.05
Dependent	0.18	0.40	0.31
All	0.17	0.14	0.15
Time-related underemployment (works fewer hours than statutory working week and would like to work more)			
Independent	0.09	0.13	0.13
Dependent	0.07	0.07	0.07
All	0.07	0.12	0.11
Working second vulnerable job outside public sector in place or premises not dedicated to the job, in firm with fewer than five people			
Independent	0.00	0.02	0.02
Dependent	0.01	0.01	0.01
All	0.01	0.01	0.01
Employment instability (on downwardly mobile or unstable career path)			
Independent	0.01	0.03	0.03
Dependent	0.08	0.08	0.08
All	0.07	0.04	0.05
Unwanted job (involuntary departure from previous job or job dissatisfaction)			
Independent	0.05	0.06	0.06
Dependent	0.09	0.06	0.07
All	0.09	0.06	0.06

(continued next page)

Table 4.2 (continued)

	Criterion/job status		
Criterion	Formal private sector	Informal sector	All private sector
Vulnerable (meets at least one of the vulnerability criteria)			
Independent	0.42	0.87	0.86
Dependent	0.62	0.98	0.82
All	0.60	0.90	0.85

Sources: Based on Phase 1 of the 1-2-3 surveys of selected countries (see table 4.1 for details).
Note: The mean of the contractual insecurity variable for the subsample of formal private sector dependent workers who report strictly positive earnings is 0.49. This means that 49 percent of dependent workers in the formal private sector do not have a written contract or do not receive a payslip. n.a. = not applicable.

The second variable concerns independent workers only. It is equal to 1 if an independent worker has no employees, wage-earning or otherwise. Self-employed professionals working alone in intellectual professions (computer engineers, doctors, notaries, lawyers) are not considered to be vulnerable.

Adverse working conditions are assessed in terms of the place or premises where the individual works. This variable is equal to 1 if the individual's main job is itinerant, worked from a makeshift or fixed street post, at the customer's home, or from the individual's own home without having a dedicated set-up for the job. It is equal to 0 if the individual works from a vehicle, from home with a dedicated set-up for the job, in a public market, or on business premises (including fields, in the case of urban market gardening). Where jobs do not require premises even though they are not physically strenuous, the existence of premises, an office, or a surgery is taken as an indication of stability and nonadverse working conditions. Excluding all intellectual professions from vulnerability in terms of working conditions would be tantamount to defining a vulnerable worker profile as consisting mainly of roving street vendors and servants. Doing so would be inconsistent with the analysis of the many forms of vulnerability and the link with earnings.

Casual labor is a source of vulnerability. According to Pagès (2003), vulnerability in employment covers both various forms of underemployment and the lack of socioeconomic security at work associated with institutional variables (employment contracts, compliance with labor code, and so forth) and their time-related factors (casual and unstable employment). Thus, even if a job is protected or offers good conditions, the casual nature of employment means that this protection is not guaranteed over time and that the risk of visible underemployment is high. Therefore, a casual job is deemed a criterion of vulnerability. The casual labor variable is equal to 1 if the individual works for a piece rate or as a day or seasonal worker. It is equal to 0 if the individual has a steady job.

The unstable remuneration variable is equal to 1 if a dependent worker is not paid a fixed wage or if an independent worker is not paid in the form of a fixed wage or profits (by the day or hour, piece rate, commission, or in kind). This variable differs from the variable describing casual jobs. A worker in a steady job may be paid erratically (as is frequently the case). Such workers are assumed to be more vulnerable, because they cannot predict what their situation will be in the coming days or weeks.

Pagès (2003) defines vulnerability as underemployment or the probability of becoming underemployed. Time-related underemployment corresponds to the situation in which individuals work less than the statutory working week when they would like to work more. Time-related underemployment is similar to structural unemployment (see chapters 1 and 2). The underemployment variable is equal to 1 if the individual works less than 35 hours and would like to work more. It is equal to 0 otherwise.

Working a second job could, in certain cases, reflect underemployment or instability in the main job. Time-related or invisibly underemployed individuals or piece-rate workers may hold second jobs to keep money coming in when they are temporarily laid off from their main job.[8] Working a second job may be a way of reducing or spreading the risks of an income loss or decrease. The second job variable is equal to 1 if the individual works a vulnerable second job—that is, a job outside the public sector, in a place or premises not dedicated to this job and in a firm of less than five people—and if the number of cumulative hours worked in the two jobs is 70 hours or more a week. It is equal to 0 otherwise.

Pagès (2005) emphasizes the importance of considering the dynamic aspect of vulnerability. The above employment situations affect workers' capacities and behavior (the skills-employment causality is reversed). We define two dynamic vulnerability criteria. Instability in employment is defined by a change of job in the last five years without an improvement or with a drop in status.[9] This variable is equal to 0 if the individual is in his or her first job or found a job following a period of unemployment or inactivity over the last five years. It is also equal to 0 if the individual has been in the same job for five years or the individual upgraded his or her job status (from the point of view of socioeconomic group, reflecting upward professional mobility) in the last five years. It is equal to 1 when the individual changed job in the last five years without an improvement in status. In the case of a transition from independent to dependent worker (or vice versa), the reason for the change of job (voluntary or involuntary) is used to determine whether or not the transition represents an upwardly mobile professional move.

An unwanted job is defined as a job with which the worker is dissatisfied and that he or she accepted following an involuntary departure from the previous job. Job dissatisfaction is measured by the answer to a question about the individual's aspirations (keep or change job and, if the respondent indicates the desire to change, for what type of job; see chapter 3). An unwanted job is more likely to be worked because of constraints and is hence mismatched with the worker's expertise, skills, and preferences. Workers may be dissatisfied because they are overqualified for their job, because working conditions are physically strenuous, because the hours are unsuitable, or for other reasons. Working an unwanted job may indicate that a worker has taken a "stopgap job" in the hope of immediate gains.

Other potential vulnerability criteria were not taken into account. For example, we do not create a social security variable, because our income variable includes all welfare benefits. Unstable remuneration or lack of a written contract, for example, should be enough to reflect social insecurity. Membership in a union and access to in-house training are variables of interest. However, these phenomena are so rare in the cities studied that we deemed them negligible.

For each employment status (dependent or independent), we define the intensity of vulnerability as the sum of the eight previously defined criteria applicable to this status. Maximum vulnerability intensity ranges from 4 to 7 depending on the city and sector. No city posts the maximum score of 8 (table 4.3).

A dichotomous dummy variable for vulnerability, built by setting a vulnerability threshold (a minimum number of vulnerability criteria to be met to be deemed vulnerable) would have simplified our measurement. However, the effect of vulnerability on earnings might be nonlinear, which would not be revealed by a dichotomous dummy variable. The fact that a worker meets one or two vulnerability criteria may reflect constraints imposed by the labor market. However, workers may choose to accept more vulnerable working conditions if doing so yields higher earnings.

Descriptive Statistics

Contractual insecurity affects 97 percent of dependent workers in the informal sector (see table 4.2). Surprisingly, it also affects half of employees in the formal private sector, 49 percent of whom do not have written contracts or receive payslips. Similarly, 18 percent of dependent workers in the formal private sector and 40 percent of dependent workers in the informal sector do not receive a fixed wage. These figures suggest that the distinction between formal private firms and informal firms is not sufficient for analyzing workers' living and working conditions: worker vulnerability needs to be examined in all institutional sectors.

The main sources of vulnerability among independent workers in the informal sector are adverse working conditions (faced by 60 percent of independent workers), including the lack of dedicated premises or workplace, and own-account employment (that is, not having any employees, 68 percent of independent workers). These percentages are small in the formal private sector, where

Table 4.3 Intensity of Job Vulnerability in Seven Cities in West Africa

Sector/intensity (0–8)	Abidjan Number of workers	Percent	Bamako Number of workers	Percent	Cotonou Number of workers	Percent	Dakar Number of workers	Percent	Lomé Number of workers	Percent	Niamey Number of workers	Percent	Ouagadougou Number of workers	Percent
Formal private sector														
0	321	38.9	185	40.9	194	38.1	424	44.6	90	29.8	136	33.3	129	38.4
1	280	33.9	175	38.7	199	39.1	243	25.6	116	38.4	112	27.4	110	32.7
2	145	17.6	68	15.0	69	13.6	160	16.8	58	19.2	87	21.3	55	16.4
3	42	5.1	19	4.2	35	6.9	88	9.3	27	8.9	46	11.3	26	7.7
4	28	3.4	5	1.1	11	2.2	29	3.1	7	2.3	23	5.6	16	4.8
5	8	1.0	0	0.0	0	0.0	6	0.6	3	1.0	4	1.0	0	0.0
6	1	0.1	0	0.0	1	0.2	0	0.0	1	0.3	1	0.2	0	0.0
7	0	0.0	0	0.0	0	0.0	0	0.0	0	0.0	0	0.0	0	0.0
Total	825	100	452	100	509	100	950	100	302	100	409	100	336	100
Informal sector														
0	347	12.2	263	9.1	306	9.5	286	8.2	267	9.4	126	5.7	329	12.0
1	995	35.0	933	32.1	1,029	31.8	1,077	30.8	738	25.8	502	22.5	848	30.9
2	972	34.2	1,035	35.6	1,241	38.4	1,102	31.6	1,052	36.8	761	34.1	907	33.0
3	372	13.1	495	17.0	488	15.1	644	18.4	508	17.8	502	22.5	450	16.4
4	124	4.4	154	5.3	151	4.7	300	8.6	235	8.2	263	11.8	166	6.1
5	23	0.8	25	0.9	19	0.6	72	2.1	49	1.7	68	3.1	40	1.5
6	8	0.3	1	0.0	2	0.1	10	0.3	8	0.3	8	0.4	5	0.2
7	1	0.0	0	0.0	0	0.0	1	0.0	0	0.0	0	0.0	0	0.0
Total	2,842	100	2,906	100	3,236	100	3,492	100	2,857	100	2,230	100	2,745	100

Sources: Based on Phase 1 of the 1-2-3 surveys of selected countries (see table 4.1 for details).
Note: The lines cutting across the distributions represent the average vulnerability intensity position. For example, in the formal private sector in Niamey, average vulnerability is 1.3, so a line is drawn between 1 and 2.

self-employed workers represent less than 20 percent of workers in all cities studied. Working conditions for independent and dependent workers in the informal sector are very similar. Most independent workers are self-employed street vendors; others are tailors, hairdressers, repairers, mechanics, masons, carpenters, and metalworkers. Similarity in working conditions justifies analyzing all informal workers in one category, controlling for their dependency status as a covariate.

Some 17 percent of dependent private sector workers and 14 percent of independent private sector workers are not vulnerable (do not meet any vulnerability criteria). These rates mask huge differences between the formal and informal sectors. In the informal sector, just 2 percent of dependent workers and 12 percent of independent workers are not vulnerable. In all, 85 percent of the private sector workers in the cities studied meet at least one vulnerability criterion.

Testing the Existence of Compensating Mechanisms for Vulnerability

In a first step, the determinants of vulnerability are analyzed using a simple linear model whose dependent variable is the intensity of vulnerability. The explanatory variables introduced are dummy variables for the individual's status in the household (1 if household head) and the institutional sector of the individual's father when the individual was 15 years old (public, formal private, or informal private). These first variables are denoted Z. The set of control variables included in all the estimated equations (X) covers gender; education (number of years of completed education) and its square; potential experience and its square; religion; migrant status (rural, urban, or foreign migrant); marital status; seniority in the firm or main job and its square; and independent versus dependent worker status.

To test the existence of compensating earnings differentials for vulnerability, we estimate the log of the hourly earnings rate for the main job for each city. Included in this earnings rate are benefits such as year-end bonuses, profit-sharing, paid leave, medical benefits, social security, bonuses, and benefits in kind, such as housing, electricity, and transport. Earnings are calculated based on the monthly earnings for the reference month and the number of hours worked per week.

Approach at the Mean
An approach at the mean studies the impact of vulnerability intensity on average earnings. In this approach, what counts is the cumulative number of vulnerability criteria met by an individual.

Let h be an indicator of four institutional sector categories ($h = 1$: zero earnings, $h = 2$: public sector, $h = 3$: formal private sector, and $h = 4$: informal sector). Our purpose is to estimate the effect $\varphi_h = (\varphi_{1h}, \varphi_{2h})$ of vulnerability index I on earnings in the formal and informal private sectors using

$$Y_h = \beta_h X + \varphi_{1h} I + \varphi_{2h} I^2 + \varepsilon_h \ \forall h = 3,4. \tag{4.1}$$

Introduction of a second-degree vulnerability intensity polynomial I^2 is designed to take into account any nonlinearity in the effect of vulnerability on earnings. Y_h is observed only if the individual has a paid job and chooses sector h.

Given that the labor markets in developing countries are segmented, sector entry selection may exist in addition to labor market entry selection (see chapters 5 and 6). A selection model is therefore needed. We use Lee (1983), an extension of Heckman's method, to estimate the earnings equation with multinomial selection. This method corrects the selection bias, by estimating

$$Y_h = \beta_h X + \varphi_{1h} I + \varphi_{2h} I^2 + \lambda_h + \kappa_h \ \forall h = 3,4 \tag{4.2}$$

where λ_h, a generalization of the inverse Mills ratio in Heckman's method, corrects the selection bias generated by the fact that belonging to sector h rather than sector k ($k \neq h$) may reflect the action of unobservable variables also associated with income. The selection effect is interpreted as the difference between the earnings of a first individual in sector h and the income that would have been earned by a second individual—drawn randomly from the first equation sample (that is, an individual from any sector) and with the same observable characteristics as the first individual—had he or she belonged to sector h.

The identifying variables (M) required for the robustness of the selection model are the inverse of the dependency ratio (the ratio of the number of employed workers to household size); a dummy variable for whether the individual's father went to primary school; and a dummy variable for whether the individual's head of household is a woman. These variables are introduced into the selection equation (multinomial logit model with four categories for h: 1,..., 4), but not into the earnings equation. The assumption is that these variables influence earnings only through sector allocation.[10]

A second problem that needs to be addressed is the potential endogeneity of the intensity of vulnerability. Unobservable characteristics may affect both the explanatory variable for vulnerability and the level of earnings. This would be the case, for example, if "poor" workers were selected for employment statuses in which vulnerability is greatest. In this case, any positive effect vulnerability might have on earnings could be underestimated. As disregarding this factor could produce nonconvergent estimators of $\varphi_h = (\varphi_{1h}, \varphi_{2h})$, the vulnerability intensity indicator needs to be instrumented.

To do so, we use the control function method rather than the two-stage least squares estimator (Garen 1984; Wooldridge 2005). Where earnings are nonlinear in the potentially endogenous variable (here vulnerability intensity), this method provides more accurate estimators than the two-stage least squares method (Card 2001). The control function method involves regressing the intensity of vulnerability on the individual characteristics X and the instrumental variables Z, not correlated with κ, the residual from the earnings equation (equation 4.2) and (partially) correlated with I (equation 4.3). These instruments are the dummy variables for the status of the head of household and the dummy variables for the institutional sector of the individual's father when the individual was 15. In principle, these variables do not have a direct impact on earned income, because they have nothing to do with productivity, the worker's capacities, or the type of job held. Being a head of household could create an incentive to accept a more vulnerable job when faced with urgent family needs, but it is more likely that household heads would search for a less vulnerable job to guarantee household income stability. All things equal, heads of household may adopt long-term strategies and be less drawn by immediate gains at the cost of a vulnerable job.

Another exogenous source of variation in job search can be obtained with the father's occupation when the worker was 15. The father's occupation is likely to influence the child's aversion, attraction, or resistance to job vulnerability. Let the vulnerability index I be regressed on X and Z such that

$$I = \alpha_h X + \gamma_h Z + \mu_h \ \forall h = 3,4. \tag{4.3}$$

The estimated residual from this first linear regression, $\hat{\mu}$, is introduced as an explanatory variable, controlling for unobserved heterogeneity, into the earnings equation:

$$Y_h = \beta_h X + \varphi_{1h} I + \varphi_{2h} I^2 + \lambda_h + \hat{\mu}_h + \kappa_h \ \forall h = 3,4. \tag{4.4}$$

The resulting estimators of $\varphi_h = (\varphi_{1h}, \varphi_{2h})$ are convergent if the model satisfies the classic identification conditions and the instruments are independent of $\hat{\mu}$ and not correlated with the earnings equation residual κ_h.

For all estimations, the bootstrap method (500 replications) was used to estimate the standard deviations, which are biased by the nature of the two-stage estimations.

Distributional Approach

The impact of vulnerability on earnings may differ across the earnings distribution. Quantile regressions are used to take these potential effects into account. First, equation (4.1) is reestimated using conditional quantiles, such that

$$q_\tau(Y_h | X, I, I^2) = \beta_h(\tau) X + \varphi_{1h}(\tau) I + \varphi_{2h}(\tau) I^2 \ \forall h = 3,4 \tag{4.5}$$

where $q_\tau(Y_h | X, I, I^2)$ is the τth conditional quantile of Y_h, and vector $\hat{\beta}_h(\tau)$ and the estimated coefficients $\hat{\varphi}_{1h}(\tau)$ and $\hat{\varphi}_{2h}(\tau)$ provide the effects of the different regressors at the th quantile of the earnings distribution in sector h.

This framework does not take selection effects into account. Whereas the control function method can also be used in the case of quantile regression, to our knowledge no models exist that can estimate quantile regressions with multinomial selection. Moreover, this distributional approach corrects only the supposed endogeneity of vulnerability. Our approach is not a major drawback, because, as shown below, the results of the quantitative approach are not sensitive to the consideration of a possible selection effect.

Results

Approach at the Mean

Table 4.4, based on models (4.1), (4.2), and (4.4), shows the marginal effects of the vulnerability indicator on earnings, calculated at the average vulnerability point.[11] Whether or not the sample selection and endogeneity of vulnerability are corrected, the marginal effect of average vulnerability is negative in both sectors for all cities except the informal sector in Dakar, where this effect is slightly positive. In both the formal private and informal sectors, the selection correction barely alters the results. However, the correction for the endogeneity

Table 4.4 Marginal Effects of Vulnerability Intensity on Earnings in Seven Cities in West Africa (percent)

Sector	Abidjan	Bamako	Cotonou	Dakar	Lomé	Niamey	Ouagadougou
Formal private sector							
No selection correction, exogenous vulnerability	−12.6	−13.9	−10.9	−16.2	−7.4	−14.3	−9.3
Selection correction, exogenous vulnerability	−12.5	−13.8	−10.9	−16.2	−7.0	−14.2	−9.3
Selection correction, endogenous vulnerability	−24.2	−37.3	−15.5	−33.5	−24.8	−23.0	−22.5
Number of observations	825	452	509	950	302	409	336
Average intensity	1.035	0.858	0.967	1.024	1.199	1.325	1.077
Informal sector							
No selection correction, exogenous vulnerability	−2.8	−1.3	−0.6	0.2	−0.1	−1.0	−1.7
Selection correction, exogenous vulnerability	−2.9	−1.3	−0.7	0.2	−0.3	−1.0	−1.6
Selection correction, endogenous vulnerability	−19.9	−17.2	−3.4	1.0	−13.1	−9.7	−15.6
Number of observations	2,842	2,906	3,236	3,492	2,857	2,230	2,745
Average intensity	1.661	1.801	1.757	1.959	1.960	2.229	1.787

Sources: Based on Phase 1 of the 1-2-3 surveys of selected countries (see table 4.1 for details).
Note: The marginal effect at the average point of intensity (denoted $\bar{I}$) was calculated using the following equation:

$$\log(y) = aI + bI^2 \Rightarrow y = \exp(aI + bI^2) \Rightarrow em(\bar{I}) = \frac{\partial y}{\partial I}(\bar{I}) = (\hat{a} + 2\hat{b}\bar{I})\exp(\hat{a}\bar{I} + \hat{b}\bar{I}^2).$$

of vulnerability alters the magnitude of the marginal effects. The marginal effect of vulnerability on earnings is already markedly negative before correcting for endogeneity. After endogeneity is taken into account, the impact remains negative and increases.

In the formal private sector, one additional point of vulnerability reduces income by 16–34 percent. The effect is smaller in the informal sector; if the endogeneity of vulnerability had not been taken into account, the effect would have been negligible. Once the endogeneity of vulnerability is included, vulnerability has a large impact on earnings, with one additional point of vulnerability reducing income by 3–20 percent. The marginal effect is positive only in Dakar.

These marginal effects are calculated for average vulnerability intensity. In the formal private sector, workers satisfy one in eight vulnerability criteria on average. In the informal sector, the average vulnerability point is close to 2. Hence, if we want to identify any compensating effects for higher than average vulnerability levels, we have to study the coefficients estimated for the second-degree vulnerability intensity polynomial.

Regression results (not shown here but reflected in figure 4.1) show that, regardless of the model used, vulnerability has a negative effect on earnings in all cities except Dakar and in both institutional sectors. However, the effect of vulnerability is nonlinear and convex, as the coefficient of I^2 is positive and significant. This quadratic effect is significant at the 5 percent level, at least, and mostly at the 1 percent level in all cities and sectors except the formal private sector in Bamako, where vulnerability squared has no significant impact on earnings.

The convexity observed in the descriptive analysis holds in the formal and informal private sectors once individual characteristics, selection, and endogeneity are controlled for. It can be seen in figure 4.2, which shows the average income predicted by the Lee model with endogeneization of vulnerability by vulnerability level (the curves produced by the ordinary least squares model and the simple Lee model are similar).

In the formal private sector, earnings are convex in vulnerability intensity in all cities, albeit in a markedly decreasing manner. The curve is convex, but the slope does not change sign for low levels of vulnerability. A change of sign appears only at vulnerability levels that are not well represented in terms of the number of workers (four or more). In other words, income losses associated with vulnerability are lower for high levels of vulnerability but do not translate into gains. In Cotonou, however, the level of gains for a vulnerability level of 4 is similar to the level of gains obtained for zero vulnerability.

In the informal sector, convexity is observed in all cities, with the slope of the earnings curves rising above a vulnerability level of 2. In all cities, average predicted earnings for a vulnerability level of 4 or 5 are higher than average predicted earnings for a vulnerability level of 2. In Cotonou, the average predicted

Figure 4.1 Marginal Effect of Vulnerability on Earnings in Seven Cities in West Africa, by Income Decile

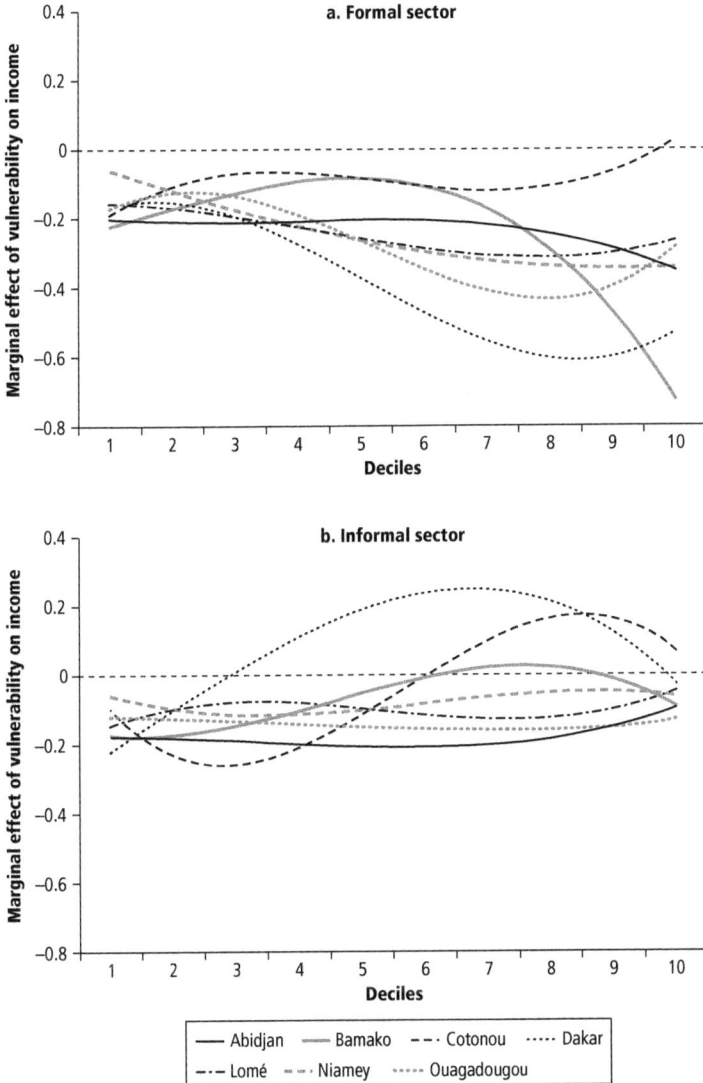

Sources: Based on Phase 1 of the 1-2-3 surveys of selected countries (see table 4.1 for details).

Figure 4.2 Average Predicted Earnings by Vulnerability Intensity in Seven Cities in West Africa

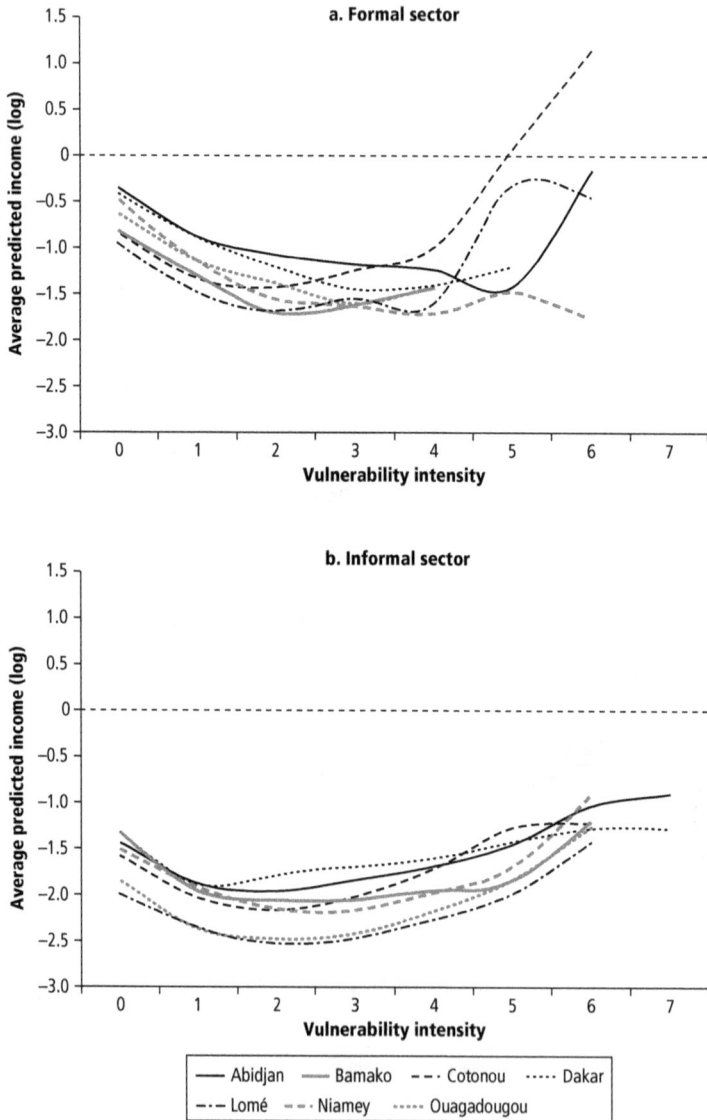

a. Formal sector

b. Informal sector

Legend: Abidjan — Bamako — Cotonou — · Dakar ····· Lomé — · Niamey — — Ouagadougou

Sources: Based on Phase 1 of the 1-2-3 surveys of selected countries (see table 4.1 for details).
Note: Figure shows the Lee model with endogeneization of vulnerability.

earnings for a vulnerability level of 5 is even higher than the average predicted earnings for workers who are not vulnerable at all.

The assumption that earnings can compensate for a certain level of vulnerability therefore holds in the informal sector. More-vulnerable workers are better paid. In keeping with the theory of compensating wage differentials, this finding can be explained by the fact that employers offer higher earnings to find employees prepared to work in vulnerable jobs. For independent workers, vulnerability can be a way of earning more immediate gains from their work.

In the informal sector, the marginal effect at average vulnerability is negative in all cities except Dakar, where it is slightly positive. The average vulnerability level (about 2) is close to the minima of the convex curves. At these average points, income is a decreasing function of vulnerability. Above these points, earnings are an increasing function of vulnerability. A significant proportion of workers are above the average vulnerability level. Depending on the city, 27–62 percent of workers in the formal private sector and 38–65 percent of workers in the informal sector are more vulnerable than average.

Employers do not compensate workers for the average level of vulnerability; it is simply a feature of the job market in a particular city. Workers can negotiate wage compensation for higher levels of vulnerability. If dependent workers believe that they are more vulnerable than average, they may be in a position to negotiate premium pay. If the market imposes a certain level of vulnerability on independent workers, they will be inclined to make their job a bit more vulnerable to earn a higher income.

Distributional Approach

The distributional approach involves estimating model 4.5 for a certain number of earnings quantiles. For simplicity of presentation, we report only the series of marginal effects of vulnerability, calculated by deciles (figure 4.1). The curves presented are the third-degree trend curves, which are more flexible than the quadratic function. The marginal effects are calculated using the coefficients resulting from the quantile regressions, taking into account the endogeneity of vulnerability. In all cities, the marginal effect of vulnerability on earnings at the average vulnerability point varies depending on its position in the earnings distribution.

In the formal private sector, the marginal effect of average vulnerability is negative across the entire distribution, meaning there is no compensating mechanism in the formal private sector at the average point. The cities of Cotonou, Dakar, Lomé, Niamey, and Ouagadougou present the same concave and then convex marginal effect curves; the points of inflection are close to median earnings in the distributions. The curve in Bamako differs. It is solely concave, reaches its maximum at the median earnings. One additional point of vulnerability is associated with a 10 percent decrease in the earnings of an individual with average vulnerability in the fifth decile of the distribution. Abidjan's curve is slightly convex at the lower tail of the distribution and then concave. The marginal effect of vulnerability on earnings varies little along the distribution (20–30 percent income loss).

In the informal sectors of Bamako, Cotonou, and Dakar the marginal effect of vulnerability along the conditional distribution of earnings is rising and mainly concave. It becomes positive as of the third decile in Dakar and as of the sixth decile in Bamako and Cotonou. Hence, for Dakar workers in the seventh decile with an average level of vulnerability, a one-point increase in vulnerability is associated with average increased earnings of 25 percent. In Cotonou, a one-point increase in the vulnerability of workers in the ninth decile with average vulnerability is associated with an average increase in earnings of 15–20 percent. In Bamako the effect is lower, but not negligible, as the increase in earnings can be as high as 5 percent for workers in the eighth decile. In the other cities (Abidjan, Lomé, Niamey, and Ouagadougou), one additional point of vulnerability is associated with no increase in earnings compared with average vulnerability, regardless of the position in the distribution. In Niamey, however, the income losses caused by a one-point increase in vulnerability are smaller for the eighth and ninth deciles.

In Dakar, Cotonou, and Bamako, the marginal effect of average vulnerability is positive for higher deciles of the earnings distribution. Dakar, Cotonou, and—to a lesser extent—Bamako display both the highest compensation for vulnerability and positive effects of vulnerability on high earnings for average levels of vulnerability. In the informal sectors of these cities, vulnerability has a different effect on earnings depending on the worker's relative position on the remuneration scale. For similar observable characteristics, workers at the lower tail of the earnings distribution (poor) are penalized in monetary terms for their vulnerability whereas workers at the upper tail of the distribution receive compensation for their vulnerability. This difference can be explained by greater bargaining power among workers at the upper tail of the earnings distribution. Dependent workers with higher skills may be in a better position to negotiate their wages. Among independent workers (the majority in the informal sector), the poorest cannot raise their income to compensate for the vulnerability of their work (by increasing the prices of goods or services they sell, for example). In contrast, independent workers at the upper tail of the earnings distribution can more easily make trade-offs between working conditions and earnings by keeping prices high. Furthermore, labor supply may well outstrip demand in low-income activity sectors. In this case, employers would not have to financially compensate workers for adverse working conditions, and own-account workers would not be able to raise their mark-up.

Conclusion

In this chapter, we develop indicators of employment vulnerability in seven West African economic capitals and study their links with individual earnings from the main job. According to the theory of compensating differentials, workers receive pecuniary compensation commensurate with the strenuous or hazardous nature of their tasks or the adverse nature of their working conditions. This chapter draws on this theory, applying it to working conditions and more broadly to vulnerability in employment (contractual insecurity, working conditions, underemployment, and stopgap jobs mismatched with individual characteristics), a dominant characteristic of urban labor markets in Sub-Saharan Africa.

Indicators of employment vulnerability in seven West African cities (Abidjan, Bamako, Cotonou, Dakar, Lomé, Niamey, and Ouagadougou) reveal that in the private sector, 83 percent of dependent workers and 86 percent of independent workers are vulnerable. These percentages mask huge differences between the formal private and informal sectors, where 98 percent of dependent and 87 percent of independent workers are vulnerable. Among workers in the private sector, 85 percent meet at least one criterion for vulnerability.

The quantitative analysis finds that the impact of vulnerability on earnings is negative for an average level of vulnerability (except in Dakar, where it is slightly positive). In the formal private sector, income losses associated with vulnerability are lower for high levels of vulnerability. In Cotonou, for example, the level of earnings for average vulnerability is close to the level of earnings obtained for zero vulnerability. In the informal sector, however, the average predicted earnings for workers with high vulnerability scores are higher than the average predicted earnings for workers with relatively low vulnerability scores. In Cotonou, the average predicted earnings for level 5 vulnerability (on a scale of 1–8) is even higher than the average predicted earnings for workers who are not vulnerable. The assumption that average earnings may compensate for a certain level of vulnerability is thus confirmed in the informal sector. This compensation or lesser-loss mechanism for high levels of vulnerability affects a significant share of workers. Average vulnerability is not compensated for; it is an inherent characteristic of the job markets in these cities.

The marginal effect is estimated through regressions on the earnings average, which conceal variations in the magnitude of the impact of vulnerability along the earnings distribution. Quantile regressions find evidence that the impact of vulnerability on earnings is not uniform, particularly in the informal sector. For example, in the informal sectors of Dakar, Cotonou, and Bamako, the marginal effect of average vulnerability is positive for the upper deciles of the earnings distribution. Dakar, Cotonou, and, to a lesser extent, Bamako display both the highest compensation for high levels of vulnerability and the positive effects of average vulnerability on earnings among the highest earnings.

For average levels of vulnerability, compensating wage differentials are found at the upper tail of the distribution. However, the compensating mechanism does not concern the poorest workers. Although the poorest dependent workers should be the most forceful in wage bargaining in an endeavor to earn a living wage, they have less bargaining power because of the urgent nature of their needs. Urban labor market imbalances could also explain this absence of compensating wage differentials at the lower tail of the distribution, where labor supply probably far exceeds demand. Similarly, the poorest independent workers suffer more from their vulnerability and do not adopt strategies to compensate for it by increasing their profits (raising receipts or reducing expenditure). An independent worker at the upper tail of the earnings distribution could more easily make trade-offs between working conditions and earnings.

Notes

1. The still-developing economic literature on vulnerability includes a range of definitions. Wilson and Ramphele (1989) define vulnerability as the risk of destitution, famine, or death. The concept of vulnerability moved forward with Sen's capability approach (1992, 1999). Cheli and Lemmi (1995) refer subsequently to exposure to the risk of poverty. Qizilbash (2003, 2006) views vulnerability as an individual's distance from an unambiguous state of poverty. Dubois and Rousseau (2001) view vulnerability in terms of the structure of "capabilities" that enables individuals to replace (or not) one capability with another in the event of an exogenous shock. The loss of a job would therefore have a greater impact on an individual with less leeway to work in different occupations and a low level of economic and social capital. The notion of vulnerability adopted in this chapter is similar to that developed by Cheli and Lemmi (1995) and Qizilbash (2006), as it remains vague about the exact level of the state of poverty and its multidimensional aspect.
2. Health hazards are not considered, because the data used did not include them.
3. However, there is not a great deal of empirical evidence to support this point. See in particular Poggi (2007) and Fernández and Nordman (2009).
4. In the more developed version of this chapter (Bocquier, Nordman, and Vescovo 2010), we used a qualitative approach, conducting a principal component factor analysis on the different aspects of vulnerability. The main components were then used as vulnerability variables. We thus relaxed the assumption that all the criteria involved in vulnerability have the same weight. Technical details on our econometric procedure, additional tables, and results are also reported in this version.
5. Although Abidjan and Cotonou are not administrative capitals, we refer to them as capitals because they are the most important economic centers in their countries (Cotonou is also the seat of government).
6. See Katz (1986) for a review of efficiency wage theories, Lindbeck and Snower (1989) for a review of insider-outsider models (labor market segmentation theory), and Akerlof and Yellen (1990) for an extended version of efficiency wage theory.

7. The studies on this issue reach conflicting conclusions. See, for example, French and Dunlap (1998); Groot and Maassen van den Brink (1998); Lanfranchi, Ohlsson, and Skalli (2002); Magnani (2002); Clark and Senik (2006); Bockerman and Ilmakunnas (2006); and Poggi (2007).

8. Not all second-job holders are vulnerable. Public and private sector wage-earners sometimes work second jobs to earn money for retirement or for their children.

9. The status hierarchy is as follows: senior executives, engineers, or equivalent; middle managers and supervisors and skilled and semi-skilled nonmanual and manual employees; unskilled workers; apprentices and family workers.

10. See Bocquier, Nordman, and Vescovo (2010) for further discussion of our identification strategies.

11. Detailed regression tables are available from the authors.

References

Akerlof, G., and J. Yellen. 1990. "The Fair Wage–Effort Hypothesis and Unemployment." *Quarterly Journal of Economics* 105 (2): 255–83.

Bockerman, P., and P. Ilmakunnas. 2006. "Do Job Disamenities Raise Wage or Ruin Job Satisfaction?" *International Journal of Manpower* 27 (3): 290–302.

Bocquier, P., C. J. Nordman, and A. Vescovo. 2010. "Employment Vulnerability and Earnings in Urban West Africa." *World Development* 38 (9): 1297–314.

Brown, C. 1980. "Equalizing Differences in the Labor Market." *Quarterly Journal of Economics* 94 (1): 113–34.

Burdett, K., and D. T. Mortensen. 1998. "Wage Differentials, Employer Size, and Unemployment." *International Economic Review* 39 (2): 257–73.

Card, D. 2001. "Estimating the Return to Schooling: Progress on Some Persistent Econometric Problems." *Econometrica* 69 (5): 1127–60.

Cheli, B., and A. Lemmi. 1995. "A 'Totally' Fuzzy and Relative Approach to the Measurement of Poverty." *Economic Note* 94: 115–34.

Clark, A., and C. Senik. 2006. "The (Unexpected) Structure of 'Rents' on the French and British Labour Markets." *Journal of Socioeconomics* 35 (2): 180–96.

Daniel, C., and C. Sofer. 1998. "Bargaining, Compensating Wage Differentials, and Dualism of the Labor Market: Theory, and Evidence for France." *Journal of Labor Economics* 16 (3): 546–75.

Dubois, J.-L., and S. Rousseau. 2001. "Reinforcing Household's Capabilities as a Way to Reduce Vulnerability, and Prevent Poverty in Equitable Terms." Paper presented at the conference "Justice and Poverty: Examining Sen's Capability Approach," Cambridge University, June 5–7.

Fernández, R. M., and C. J. Nordman. 2009. "Are There Pecuniary Compensations for Working Conditions?" *Labour Economics* 16 (2): 194–207.

French, M. T., and L. J. Dunlap. 1998. "Compensating Wage Differentials for Job Stress." *Applied Economics* 30 (8): 1067–75.

Garen, J. 1984. "The Returns to Schooling: A Selectivity Bias Approach with a Continuous Choice Variable." *Econometrica* 52 (5): 1199–218.

Groot, W., and H. Maassen van den Brink. 1998. "The Price of Stress." *Journal of Economic Psychology* 20: 83–103.

Hwang, H., D. T. Mortensen, and W. R. Reed. 1998. "Hedonic Wages and Labor Market Search." *Journal of Labor Economics* 16 (4): 815–47.

Katz, L. F. 1986. "Efficiency Wage Theories: A Partial Evaluation." In *NBER Macroeconomics Annual,* ed. S. Fisher, 1:235–90, Cambridge, MA: MIT Press.

Lanfranchi, J., H. Ohlsson, and A. H. Skalli. 2002. "Compensating Wage Differentials and Shift Work Preferences." *Economics Letters* 74 (3): 393–98.

Lee, L.-F. 1983. "Generalized Econometric Models with Selectivity." *Econometrica* 51(2): 507–12.

Lindbeck, A., and D. J. Snower. 1989. *The Insider-Outsider Theory of Employment and Unemployment.* Cambridge, MA: MIT Press.

Magnani, E. 2002. "Product Market Volatility and the Adjustment of Earning to Risk." *Industrial Relations* 41: 304–28.

Maloney, W. 2004. "Informality Revisited." *World Development* 32 (7): 1159–78.

Manning, A. 2003. *Monopsony in Motion: Imperfect Competition in Labor Markets.* Princeton, NJ: Princeton University Press.

Mortensen, D. T. 2003. *Wage Dispersion: Why Are Similar Workers Paid Differently?* Cambridge, MA: MIT Press.

Murphy, K. M., and R. Topel. 1987. "Unemployment, Risk, and Earnings: Testing for Equalizing Wage Differences in the Labor Market." In *Unemployment, and the Structure of Labor Markets,* ed. K. Lang and J. Leonard, 103–40. London: Basil Blackwell.

Pagès, N. 2003. "Hétérogénéité des systèmes d'emploi urbain et vulnérabilité au travail: application aux entreprises et aux petites unités productives en Côte d'Ivoire." Paper presented at the Third Conference on "Approaches to Capacity: From Viable Development to Durable Liberty," University of Pavia, Italy, September 8–10.

———. 2005. *Hétérogénéité du système d'emploi et développement: une application aux entreprises et aux petites unités productives urbaines en Côte d'Ivoire,* PhD diss., Université Paris X-Nanterre.

Pissarides, C. 2000. *Equilibrium Unemployment Theory,* 2nd ed. Cambridge, MA: MIT Press.

Poggi, A. 2007. "Do Satisfactory Working Conditions Contribute to Explaining Earning Differentials in Italy? A Panel Data Approach." *Labour* 21 (4–5): 713–33.

Qizilbash, M. 2003. "Vague Language and Precise Measurement: The Case of Poverty." *Journal of Economic Methodology* 10 (1): 41–58.

———. 2006. "Philosophical Accounts of Vagueness, Fuzzy Poverty Measures, and Multidimensionality." In *Fuzzy Set Approach to Multidimensional Poverty Measurement,* ed. A. Lemmi and G. Betti, 9–28. New York: Springer.

Rosen, S. 1986. "The Theory of Equalising Differences." In *The Handbook of Labor Economics,* vol. 1, ed. O. Ashenfelter and R. Layard, 641–92. Amsterdam: Elsevier Science.

Sen, A. K. 1992. *Inequality Reexamined.* Oxford, U.K.: Oxford University Press.

————. 1999. *Development as Freedom.* New York: Knopf.

Wilson, F., and M. Ramphele. 1989. *Uprooting Poverty: The South African Challenge.* New York: Norton.

Wooldridge, J. M. 2005. "Unobserved Heterogeneity and Estimation of Average Partial Effects." In *Identification and Inference for Econometric Models,* prepared under the direction of D. W. K. Andrews and J. H. Stock, 27–55. Cambridge, U.K.: Cambridge University Press.

Part III

The Many Dimensions of Labor Market Inequalities

Chapter 5

Education and Labor Market Outcomes in Urban West Africa

Mathias Kuépié, Christophe J. Nordman, and François Roubaud

Education in Sub-Saharan Africa is often seen as the main policy instrument in the fight against poverty. In practice, however, although education is an intrinsic component of development and well-being, its economic value is not clear, as urban unemployment in Sub-Saharan Africa is rising, especially among educated workers.

The mismatch between (increasing) investment in schooling on the one hand and actual labor market opportunities on the other represents a major challenge for policy makers. For years, the existence of significant rents in the formal sector (especially in the dominant public sector) were so high that it made sense for individuals to "queue" and to undervalue returns in the informal sector. Today, education no longer seems to guard against poverty and social exclusion. It is therefore critical to reappraise the external efficiency of investment in schooling in these countries.

Traditional studies of the external efficiency of education systems look at the impact of education on individuals after they leave school.[1] They examine two types of impacts, economic and social, which can be interpreted either from the individual or the collective standpoint. This chapter focuses solely on the economic and private dimensions of the efficiency of education.

The analysis of private returns to education is based on standard human capital theory, according to which earnings differentials between individuals result from differences in wage compensation for different human capital endowments. This theory suggests that investment in education is an explanatory factor in the distribution of individual earnings.

This principle has substantial implications for low-income countries, because it explains the existence of earnings differences between individuals in the labor market. From a policy viewpoint, if returns to education are high for individuals from poor households, poverty reduction policies designed to promote equal opportunities in access to schooling would be appropriate.

Numerous objections and criticisms have been made regarding the assumption that education—and hence productivity—is the main determinant of differences in individuals' earnings. Many authors have shown that traditional theories postulating the leveling of income levels by individuals with identical levels of human capital do not describe reality when markets are imperfect or segmented.

Markets in African countries are imperfect, and the nature of work contracts interferes significantly in the relationship between human capital endowments and earnings. There are four types of labor markets in developing countries: rural, public, private formal, and informal. Each type of market has its own characteristics, such as job seasonality and uncertainty about the level of demand, the nature of contracts, and the structure of wages and earnings. However, many studies on the link between education and labor market outcomes in Africa overlook the fact that the existence of different employment segments, especially in the rural and informal sectors, may have major implications regarding the role of education in labor market integration.[2]

This chapter analyzes the effects of education on remuneration in seven cities in the West African Economic and Monetary Union (WAEMU).[3] Using Phase 1 of the 1-2-3 surveys in these capitals, we broaden the scope and refine the indicators generally used to assess the efficiency of education for labor market integration in Sub-Saharan Africa, using the same method for each city.[4] In particular, we estimate the determinants of earnings, especially the effect of education. The data allow us to compare the returns to vocational versus general education at different levels of the schooling path, shedding light on the debate over whether general education or vocational training yields higher returns. The household survey data enable us to account for two persistent econometric problems: the possible sample selectivity biases introduced by endogenous sector choices and the possible endogeneity of the education variable in the earnings function.

The results show that returns to schooling generally increase once an endogenous education variable is accounted for. This effect is particularly strong in the informal sector. In most cities in the sample, the returns to education are highest in the public sector, followed by the formal private sector and then the informal sector. We also shed light on the finding that returns to education are convex in all cities and sectors, including the informal sector. We provide evidence of significant effects of education on individual earnings in the informal sectors of the major WAEMU cities, even at high levels of schooling.

The chapter is organized as follows. The first section describes the econometric models. The second section analyzes and discusses the findings. The last section presents the conclusions and offers some policy recommendations.[5]

Econometric Methods

Our methodological approach consists of estimating different models to evaluate the impact of education (years of education, type of education [general versus vocational], level reached, and qualifications obtained) on earnings. The surveys enable us to estimate Mincer-type earnings models, taking account of the sample selection effects associated with individuals' participation and sector choices. In addition, the data allow us to address the possible endogeneity of the education variable in the earnings function using alternative techniques that make use of information on family background.

Earnings Equations with Selection Bias Correction

Let S_j be the sectoral situation ($j = 0$–3), where S_0 = no work, S_1 = public sector, S_2 = formal private sector, and S_3 = informal private sector. We can view S_j as a "response function" to a set of latent continuous variables S^*_j that measure the propensities to have the sectoral situations S_j:

$$S^*_{ij} = \beta'_j \mathbf{X}_i + \varepsilon_{ij} \tag{5.1}$$

and

$$Y_{ij} = \zeta'_j \mathbf{Z}_i + \eta_{ij}, \tag{5.2}$$

where S^*_{ij} measures the propensities of individual i to have the sectoral situation S_j; Y_{ij} denotes the income individual i earns by working in sector j, where $j = 1$ (public sector), 2 (formal sector), and 3 (informal sector); $\mathbf{X}_i$ and $\mathbf{Z}_i$ are vectors of observable individual characteristics (including education); β_j and ζ_j are vectors of parameters to be estimated; and ε_{ij} and η_{ij} are error terms. The aim is to estimate the coefficients ζ_j for each sector. Y_j is observed only if sector j is chosen; η_j and ε_j are therefore not independent. As a result, the ordinary least squares estimator is potentially biased.

In the first stage, multinomial logit models are used to compute the correction terms λ_{ij} from the predicted probability of individual i working in sector j. The generalized forms of the inverse Mills ratios are then introduced into the earnings equation for each sector j, yielding consistent estimators of β_j. Lee's method has been criticized because it relies on a strong assumption regarding the joint distribution of error terms of the equations of interest (see Vijverberg 1993; Dahl 2002; Bourguignon, Fournier, and Gurgand 2007). However, the alternative methods we tried (Dubin and McFadden 1984; Dahl 2002) did not appear more efficient given the small size of the sectoral subsamples.[6] We therefore chose Lee's correction method, which has the advantage of providing an easier interpretation of the correction terms.

Another potential problem is that the multinomial logit may suffer from the independence of irrelevant alternatives (IIA) assumption, which in most cases is questionable. The Hausman-type tests performed for each city and sector provide overwhelming evidence that the IIA assumption was not violated, except in the informal sector in Bamako.[7]

In both Heckman's and Lee's procedure, identification is achieved using exclusion restrictions (that is, by the inclusion of additional regressors in the first-stage selection equations). In order to preserve comparability across countries as much as possible, we rely on the same exclusion restrictions for each city. However, after considering tests of appropriateness of the exclusion restrictions, we relaxed such constraints at the sector level (that is, we use different sets of identifying variables for selection into the informal sector and the formal sectors [public and private]).[8] In the formal sectors, we use six dummy variables describing the individual's relationship to the household head (child, spouse), together with the household's inverse dependency ratio (the number of working individuals divided by the total number of people in the household). For the informal sector, we excluded only the dependency ratio from the second-step regressions, where the individual's situation in the household often appeared significant. We tested the appropriateness of this identification strategy using Wald tests of joint significance of the identifying variables in the first stage and insignificance in the second stage for each sector in all cities (21 cases). The tests highlighted the appropriateness of this choice in 19 cases.[9] However, bearing in mind the methodological controversies surrounding the choice of identifying variables in general, we report summary results from uncorrected earnings functions (ordinary least squares) as well, which makes it easier to compare our results with the results of other studies.

Endogenous Education

It is widely recognized in the literature that using ordinary least squares to estimate the returns to education from cross-sectional data is potentially problematic. The standard concern is that education may be an endogenous variable—that is, correlated with the residual of the earnings function because of unobserved individual heterogeneity. To address this issue, researchers commonly use instrumental variables techniques, which involve finding variables that are uncorrelated with the individuals' unobserved heterogeneity but correlated with their education. The instrumentation is often based on household and demographic characteristics that are assumed to be uncorrelated with the error term of the earnings equation. These instruments, which are popular in analyses of developing country data, may capture various genetic and environmental influences (Sahn and Alderman 1988).[10]

We tackle the issue of endogeneity using various techniques. First, we use father's schooling and main occupation as instruments and adopt a control function approach (Garen 1984; Wooldridge 2005; Söderbom and others 2006). This method is adopted when the earnings-education profile is nonlinear in the estimated parameters. As our results show, the marginal effects of education are nonconstant (for details and discussion of the implementation of this method, see Kuépié, Nordman, and Roubaud 2009).

Following Blackburn and Neumark (1995), Lam and Schoeni (1993), and Ashenfelter and Zimmerman (1997), we also use family background information differently, introducing it directly into the earnings functions. Doing so is another way of applying the control function procedure (see Kuépié, Nordman, and Roubaud 2009).

All of these techniques are interesting, because the different hypotheses behind them may lead to common features in the results that can be considered relatively robust. Thus, even if endogeneity issues are not perfectly corrected, the similarity of results from the different methods should help convince readers of their soundness.

Impact of Education on Labor Market Outcomes

This section examines the effect of education on labor market insertion and inter-individual earnings differentials. In the first subsection, we present some figures on the link between labor market integration (unemployment, sector choice) and education. In the second subsection, we report results from pooled and sectoral earnings functions and examine summary results obtained with different econometric methodologies, considering in particular selectivity-corrected earnings functions and the education variable as an endogenous regressor. In the third subsection, we focus on the cross-country comparison, using a set of estimates deemed most reliable for each city and sector. In the last subsection, we provide an overview of the marginal returns to different qualifications.

Education, Unemployment, and Labor Market Insertion

The subsection presents findings on the efficiency of education in terms of exits from unemployment and integration into different labor market segments (formal versus informal). For the seven cities, the unemployment rate is lowest (15 percent) among people with the least education. It rises to 20–21 percent for people with levels ranging from completed primary schooling to completed secondary schooling.[11] It drops slightly (to 19 percent) for people who completed at least one year of higher education.

The fact that human capital is thin on the ground does not appear to protect people who have it against unemployment. This is particularly true in Lomé, where unemployment increases strictly with the level of education (from 8 percent among people with no education to 23 percent among people with higher education). The trends are less linear in other cities. In most cases, unemployment tends first to increase with the level of education, before decreasing with completion of secondary school and entry into higher education. This pattern is particularly strong in Cotonou, Dakar, and Ouagadougou, where higher education somewhat reduces the extent of unemployment.

Findings from a logit of the probability of being unemployed (controlling for individual and household characteristics such as age, gender, migrant status, marital status, household per capita income, the individual's relationship to the head of household, and the household's dependency ratio) are similar to the findings of the descriptive analysis.[12] All else equal, individuals with little or no education appear to be less exposed to unemployment than individuals who have at least completed primary school, probably indicating lower job aspirations. Lomé shows a strong positive relation between unemployment and education. Abidjan and Cotonou also follow this trend. In the other cities, the link between unemployment and the level of education takes the bell shape observed previously.

The fact that investment in human capital does not always open the door to employment reflects deterioration of African urban labor markets, the result of the failure (or absence) of urbanization policies to set in motion a drive to create skilled jobs. It is also a consequence of structural adjustment policies that reduced staff in the civil service. Evidence of the effect of these policies is found in the fact that among people 45–59, who entered the labor market before the urban boom and the full force of the structural adjustment plans was felt, higher education is associated with a low risk of unemployment in all seven cities.

Although being unemployed is an indicator of exclusion from the labor market, having a job does not always guard against precariousness (see chapters 1, 2, and 4). In the following subsections, we look at the link between education and the quality of the job held in addition to its impact on unemployment.

A quantitative analysis of the balance in the labor markets reveals the existence of significant unemployment against which human capital accumulation is no shield, especially among young people. An analysis of external efficiency should consider the correspondence between the level of education and job quality. Job quality is studied here in terms of the employment sector: public formal, private formal, and informal (for another approach, see chapter 2).

There is a very close link between the level of education and the employment sector. For the sample as a whole, 91 percent of employed workers who did not start or complete primary school work in the informal sector. Completed primary schooling brings the proportion in the informal sector down to 75 percent; completed middle school reduces it to 50 percent. Only 19 percent of people who entered higher education work in the informal sector. This pattern holds for all cities except Lomé. In Lomé, the formal sector clearly supplants the informal sector as the level of education rises, but the correlation is weaker than in the other cities and a significant proportion of people with higher education (39 percent) work in the informal sector (95 percent of people who did not start or complete primary school work in the informal sector).

We decompose the formal sector into public and private formal sectors and then run a multinomial logit model to measure the net influence of education on sector allocation (table 5.1).[13] The results show that for all cities and school grades, an additional year of education tends to yield the maximum impact for integrating the public sector, followed by the private formal sector. In three cities (Bamako, Lomé, and Ouagadougou), additional years of higher education (more than 13 years of schooling) have no influence on the probability of integrating into the formal private sector. This result may reflect the incapacity of formal private firms to create highly qualified jobs for people with higher education.

The type of education also plays an important role in providing access to the formal sector. Only 37 percent of individuals who complete at least four years of vocational education—after which they receive an occupational proficiency certificate (the *Certificat d'aptitude professionnelle* [CAP])—work in the informal sector, as opposed to nearly 50 percent of individuals who reached an equivalent level in the secondary school system (that is, completed middle school without starting secondary school). Vocational education is more effective for integrating people into the formal sector than general education in Niamey, Dakar, Bamako, Cotonou, and Lomé. The share of workers with vocational training who work in the formal sector is 82 percent in Niamey, 71 percent in Dakar and Bamako, 58 percent in Cotonou, and 50 percent in Lomé. By way of comparison, the proportion of individuals who completed general studies at middle school and worked in the formal sector stood at 68 percent in Niamey, 55 percent in Dakar, 41 percent in Bamako, 44 percent in Cotonou, and 30 percent in Lomé. In Abidjan and Ouagadougou, vocational education shows no advantage over general education in terms of the chances of entering the formal sector.

Specifications of Earnings Functions

The earnings regressions assess the seven cities separately. The estimates are obtained using the log of hourly rather than monthly earnings to take account of the heterogeneity of working hours in different sectors. The additional explanatory variables in the models are migrant status (dummies for rural, urban, and foreign migrants); marital status (dummies for single, monogamous married, polygamous married, widowed, free union, divorced); and religion (dummies for Muslim and Christian).

In most studies, log earnings are assumed to be linear or quadratic in years of education. Here we seek to document the shape of the entire earnings-education

Table 5.1 Multinomial Logit Models of Impact of Education on Allocation of Labor to Public or Formal Private Sector in Seven Cities in West Africa, 2001/02

Variable	Abidjan Public	Abidjan Formal private	Bamako Public	Bamako Formal private	Cotonou Public	Cotonou Formal private	Dakar Public	Dakar Formal private	Lomé Public	Lomé Formal private	Niamey Public	Niamey Formal private	Ouagadougou Public	Ouagadougou Formal private
Years of education														
0–6 (*primaire*)	0.266*** (3.36)	0.165*** (6.04)	0.259*** (5.65)	0.102*** (3.21)	0.305*** (4.98)	0.183*** (4.36)	0.328*** (8.32)	0.190*** (8.79)	0.265*** (4.44)	0.204*** (3.83)	0.267*** (7.31)	0.195*** (5.84)	0.320*** (8.80)	0.215*** (6.24)
7–9 (*collège*)	0.558*** (6.74)	0.243*** (5.63)	0.489*** (6.36)	0.195*** (2.92)	0.417*** (6.72)	0.282*** (5.59)	0.409*** (8.46)	0.250*** (7.01)	0.333*** (5.64)	0.220*** (4.16)	0.518*** (8.54)	0.242*** (4.07)	0.573*** (11.14)	0.374*** (6.87)
10–13 (*lycée*)	0.449*** (4.51)	0.183*** (2.38)	0.593*** (6.54)	0.445*** (4.84)	0.335*** (3.98)	0.327*** (4.35)	0.365*** (5.09)	0.235*** (3.72)	0.525*** (6.46)	0.382*** (4.89)	0.343*** (4.05)	0.331*** (3.57)	0.383*** (4.62)	0.265*** (2.76)
13+	0.402*** (4.70)	0.326*** (4.18)	0.179** (2.28)	0.076 (0.91)	0.420*** (7.03)	0.305*** (5.34)	0.319*** (4.67)	0.280*** (4.30)	0.132** (2.10)	0.070 (1.08)	0.158** (2.39)	0.121* (1.72)	0.159** (2.33)	0.096 (1.22)
Potential experience														
Potential experience	0.210*** (6.14)	0.096*** (5.73)	0.208*** (8.84)	0.088*** (4.48)	0.125*** (5.45)	0.040** (2.20)	0.169*** (8.14)	0.077*** (6.11)	0.148*** (5.67)	0.068*** (3.16)	0.100*** (5.24)	0.056*** (2.83)	0.155*** (7.75)	0.139*** (6.36)
(Potential experience)²/100	-0.297*** (-4.35)	-0.129*** (-4.37)	-0.244*** (-6.61)	-0.132*** (-4.34)	-0.129*** (-3.36)	-0.038 (-1.27)	-0.197*** (-5.64)	-0.081*** (-4.24)	-0.157*** (-3.51)	-0.069* (-1.85)	-0.109*** (-3.88)	-0.092*** (-3.02)	-0.169*** (-5.23)	-0.179*** (-5.04)
Gender														
Woman	-0.701*** (-2.86)	-1.058*** (-8.11)	-0.536* (-1.94)	-1.319*** (-5.38)	-0.508*** (-2.74)	-0.550*** (-3.71)	-0.395** (-2.50)	-0.768*** (-7.22)	-0.743*** (-3.57)	-1.010*** (-5.12)	-0.299 (-1.37)	-0.633*** (-3.20)	-0.405** (-1.97)	-0.541** (-2.55)
Pseudo R²	0.285		0.287		0.268		0.231		0.227		0.259		0.289	
Number of observations	4,259		4,015		4,397		5,291		3,911		3,575		4,192	

Sources: Based on Phase 1 of the 1-2-3 surveys of selected countries in the West African Economic and Monetary Union (WAEMU) conducted in 2001/02 by the Observatoire économique et statistique d'Afrique Subsaharienne (AFRISTAT); Développement, Institutions et Mondialisation (DIAL); and national statistics institutes.

Note: The base category is the informal sector. The additional explanatory variables are migrant status (dummies for rural, urban, or foreign migrants); marital status (dummies for single, monogamous married, polygamous married, widowed, free union, divorced); and dummies for religion (Muslim, Christian). Figures in parentheses are student statistics.
* significant at the 10 percent level, ** significant at the 5 percent level, *** significant at the 1 percent level.

profile. We therefore adopt a more flexible approach, specifying education as a piecewise linear spline function (see below) that allows the strength of the relationship between education and earnings to vary across different parts of the educational distribution. We distinguish four levels of education: primary, lower secondary (*collège*), upper secondary (*lycée*), and tertiary. The education variables introduced have the form $s_k(e)$, where e is years of completed schooling at the k level (k: 1,...,4):

$$s_1(e) = \begin{cases} e & e \leq 6 \\ 6 & e \leq 6, \end{cases} \quad s_2(e) = \begin{cases} 0 & e \leq 6 \\ e-6 & 6 < e \leq 10 \\ 4 & e > 10, \end{cases}$$

$$s_3(e) = \begin{cases} 0 & e \leq 10 \\ e-10 & 10 < e \leq 13 \\ 3 & e > 13, \end{cases} \quad s_4(e) = \begin{cases} 0 & e \leq 13 \\ e-13 & e > 13. \end{cases}$$

(5.3)

Table 5.2 reports the pooled earnings functions estimates across sectors using Heckman's two-step approach and endogenous education with the control function method. The use of a single model for all gainfully employed individuals provides only the average effect of education on earnings, masking specific education effects in each employment sector. Where differences in these effects across sectors are small, a pooled model is sufficient to be able to draw conclusions about each labor market segment. Where these effects vary widely, the returns to education must be estimated separately for each sector.

Tables 5.3–5.5 report the estimates corrected for potential endogenous sector selection (using Lee's method).[14] To ease reading, given the number of countries studied and the set of alternative estimation techniques, we also present a synthesis table (table 5.6) reporting the average marginal returns to schooling using different methods.[15] Before turning to the comments on the returns to human capital, we briefly discuss the results obtained with different estimation strategies.[16]

Ordinary least squares versus selectivity-corrected earnings functions. Using a pooled population of paid-work participants across the three sectors, the selection-correction terms stemming from a probit equation of paid-work participation in the first stage are generally insignificant, except in Abidjan at the 1 percent level (this finding means that the mechanism of allocation of paid-work participants versus nonparticipants is not random and affects earnings significantly). Paid-work participation is associated with unobserved characteristics that are negatively correlated with earnings. If sample selectivity is not accounted for, ordinary least squares estimates would yield biased estimates of the returns to observed characteristics, notably human capital.

Table 5.2 Earnings Functions with Endogenous Education and Selectivity Correction in All Sectors in Seven Cities in West Africa, 2001/02
(dependent variable: log of hourly earnings)

Variable	Abidjan	Bamako	Cotonou	Dakar	Lomé	Niamey	Ouagadougou
Years of education							
0–6 (*primaire*)	0.037***	0.058***	0.080***	0.092***	0.064***	0.052***	0.103***
	(3.44)	(5.34)	(9.24)	(9.00)	(4.82)	(4.23)	(9.66)
7–9 (*collège*)	0.112***	0.104***	0.077***	0.106***	0.102***	0.158***	0.182***
	(6.92)	(4.78)	(5.42)	(6.92)	(5.80)	(7.44)	(11.55)
10–13 (*lycée*)	0.187***	0.171***	0.174***	0.134***	0.215***	0.182***	0.201***
	(7.62)	(6.13)	(7.98)	(5.85)	(8.41)	(6.21)	(8.76)
13+ (higher education)	0.166***	0.138***	0.141***	0.166***	0.154***	0.103***	0.157***
	(7.99)	(6.44)	(8.46)	(8.80)	(4.90)	(6.23)	(8.42)
Experience							
Potential experience	0.014**	0.029***	0.011*	0.033***	0.025***	0.028***	0.044***
	(2.31)	(5.10)	(1.78)	(5.65)	(3.80)	(4.47)	(7.73)
Potential experience squared/100	–0.002	–0.036***	–0.008	–0.040***	–0.030***	–0.030***	–0.052***
	(0.22)	(4.33)	(0.81)	(4.59)	(2.79)	(3.44)	(6.34)
Seniority in current job	0.027***	0.025***	0.024***	0.028***	0.032***	0.030***	0.030***
	(4.76)	(5.03)	(4.87)	(5.65)	(5.76)	(5.60)	(5.82)
Seniority in current job squared/100	–0.058***	–0.033**	–0.040**	–0.041***	–0.053***	–0.047***	–0.040**
	(2.94)	(2.23)	(2.43)	(2.96)	(2.83)	(2.88)	(2.49)
Gender							
Woman	–0.325***	–0.190***	–0.330***	–0.264***	–0.229***	–0.249***	–0.210***
	(7.48)	(3.49)	(8.92)	(6.69)	(4.42)	(4.81)	(5.20)

Sector

	(1)	(2)	(3)	(4)	(5)	(6)	(7)
Public sector	0.675***	0.281***	0.383***	0.469***	0.610***	0.420***	0.640***
	(14.24)	(5.75)	(9.13)	(11.14)	(10.99)	(9.41)	(15.83)
Formal private sector	0.476***	0.229***	0.229***	0.407***	0.418***	0.397***	0.591***
	(15.03)	(4.59)	(5.64)	(11.83)	(7.39)	(8.49)	(13.16)
Corrections							
Control variable (residuals of education regression)	−0.007	−0.030***	−0.028***	−0.037***	−0.023*	−0.015	−0.038***
	(0.74)	(3.70)	(3.81)	(4.02)	(1.90)	(1.60)	(4.79)
Inverse Mills ratio	−0.240***	0.058	−0.092	0.004	−0.026	0.035	0.055
	(3.86)	(1.06)	(1.49)	(0.07)	(0.36)	(0.58)	(1.03)
Constant	−2.023***	−2.480***	−2.296***	−2.506***	−2.967***	−2.759***	−3.214***
	(19.41)	(23.18)	(21.30)	(20.02)	(24.76)	(20.51)	(28.63)
Number of observations	4,011	3,821	4,184	4,364	3,496	3,069	3,665
Pseudo R^2	0.51	0.38	0.41	0.42	0.38	0.46	0.55

Sources: Based on Phase 1 of the 1-2-3 surveys of selected countries (see table 5.1 for details).

Note: The additional explanatory variables in the models are migrant status (dummies for rural, urban, and foreign migrants); marital status (dummies for single, monogamous married, polygamous married, widowed, free union, divorced); and religion (dummies for Muslim and Christian). The inverse Mills ratio is derived from a probit estimation of labor market participation for each city (with a dummy variable of strictly positive earnings as the dependent variable) comprising age and its square, gender, years of education, migrant status, marital status, religion, and one identifying variable (the dependency ratio). The reference category is a man working in the informal sector. Figures in parentheses are student statistics. Standard errors are bootstrapped with 500 replications.

* significant at the 10 percent level, ** significant at the 5 percent, *** level significant at the 1 percent level.

Table 5.3 Earnings Functions with Endogenous Education and Selectivity Correction in the Public Sector in Seven Cities in West Africa, 2001/02
(dependent variable: log of hourly earnings)

Variable	Abidjan	Bamako	Cotonou	Dakar	Lomé	Niamey	Ouagadougou
Years of education							
0–6 (*primaire*)	0.090**	0.085**	0.063	0.069*	−0.016	0.031	0.095***
	(1.97)	(2.32)	(1.44)	(1.72)	(0.21)	(1.10)	(3.08)
7–9 (*collège*)	−0.048	0.131***	0.125**	0.034	−0.024	0.127***	0.139***
	(0.81)	(2.58)	(2.28)v	(0.74)	(0.35)	(3.42)	(3.51)
10–13 (*lycée*)	0.138**	0.157***	0.182***	0.112**	0.094	0.148***	0.141***
	(2.43)	(3.50)	(3.56)	(2.41)	(1.21)	(3.91)	(3.86)
13+ (higher education)	0.099***	0.135***	0.141***	0.127***	0.075*	0.094***	0.124***
	(2.80)	(5.33)	(3.76)	(3.89)	(1.82)	(4.37)	(5.75)
Experience							
Potential experience	−0.012	0.069***	0.041	0.015	−0.022	0.058***	0.058***
	(0.45)	(3.59)	(1.33)	(0.59)	(0.62)	(5.36)	(3.50)
Potential experience squared/100	0.064	−0.091***	−0.017	0.007	0.062	−0.078***	−0.063**
	(1.25)	(2.76)	(0.31)	(0.18)	(1.04)	(4.39)	(2.25)

Gender							
Woman	-0.017	-0.072	-0.003	-0.105	0.281*	-0.081	-0.058
	(0.20)	(1.07)	(0.03)	(1.19)	(1.88)	(1.37)	(0.97)
Corrections							
Control variable (residuals of education regression)	-0.006	-0.015	-0.008	-0.015	0.033	0.011	-0.007
	(0.26)	(1.04)	(0.51)	(0.97)	(1.13)	(0.86)	(0.59)
Inverse Mills ratio	0.493**	-0.184	-0.100	0.249	0.711*	0.016	0.003
	(2.42)	(1.03)	(0.29)	(0.92)	(1.88)	(0.12)	(0.01)
Constant	-0.176	-3.235***	-2.679**	-1.089	0.253	-2.427***	-2.716***
	(0.21)	(4.77)	(2.00)	(1.09)	(0.18)	(5.79)	(3.95)
Number of observations	306	459	411	483	313	597	595
Pseudo R^2	0.44	0.38	0.46	0.38	0.45	0.47	0.53

Sources: Based on Phase 1 of the 1-2-3 surveys of selected countries (see table 5.1 for details).

Note: The additional explanatory variables in the models are migrant status, marital status, and religion. The Lee ratio is derived from a multinomial logit model of sector choices (with, as reference category, nonpaid work participation) comprising age and its square, gender, years of education, migrant status, marital status, religion, and identifying variables (namely, dummies on the individual's relationship to the head of household and the dependency ratio). Figures in parentheses are student statistics. Standard errors are bootstrapped with 500 replications.

* significant at the 10 percent level, ** significant at the 5 percent level, *** significant at the 1 percent level.

175

Table 5.4 Earnings Functions with Endogenous Education and Selectivity Correction in the Formal Private Sector in Seven Cities in West Africa, 2001/02
(dependent variable: log of hourly earning)

Variable	Abidjan	Bamako	Cotonou	Dakar	Lomé	Niamey	Ouagadougou
Years of education							
0–6 (*primaire*)	0.040*	0.101***	0.057	0.084***	0.070	0.094***	0.127***
	(1.72)	(2.88)	(1.57)	(3.58)	(1.17)	(2.61)	(3.86)
7–9 (*collège*)	0.116***	0.184***	0.139***	0.089***	0.050	0.182***	0.114***
	(4.32)	(3.38)	(3.93)	(3.39)	(0.91)	(3.51)	(2.66)
10–13 (*lycée*)	0.218***	0.113	0.124**	0.141***	0.260***	0.171**	0.247***
	(5.84)	(1.45)	(2.54)	(4.18)	(3.55)	(2.52)	(4.79)
13+ (higher education)	0.214***	0.261***	0.175***	0.169***	0.184***	0.115**	0.205***
	(6.83)	(5.44)	(6.06)	(5.94)	(3.17)	(2.41)	(3.66)
Experience							
Potential experience	0.040***	0.020	0.019	0.032**	0.041*	0.053***	0.042**
	(3.26)	(0.98)	(1.51)	(2.39)	(1.76)	(3.05)	(1.97)
Potential experience squared/100	–0.027	0.012	0.011	–0.022	–0.026	–0.045	–0.036
	(1.26)	(0.34)	(0.50)	(1.04)	(0.62)	(1.48)	(1.06)

Gender

Woman	-0.083	0.036	-0.039	-0.058	0.031	-0.422**	-0.016
	0.040*	0.101***	0.057	0.084***	0.070	0.094***	0.127***
Corrections							
Control variable (residuals of education regression)	-0.008	-0.068***	-0.021	-0.029*	0.015	0.009	-0.042**
	(0.53)	(2.98)	(1.31)	(1.88)	(0.39)	(0.39)	(2.07)
Inverse Mills ratio	0.070	0.345	-0.093	0.203	-0.122	-0.328	0.050
	(0.62)	(1.18)	(0.56)	(1.04)	(0.44)	(1.38)	(0.21)
Constant	-1.930***	-2.081***	-2.362***	-1.778***	-3.186***	-3.491***	-2.708***
	(5.77)	(3.02)	(4.64)	(3.39)	(3.75)	(5.48)	(3.30)
Number of observations	854	455	529	957	307	414	346
Pseudo R^2	0.46	0.32	0.36	0.32	0.35	0.46	0.48

Sources: Based on Phase 1 of the 1-2-3 surveys of selected countries (see table 5.1 for details).

Note: The additional explanatory variables in the models are migrant status, marital status, and religion. The Lee ratio is derived from a multinomial logit model of sector choices (with nonpaid work participation as the reference category) comprising age and its square, gender, years of education, migrant status, marital status, religion, and identifying variables (namely, dummies on the individual's relationship to the head of household and the dependency ratio). Figures in parentheses are student statistics. Standard errors are bootstrapped with 500 replications.

* significant at the 10 percent level, ** significant at the 5 percent level, *** significant at the 1 percent level.

Table 5.5 Earnings Functions with Endogenous Education and Selectivity Correction in the Informal Sector in Seven Cities in West Africa, 2001/02

(dependent variable: log of hourly earnings)

Variable	Abidjan	Bamako	Cotonou	Dakar	Lomé	Niamey	Ouagadougou
Years of education							
0–6 (*primaire*)	0.029*	0.050***	0.081***	0.090***	0.060***	0.059***	0.093***
	(1.88)	(3.92)	(7.66)	(7.26)	(3.96)	(3.36)	(6.26)
7–9 (*collège*)	0.122***	0.067**	0.073***	0.093***	0.110***	0.138***	0.167***
	(4.64)	(2.55)	(4.54)	(3.99)	(5.49)	(4.07)	(6.67)
10–13 (*lycée*)	0.122***	0.184***	0.205***	0.130***	0.196***	0.208***	0.231***
	(2.74)	(3.75)	(5.43)	(2.88)	(5.13)	(3.44)	(4.63)
13+ (higher education)	0.225***	0.036	0.144***	0.151**	0.144**	0.141**	0.194***
	(4.10)	(0.49)	(3.40)	(2.31)	(2.39)	(2.44)	(3.54)
Experience							
Potential experience	0.022***	0.031***	0.012*	0.044***	0.030***	0.023***	0.046***
	(3.00)	(5.32)	(1.93)	(7.78)	(4.80)	(3.15)	(7.47)
Potential experience squared/100	−0.011	−0.034***	−0.008	−0.051***	−0.031***	−0.015	−0.048***
	(1.01)	(4.24)	(0.89)	(6.43)	(3.24)	(1.49)	(5.69)

178

Gender							
Woman	-0.491***	-0.254***	-0.442***	-0.320***	-0.331***	-0.269***	-0.310***
	(8.57)	(4.34)	(10.09)	(7.82)	(5.86)	(4.27)	(5.49)
Corrections							
Control variable (residuals of education regression)	0.006	-0.020*	-0.031***	-0.033***	-0.027**	-0.029*	-0.032**
	(0.39)	(1.74)	(3.43)	(2.67)	(2.01)	(1.80)	(2.38)
Inverse Mills ratio	0.233***	-0.062	0.125*	-0.018	0.047	0.054	-0.049
	(3.08)	(1.06)	(1.77)	(0.29)	(0.59)	(0.78)	(0.72)
Constant	-1.778***	-2.256***	-2.101***	-2.386***	-2.811***	-2.483***	-2.995***
	(13.61)	(17.81)	(17.60)	(19.14)	(20.07)	(13.96)	(21.99)
Number of observations	2,859	2,929	3,250	3,423	2,930	2,233	2,771
Pseudo R^2	0.25	0.24	0.26	0.20	0.22	0.17	0.31

Sources: Based on Phase 1 of the 1-2-3 surveys of selected countries (see table 5.1 for details).

Note: The additional explanatory variables in the models are migrant status; the individual's relationship to the head of household (dummies for head of household, spouse, son/daughter, father/mother, other relatives); and religion. The Lee ratio is derived from a multinomial logit model of sector choices (with nonpaid work participation as the reference category) comprising age and its square, gender, years of education, migrant status, marital status, the individual's relationship to the head of household, religion, and one identifying variable (namely, the dependency ratio). Figures in parentheses are student statistics. Standard errors are bootstrapped with 500 replications.

* significant at the 10 percent level, ** significant at the 5 percent, *** level significant at the 1 percent level.

Table 5.6 Marginal Returns to Education in Seven Cities in West Africa, Using Alternative Estimation Techniques, 2001/02

Sector	Abidjan	Bamako	Cotonou	Dakar	Lomé	Niamey	Ouagadougou
All sectors							
Ordinary least squares	0.033***	0.033***	0.058***	0.059***	0.044***	0.038***	0.069***
Selectivity corrected (Lee's method)	0.031***	0.033***	0.059***	0.059***	0.045***	0.039***	0.070***
Selectivity corrected + father's characteristics	0.031***	0.029***	0.053***	0.056***	0.041***	0.035***	0.065***
Selectivity corrected + control function	0.037***	0.058***	0.080***	0.092***	0.064***	0.052***	0.103***
Number of observations	4,011	3,821	4,184	4,364	3,496	3,069	3,665
Public sector							
Ordinary least squares	0.206***	0.114***	0.163***	0.118***	0.245***	0.142***	0.136***
Selectivity corrected (Lee's method)	0.133**	0.145***	0.175***	0.094**	0.129*	0.140***	0.136***
Selectivity corrected + father's characteristics	0.144***	0.154***	0.178***	0.093**	0.120*	0.139***	0.137***
Selectivity corrected + control function	0.138**	0.157***	0.182***	0.112**	0.094	0.127***	0.141***
Number of observations	306	459	411	483	313	597	595

Formal private sector

Ordinary least squares	0.112***	0.143***	0.104**	0.077***	0.056	0.181***	0.075**
Selectivity corrected (Lee's method)	0.108***	0.138***	0.111**	0.065***	0.063	0.191***	0.065*
Selectivity corrected + father's characteristics	0.107***	0.115**	0.099**	0.063***	0.064	0.195***	0.069*
Selectivity corrected + control function	0.116***	0.184***	0.124***	0.089***	0.050	0.182***	0.114***
Number of observations	854	455	529	957	307	414	346

Informal sector

Ordinary least squares	0.030***	0.035***	0.054***	0.062***	0.035***	0.034***	0.067***
Selectivity corrected (Lee's method)	0.033***	0.034***	0.057***	0.061***	0.037***	0.035***	0.066***
Selectivity corrected + father's characteristics	0.034***	0.030***	0.052***	0.059***	0.033***	0.032***	0.061***
Selectivity corrected + control function	0.029*	0.050***	0.081***	0.090***	0.060***	0.059***	0.093***
Number of observations	2,859	2,931	3,250	3,423	2,930	2,233	2,771

Sources: Based on Phase 1 of the 1-2-3 surveys of selected countries (see table 5.1 for details).
Note: Earnings functions include the set of characteristics reported in tables 5.3–5.5. Estimates are computed at the sample mean using the piecewise linear spline earnings function in tables 5.2–5.5.
* significant at the 10 percent level, ** significant at the 5 percent level, *** significant at the 1 percent level.

The same picture emerges from the sectoral estimates, which also report only a few significant selectivity terms (Abidjan and Lomé for the public sector, Cotonou and Abidjan for the informal sector; see tables 5.3–5.5).

Exogenous versus endogenous education. We use the father's characteristics as instruments by means of the control function method. Using the first-stage regressions, in which education is regressed on all exogenous variables, we test for the joint significance of the coefficients of father's characteristics, a necessary condition for consistency of the estimates. For all cities, we can safely reject the hypothesis that these coefficients are jointly zero.[17] Several interesting patterns emerge from the control function estimates of the returns to schooling (see tables 5.2–5.5).

Using the control function approach, we can directly identify the correlation between the endogenous variable (education) and its unobserved determinants. A significant parameter estimate of the control variable (residuals of the education regression) means that the unexplained variation in the education variable also affects variation in earnings. An insignificant parameter means that we cannot accept the hypothesis of endogeneity. Table 5.7 presents the *p*-values for *t*-tests associated with each control variable in the different specifications.

For all cities, we cannot reject the hypothesis of exogeneity of education in the public sector.[18] By contrast, we reject exogeneity in the informal sector in all cities except Abidjan. In the formal private sector, we obtain mixed results, rejecting exogeneity in Bamako, Dakar, and Ouagadougou (instrumentation for the private sector in Bamako appeared dubious, however). In Abidjan, the unexplained variation of schooling never significantly affects variation in earnings.

When exogeneity of education is rejected, we place more confidence in the instrumental variables estimates, at least the ones based on the control function

Table 5.7 Endogeneity Tests of Education in the Earnings Functions in Seven Cities in West Africa, by Sector, 2001/02

City	All sectors	Public sector	Formal private sector	Informal sector
Abidjan	0.46	0.80	0.60	0.69
Bamako	0.00	0.30	0.00	0.08
Cotonou	0.00	0.61	0.19	0.00
Dakar	0.00	0.33	0.06	0.01
Lomé	0.06	0.26	0.70	0.04
Niamey	0.11	0.39	0.70	0.07
Ouagadougou	0.00	0.56	0.04	0.02

Sources: Based on Phase 1 of the 1-2-3 surveys of selected countries (see table 5.1 for details).
Note: The null hypothesis is that education is exogenous in the earnings function. Figures show *p*-values of the *t*-test.

approach. Motivations for this choice can be found in Kuépié, Nordman, and Roubaud (2009).

Cross-Country Comparison

Chow tests for the joint equality of coefficients across sectors show that the decomposition by institutional sector is justified. Indeed, we find highly contrasting configurations. As expected, the models' explanatory power declines as one moves from the public sector (pseudo R^2 = 0.44 to the formal private sector [0.39] and the informal sector [0.23]). This hierarchy is consistent with the predictions of the standard human capital model, which is better suited to accounting for the heterogeneity of earnings in the public sector, where wages are based on a set scale that takes education and experience explicitly into account. In the informal sector, apart from the probability of greater measurement errors, factors not taken into account in our equation, such as the amount of physical capital, are likely to have a significant impact on earnings.

To synthesize the results for education, we present histograms of the marginal returns to education by sector and city at the sample means of education (figure 5.1). In six out of seven cities, the return to education is highest in the public sector, with a marginal return ranging from 9.4 percent (in Dakar) to 17.5 percent (in Cotonou). This finding reflects, to a great extent, the salary scales for civil servants, which are determined based on diploma and length

Figure 5.1 Marginal Returns to Education in Seven Cities in West Africa, by Sector, 2001/02

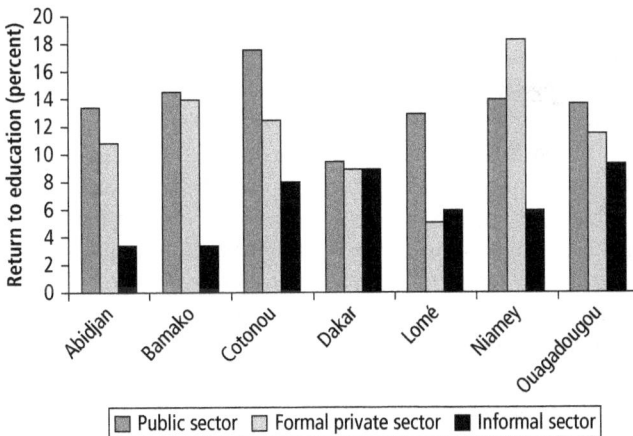

Sources: Based on Phase 1 of the 1-2-3 surveys of selected countries (see table 5.1 for details).
Note: Returns are calculated at the sample mean. Estimates are based on results reported in table 5.6. Returns are for the exogenous education variable for the public sector of all cities and for the private sectors of Abidjan and Bamako.

of service. The formal private sector comes next (except in Niamey, where it ranked first), followed by the informal sector (except in Lomé, where returns to education are higher in the informal sector [6 percent] than in the formal private sector [5 percent], and in Dakar, where the marginal returns across sectors are roughly the same in the two sectors).

Convexity of returns. The results show strong evidence that earnings are non-linear in education, with a convex profile. For all the regressions reported in tables 5.3–5.6, we can reject the linear model at the 10 percent level or lower.[19] Convex marginal returns mean that education has a growing impact on remuneration. In almost all cases, a completed year of *lycée* (10–13 years completed) provides a greater return than a year of *collège* (7–9 years), especially in the private sectors.

In figure 5.2, we present predicted earnings in each sector based on years of completed schooling. For all sectors, earnings are roughly constant until about the 8th year of education and sharply increase around the 11th year, with small differences across cities. This rise in earnings occurs slightly earlier for informal sector workers (about the eighth year of schooling). These patterns indicate that, to a large extent, the convex profile reflects the surge in income observed when individuals make the transition from secondary to higher education in the formal sectors and the completion of *collège* in the informal sector.

These results are inconsistent with the traditional model of human capital accumulation, in which the marginal return to education is assumed to be constant or decreasing. Schultz (2004) highlights this convexity, using household surveys for six African countries (Burkina Faso, Côte d'Ivoire, Ghana, Kenya, Nigeria, and South Africa); Söderbom and others (2006) observe it in samples of employees of manufacturing firms in Kenya and Tanzania. To our knowledge, this feature of Africa's labor markets has not been documented before at the sectoral level using representative samples from urban Africa.

This result is important, because it has been advocated that not accounting for the high proportion of workers in the informal sector may lead to overestimates of the returns to primary education and underestimates of the returns to higher education (Bennell 1996). Convexity is revealed here in all sectors, including the informal sector. In our estimates, the marginal return to primary education is lower than the returns to secondary and higher education in all sectors, and the return to primary school is lower in the informal sector (6.6 percent) than in the formal private sector (7.2 percent). Similarly, the average return to a year of *lycée* is higher in the informal sector (18.3 percent) than in the formal (public and private) sector (on average, 15.5 percent). Hence, not accounting for earnings in the informal sector indeed yields an overestimation of the returns to primary education, as Bennell (1996) predicted, as well as possibly an underestimation of returns to higher levels of education.[20]

Figure 5.2 Estimated Hourly Earnings in Seven Cities in West Africa, by Sector, 2001/02

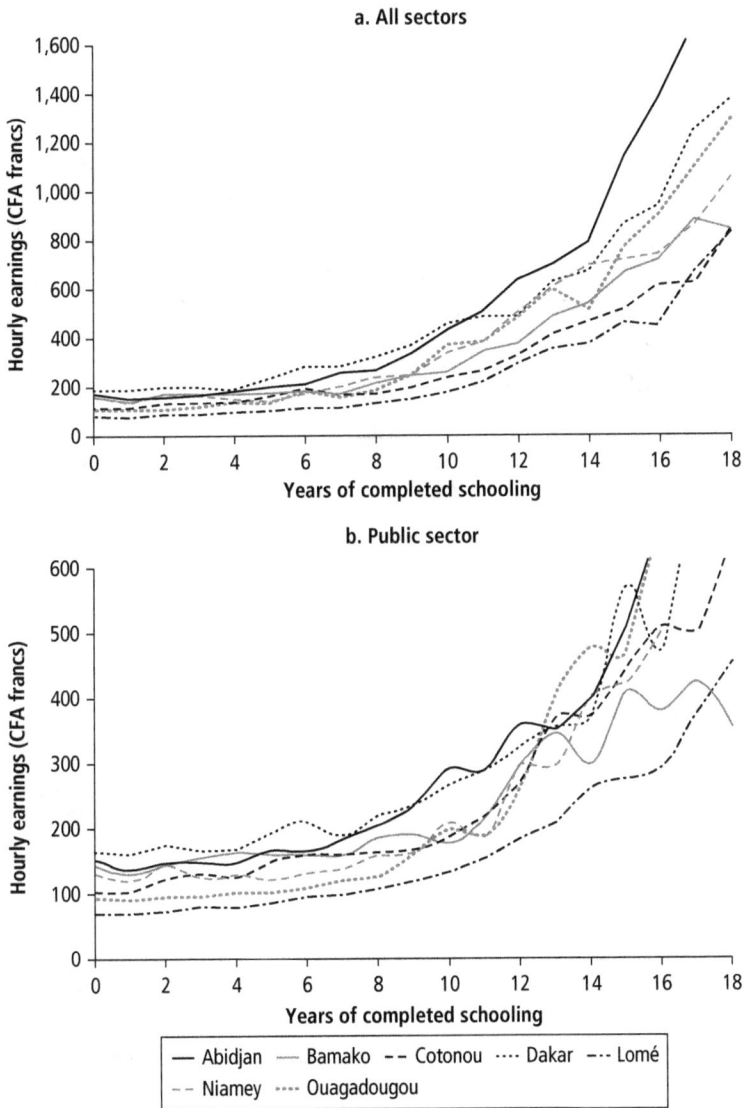

a. All sectors

b. Public sector

Legend: Abidjan — Bamako — Cotonou ···· Dakar ─·· Lomé ─ ─ Niamey ····· Ouagadougou

(continued next page)

Figure 5.2 (continued)

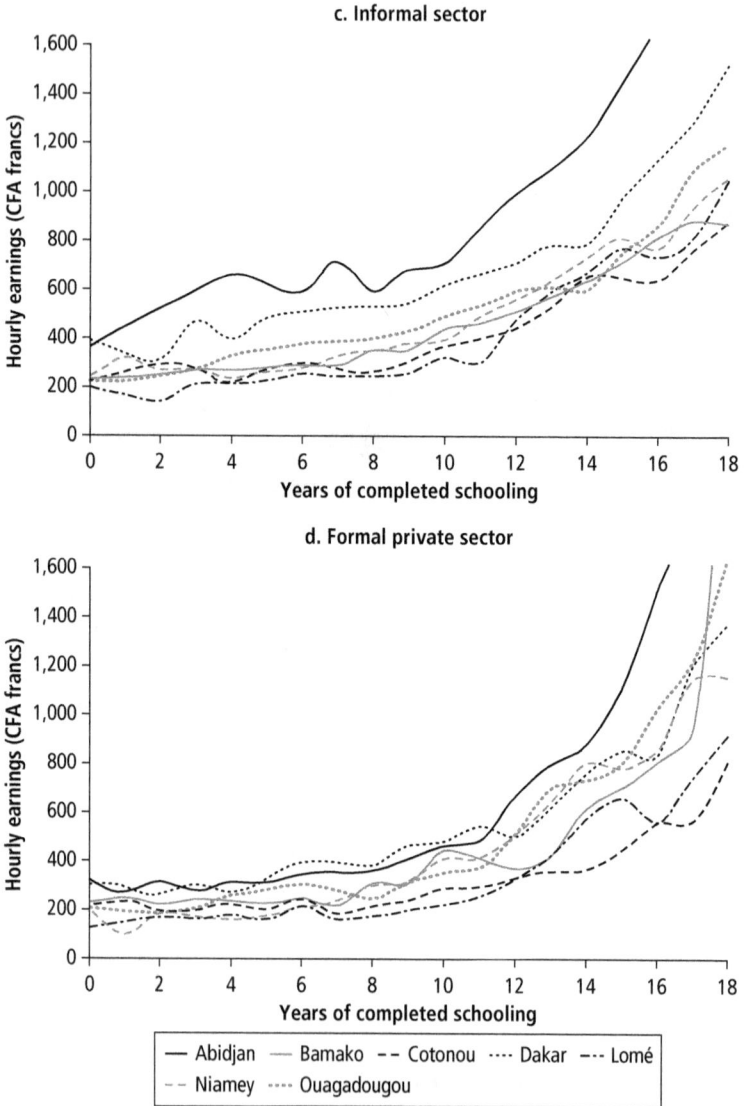

c. Informal sector

d. Formal private sector

Legend: — Abidjan — Bamako -- Cotonou ···· Dakar -·· Lomé -- Niamey ···· Ouagadougou

Sources: Based on Phase 1 of the 1-2-3 surveys of selected countries (see table 5.1 for details).

Observing increasing returns to education by levels is important, because the idea that primary education is an effective instrument for fighting poverty is based partly on the hypothesis of a concave earnings function—that is, the notion that investing in education is more profitable during the first years of schooling. Recommendations for policies aimed at promoting primary education in Sub-Saharan Africa were drawn up on the basis of this premise, among others (Psacharopoulos and Patrinos 2004).

Various arguments have been posited to explain convexity in the returns to schooling (Bennell 1996, 2002; Schultz 2004). One is that primary education has been overexpanded, reducing the returns relative to higher levels. Another is that over time the quality of primary school has declined, reducing returns (Behrman, Ross, and Sabot 2008). The slowdown in formal sector growth, which may have reduced the demand for educated labor and perhaps affected less educated individuals more strongly, has also been mentioned.

Returns to Qualifications

The fact that the earnings function is convex prompted us to make more detailed analyses, measuring the returns to different levels of qualification and not just to average years. To do so, we estimated the marginal returns to holding a diploma, thus accounting for the quality of the school career. In the private sector, we controlled for the endogeneity of schooling using the control function method (except in Abidjan and Bamako).

Returns to qualifications can be studied in at least two ways. One way is to directly consider the regression model coefficients. In this case, the coefficient associated with each qualification dummy is interpreted as the rate of increase in earnings between individuals with no qualifications (the reference) and individuals with a particular qualification. Another way is to calculate the marginal returns obtained by subtracting from the considered qualification's coefficient (qualification d) the value of the coefficient for the qualification immediately below it (qualification $d - 1$). For example, the marginal return to a *baccalauréat* plus two years of higher education (BAC+2) is the difference between the coefficient for the BAC+2 and the coefficient for the *baccalauréat* alone. The return to a primary certificate (*Certificat d'études primaires* [CEP]) is the difference in average earnings between someone with a CEP and someone with no diploma, the return to the middle school certificate (*Brevet d'études du premier cycle du second degré* [BEPC]) is the difference in average earnings between someone with a BEPC and someone with a CEP, and so forth. Marginal returns hence correspond to the increases in earnings generated by the acquisition of the next level of qualifications. In this study, we rely on marginal returns, because they measure the additional value of each qualification rather than the value compared with "no qualifications" which is almost always positive.

Kuépié, Nordman, and Roubaud (2009) report the results of this exercise using histograms of the marginal returns to various qualifications for each sector. Not surprisingly, the effect of each qualification on earnings is positive overall, with a huge quantitative leap for secondary and higher education, as already shown using continuous variables for schooling. The most striking result is that, depending on the city, some diplomas (such as the *baccalauréat*) do not yield positive marginal returns. This situation reflects either the inadequacy of the training considered with respect to the labor market or the fact that certain diplomas have no value in the labor market but are aimed solely at providing access to higher levels of education. This hypothesis might explain the low marginal profitability of some diplomas in the public sector. But the fact that for many diplomas, additional earnings are nil or negative in the formal private sector suggests that many training schemes do not correspond to the needs of the labor market in this sector.

This lack of connection between the level of training revealed by a diploma and the remuneration obtained in the formal private labor market is evident in all of the cities studied. Marginal earnings seem to correspond more closely to the level of training in the informal sector than in the formal private sector (but less than in the public sector). This result is inconsistent with the idea that the informal sector does not value educational capital. The profitability of education in the informal sector is illustrated by the earnings premium received by individuals with vocational diplomas (in particular the *Brevet d'études profession-nelles* [BEP]). In fact, returns to vocational training in the informal sector often exceed returns in the formal private sector. Vocational education qualifications are also often more profitable than general education qualifications, which take longer to obtain. For example, although it generally takes one year less to obtain a BEP (on average 11.6 years) than to obtain the *baccalauréat* (on average 13.0 years), the BEP is often more profitable than the *baccalauréat*, especially in the informal sector. The returns to the BEP are more than 40 percent higher than the returns to the *baccalauréat* in the formal private sector of Cotonou and in the informal sectors of Ouagadougou, Bamako, Niamey, and Lomé. The same result holds if we compare the premium for obtaining the CAP (a vocational certificate equivalent to completed primary school) versus the BEPC (a general certificate of completed primary education).

Conclusion

Using a series of comparable labor force surveys in urban West Africa, we estimate the impact of education on labor market outcomes among representative samples of workers in seven economic capitals. The data provide a unique cross-country comparison using the same variables and methodology for each city.

We tackle two recurrent econometric issues that arise in assessing the effect of education on individual earnings. First, we address the issue of endogenous sector allocation (public, formal private, and informal sectors) in the earnings functions estimates and provide evidence that correcting for this sample selectivity refines the returns to education in all cities and sectors. Second, for most cities, we reject the assumption of exogeneity of the education variable, except in the public sector. Using the workers' family background as an instrument for education, we find that the returns to schooling usually increase once endogeneity is accounted for. This effect is particularly strong in the informal sector.

Traditional theories assume constant or concave marginal returns to education, which ensure immediate, high profitability from the first years of schooling. The data from the 1-2-3 surveys of West Africa reveal convex returns in all sectors, including the informal sector. This finding casts doubts on the suitability of estimating average marginal returns and calls for disaggregated estimates at each level of the educational path. We provide evidence that the convex profile reflects the surge in income observed when individuals make the transition from secondary to higher education in the formal sectors; for informal sector workers, it mainly reflects completion of the first secondary cycle. In Abidjan, Bamako, Dakar, and Lomé, the earnings-education profile observed is particularly convex for young workers, especially in the informal sector.

Even at high levels, education substantially increases earnings in informal sector jobs in most of the cities studied.[21] To our knowledge, these features of Africa's labor markets have never before been documented at the sectoral level using representative samples of urban areas.

Convexity of the returns to schooling means that stimulating access to primary education is effective in reducing poverty only if primary school graduates can continue their studies in order to take full advantage of the high marginal returns associated with many years of education. Management of the flows of students completing general secondary and higher education could benefit from an in-depth review of the (too) general content of schooling programs, with an eye toward adapting it to the needs of the labor market. In the meantime, to increase the returns to low levels of schooling, improving primary school quality should remain at the top of any agenda for education.

That said, unemployment is growing in West African cities, especially among educated workers. This mismatch between (increasing) investment in schooling and actual labor market opportunities represents a major challenge. Would an increase in education generate its own demand? Or would more educated people simply add to the pool of disenfranchised and disillusioned workers, whose only hope is to migrate and find employment elsewhere? If our findings provide insight into the question of where specific bottlenecks arise on the labor demand side, they also provide evidence of the existence of significant returns to education in the informal sector that may counterbalance the incentive for job queuing. More specifically, if schooling helps workers in the informal sector be more productive (probably thanks to innovation and adaptability), then household and government investments in their education are not being made in vain. Given that the informal sector has created more than 80 percent of urban jobs in West Africa in recent years, concentrating public investments in employment in this sector with attractive policies for the most qualified people could represent a serious alternative to the lack of employment observed in the formal sectors, at least in the short term. Coupled with continued support to primary school quality and postprimary education, such a policy could also pay off in the medium to long term by generating the human capital accumulation required for the modern economy to take off in African cities.

Notes

1. By way of comparison, analyses of the internal efficiency of education systems concern school processes and the way the teaching establishments operate: generally speaking, they compare the schools' activities and organizational methods with the results obtained by pupils while they are still in the system, looking for the most cost-effective situations (Mingat and Suchaut 2000).
2. See Kuépié, Nordman, and Roubaud (2009) for further development of this point and for additional or more complete analyses of the findings presented in this chapter.
3. The cities are Abidjan, Côte d'Ivoire; Bamako, Mali; Cotonou, Benin; Dakar, Senegal; Lomé, Togo; Niamey, Niger; and Ouagadougou, Burkina Faso. Although Abidjan and Cotonou are not administrative capitals, we refer to them as capitals because they are the most important economic centers in their countries (Cotonou is also the seat of government).
4. For a description of the 1-2-3 surveys, see box O.1 in the overview.
5. For a presentation of descriptive statistics (education, earnings, and so forth), see chapter 1.
6. Based on Monte Carlo simulations, Bourguignon, Fournier, and Gurgand (2007) conclude that Lee's method is adapted to small samples.
7. Bourguignon, Fournier, and Gurgand (2007, p. 192) argue that correcting for selection bias based on the multinomial logit model is a "reasonable alternative to multinomial normal models when the focus is on estimating an outcome over selected populations rather than on estimating the selection process itself. This seems true even when the IIA hypothesis is severely at odds." As we are interested primarily in results in the second-stage regression, this argument allows us to be confident regarding the choice of a multinomial logit.
8. The results of the probits and multinomial logits are not reported, in order to save space. They are available on request from the authors.

9. The exceptions were the formal private sectors in Niamey and Dakar, where the appropriateness of the excluding conditions in the second stage was rejected (at the 10 percent level in Niamey and the 1 percent level in Dakar). In these two cases, we then tried to restrict the number of exclusions, using as identifying variables only a dummy variable indicating whether the respondent was the household head (together with the dependency ratio). The test was satisfied, and the results in the second step did not differ from the results obtained previously. We hence report the results including the full set of exclusions in order to ensure perfect comparability across countries. For all cities and sectors, Wald tests of joint significance of the instruments in the first stage never rejected the null hypothesis at the 1 percent level. The second-stage equation is still identified without excluding conditions for the need of the tests, as identification relies on the distributional assumption of Lee's model (see Bourguignon, Fournier, and Gurgand 2007).

10. For example, Ashenfelter and Zimmerman (1997) use parental education, Butcher and Case (1994) exploit the presence of any sister within the family, and Card (1995) draws on proximity to a four-year college as instruments.

11. These figures are slightly different from the figures presented in chapter 1 because of changes in education brackets.

12. These findings are available from the authors upon request.

13. The same set of control variables used for the analysis of unemployment is used here.

14. We drop the tenure variable from the set of covariates in the sectoral estimates, because seniority in the current job makes less sense in the informal sector.

15. Assuming that the marginal return to education varies across educational levels but is constant within each cycle, the marginal return to education around the sample's education mean is defined as follows:

$$R = \sum_{k=1}^{4} \alpha_k I(\overline{educ} \in C_k),$$ where α_k is the estimated coefficients of the k education

variables corresponding to the four cycles, $I(.)$ is the indicator function, $\overline{educ}$ is the average years of schooling, and C is the educational group.

16. Interested readers should see Kuépié, Nordman, and Roubaud (2009).

17. In 18 out of 21 cases, Sargan tests on overidentifying restrictions cannot reject at the 10 percent level the null hypothesis that the instruments are valid. The three cases where validity is not supported are the formal private and informal sectors of Bamako and the public sector of Niamey, suggesting that uncorrected education returns be considered in these cases. The results of these tests are available upon request.

18. Tests for exogeneity based on Hausman tests confirm these findings.

19. We investigated whether our findings are sensitive to functional form by considering the effects of modeling the earnings-education profile as second- and third-order polynomials. The quadratic function systematically produced significant squared education coefficients; the cubic form appeared less appropriate in the majority of cases.

20. These cross-country averages mask some country specificities.

21. The heterogeneity of the informal sector in this respect, notably the possible coexistence of different employment segments with specific features, deserves consideration (see chapter 4).

References

Ashenfelter, O., and D. Zimmerman. 1997. "Estimating of Return to Schooling from Sibling Data: Fathers, Sons, and Brothers." *Review of Economics and Statistics* 79 (February): 1–9.

Behrman, J. R., D. Ross, and R. Sabot. 2008. "Improving Quality versus Increasing Quantity of Schooling: Estimates of Rates of Return from Rural Pakistan." *Journal of Development Economics* 85 (1–2): 94–104.

Bennell, P. 1996. "Rates of Return on Education: Does the Conventional Pattern Prevail in Sub-Saharan Africa?" *World Development* 24 (1): 183–99.

———. 2002. "Hitting the Target: Doubling Primary School Enrolments in Sub-Saharan Africa by 2015." *World Development* 30 (7): 1179–94.

Blackburn, M., and D. Neumark. 1995. "Are OLS Estimates of the Return to Schooling Biased Downward? Another Look." *Review of Economics and Statistics* 77 (2): 217–29.

Bourguignon, F., M. Fournier, and M. Gurgand. 2007. "Selection Bias Correction Based on the Multinomial Logit Model: Monte-Carlo Comparisons." *Journal of Economic Surveys* 21 (1): 174–205.

Butcher, K. F., and A. Case. 1994. "The Effects of Sibling Composition on Women's Education and Earnings." *Quarterly Journal of Economics* 109: 443–50.

Card, D. 1995. "Using Geographic Variation in College Proximity to Estimate the Return to Schooling." In *Aspects of Labour Market Behavior: Essays in Honor of John Vanderkamp,* under the direction of L. N. Christofides, E. K. Grant, and R. Swidinsky, 201–22. Toronto: University of Toronto Press.

Dahl, G. B. 2002. "Mobility and the Return to Education: Testing a Roy Model with Multiple Markets." *Econometrica* 70 (6): 2367–420.

Dubin, J. A., and D. L. McFadden. 1984. "An Econometric Analysis of Residential Electric Appliance Holdings, and Consumption." *Econometrica* 52 (2): 345–62.

Garen, J. 1984. "The Returns to Schooling: A Selectivity Bias Approach with a Continuous Choice Variable." *Econometrica* 52 (5): 1199–218.

Kuépié, M., C. J. Nordman, and F. Roubaud. 2009. "Education and Earnings in Urban West Africa." *Journal of Comparative Economics* 37 (3): 491–515.

Lam, D., and R. F. Schoeni. 1993. "Effects of Family Background on Earnings and Returns to Schooling: Evidence from Brazil." *Journal of Political Economy* 1001: 710–40.

Mingat, A., and B. Suchaut. 2000. *Les systemes éducatifs africains: Une analyse économique comparative.* Brussels: De Boeck University.

Psacharopoulos, G., and H. A. Patrinos. 2004. "Returns to Investment in Education: A Further Update." *Education Economics* 12 (2): 111–34.

Sahn, D. E., and H. Alderman 1988. "The Effects of Human Capital on Wages, and the Determinants of Labor Supply in a Developing Country." *Journal of Development Economics* 29 (2): 157–83.

Schultz, T. P. 2004. "Evidence of Returns to Schooling in Africa from Household Surveys: Monitoring, and Restructuring the Market for Education." *Journal of African Economies* 13: ii95–148.

Söderbom, M., F. Teal, A. Wambugu, and G. Kahyarara. 2006. "Dynamics of Returns to Education in Kenyan and Tanzanian Manufacturing." *Oxford Bulletin of Economics, and Statistics* 68 (3): 261–88.

Vijverberg, W. P. 1993. "Educational Investments and Returns for Women and Men in Côte d'Ivoire." *Journal of Human Resources* 28 (4): 933–74.

Wooldridge, J. M. 2005. "Unobserved Heterogeneity and Estimation of Average Partial Effects." In *Identification and Inference for Econometric Models,* prepared under the direction of D. W. K. Andrews and J. H. Stock, 27–55. Cambridge U.K.: Cambridge University Press.

Chapter **6**

Urban Labor Market Segmentation in West Africa

Muriel Barlet

Most developing countries have large informal sectors: according to one study, the informal economy produces 39 percent of gross domestic product (GDP) in developing countries, 40 percent in transition economies, and 16 percent within the Organisation for Economic Co-operation and Development (OECD) (Schneider 2004). A better understanding of this sector is therefore critical.

This chapter examines the informal sector through the lens of the urban labor market in seven capitals in the West African Economic and Monetary Union (WAEMU): Abidjan, Bamako, Cotonou, Dakar, Lomé, Niamey, and Ouagadougou.[1] The chapter describes labor market segmentation—the phenomenon in which some individuals are prevented from working in the most financially rewarding sector, usually the formal sector. It examines the heterogeneity of the informal sector by splitting it into two segments, dependent workers and workers who are self-employed, including workers who work alone and workers who employ others.

The literature provides two divergent points of view on the informal sector (Fields 2005). On the one hand, it is regarded as a subsistence sector without entry costs that is attractive for individuals while they search for more rewarding work (Tokman 2007). On the other hand, it is viewed as a rewarding sector with many advantages and opportunities (flexibility, self-employment). The first view is supported by the existence of poor working conditions and low wages, which suggest low-quality jobs. Supporters of the second view claim that the social protection provided by the formal sector does not outweigh the opportunities provided by the flexibility afforded by the informal sector (Bromley 1990; Maloney 1999, 2004). The two views highlight the heterogeneity of the informal sector, which pools badly paid employees with no protection and successful employers.

Taking this heterogeneity into account is essential to provide relevant results. We thus divide workers into three groups: formal sector workers, informal sector employers, and informal sector workers (including the self-employed). We test whether individuals choose their working sector. If they do not, labor market segmentation exists. The results suggest that all labor markets examined are segmented.

Why is it important to divide the informal sector when testing for segmentation? When informal workers and informal employers are pooled, predicted earnings for the sector are low, suggesting that the informal sector is less attractive than the formal sector. Observing a large informal sector can thus be explained only by the rationing of jobs in the formal sector.[2] When only informal sector employers are examined, predicted earnings are rather high. Thus, two sectors appear attractive, the formal sector and the sector of informal employers. A large number of informal sector workers may thus reflect barriers to entry in entrepreneurship, not only the rationing of formal sector jobs. Splitting up the informal sector does not change the conclusion regarding segmentation (at least in our samples). However, it highlights two different rationing processes and consequently implies different public policies (increasing access not only to formal sector jobs but also to entrepreneurship, for instance).

Several studies divide the informal sector into two segments (Alderman and Kozel 1989; Azevedo 2005; Günther and Launov 2006). We go a step farther, by precisely identifying both segments of the informal sector. In our set-up, informal workers comprise wage workers and self-employed workers working alone. Günther and Launov (2006) establish the existence of two segments but do not define them. Our division is more relevant than the one proposed by Alderman and Kozel (1989) or Azevedo (2005). They separate wage workers from all own-account workers (self-employed and employers), whereas we separate employers from other workers. Our choice is supported by the work of De Mel, McKenzie, and Woodruff (2008) and Parga and Mondragn-Vlez (2008), who show that self-employed workers with no employees are closer to employed workers than to employers. One of our robustness checks also supports our choice.

We simulate a labor market in which individuals are allocated to the sector that is most rewarding for them. We then predict the size of each sector under the assumption of a competitive labor market and compare it to what is observed.

In order to provide relevant predictions, we need accurate earnings equation estimation. Estimating earnings equations for the different working sectors is tricky, because a rational self-selection process, as in the model developed by Roy (1951), may bias the coefficients. The main challenge is to correctly take this selection bias into account. Our estimations rely mainly on the selection bias correction method proposed by Lee (1983). We test the robustness of our results by also applying the method proposed by Dubin and McFadden (1984). We pay particular attention to the identification problem, suggesting several excluding variables (that is, variables that explain sector choice but not earnings) and testing each of them for each city and gender.

We apply our methodology to the seven comparable data sets from the 1-2-3 surveys (for a description of these surveys, see box O.1 in the overview). The results are for countries on which the literature is very thin.[3] We show that for all seven cities, the lower informal sector segment (wage workers and self-employed workers working alone) is significantly larger than predicted by our simulations of competitive labor markets; the employment shares of the formal sector and the sector of informal employers are generally smaller than predicted. These results suggest that labor markets are segmented. This conclusion is robust to the empirical strategy and the distribution of unobserved abilities.

The rest of this chapter is organized as follow. The first section describes the empirical method. The second section provides details on the data used. The third section presents the results and some robustness checks. The last section summarizes the conclusions and draws some policy implications.

Empirical Strategy: Predicting Sector Shares in a Hypothetical Competitive Labor Market

This section compares the observed shares of individuals in each sector (formal sector, informal sector workers, and informal sector employers) and the shares predicted by a model simulating a hypothetical competitive labor market. To simulate these shares, we allocate each individual to the sector that yields the highest predicted income, given the individual's characteristics. If at least one of the observed shares is outside the confidence interval of the corresponding simulated share, we can claim that some individuals are prevented from working in the sector that is most financially rewarding. We then conclude that labor market segmentation exists.[4]

Providing an unbiased prediction of income in each sector is tricky. Indeed, as individuals probably try to work in their favorite sector, the distribution of individuals across sectors may be far from random. The decision to participate in the labor market also affects earnings in the different sectors. We thus need to correctly take into account selection biases. To do so, we rely on the selection bias correction methods proposed by Lee (1983) and Dubin and McFadden (1984).

Sector-Choice Equation

We first estimate a sector choice equation, in order to calculate the correction terms for the earnings equation estimation. The equation is estimated with a multinomial logit. Individuals face four possible choices: not working, working in the formal sector, working in the informal employer sector, or working in the informal worker sector. The selection equation is

$$S_i = \gamma Z_i + \mu_i \qquad (6.1)$$

where S_i is the segment of individual i (nonworking, formal, informal sector workers, or informal employers); Z_i is a set of explanatory variables listed below; and μ_i is a residual term.

The explanatory variables in the first step are age; education; reading and writing French; reading and writing another language; father's sector when the individual was 15 years old; father's education (years); migrant status; belonging to the dominant religious community; belonging to the dominant ethnic group; total nonlabor income of the household; number of children in the household (for women only); and number of women older than 13 in the household (for women only).

These variables are gender but not city specific. Age and education (measured by years of schooling) are the usual determinants of sector choices. To complete the information on education, we add two measures of literacy. As most West Africans spend only few years in school, the years of schooling may be a weak determinant of the level of education (see chapter 5).

We also control for several other features that could affect sector choice. We first control for social and family background. The variables regarding the father, migrant status, religious community, and ethnic group are proxies that describe the individuals' social networks. These social networks are of primary interest here because they may ease access to some segments of the labor market (see chapters 9 and 10). As one of the working sectors is entrepreneurship, we then add a measure of the wealth of the household (total nonlabor income). It can be a strong determinant for entrepreneurship, as the credit market is poorly developed in the cities studied. It is also a determinant for inactivity. Finally, for women only, we know that there is a trade-off between working and performing household chores (see chapters 9 and 13). The number of children may increase the burden of household chores, whereas the number of adult women in the household may reduce it.

We run estimations separately for each city and gender. The sample consists of all individuals between the ages of 15 and 64.

The multinomial logit estimator relies on the assumption of independence of irrelevant alternatives. This assumption may be violated, especially if the choices under scrutiny are not simultaneous. However, Bourguignon, Fournier, and Gurgand (2007) use Monte Carlo simulations to show that the results of the second step are robust to the violation of that assumption.

Earnings Equation

For the second step, we estimate an earnings equation for each sector (except inactive). To correct for the selection bias, we mainly use Lee's methodology. The earnings equation can be written as follows:

$$\ln w_{is} = \beta_s . X_i + \alpha_s . m_i + \varepsilon_i \tag{6.2}$$

where w_{is} the income of individual i in sector s; X_i is a set of explanatory variables listed below; m_i is the selection term calculated from the first-step estimation; and ε_i is a residual error from a normal distribution with zero mean and a variance σ_s. The common explanatory variables in the second step are potential experience (age minus education minus 7); education; reading and writing French; and reading and writing another language.

For each city and gender, we test whether the other explanatory variables of the first step (father's sector and education, nonlabor income, number of children, number of women older than 13, and so forth) are significantly different from zero. We test each variable separately. When a test is rejected, we add the variable to the set of explanatory variables of the second step and rerun the test for all other variables. We carry out this procedure until all tests are accepted.[5] Consequently, the set of explanatory variables of the second step is city-gender specific. The variables for which the test is accepted are considered excluding variables. If such variables exist, the model is nonparametrically identified, as some variables appear only in the first step of the estimations. (In the last section, we discuss the validity of the excluding variables and present the most reliable results.)

Other methodologies could have been used to correct for selection bias (Dahl 2002; Dubin and McFadden 1984). However Bourguignon, Fournier, and Gurgand (2007) show that Lee's methodology performs best on very small samples. For women, the samples are relatively small (about 200 in the formal or informal entrepreneur sector). Bourguignon, Fournier, and Gurgand (2007) conclude that Lee's methodology is more efficient on samples with 50 observations but that the methodology of Dubin and McFadden should be used on samples with 500 observations or more. As the number of observations here lies between these two bounds, we tested both strategies, using Lee's methodology for the main results and a variant of the Dubin and McFadden methodology proposed by Bourguignon, Fournier, and Gurgand (2007) as a robustness check.

Predicting the Share of Each Sector

From the earnings function estimation, we compute a potential income w_{is}^* for each individual in each sector. We add to the mean predicted income a random term, $\hat{u}_{is}$, drawn from the estimated distribution of the residuals ($N(0, \hat{\sigma}_s^2)$). We then match each individual is with the sector that yields the highest potential income, $S_i^* = \arg\max_s \{w_{is}^* + \hat{u}_{is}\}$, and calculate the share of workers predicted in each sector. To obtain a confidence interval, we compute those shares with 20 drawings of random terms and 200 different sets of parameters. The different parameter sets are obtained by bootstrapping the observation sample. We then compare observed shares and simulated confidence intervals. If, for example, the formal sector share is outside its confidence interval (probably smaller than the prediction), we conclude that the labor market is segmented.

We adopt the following restrictive assumption: we consider that utility depends only on income. This restrictive assumption, which is standard in the literature on segmentation, results from the lack of adequate data to account for nonmonetary determinants of preferences.

Disaggregating the Informal Sector and Descriptive Statistics

The data are taken from Phase 1 of the 1-2-3 surveys conducted in the French-speaking countries of the WAEMU zone. These data allow the precise identification of the employment sector of the surveyed individuals. For people who work in the informal sector, it is also possible to distinguish between wage workers, self-employed workers working alone, and informal employers (the head of an independent production unit with at least one worker). We explain below the identification criteria in the informal sector and provide the main descriptive statistics.

Sorting informal sector workers between an upper and a lower segment is tricky. The underlying idea is that some informal sector workers benefit greatly from informality and thus belong to an upper segment. We assume that informal firm managers who employ at least one person (paid or unpaid) benefit from informality. They do not have to provide social security coverage or formal employment contracts, they are not required to pay the minimum wage, and they can hire and fire employees whenever they need to.

There are at least two other ways of dividing the informal sector. A more restrictive definition of the upper segment would include only employers of paid workers. Doing so reduces the sample too much, however, as employers of paid workers represent less than 10 percent of the labor force. A less restrictive definition would allocate self-employed workers with no employees to the upper segment. This solution is less appealing, as the advantage of informality is lower for such workers than it is for people with employees. Moreover, the studies by De Mel, McKenzie, and Woodruff (2008) and Parga and Mondragn-Vlez (2008) lend support for excluding self-employed workers from the upper segment. Based on Colombian data, Parga and Mondragn-Vlez (2008) conclude that employers (defined as business owners) differ from self-employed workers (who work for themselves). They find an earnings premium for employers (over wage workers) but not for self-employed workers. They also suggest that self-employment does not lead to entrepreneurship. Based on data from Sri Lanka, De Mel, McKenzie, and Woodruff (2008) show that self-employed workers are closer to wage workers than to employers. One of our robustness checks is to modify the definition of the upper segment by adding self-employed workers. The results change dramatically, suggesting that employers and self-employed workers are too different to be pooled. This test provides additional justification for including only employers in the upper informal sector segment.

The classification can be summed up as follows:

1. Formal sector: civil servants and employees and owners of registered firms
2. Informal sector: employees and owners of unregistered firms (or associations)
   - upper informal sector segment (informal employers sector): own-account workers employing at least one other person (paid or unpaid)
   - lower informal sector segment (informal workers sector): informal sector workers and self-employed workers working alone
3. Inactive sector: people out of the labor force or unemployed.

Table 6.1 shows the distribution of men and women across sectors in each city.

The most striking fact about urban labor markets in the WAEMU countries is the gap between mean incomes in the formal and informal sectors, especially for women. The distribution for informal employers lies between the distributions of the formal sector and the informal workers sector. As an example, figure 6.1 displays the density distribution of earnings in Cotonou.[6]

Table 6.2 presents summary statistics on individual characteristics for Cotonou. As expected, workers' abilities explain much of the income gap across sectors. Relative to workers in other sectors, workers in the formal sector are more educated and are more likely to have fathers who worked in the formal sector and had more education. Formal workers also are more likely to practice the dominant religion (Catholicism in Cotonou). Women in the formal sector also have fewer young children at home.

Table 6.1 Distribution of Labor Force across Sectors in Seven Cities in West Africa, by Gender, 2001/02
(percent)

Gender/sector	Abidjan	Bamako	Cotonou	Dakar	Lomé	Niamey	Ouagadougou
Men							
Inactive	31	30	30	30	36	37	33
Formal workers	24	22	20	19	19	21	22
Informal workers	34	34	35	37	34	33	32
Informal sector employer	11	14	14	14	10	9	13
Women							
Inactive	42	49	31	30	60	68	52
Formal workers	7	5	7	5	6	6	8
Informal workers	43	40	51	52	31	21	34
Informal employer	8	5	11	12	4	5	6

Sources: Based on Phase 1 of the 1-2-3 surveys of selected cities in the West African Economic and Monetary Union (WAEMU) conducted in 2001/02 by the Observatoire économique et statistique d'Afrique Subsaharienne (AFRISTAT); Développement, Institutions et Mondialisation (DIAL); and national statistics institutes.
Note: Figures are for working individuals 15–65.

Figure 6.1 Hourly Wage Densities of Men and Women in Cotonou, by Sector, 2001/02

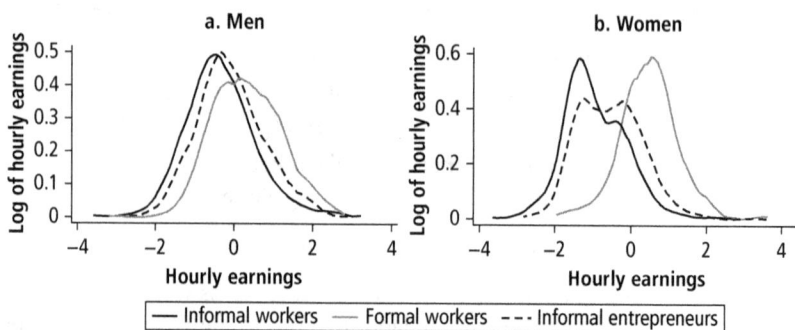

Sources: Based on Phase 1 of the 1-2-3 surveys of selected cities (see table 6.1 for details).

Table 6.2 Summary Statistics on Men and Women in Cotonou, by Sector, 2001/02
(percent, except where otherwise indicated)

Variable	Inactive sector	Formal sector	Informal sector Employers	Informal sector Workers
Men				
Hourly income (1,000 CFAF)	n.a.	2.08	1.46	1.16
Age (years)	26	38	36	30
Education (years)	9.43	11.29	6.65	5.78
Writes and reads French	94	94	78	70
Writes and reads other language	48	47	24	22
Belongs to dominant religion	69	71	59	58
Belongs to dominant ethnic group	59	61	55	57
Inactive father	23	26	26	25
Father worked in informal sector	34	35	48	47
Father worked in formal sector	42	40	27	28
Father's education (years)	6.77	4.84	3.05	3.33
Household nonlabor income (1,000 CFAF a month)	63.1	34.2	12.2	11.8
Women				
Hourly income (1,000 CFAF)	n.a.	1.87	0.81	0.52
Age (years)	28	37	39	31
Education (years)	6.61	11.54	3.99	3.32
Writes and reads French	72	95	51	44
Writes and reads other language	33	60	13	10
Belongs to dominant religion	68	78	66	64

(continued next page)

Table 6.2 (continued)

Variable	Inactive sector	Formal sector	Informal sector Employers	Workers
Belongs to dominant ethnic group	58	68	55	59
Inactive father	21	21	25	25
Father worked in informal sector	40	23	43	51
Father worked in formal sector	40	56	32	23
Father's education (years)	5.69	7.27	3.43	2.93
Household nonlabor income (1,000 CFAF a month)	62,400	12,400	30,800	26,500
Children less than 1 year	0.15	0.15	0.13	0.18
Children 1–3	0.14	0.12	0.16	0.17
Children 4–9	0.51	0.48	0.55	0.62
Women 13 or older	2.57	2.21	2.31	2.32

Sources: Based on Phase 1 of the 1-2-3 surveys of selected cities (see table 6.1 for details).
Note: Figures are for individuals 15–65. n.a. = not applicable.

More education may contribute to higher income and thus explain a large part of the income gap between sectors. These differences are observed for both men and women, but they are larger for women, probably because their participation rate in the labor market is lower and the selection process is more stringent than it is for men.

Econometric Results

We first apply our methodology without dividing the informal sector into segments, in order to obtain a benchmark for our full four-sector model. People are allocated to the inactive, formal, or informal sectors. We present only the final results: the share of people predicted by the model in the formal sector. The steps of the estimation (estimation of a sector choice model, estimation of earnings functions) are detailed in the section on the model with four sectors.

The Three-Sector Model
We match individuals to the sector that is most lucrative for them in order to predict the size of the formal sector. We compute the 2.5 percentile and the 97.5 percentile of the predicted size in order to obtain the 95 percent confidence interval (in brackets in table 6.3). We then check whether the observed shares fall within the confidence interval.[7]

None of the observed values falls within the 95 percent confidence interval, indicating that the labor market is segmented and formal jobs are rationed in all cities. If active people worked in the sector in which they would earn the

Table 6.3 Observed and Predicted Shares of Men and Women Working in Formal and Informal Sectors in Seven Cities in West Africa, 2001/02
(percent)

Gender/sector	Abidjan	Bamako	Cotonou	Dakar	Lomé	Niamey	Ouagadougou
Men							
Formal sector	35 [60–67]	32 [54–62]	29 [43–51]	30 [57–66]	28 [48–60]	33 [56–66]	32 [66–74]
Informal sector	65 [33–40]	68 [38–46]	71 [49–57]	70 [34–42]	72 [40–52]	67 [34–44]	68 [26–34]
Women							
Formal sector	12 [52–80]	11 [24–79]	10 [66–88]	14 [47–77]	8 [48–83]	19 [47–85]	16 [78–92]
Informal sector	88 [20–48]	89 [21–76]	90 [12–34]	86 [23–53]	92 [17–52]	81 [15–53]	84 [8–22]

Sources: Based on Phase 1 of the 1-2-3 surveys of selected cities (see table 6.1 for details).
Note: Figures are for individuals 15–65. Figures in brackets are 95 percent confidence intervals.

highest income, they would work mainly in the formal sector. In fact, most men and women work in the informal sector. For all cities, the confidence intervals are smaller for men than women. Relevant determinants of both earnings and sector choice are harder to identify for women. Consequently, estimations for men are more accurate.

The Four-Sector Model

Some authors believe that the informal sector consists of two distinct segments: disadvantaged workers and prosperous employers. If this is the case, agglomerating the two segments is misleading. For instance, if the nonemployers segment of the informal sector is a kind of subsistence sector, the predicted size of the overall informal sector will be relatively small even if informal entrepreneurship is very lucrative. In this case, pooling employers and nonemployers may underestimate the attractiveness of entrepreneurship. In what follows, we show the different steps in the estimation for our model with four sectors (inactivity, formal, informal sector workers, and informal employers).

Tables 6.4 and 6.5 show the sector choice estimations for men and women. The reference category is informal sector workers. Concerning age and education, the results are relatively consistent with what has been reported in the literature. The older a worker is, the more likely he or she is to belong to the formal or informal employers sector. Age has a significant impact on sector choice. Young people are more likely to be inactive, probably because many of them are looking for their first job. After entering the labor market, young people have a greater probability of working in the informal workers sector than in the formal sector or the informal employer sector. This finding suggests that the informal workers sector is a waiting sector before entry into a more desirable sector.

The number of years of education increases the probability of accessing the formal sector or remaining inactive. It does not seem to affect the probability of being an informal employer (rather than working in the informal worker

Table 6.4 Sector Allocation Equation Results for Men in Seven Cities in West Africa, 2001/02

Variable	Abidjan	Bamako	Cotonou	Dakar	Lomé	Niamey	Ouagadougou
Inactive versus informal workers							
Age (years)	−0.356***	−0.370***	−0.557***	−0.235***	−0.407***	−0.311***	−0.241***
Age squared	0.005***	0.005***	0.007***	0.003***	0.006***	0.004***	0.003***
Education (years)	0.188***	0.143***	0.234***	0.127***	0.148***	0.143***	0.169***
Reads and writes French	−0.168	0.216	0.374**	0.196	0.211	−0.261*	−0.034
Reads and writes another language	0.342***	0.132	0.295**	0.407***	0.192	0.416***	0.485***
Father worked in informal sector	−0.087	−0.091	0.118	−0.334***	−0.394***	−0.267**	−0.300***
Father worked in formal sector	0.124	0.081	−0.078	0.218	−0.015	0.364**	−0.071
Father's education (years)	0.044***	0.032**	0.062***	0.026***	0.011	−0.002	0.018
Belongs to dominant religion	−0.391***	0.423	0.002	−0.639***	0.108	0.249	−0.060
Belongs to dominant ethnic group	0.195	−0.215	−0.042	0.019	−0.018	0.004	−0.112
Migrant	−0.271**	−0.160	−0.127	−0.275**	−0.301***	−0.227**	−0.082
Household nonlabor income	0.085***	0.057***	0.079***	0.049***	0.053***	0.053***	0.04***
Intercept	4.191***	4.429***	5.768***	3.053***	4.728***	4.233***	2.904***
Formal employees versus informal workers							
Age (years)	0.303***	0.275***	0.296***	0.309***	0.227***	0.292***	0.384***
Age squared	−0.003***	−0.003***	−0.003***	−0.003***	−0.002***	−0.003***	−0.004***
Education (years)	0.169***	0.169***	0.229***	0.163***	0.169***	0.176***	0.22***
Reads and writes French	0.314*	0.037	0.21	0.522***	0.165	0.385***	0.179
Reads and writes another language	−0.009	0.315**	−0.018	0.081	0.163	0.26*	0.334**
Father worked in informal sector	0.403***	0.089	−0.089	−0.123	−0.054	−0.059	−0.347***
Father worked in formal sector	0.398**	0.376**	−0.004	0.441***	0.049	0.326*	−0.168

(continued next page)

Table 6.4 (continued)

Variable	Abidjan	Bamako	Cotonou	Dakar	Lomé	Niamey	Ouagadougou
Father's education (years)	0.024*	0.013	0.038***	0.028***	-0.002	0.008	-0.002
Belongs to dominant religion	-0.301**	0.166	0.34***	-0.239	0.326***	1.464***	-0.256**
Belongs to dominant ethnic group	0.213	0.021	-3.000	-0.090	-0.129	0.138	-0.142
Migrant	0.025	-0.041	0.405***	0.033	0.393***	-0.032	0.297**
Household nonlabor income	0.017	-0.026	-0.017	0.002	-0.022	-0.002	0.006
Intercept	-8.359***	-7.581***	-9.708***	-8.557***	-7.842***	-9.504***	-9.222***
Informal employers versus informal workers							
Age (years)	0.211***	0.207***	0.261***	0.247***	0.113***	0.116***	0.302***
Age squared	-0.002***	-0.002***	-0.003***	-0.003***	-0.001*	-7*	-0.003***
Education (years)	0.009	-0.033	0.032*	-0.027	0.034*	-0.007	-0.030
Reads and writes French	0.279	0.449**	0.229	0.235	0.132	0.252	0.547***
Reads and writes another language	0.333**	0.216	-0.054	0.289*	0.201	0.339**	0.247
Father worked in informal sector	0.139	-0.094	0.028	-0.106	0.271*	0.125	-0.457***
Father worked in formal sector	0.457**	-0.217	-0.100	-0.078	0.058	-0.090	-0.564***
Father's education (years)	-0.012	0.042***	0.008	0.006	-0.004	0.09	0.04**
Belongs to dominant religion	0.043	0.057	0.071	-0.017	-0.220*	0.361	0.210*
Belongs to dominant ethnic group	-0.138	0.053	-0.089	0.161	-0.075	-0.178	0.443***
Migrant	-0.080	-0.309**	0.174	-0.548***	-0.157	-0.445***	-0.045
Household nonlabor income	-0.024	0.009	-0.005	0.032*	-0.016	-0.028	-0.049**
Intercept	-5.948***	-5.140***	-6.569***	-5.981***	-3.831***	-4.677***	-7.420***
Number of observations	3,606	3,013	3,438	3,179	2,763	3,428	3,787

Sources: Based on Phase 1 of the 1-2-3 surveys of selected cities (see table 6.1 for details).
Note: Figures are for individuals 15–65.
* significant at the 10 percent level, ** significant at the 5 percent level, *** significant at the 1 percent level.

Table 6.5 Sector Allocation Equation Results for Women in Seven Cities in West Africa, 2001/02

Variable	Abidjan	Bamako	Cotonou	Dakar	Lomé	Niamey	Ouagadougou
Inactive versus informal workers							
Age (years)	−0.169***	−0.142***	−0.240***	−0.131***	−0.267***	−0.080***	−0.134***
Age squared	0.243***	0.196***	0.311***	0.17***	0.372***	0.079***	0.179***
Education (years)	0.151***	0.103***	0.178***	0.099***	0.172***	0.111***	0.135***
Reads and writes French	−0.354***	−0.143	−0.181	−0.070	0.036	−0.355**	−0.126
Reads and writes another language	0.628***	0.166	0.507***	0.126	0.238**	0.011	−0.075
Father worked in informal sector	−0.091	−0.065	0.208*	−0.201**	−0.182	−0.023	−0.191**
Father worked in formal sector	−0.102	−0.100	0.209*	0.069	−0.052	−0.364***	−0.130
Father's education (years)	0.035***	0.041***	0.032***	0.02***	0.004	0.035**	0.028**
Belongs to dominant religion	0.055	0.092	−0.138	0.221	0.046	0.849***	0.116
Belongs to dominant ethnic group	−0.069	−0.044	−0.141	0.0005	−0.083	0.273***	−0.304***
Migrant	−0.181**	−0.201**	−0.202**	−0.242***	−0.167*	−0.060	−0.087
Household nonlabor income	0.021**	−0.009	0.031***	0.014	0.007	0.019	0.014
Children less than 1 year	0.47***	0.151**	0.071	0.159	0.393***	0.287***	0.122
Children 1–3	0.122	0.081	0.132	0.099	0.112	0.327***	−0.020
Children 4–9	−0.057	0.027	0.015	0.056	−0.137**	0.075**	0.052
Women 13 or older	0.015	−0.008	−0.032	−0.051***	0.091***	−0.027	−0.027
Intercept	1.887***	2.037***	2.416***	2.423***	2.451***	1.403***	2.406***
Formal employees versus informal workers							
Age (years)	0.396***	0.388***	0.373***	0.339***	0.186***	0.486***	0.464***
Age squared	−0.401***	−0.400***	−0.419***	−0.392***	−0.166***	−0.551***	−0.510***
Education (years)	0.319***	0.443***	0.402***	0.316***	0.315***	0.33***	0.391***
Reads and writes French	0.749**	−0.114	−0.090	−0.322	0.482	1.329***	0.547
Reads and writes another language	0.637***	−0.022	0.663***	0.053	−0.007	0.407*	0.107
Father worked in informal sector	−0.110	0.195	−0.016	0.079	−0.134	−0.350	−0.428*
Father worked in formal sector	−0.160	0.492	0.321	0.278	0.004	−0.433	−0.079
Father's education (years)	0.061***	0.014	0.016	0.016	0.013	0.027	0.030
Belongs to dominant religion	−0.013	0.215	0.165	−0.212	−0.173	1.319***	−0.331*

(continued next page)

Table 6.5 (continued)

Variable	Abidjan	Bamako	Cotonou	Dakar	Lomé	Niamey	Ouagadougou
Belongs to dominant ethnic group	0.370*	0.062	0.353*	-0.073	0.007	0.196	-0.116
Migrant	-0.150	-0.068	0.193	0.016	0.170	0.311	-0.246
Household nonlabor income							
Children less than 1 year	-0.040**	-0.021	0.070	0.004	-0.026	-0.015	-0.007
Children 1–3							
Children 4–9	0.428	0.100	0.172	0.095	0.217	0.308	-0.266
Women 13 or older	-0.645**	-0.308	-0.154	-0.254	0.092	-0.012	-0.016
Intercept	-0.356***	-0.035	-0.136	-0.197*	-0.224	-0.075	-0.057
Informal employers versus informal workers							
Age (years)	0.237***	0.241***	0.239***	0.148***	0.122***	0.28***	0.289***
Age squared	-0.214***	-0.280***	-0.238***	-0.151**	-0.104**	-0.315***	-0.330***
Education (years)	0.030	0.045	0.018	0.053	0.096***	-0.028	0.040
Reads and writes French	0.243	0.083	0.133	-0.195	-0.243	0.091	0.012
Reads and writes another language	0.282	-0.543	0.092	-0.096	0.074	0.136	0.355
Father worked in informal sector	0.065	-0.118	-0.122	0.299	0.224	0.314	0.155
Father worked in formal sector	-0.125	-0.160	0.285*	0.454*	-0.002	0.156	0.407
Father's education (years)	0.029	0.031	0.018	0.0005	-0.016	-0.010	0.003
Belongs to dominant religion	0.169	-0.476	-0.019	-0.317	-0.327***	-0.718**	0.207
Belongs to dominant ethnic group	0.382**	-0.042	-0.255**	-0.098	-0.053	-0.251	-0.206
Migrant	0.089	-0.375**	0.19	-0.408**	0.010	-0.268	-0.392**
Household nonlabor income	-0.050***	0.0009	0.009	0.021	-0.003	-0.003	-0.004
Children less than 1 year	-0.046	0.142	-0.044	-0.094	0.073	0.419**	-0.595***
Children 1–3	0.142	-0.197	0.219	0.452**	-0.008	0.315**	-0.046
Children 4–9	0.010	-0.154*	-0.071	0.023	0.080	-0.010	0.033
Women 13 or older	0.035	0.025	0.065*	0.029	0.201***	-0.003	0.035
Intercept	-7.482***	-5.916***	-6.987***	-5.206***	-4.925***	-6.386***	-7.390***
Number of observations	3,600	3,166	3,724	3,363	3,029	3,757	3,754

Sources: Based on Phase 1 of the 1-2-3 surveys of selected countries (see table 6.1 for details).
Note: Figures are for individuals 15–65.
* significant at the 10 percent level, ** significant at the 5 percent level, *** significant at the 1 percent level.

sector). Educated workers who do not find jobs in the formal sector prefer to stay inactive. Writing and reading French or another language may reinforce the effect of education, although it does not do so in all cities. For men, education in years (Cotonou and Lomé), writing and reading French (Bamako and Ouagadougou), and writing and reading another language (Abidjan, Dakar, and Niamey) have a positive impact on the probability of being an informal employer. Education thus seems to matter, but in a way that is not as clear as it is in the choice between the formal sector and the informal workers sector.

Other explanatory variables in the sector choice model are proxies of household wealth (household nonlabor income); household composition (for women only); and social and family networks captured by variables such as father's occupation, religious and ethnic community, and migrant status. These variables can affect sector choice by increasing the opportunity of working in a sector without necessarily influencing earnings. They are of interest here because they provide evidence that the labor market is not competitive, yield insights on the rationing process, and are necessary for the model to be nonparametrically identified.

In contrast to some other authors, we do not impose a fixed set of exclusion variables. For each city and gender group, we test whether the coefficients of the potential exclusion variables are significant in the earnings equation. If they are, we use the variable as an explanatory variable; if they are not, we use them as exclusion variables.

Several variables affect sector choice but have no influence on earnings:

- Having a father who worked in the formal sector increases the probability of working in the formal sector (relative to the informal workers sector) in four of seven cities (see the results at the bottom of table 6.4). Father's education increases the probability of working in the formal sector in three cities. The probability of working in the formal sector also increases for men belonging to the dominant religious community. This variable is not really discriminatory in most cities, however, as the dominant group represents more than 90 percent of the population.

- Migrant status increases the probability of working in the informal workers sector or the formal sector. This result may hide two different phenomena. Some people migrate because they are transferred to the economic capital (in which case they are most likely employed in a formal firm or the public sector) or because they are in school and then find a job in the formal sector. Others migrate to find better opportunities, but lacking valuable social networks they are unable to access the most profitable sectors.

- Household nonlabor income has a positive effect on the probability of being inactive but not on the probability of becoming an informal employer, except in Dakar, where the positive effect is marginal.

For women, the results are less clear. Belonging to the dominant ethnic group or religious community increases the probability of working in the formal sector. Belonging to a household with children increases the probability of being an informal sector worker. This result can be explained by the fact that the workplace for some informal jobs is the home.

The model is always identified because of the nonlinearity of the correction term in Lee's methodology. However, a nonparametric identification with an exclusion variable is more convincing. Such an identification implies that some variables determine sector choice but not earnings. Such variables always exist for men. The models are less reliable for women, mainly because few women work in some cities and even fewer work in the formal sector. However, we believe it is meaningful to separate men and women in our estimations, because the sector choice and income determinants are not the same, especially with respect to inactivity.

Estimation of Earnings

We estimate earnings using the method proposed by Lee (1983). For each variable in the sector choice equation, we test whether the corresponding coefficients are significantly different from zero. We also report the p-values of the test. If a p-value is greater than 0.05, we add the corresponding variable to the set of explanatory variables. We apply this procedure for each city-gender pair, yielding a set of explanatory variables that is city and gender specific.

Regarding the usual variables of the Mincer equation (experience and education), the returns differ across cities (tables 6.6 and 6.7). However, the general pattern is almost always similar. The returns to experience are positive, significant, and decreasing for formal and informal workers sectors. In the informal employers sector, most of the returns to experience are not statistically significant. The returns to education are almost always significantly positive. These returns are usually higher in the formal sector than in the informal workers sector, and they differ for men and women. For the informal workers sector, the returns to education are greater for men. When significant, migration has a negative impact on earnings in the informal workers sector.

Are Labor Markets Segmented?

We are now able to allocate each individual to the sector that provides him or her with the highest predicted earnings, under the hypothesis that labor markets are competitive and the assumption that only income differences matter in sector choice. We compute earnings for each sector (formal workers, informal workers, informal employers) by adding a random term to the expected value given by the estimated earnings equation. We then allocate individuals to the sector in which their earnings are highest. We repeat this procedure 4,000

Table 6.6 Estimation of Men's Earnings in Seven Cities in West Africa, by Sector, 2001/02

Variable	Abidjan			Bamako			Cotonou			Dakar			Lomé			Niamey			Ouagadougou		
	FW	IW	IE	FW	IW	IE	FW	IW	IE	FW	IW	IE	FW	IW	IE	FW	IW	IE	FW	IW	IE
Experience (years)	0.045***	0.058***	0.108***	0.030*	0.076***	0.069*	0.048***	0.035***	0.015	0.057***	0.074***	0.023	0.035***	0.035***	0.039	0.019	0.061***	0.039	0.029**	0.082***	0.034
Experience^2	-0.025	-0.060***	-0.149***	0.006	-0.083***	-0.080	-0.037	-0.014	0.015	-0.045	-0.091***	-0.008	-0.018	-0.018	-0.032	0.015	-0.056***	-0.032	0.011	-0.112***	-0.019
Education (years)	0.141***	0.100***	0.072***	0.110***	0.099***	0.020	0.115***	0.116***	0.066***	0.095***	0.088***	0.051***	0.152***	0.135***	0.108***	0.116***	0.168***	0.057***	0.138***	0.080***	0.095***
Reads and writes French	-0.285***	-0.051	-0.189	-0.051	-0.136	0.228	-0.207	-0.044	-0.005	-0.041	-0.132	0.098	-0.169	-0.036	-0.178*	0.083	-0.450***	-0.181	-0.081	-0.095	-0.123
Reads and writes another language	0.107**	0.172**	0.075	0.116	0.160	0.465***	0.117**	0.157**	0.120	0.177**	0.046	0.151				0.187**	-0.029	-0.066	0.137**	0.063	0.162
Father worked in informal sector																			-0.051	0.141*	-0.034
Father worked in formal sector																			0.099*	0.287	0.159
Father's education				0.014**	0.013	0.005															
Belongs to dominant religion	0.026	0.147	0.145																		
Belongs to dominant ethnic group	0.059	0.228	0.102							0.125**	-0.010	-0.168									
Migrant	-0.014	-0.129*	-0.047										-0.035	-0.161*	-0.053	0.018	0.030	0.247**	0.047	0.117	-0.125
Household nonlabor income													0.029	0.019	0.010	0.020**	0.031**	-0.004***	0.016*	-0.007	0.027*
Lee's correction term	-0.126	0.117	0.371	-0.378*	0.146	0.185	0.086	0.282	0.103	-0.244	-0.037	-0.118	-0.103	0.504*	-0.234	-0.517***	0.277	0.191	-0.534***	-0.573***	-0.236
Father's sector test	1	0.382	0.431	0.981	0.316	0.053	0.312	0.543	0.284	0.925	0.703	0.473	0.704	0.409	0.340	0.133	0.962	0.676			
Father's education test	0.21	0.908	0.747				0.990	0.787	0.999	0.618	0.890	0.950	0.758	0.779	0.656	0.556	0.979	0.979			
Household nonlabor income test	0.783	0.460	0.235	0.145	0.070	0.810	0.673	0.292	0.451	0.232	0.499	0.337									
Religion test				0.524	0.646	0.092	0.149	0.699	0.118	0.157	0.300	0.929	0.316	0.466	0.366	0.416	0.162	0.532	0.175	0.127	0.829
Ethnic group test				0.116	0.802	0.337	0.256	0.361	0.582				0.642	0.455	0.792	0.204	0.328	0.577	0.466	0.295	0.891
Migrant test				0.333	0.636	0.311	0.984	0.573	0.470	0.444	0.355	0.735									
Number of observations	864	1,061	378	673	947	429	679	925	487	590	791	314	534	844	375	727	976	312	808	1,003	478

Sources: Based on Phase 1 of the 1-2-3 surveys of selected cities (see table 6.1 for details).
Note: Figures are for individuals 15–65. FW = formal worker; IW = informal worker; IE = informal employer.

211

Table 6.7 Estimation of Women's Earnings in Seven Cities in West Africa, by Sector, 2001/02

Variable	Abidjan FW	Abidjan IW	Abidjan IE	Bamako FW	Bamako IW	Bamako IE	Cotonou FW	Cotonou IW	Cotonou IE	Dakar FW	Dakar IW	Dakar IE	Lomé FW	Lomé IW	Lomé IE	Niamey FW	Niamey IW	Niamey IE	Ouagadougou FW	Ouagadougou IW	Ouagadougou IE
Experience (years)	0.022	0.045***	0.003	0.108***	0.063***	0.016	-0.010	0.037***	0.041	0.055**	0.067***	0.101**	0.035	0.030***	0.042	0.055**	0.050***	-0.062	0.043**	0.075***	0.130**
Experience²	0.015	-0.047***	0.021	-0.144**	-0.081***	-0.025	0.083**	-0.055***	-0.054	-0.084	-0.085***	-0.116	0.012	-0.026	-0.040	-0.044	-0.052**	0.078	-0.022	-0.106***	-0.220***
Education (years)	0.176***	0.093***	0.034	0.172***	0.042**	0.051*	0.096***	0.027	0.040**	0.103***	0.048***	0.059*	0.147***	0.054***	0.099***	0.130***	0.144***	-0.014	0.107***	0.096***	0.112**
Reads and writes French	-0.302	-0.115	0.114	-0.345	0.291**	-0.202	0.213	0.025	-0.058	0.292	0.099	0.141	0.292	-0.007	-0.006	0.352	-0.416***	-0.050	0.534***	-0.159	-0.582**
Reads and writes another language	0.240**	0.324***	0.172	0.026	0.236*	0.167	0.142	-0.143	-0.130	-0.008	0.013	-0.685***	0.167	0.054	0.016	0.004	0.20	-0.301	0.144	0.123	0.267
Father worked in informal sector							-0.113	-0.047	-0.028	0.178	0.016	0.130							0.041	0.178***	0.351**
Father worked in formal sector							-0.035	-0.078	0.240*	0.318	-0.031	0.053							0.017	0.213**	-0.001
Father's education													0.015	0.018	-0.020						
Women 13 and older	0.013	-0.035***	-0.055*	-0.021	-0.035**	0.037	-0.007	-0.031**	0.074**				-0.087***	-0.012	0.008						
Children less than 1 year																0.012	-0.086	-0.182	0.238**	-0.117**	-0.008
Children 1–3																0.189**	0.079	0.192	0.076	-0.0007	0.117
Children 4–9																0.009	-0.057*	-0.126	0.086*	-0.025	-0.031
Belongs to dominant religion	0.047	0.039	-0.244**	-0.098	0.077	1.138**													0.076	0.124**	-0.319*

Belongs to dominant ethnic group				0.021	-0.120**	-0.124				0.127	0.132	0.228				0.011		0.363**			
Migrant	-0.055	-0.112**	-0.017	-0.005	-0.266***	-0.048				0.319**	-0.134*	-0.108					-0.043				
Household nonlabor income				-0.006	-0.005	-0.038**															
Lee's correction term	-0.302	0.191	0.003	0.387	-0.531	0.097	-0.297	-0.605***	0.160	0.089	-0.289	1.145	-0.299	0.134	-0.035	0.149	-0.044	-0.421	-0.490**	-0.745***	2.082***
Father's sector test	0.904	0.872	0.604	0.278	0.996	0.36	0.176	0.891		0.967	0.780	0.996	0.512	0.554	0.616	0.985	0.675	0.976	0.616	0.997	0.981
Father's education test	0.787	0.983	1		0.874	0.712		0.442	0.410	0.867	0.449	0.638		0.716		0.640	0.131	0.920	0.874	0.974	0.886
Children test	0.575	0.470	0.629	0.709	0.881	0.447	0.152	0.807					0.155		0.114		0.084	0.120			
Women test										0.800	0.285	0.446				0.88					
Household nonlabor income test	0.676	0.486	0.755				0.697	0.688	0.130	0.996	0.668	0.309	0.442	0.849	0.588	0.06	0.295	0.984	0.947	0.327	0.861
Religion test							0.708	0.636	0.548	0.576	0.458	0.667	0.461	0.919	0.297	0.066	0.130	0.612			
Ethnic group test	0.915	0.890	0.690				0.147	0.356	0.617				0.670	0.309	0.740				0.155	0.171	0.220
Migrant test							0.390	0.780	0.274				0.441	0.317	0.351	0.154	0.624	0.230	0.875	0.170	0.945
Number of observations	1,299	252	271	174	1,232	156	254	1,493	396	177	939	134	160	1,344	376	224	686	186	278	1,115	215

Sources: Based on Phase 1 of the 1-2-3 surveys of selected cities (see table 6.1 for details).

Note: Figures are for individuals 15–65. FW= formal worker; IW = informal worker; IE = informal employer.

times in order to account for the multistep estimation procedure and to ensure that the results do not depend on a particular draw of the residuals. For each allocation, we compute the share of the three sectors. For each sector, we then calculate the mean share and the 95 percent confidence interval. We then check whether the observed shares fall within the confidence interval of the predicted shares. If they do not, we reject the competitive assumption.

For men, the overall picture is fairly clear: labor markets are segmented (table 6.8). The formal sector and the informal employers sector appear to be sectors of choice: except for Cotonou, the observed shares are smaller than the predicted and fall outside the confidence interval. In contrast, the observed sizes of the informal workers sector are about twice the predicted sizes and fall outside the confidence interval. These figures mean that if people were free to enter the sector that provides them with the highest income, the share of the informal workers sector would be smaller.

For women, the observed size of the informal workers sector (about 75 percent) is always larger than the upper bound of the confidence interval (which never exceeds 35 percent), and the employment share of the formal sector is below the predicted one. The observed size of the informal employers sector falls within the confidence interval in three of seven cities (Lomé, Niamey, and Ouagadougou). The confidence intervals are very large for women, because most of the earnings estimations are based on very small samples.

To sum up, the labor markets in all seven cities are segmented. The informal sector workers segment is larger than it would be in a competitive labor market, because jobs in both the formal and informal employers sector are rationed. For

Table 6.8 Simulation Results of Four-Sector Model of Sector Allocation in Seven Cities in West Africa, 2001/02
(percent)

Gender/sector	Abidjan	Bamako	Cotonou	Dakar	Lomé	Niamey	Ouagadougou
Men							
Formal workers	35 [43, 48]	32 [33, 44]	**29** [25, 34]	30 [36, 44]	28 [31, 41]	33 [38, 48]	32 [42, 55]
Informal workers	49 [22, 27]	48 [22, 29]	51 [29, 36]	54 [16, 21]	53 [24, 31]	52 [22, 30]	49 [14, 19]
Informal employers	15 [27, 32]	20 [32, 39]	21 [36, 41]	16 [37, 44]	19 [33, 40]	14 [28, 37]	19 [28, 44]
Women							
Formal workers	12 [32, 64]	11 [15, 66]	10 [46, 78]	14 [29, 59]	8 [34, 74]	19 [30, 74]	16 [53, 84]
Informal workers	74 [13, 28]	79 [14, 35]	74 [7, 19]	76 [15, 29]	75 [10, 29]	66 [11, 28]	72 [5, 15]
Informal employers	14 [22, 43]	10 [20, 52]	**16** [15, 37]	10 [26, 45]	**18** [16, 38]	**16** [14, 44]	**12** [10, 33]

Sources: Based on Phase 1 of the 1-2-3 surveys of selected cities (see table 6.1 for details).
Note: Figures are for individuals 15–65. Figures in brackets are 95 percent confidence intervals of the predicted share under the competitive model assumptions. Results falling within the confidence interval are in bold.

women, in some cities (Abidjan, Dakar, and Lomé), only formal jobs seem to be rationed.

How Robust are the Results?

We provide three robustness checks. We first compute our results with another form for the correction terms in the earnings equation estimation. Instead of using the empirical strategy developed by Lee (1983), we use the strategy developed by Dubin and McFadden (1984).

For men, the broad picture of segmentation remains unchanged (table 6.9). For each city, the observed share of informal sector workers lies outside the confidence interval, and the observed share of informal employers is smaller than predicted. However, the formal sector appears less attractive than previously. In four of seven cities (Abidjan, Bamako, Cotonou, and Niamey), the observed share of formal workers is consistent with the predictions of our model. When properly taken into account, the informal employers sector reduces the attractiveness of the formal sector. With the Dubin and McFadden strategy, in a three-sector model, the formal sector is always smaller than predicted (as with Lee's strategy). With a four-sector model, however, this conclusion is challenged. The most rationed sector becomes the informal employers sector. For women, the results are perfectly robust to the empirical strategy.

The second assumption we want to relax is the independence of random terms across sectors, which may represent unobserved skills of individuals in

Table 6.9 Simulation Results of Sector Allocation in Seven Cities in West Africa Using the Dubin and McFadden Method, 2001/02

Gender/ model/sector	Abidjan	Bamako	Cotonou	Dakar	Lomé	Niamey	Ouagadougou
Men, four-sector model							
Formal workers	**35** [33, 46]	**32** [28, 42]	**29** [23, 32]	30 [32, 45]	28 [30, 39]	**33** [33, 48]	32 [41, 55]
Informal workers	49 [24, 34]	48 [24, 32]	51 [31, 40]	54 [16, 24]	53 [24, 30]	52 [21, 30]	49 [13, 23]
Informal employers	15 [26, 37]	20 [33, 43]	21 [32, 42]	16 [36, 46]	19 [35, 41]	14 [25, 40]	19 [29, 40]
Men, three-sector model							
Formal workers	35 [55, 68]	32 [43, 60]	29 [41, 53]	30 [54, 67]	28 [46, 59]	33 [51, 66]	32 [63, 75]
Informal workers	65 [32, 45]	68 [39, 57]	71 [47, 59]	70 [33, 46]	72 [41, 54]	67 [34, 48]	68 [25, 37]
Women, four-sector model							
Formal workers	12 [28, 62]	11 [12, 53]	10 [38, 83]	14 [23, 65]	8 [28, 73]	19 [33, 79]	16 [46, 86]
Informal workers	74 [13, 30]	79 [17, 38]	74 [6, 24]	76 [13, 34]	75 [11, 32]	66 [10, 28]	72 [5, 20]
Informal employers	14 [25, 48]	10 [28, 57]	**16** [10, 40]	10 [21, 46]	**18** [15, 44]	**16** [10, 41]	**12** [8, 34]

Sources: Based on Phase 1 of the 1-2-3 surveys of selected cities (see table 6.1 for details).
Note: Figures are for individuals 15–65. Figures in brackets are 95 percent confidence intervals of the predicted share under the competitive model assumptions. Results falling within the confidence interval are in bold.

each sector. We previously assumed that unobserved skills were not correlated across sectors. This assumption may be too strong, as some abilities may be valuable in all sectors.

To test the robustness of our results to this assumption, we now assume that random terms are perfectly correlated across sectors. If the random term increases potential earnings in the formal sector, it will also positively affect potential earnings of informal employers and informal sector workers. The results do not dramatically change with this extreme assumption (table 6.10). Regarding men, the formal sector remains significantly smaller and the informal workers sector larger than predicted. The informal employers sector is smaller than predicted in three of seven cities; in four cities, it lies within the confidence interval. As a consequence, the overall picture is still segmentation, but the insufficient size of the informal employers sector may be questioned in some cities (Abidjan, Bamako, Niamey, and Ouagadougou). However, the assumption of perfect correlation is extreme, and the fact that the results are fully robust for some cities is striking.

For women, the informal workers sector remains larger and the formal sector significantly smaller than predicted in all cities; the size of the employers sector falls within the confidence interval. The results are less accurate than the results obtained with other models (independent random terms, Dubin and McFadden methods). The largest confidence interval is [13, 97] for the formal sector in Bamako. These findings reinforce the fact that the results for women are less reliable than the results for men.

Table 6.10 Observed and Predicted Sector Shares in Seven Cities in West Africa When Random Terms Are Positively Correlated, 2001/02
(percent)

Gender/sector	Abidjan	Bamako	Cotonou	Dakar	Lomé	Niamey	Ouagadougou
Men							
Formal workers	35 [60, 83]	32 [38, 73]	**29** [9, 36]	30 [39, 72]	28 [37, 77]	33 [41, 82]	32 [61, 96]
Informal workers	49 [0, 10]	48 [0, 19]	51 [0, 35]	54 [0, 2]	53 [0, 17]	52 [1, 19]	49 [0, 4]
Informal employers	**15** [14, 37]	**20** [20, 55]	21 [53, 70]	16 [28, 60]	19 [23, 54]	**14** [6, 48]	**19** [3, 38]
Women							
Formal workers	12 [36, 96]	11 [13, 97]	10 [55, 100]	14 [25, 90]	8 [40, 100]	19 [29, 97]	16 [66, 100]
Informal workers	74 [0, 10]	79 [0, 18]	74 [0, 7]	76 [0, 17]	75 [0, 19]	66 [0, 17]	72 [0, 2]
Informal employers	**14** [4, 59]	**10** [2, 74]	**16** [0, 43]	**10** [10, 63]	**18** [0, 51]	**16** [0, 52]	**12** [0, 33]

Sources: Based on Phase 1 of the 1-2-3 surveys of selected cities (see table 6.1 for details).
Note: Figures are for individuals 15–65. Figures in brackets are 95 percent confidence intervals of the predicted share under the competitive model assumptions. Results falling within the confidence interval are in bold.

For women, all tests find evidence of a segmented labor market. However, small sample sizes cast some doubt on the reliability of the results. For men, all labor markets are also segmented. The overly large informal workers sector is robust to all specifications. However, except in Dakar and Lomé, the tests are not consistent, and all of them do not conclude that both the formal sector and the informal employers sector are too small. Because of the size of the samples and following Bourguignon, Fournier, and Gurgand (2007), the preferred test is the one based on the Dubin and McFadden strategy with uncorrelated residuals (see table 6.9). This test supports the hypothesis that the informal employer sector would be larger in a competitive labor market but rejects the hypothesis that formal jobs are rationed for some cities.

The last robustness check consists of modifying the definition of the informal employers sector. We previously argued that self-employed workers working alone should be excluded from that sector, because they benefit less from informality than people who employ others (employers and self-account workers employing at least one person). Here we modify the definition of the informal employers sector by including self-employed workers working alone (table 6.11). Pooling men and women, the results are striking. For all city-gender couple (except men in Lomé), the observed size of the newly defined informal employer sector lies above the upper bound of the confidence interval. The informal employer sector appears far less attractive than previously. Self-employed workers working alone represent the majority of the sector. These

Table 6.11 Observed and Predicted Sector Shares in Seven Cities in West Africa When Definition of Informal Employers Sector Is Broadened, 2001/02
(percent)

Gender/sector	Abidjan	Bamako	Cotonou	Dakar	Lomé	Niamey	Ouagadougou
Men							
Formal workers	35 [42, 50]	32 [36, 45]	**29** [27, 34]	28 [34, 45]	30 [40, 50]	33 [39, 50]	32 [49, 59]
Informal workers	30 [22, 28]	19 [24, 31]	23 [29, 34]	**25** [24, 31]	34 [19, 24]	**28** [21, 28]	29 [16, 21]
Informal employers	35 [26, 32]	49 [29, 36]	48 [35, 40]	48 [30, 37]	**36** [30, 38]	39 [26, 36]	39 [23, 32]
Women							
Formal workers	12 [37, 71]	11 [18, 73]	10 [49, 81]	14 [32, 63]	8 [36, 72]	19 [33, 78]	16 [66, 88]
Informal workers	31 [12, 28]	**15** [12, 38]	21 [9, 25]	31 [16, 30]	**20** [13, 30]	**20** [12, 32]	22 [6, 17]
Informal employers	57 [16, 35]	74 [14, 45]	68 [10, 27]	55 [21, 39]	73 [14, 34]	62 [10, 35]	62 [5, 18]

Sources: Based on Phase 1 of the 1-2-3 surveys of selected cities (see table 6.1 for details).
Note: Figures are for individuals 15–65. Figures in brackets are 95 percent confidence intervals of the predicted share under the competitive model assumptions. Results falling within the confidence interval are in bold.

results thus confirm that self-employed workers working alone should be allocated to the lower segment of the informal sector. If self-employment status were as attractive as employer status, adding self-employed workers working alone to the definition of entrepreneurs would not have changed the results.

Conclusion

This chapter provides a test for labor market segmentation based on the idea that the informal sector should be divided into two subsectors. In our set-up, the lower informal sector consists of informal sector dependent workers and self-employed workers working alone; the upper sector comprises informal employers. Applying our test to seven cities in WAEMU, separately for men and women, leads to the conclusion that the labor market is segmented for the 14 city-gender groups examined.

The lower informal sector is always larger than it would have been in a competitive labor market. This conclusion is remarkably robust to different specifications. The finding is particularly important because few studies have been conducted in West Africa, where labor markets are very different from those in Latin America or Asia, the site of most studies.

Within the informal sector, pooling self-employed workers working alone with employees rather than employers makes sense, as only entrepreneurship appears to be a desirable situation in this sector. The policy implications are clear: efforts to reduce poverty in the informal sector should target both employees and self-employed workers working alone; they should not target informal employers.

We test three cases regarding the rationing process. Where the informal sector is not divided, the labor market is segmented if formal sector jobs are rationed. In our set-up, segmentation means that formal jobs are rationed, that informal employers are rationed, or both. If formal jobs are rationed, a policy that aims to reduce labor costs will probably be efficient. If the employers sector is rationed, a more meaningful approach will be to improve access to capital, management skills, and accounting literacy.

Notes

1. Although Abidjan and Cotonou are not administrative capitals, we refer to them as capitals because they are the most important economic centers in their countries (Cotonou is also the seat of government).
2. Rationing can occur because of the burden of formal labor market regulations, which impose high minimum wages and high taxes. Alternatively, high wages paid by formal employers may prevent their employees from quitting their job—the so-called efficiency wage hypothesis (Krebs and Maloney 1999).

3. Most studies examine India (Banerjee 1983); Latin America (Pratap and Quintin 2006; Pagès and Stampini 2007); or South Africa (Badaoui, Strobl, and Walsh 2008).

4. If all observed and simulated shares are equal, our test is inconclusive. Indeed, our model could reproduce the observed shares by allocating a large share of the informal sector worker segment to the informal employers segment or vice versa. In this case, the observed shares would be consistent with a competitive labor market, but the way workers are allocated to each sector would not. Fortunately, this never happens in our results: in all cases, at least one observed share lies outside its simulated confidence interval.

5. We are aware that the result of our test procedure may be path dependent, but as there is no natural order between the variables, we did not see a preferable procedure.

6. Results for other countries, available in the full version of this chapter (http://www .dial.ird.fr/publications), are similar.

7. These shares are different from the ones in table 6.1, because the figures in table 6.1 are shares of the labor force, not the population as a whole.

References

Alderman, H., and V. Kozel. 1989. "Formal and Informal Sector Wage Determination in Urban Low-Income Neighborhoods in Pakistan." Paper 65, World Bank Living Standards Measurement, Washington, DC.

Azevedo, J. P. 2005. "An Investigation of the Labour Market Earnings in Deprived Areas: A Test of Labour Market Segmentation in the Slums." In *Proceedings of the 33th Brazilian Economics Meeting*, Brazilian Association of Graduate Programs in Economics, Natal, Brazil.

Badaoui, E., E. Strobl, and F. Walsh. 2008. "Is There an Informal Employment Wage Penalty? Evidence from South Africa." *Economic Development and Cultural Change* 56 (3): 683–710.

Banerjee, B. 1983. "The Role of the Informal Sector in the Migration Process: A Test of Probabilistic Migration Models, and Labour Market Segmentation for India." *Oxford Economic Papers* 35 (3): 399–422.

Bourguignon, F., M. Fournier, and M. Gurgand. 2007. "Selection Bias Correction Based on the Multinomial Logit Model: Monte-Carlo Comparisons." *Journal of Economic Surveys* 21 (1): 174–205.

Bromley, R. 1990. "A New Path to Development? The Significance and Impact of Hernando De Soto's Ideas on Underdevelopment, Production, and Reproduction." *Economic Geography* 66 (4): 328–48.

Dahl, G. B. 2002. "Mobility and the Return to Education: Testing a Roy Model with Multiple Markets." *Econometrica* 70 (6): 2367–420.

De Mel, S., D. McKenzie, and C. Woodruff. 2008. "Who Are the Microenterprise Owners? Evidence from Sri Lanka on Tokman vs. de Soto." Policy Research Working Paper 4635, World Bank, Washington, DC.

Dubin, J. A., and D. L. McFadden. 1984. "An Econometric Analysis of Residential Electric Appliance Holdings and Consumption." *Econometrica* 52 (2): 345–62.

Fields, G. 2005. "A Guide to Multisector Labor Market Models." Social Protection Discussion Paper 0505, World Bank, Washington, DC.

Günther, I., and A. Launov. 2006. "Competitive and Segmented Informal Labor Markets." IZA Discussion Paper 2349, Institute for the Study of Labor, Bonn, Germany.

Krebs, T., and W. F. Maloney. 1999. "Quitting and Labor Turnover: Microeconomic Evidence and Macroeconomic Consequences." Policy Research Working Paper 2068, World Bank, Washington, DC.

Lee, L.-F. 1983. "Generalized Econometric Models with Selectivity." *Econometrica* 51 (2): 507–12.

Maloney, W. 1999. "Does Informality Imply Segmentation in Urban Labor Markets? Evidence from Sectoral Transition in Mexico." *World Bank Economic Review* 13 (2): 275–302.

———. 2004. "Informality Revisited." *World Development* 32 (7): 1159–78.

Pagès, C., and M. Stampini. 2007. "No Education, No Good Jobs? Evidence on the Relationship between Education and Labor Market Segmentation." IZA Discussion Paper 3187, Institute for the Study of Labor, Bonn, Germany.

Parga, X. P., and C. Mondragn-Vlez. 2008. "Business Ownership, and Self-Employment in Developing Economies: The Colombian Case." Documentos Cede 004672, Universidad de los Andes-Cede, Bogota.

Pratap, S., and E. Quintin. 2006. "Are Labor Markets Segmented in Developing Countries? A Semiparametric Approach." *European Economic Review* 50 (7): 1817–41.

Roy, A. 1951. "Some Thoughts on the Distribution of Earnings." *Oxford Economic Papers* 3: 135–46.

Schneider, F. 2004. "The Size of the Shadow Economies of 145 Countries All over the World: First Results over the Period 1999 to 2003." IZA Discussion Paper 1431, Institute for the Study of Labor, Bonn, Germany.

Tokman, V. E. 2007. "Modernizing the Informal Sector." Working Paper 42, United Nations, Department of Economics and Social Affairs, New York.

Chapter 7

Domestic Work and Employment in Africa: What Is the Trade-Off for Women?

Javier Herrera and Constance Torelli

One of the keys to understanding the low labor force participation rate among women and their weaker ties with the labor market is the breakdown of domestic work and market-related work by gender. How do inequalities in the distribution of domestic work affect the type of employment integration (informal) for women and their level of participation (number of hours worked) on the labor market?[1] What are the links between inequalities in the distribution of domestic work time and employment in the informal sector? This chapter addresses these questions.

As domestic work is not considered work in official labor force indicators, activity rates are underestimated, especially for women. As defined by International Labour Organization (ILO) standards, the labor force participation rate covers only work associated with the production of goods and services included in the system of national accounts. Domestic work to produce services consumed by the household is not included; an individual in full-time domestic work is therefore considered "inactive." The time spent producing goods for domestic consumption (gathering firewood, fetching water, caring for the sick, and performing voluntary community services) is not generally considered to be work either.

This chapter focuses on the links between domestic labor and labor market participation. The first section reviews the literature on the distribution of domestic time and market time by gender in developing countries. The second section describes the databases in the 10 Sub-Saharan African countries included in the study. The third section presents the main stylized facts derived from a number of comparative findings and analyzes the determinants of the allocation of time between domestic activities and market work within the framework of family reproduction. It concludes by briefly examining the effects of the distribution of domestic work on labor market participation and household incomes. The fourth section puts forth hypotheses, describes the econometric models employed to test them, and analyzes the results of the estimates. The last section draws conclusions and discusses implications for future research.

To our knowledge, no other study has conducted a comparison of this kind across a large number of Sub-Saharan African countries. This study is also the first to link inequalities in the distribution of domestic work time and employment on the labor market (especially the informal sector).

Review of the Literature

Empirical studies of household allocations of time are based on Becker (1965, 1981) and Gronau (1977), who propose a unitary model of the household in which the ratio of each member's relative productivity to his or her expected wage dictates specialization in domestic or market activities. The variables considered are the individuals' human capital and the opportunity cost of domestic activities (generally measured by proxies such as the number of children, household wealth, and spouse's level of education).

Most empirical studies examine developed countries and focus on the intrahousehold division of labor and its link with the determinants of the labor supply (of married women, for example). One of the focal points of this literature is to test the hypothesis of the unitary household, which posits that the cross-effect of a balanced increase in income from the wife's wage on the husband's labor supply is identical to the effect of an increase in the husband's wage on the wife's labor supply (see, for example, Browning and others 1994; Alderman and others 1995; Browning and Chiappori 1998; Bourguignon and Chiuri 2005).

Empirical studies reject the "shared or common preferences" hypothesis underlying the unitary model of the household (Ilahi 2000). Quisumbing and Maluccio (2000) show the importance (to varying extents) of women's bargaining power in the allocation of household spending in four developing countries (Bangladesh, Ethiopia, Indonesia, and South Africa). But very few studies have looked into intrahousehold time use.

In developing countries, a major feature of the studies based on surveys combining time use with labor market participation is the exploration of the links between child labor (domestic and market work) and children's education (see chapter 12). This work has qualified the idea that work and education are two incompatible activities. Canagarajah and Coulombe (1998) do not include the time children spend on domestic work in their econometric estimates (a bivariate probit model) of the probability of children working as opposed to studying. As Ilahi (2001) shows in his panel study of Peruvian households, failing to do so underestimates the time children, especially girls, spend working. He shows that changes in the household's level of wealth (ownership of assets), the employment of women, and sickness of a household member have a stronger impact on time spent at school and work for girls than for boys (Ilahi 2001). Ritchie, Lloyd, and Grant (2004) consider the impact of adolescents' schooling on the gender division of labor in India, Kenya, Pakistan, and South Africa.

A number of authors point out that part of the household production (mainly produced by women) is not counted. They seek to include domestic work in the system of national accounts and to incorporate female participation in domestic production into the measurement of the labor force participation rate in order to accurately measure women's economic contribution.

Different classifications and breakdowns of working time have been proposed, but the distinction between work and nonwork remains hazy. For example, Kes and Swaminathan (2006) posit that individuals' time use can be classified as market and nonmarket work. Nonmarket work covers subsistence production, reproductive work, and volunteer work. Reproductive work comprises domestic work and care work. Domestic activities include activities such as preparing meals, doing laundry, cleaning, maintaining the household, and providing personal care. This misclassification clearly illustrates the confusion over the distinction between work and nonwork: although personal care is an essential activity, like leisure and sleep, none of these activities is defined as work for the purpose of national accounts.[2]

Few empirical household time use studies have been conducted on developing countries. In Sub-Saharan Africa, surveys do not collect enough economic and demographic data for an in-depth analysis of time use by men and women.

Kes and Swaminathan (2006) update the review by Brown and Haddad (1995) to summarize the findings of 17 studies on time use by gender. They find that different instruments are used to collect the data (simplified diaries, prelisting of 77 activities classified and not classified as in a system of national accounts, participant observation, seven-day recall, two-day recall, 24-hour diary, and so forth). Sample sizes range from 44 women to 5,938 households and cover different age ranges.

In a move to overcome these shortcomings, the United Nations Development Programme (UNDP) supported four surveys on time use in Sub-Saharan Africa, in Benin (1998), South Africa (2000), Madagascar (2001), and Mauritius (2003). The findings are summarized in a report titled *Gender, Time Use and Poverty in Sub-Saharan Africa* (World Bank 2006). This report merely describes the working time included in and excluded from the system of national accounts. Except for gender and country variables, the findings are not broken down by age bracket, level of education, household demographic structure, household poverty status, income level, occupational status, or type of employment.[3]

Empirical studies agree on three stylized facts:

- Women spend more time working than men in nearly all regions.[4]
- The distribution of tasks is very different for men and women, with women performing virtually all domestic tasks and men specializing in income-earning activities (Ilahi 2000).
- There is very little total specialization. Fafchamps and Quisumbing (2003) show that less than 2 percent of people in Pakistan perform all the domestic work in their household and less than 8 percent perform no work at all.

Description of the Data

The data used in this chapter combine samples from 1-2-3 surveys conducted in seven West African Economic and Monetary Union (WAEMU) capitals; Antananarivo, Madagascar; Kinshasa, Democratic Republic of Congo; Douala and Yaoundé, Cameroon (for a description of these surveys, see box O.1 in the overview).[5] The sample covers 95,220 individuals 10 and older, including 68,428 in WAEMU cities (table 7.1). The 1-2-3 surveys share the same methodological

Table 7.1 Sample Characteristics and Descriptive Statistics
(percentage of total, except where indicated otherwise)

Variable	All countries	West African Economic and Monetary Union (WAEMU) subtotal
Gender		
Women	50.8	50.8
Men	49.2	49.2
Number of people (thousands)		
Number of people in areas sampled	18,880.8	9,216.0
Number of people in sample	127.4	91.8
Age bracket		
<6	15.1	14.4
6–9	10.7	10.6
10–14	11.6	11.8
15–24	23.0	24.2
25–64	37.5	37.3
65+	2.1	1.8
Total	100	100
Household size (thousands)		
Total number of people 10 and older in cities sampled	14,009.1	6,920.3
Number of people 10 and older in sample	95.2	68.4

(continued next page)

Table 7.1 (continued)

Variable	All countries	West African Economic and Monetary Union (WAEMU) subtotal
Household type		
One person	12.4	14.4
Couple without children	4.3	4.4
Couple with children	32.6	27.5
Nuclear single parent	8.4	7.9
Extended single parent	9.9	10.7
Extended household	32.4	35.1
Total	100	100
Number of households (thousands)		
Number of households in cities sampled	3,635	1,770
Number of households in sample	25.5	17.8
Percentage of households headed by a woman	20.5	20.5
Average household size	5.1	5.1
Relation to head of household		
Head of household	19.3	19.2
Spouse	12.4	12.3
Child	47.5	45.3
Father/mother	0.6	0.5
Other relative	18.5	19.9
Other unrelated member	1.1	1.7
Servant	0.6	1.1
Institutional sector		
Administration	8.3	6.7
Public enterprise	2.6	1.8
Formal private sector	16.4	14.1
Informal sector	71.0	76.2
Association, nongovernmental organization	1.7	1.2
Religion		
Muslim	28.7	58.7
Catholic	32.4	24.4
Protestant	16.8	5.0
None	2.7	3.6
Other	19.4	8.3
Number of years of education (people 10 and older)		
Women	6.3	4.3
Men	7.8	6.3
All	7.0	5.3

Sources: Based on Phase 1 of the 1-2-3 surveys of selected countries in the West African Economic and Monetary Union (WAEMU) conducted in 2001/02 by the Observatoire économique et statistique d'Afrique Subsaharienne (AFRISTAT); Développement, Institutions et Mondialisation (DIAL); and national statistics institutes.

approach to their measurement of working weeks for people 10 and older in the 11 cities. This means that the harmonized data taken from these surveys can be used to conduct the first ever rigorously comparable assessment.

Household members were asked to recall the time spent on each activity over the reference period. The information obtained is not as accurate as the information obtained from journals filled in by household members. This method was used because it is less expensive and because the one-week period has the advantage of covering activities that are not daily, which prevents underestimation of their weight.

Six types of activities are defined:

- Studying
- Unpaid domestic work in own house and caring for children, the elderly, and the sick
- Fetching water or wood and going to the market
- Building own house
- Performing voluntary community services
- Spending time in employment (in main and second job).

Time spent on leisure, family time, and sleeping was not collected directly but can be estimated residually (table 7.2). The sample covers urban households only; it thus largely avoids seasonality issues.

The other recurring problem with empirical studies on time use is that the sum of the time spent on different activities is sometimes greater than the maximum number of hours available in a day (because two activities, such as caring for children and performing domestic tasks and even market activities, can be performed simultaneously). In our sample, this risk is limited (albeit not eliminated) because caring for children, the elderly, and the sick is grouped with domestic activities. In order to correct for the overestimation of time spent on different activities and hence deal with the double counting problem, we placed a ceiling on the maximum time individuals could spend on activities, so that the sum of weekly activity time does not exceed 112 hours ([24–8] * 7). When the total time individuals reported spending on different activities exceeded the maximum, we applied a correction factor (total time/112) to each of the components, so that the sum does not exceed 112 hours.[6]

Stylized Facts on Time Use by Gender

We first look at the breakdown of working time spent producing domestic goods and services, in order to examine the links between the distribution of

Table 7.2 Allocation of Time in 11 Cities in Sub-Saharan Africa, by Type of Activity
(weekly hours, except where otherwise indicated)

City	Domestic work and caring for children	Gathering wood, fetching water, and shopping	Building home	Studying	Performing voluntary community services	Working in main job	Working in second job	Total
Abidjan	5.8	1.6	0.0	5.0	0.1	26.9	0.4	39.8
Antananarivo	6.1	4.0	1.3	9.9	0.1	24.1	0.8	46.4
Bamako	7.3	1.7	0.1	0.4	0.1	21.3	0.7	31.5
Cotonou	8.3	3.1	0.0	3.5	0.1	26.0	1.0	42.1
Dakar	7.5	1.3	0.1	1.6	0.2	19.9	0.3	30.9
Douala	9.9	3.3	0.2	3.6	0.3	24.3	1.0	42.6
Kinshasa	6.4	2.5	0.1	2.9	0.3	16.5	0.4	29.1
Lomé	11.5	3.9	0.1	2.1	0.4	30.3	0.9	49.2
Niamey	9.1	1.7	0.1	2.0	0.1	19.3	0.7	33.0
Ouagadougou	7.3	2.0	0.0	1.1	0.1	23.0	0.7	34.2
Yaoundé	9.0	3.3	0.1	4.7	0.5	22.5	0.9	41.1
West African Economic and Monetary Union (WAEMU)	7.4	1.9	0.1	2.8	0.1	24.1	0.6	37.0
WAEMU countries	7.4	2.5	0.2	3.6	0.2	21.9	0.6	36.4
Distribution of time (percentage of total)								
WAEMU	20.1	5.2	0.2	7.5	0.4	65.2	1.5	100
All	20.4	6.8	0.5	9.9	0.6	60.2	1.7	100

Sources: Based on Phase 1 of the 1-2-3 surveys of selected countries (see table 7.1 for details).

domestic and market time and the female labor market participation rate and define the relative weight of the activities not counted by the national accounts. We then focus on the extent and determinants of intrahousehold inequalities, an aspect rarely studied in the developing countries.

Time Spent on Domestic and Market Work

One of the keys to understanding low female labor force participation rates and the marginal nature of female employment on the labor market (mainly in the informal sector) is the allocation of time between domestic and market work. The more women are taken up with domestic tasks, the less time they spend on the labor market (figure 7.1). This notion suggests that a trade-off exists between domestic and market-based work. A different picture emerges from examination of the cities individually.

Time Spent on Domestic Work as a Percentage of Total Working Time

Across all 11 cities, nearly one-third (31 percent) of total working time is spent performing domestic activities not included in national accounts (28 percent for WAEMU cities) (figure 7.2). Official per capita gross domestic product (GDP) figures therefore underestimate the real standard of living. It is impossible to quantify the amount by which GDP is underestimated without assigning a monetary value to the time spent on domestic work. Imputing such a value is difficult, however, because there is little if any market for household services in

Figure 7.1 Female Labor Force Participation Rate and Share of Working Time Spent on Domestic Activities in 11 Cities in Sub-Saharan Africa

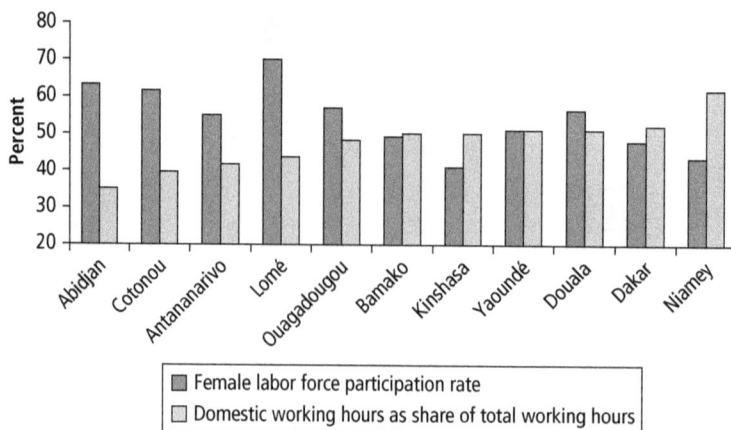

Sources: Based on Phase 1 of the 1-2-3 surveys of selected countries (see table 7.1 for details).

Figure 7.2 Allocation of Time in 11 Cities in Sub-Saharan Africa

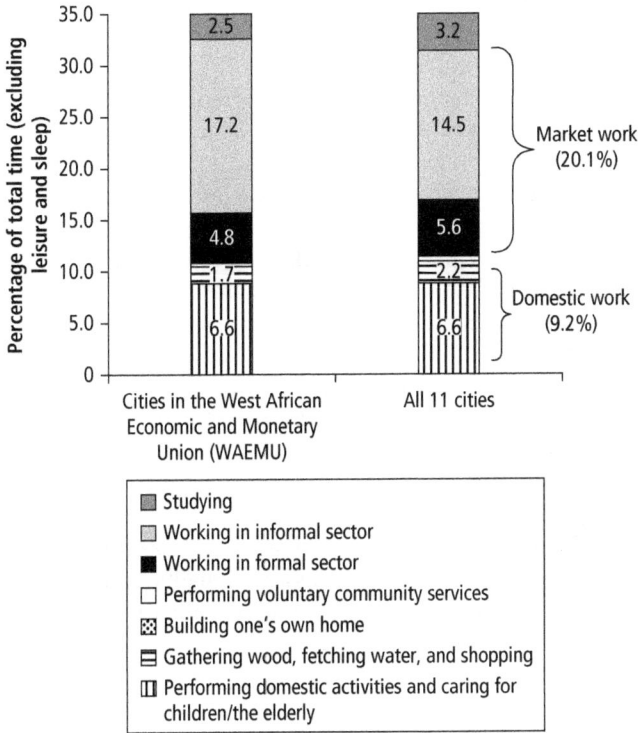

Sources: Based on Phase 1 of the 1-2-3 surveys of selected countries (see table 7.1 for details).

Sub-Saharan Africa. However, given that productivity for domestic production tasks is probably lower than it is for market-based work, GDP cannot be underestimated by more than 30 percent.

Working in the formal sector (often the only working time visible to labor market statistics) accounts for just one-quarter of "market-based" work in both the WAEMU cities and all 11 cities in the sample (the other three-quarters is in the informal sector).[7] On average, more time is spent on domestic activities than on production-related activities in the formal sector. The time-use survey approach provides another way of assessing the extent to which activities outside the formal sector are excluded from both GDP and labor market indicators.

The populations studied spend nearly 70 percent of their time on leisure, sleep, studying, and other activities counted as nonwork. In the WAEMU cities, the time spent studying (2.5 percent) is below the average for all 11 cities (Antananarivo, 7.9 percent; Yaoundé, 4.2 percent; Douala, 3.3 percent).

Cross-Country Differences

The cities display sharp variations around an average working week of 34.2 hours within WAEMU and 32.8 hours for all 11 cities considered. In the capitals of Benin, Côte d'Ivoire, and Togo; Cameroon's two main cities; and Madagascar's capital, people spend more time working (domestic or market-based) than do people in the capitals of Burkina Faso, the Democratic Republic of Congo, Mali, Niger, and Senegal (figure 7.3).

One explanation for the differences in time allocation across cities could be differences in demographic structures and household types. Extended households, polygamy, and the prevalence of child labor may all have an impact on the observed heterogeneity in working hours across countries.

For the sample as a whole, women account for 56 percent of the household's total working time (figure 7.4). Domestic working time is more unevenly spread by gender than market-based work. Women perform 82 percent of domestic work in the household. They also account for 42 percent of the household's market-based working time.

In every city considered, women account for more than half of the household's working time, but there are large differences across countries. Gender differences are greatest in Cotonou and Lomé, where the rates of female specialization in domestic activities are lowest. Gender inequalities occur not principally because women specialize in domestic work but rather because they perform both domestic and market work (figure 7.5).

Figure 7.3 Time Spent on Domestic Work, Market Work, and Studying in 11 Cities in Sub-Saharan Africa

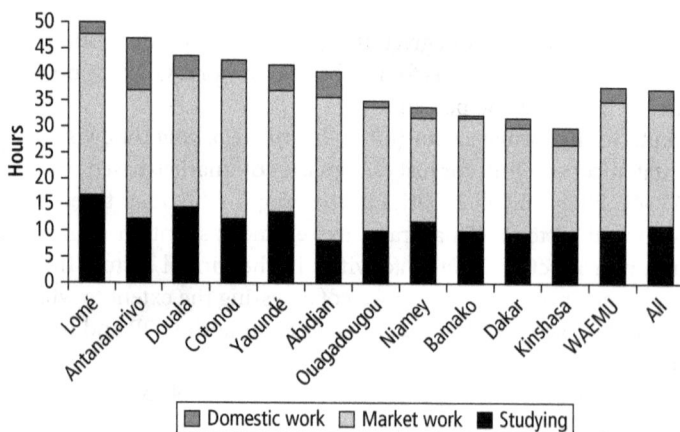

Sources: Based on Phase 1 of the 1-2-3 surveys of selected countries (see table 7.1 for details).
Note: WAEMU = West African Economic and Monetary Union.

Figure 7.4 Division of Labor within Households by Gender in 11 Cities in Sub-Saharan Africa

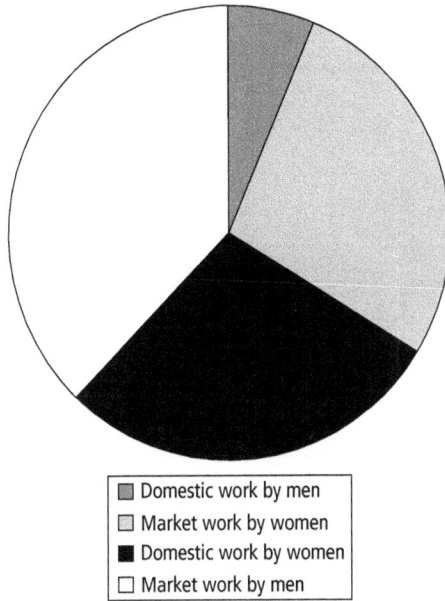

Legend:
- Domestic work by men
- Market work by women
- Domestic work by women
- Market work by men

Sources: Based on Phase 1 of the 1-2-3 surveys of selected countries (see table 7.1 for details).

Figure 7.5 Percentage of Total Working Time Men and Women in 11 Cities in Sub-Saharan Africa Spend Performing Domestic and Market Work

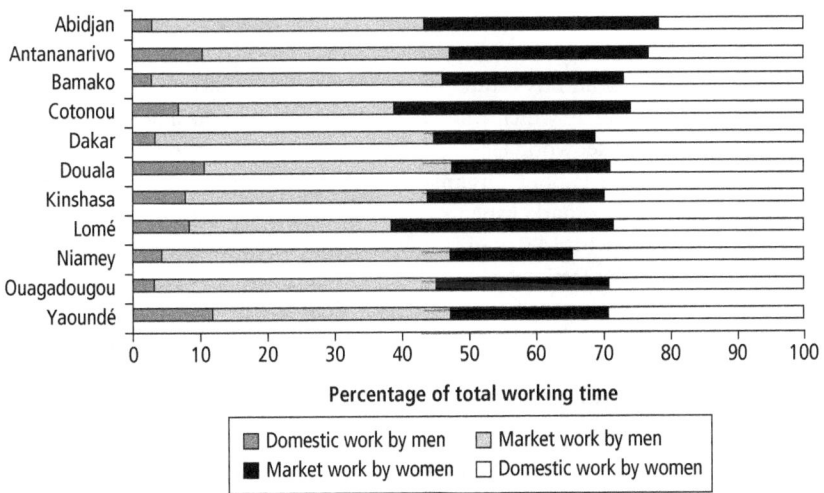

Percentage of total working time

Legend:
- Domestic work by men
- Market work by women
- Market work by men
- Domestic work by women

Sources: Based on Phase 1 of the 1-2-3 surveys of selected countries (see table 7.1 for details).

Table 7.3 Gini Coefficients for Differences in Working Time by Men and Women in 11 Cities in Sub-Saharan Africa

Hours	Including individuals with zero hours			Excluding individuals with zero hours		
	Total	Women	Men	Total	Women	Men
Total working hours	0.520	0.500	0.539	0.389	0.413	0.356
Hours spent on domestic work	0.701	0.571	0.809	0.483	0.444	0.496
Hours spent on market work	0.642	0.696	0.586	0.223	0.240	0.206

Sources: Based on Phase 1 of the 1-2-3 surveys of selected countries (see table 7.1 for details).
Note: Figures are for individuals 10 and older.

Given the small contribution to domestic work by men and the sizable participation of women in market work, it comes as no surprise to find that inequalities (measured by the Gini coefficient) are greater in domestic work than in market work, although both are significant (table 7.3). This result holds when individuals who do not take part in domestic tasks or market tasks are excluded. However, the inequalities are sharper for women in the distribution of market work and for men in the distribution of domestic work. Inequalities in the breakdown of domestic working time are largest for both men and women when zero values are excluded. When we decompose the Theil inequality index, intragroup (male/female) inequalities account for virtually all the inequalities in the distribution of working time (88.7 percent for domestic work, 98.3 percent for market work, and 99.9 percent for total working time).

Women's Double Days

The data in table 7.4 bluntly refute the notion that inequality in domestic work reflects specialization, in which women who participate in the labor market specialize solely in market work, leaving the domestic workload to women defined by the International Labour Organization as economically inactive. Women employed in the labor market spend an average of 16.6 hours a week on domestic tasks, compared with 14.9 hours for women out of the labor force (11 percent more time). This domestic working time is in addition to their market working time. Many African women thus work a double day. Their involvement in domestic work does not appear to be an obstacle to their participation in the labor market.

These average figures mask cross-county differences. The double day is a significant phenomenon in the capitals of Benin, Côte d'Ivoire, Mali, Madagascar, and Togo; the time working women spend on domestic tasks does not differ greatly among women out of the labor force in the other African capitals in our sample.

Table 7.4 Employment, Unemployment, and Inactivity of Women in 11 Cities in
Sub-Saharan Africa, according to Different Definitions
(weekly hours)

City	Employed	Unemployed International Labour Organization (ILO) definition	Broad definition[a]	Inactive	All
Abidjan	13.4	16.6	21.7	11.6	13.3
Antananarivo	16.4	21.2	30.5	14.0	15.6
Bamako	18.2	20.8	18.5	15.1	16.7
Cotonou	20.4	18.1	27.7	13.6	17.8
Dakar	13.5	20.5	23.8	15.8	15.9
Douala	20.5	24.6	30.8	19.0	20.6
Kinshasa	14.4	17.5	16.7	13.8	14.3
Lomé	25.1	26.3	27.9	20.3	23.7
Niamey	19.7	18.7	23.2	18.7	19.4
Ouagadougou	16.6	21.8	24.6	16.1	17.5
Yaoundé	18.2	25.5	27.1	16.4	18.3
West African Economic and Monetary Union (WAEMU)	16.7	18.9	23.2	14.9	16.4
Average all countries	16.6	20.3	22.1	14.9	16.3

Sources: Based on Phase 1 of the 1-2-3 surveys of selected countries (see table 7.1 for details).
a. Includes workers defined by the International Labour Organization (ILO) as unemployed and discouraged.

This observation comes with two reservations. First, unemployed women spend more time than working women on domestic work (3.7 hours more a week using the ILO definition of unemployment, 5.5 hours more using a broader definition of unemployment). The gap in time devoted to domestic activities between inactive and active women narrows when unemployed women (broadly defined) are included (17.5 versus 14.9 hours per week).

Second, the differences between employed and economically inactive females occur mainly because of large differences among girls 10–14: girls 10–14 who work devote very little time (1.5 hours a week) compared with economically inactive girls the same age (8.5 hours a week). In fact, working girls perform more domestic work (16.1 hours) a week than girls who are not in the labor force (9.4 hours). The differences are insignificant among women 15 and older (0.3 hours). All in all, however, working women work five hours more on average (market and domestic working time) than their male counterparts.

The explanatory models of Becker and Gronau focus on economic factors (the opportunity cost associated with different human capital endowments). Another approach concentrates on the importance of social standards. In this approach, the household is seen as a unit in which members share the same preferences or as a group led by a "benevolent dictator" (Ilahi 2000).

Many authors have pointed to the importance of social standards and roles, overlooked by the Becker-Gronau approach. Women, they suggest, specialize in domestic activities and men in market activities because of culturally determined social standards and roles rather than economic factors. These social standards depend on religion, ethnicity, position in the household hierarchy, and other factors. For example, in their study on Pakistan, Fafchamps and Quisumbing (2003) highlight the importance of the position in the household hierarchy. They find that the wife accounts for the bulk of domestic work and that daughters-in-law take on a heavier load in the domestic activities than the daughters of the head of household. If social standards predominate, differences in human capital may have a minor effect on the gender-based division of labor.

A higher level of education is associated with a larger male contribution to domestic work (table 7.5). Women's contribution, however, remains virtually the same for both domestic tasks and market work regardless of their level of education. This finding tends to support the hypothesis of the minor role played by economic factors in the gender-based division of labor between market and domestic work.

One of the distinguishing factors in the cities in the sample is the predominance of Islam in some and Christianity in others. Religion affects the demographic composition of households; in some countries, it dictates a more traditional role for women. Islam is associated with greater task specialization by gender (table 7.6). The proportion of hours devoted to market work is slightly lower for Muslim women; much larger inequalities are found in the tiny contribution made by Muslim men to domestic activities, an area "reserved" for Muslim women.

Table 7.5 Weekly Hours Men and Women in 11 Cities in Sub-Saharan Africa Spend Performing Domestic and Market Work, by Level of Education
(percent)

Years of education	Domestic work/total household working hours			Market work/total household working hours		
	Men	Women	All	Men	Women	All
None	2.8	27.5	30.3	42.3	27.4	69.7
1–5	5.8	27.5	33.3	37.6	29.1	66.7
6–10	7.4	28.1	35.5	36.9	27.5	64.5
11 or more	8.9	27.4	36.4	37.0	26.7	63.6
All	6.7	27.7	34.4	37.9	27.7	65.6

Sources: Based on Phase 1 of the 1-2-3 surveys of selected countries (see table 7.1 for details).

Table 7.6 Weekly Hours Men and Women in 11 Cities in Sub-Saharan Africa Spend Performing Domestic and Market Work, by Religion
(percent)

Religion	Hours domestic work/total household working hours			Hours market work/total household working hours		
	Men	Women	Total	Men	Women	Total
Muslim	3.1	28.0	31.1	43.7	25.2	68.9
Catholic	8.3	28.0	36.3	34.7	29.1	63.7
Protestant	9.0	27.2	36.2	35.5	28.4	63.8
No religion	5.9	20.8	26.7	44.0	29.4	73.3
Other	7.3	28.5	35.7	35.4	28.8	64.3
West African Economic and Monetary Union (WAEMU)	3.7	26.6	30.3	39.9	29.8	69.7
All	6.7	27.8	34.5	37.7	27.8	65.5

Sources: Based on Phase 1 of the 1-2-3 surveys of selected countries (see table 7.1 for details).

Social standards are also expressed through the roles assigned to individuals at different stages in their lives. School-age (10–14) children concentrate mainly on their studies, while providing considerable assistance with domestic tasks and working in the labor market. The gender-based division of labor is forged from a very young age: girls spend twice as much time on domestic activities as boys. Although the domestic work time curve is relatively flat for men over their life cycle (it dips slightly when they marry, before stabilizing), it takes the form of a bell curve for women, reaching its peak in the 26–35 age bracket before gradually falling off as the household grows and children are able to contribute (figure 7.6).

The market work curve is more concave for men than for women. Gender differences start to widen in adolescence, reaching their peak in adulthood, the most productive period (36–45). Women withdraw more gradually from working life than men. Entry into the labor market is problematic for young people (16–25), judging from the small number of hours of market work. Schooling beyond secondary education accounts for only a smart part of the low level of market work (the average number of years of education for this age bracket is just eight for all 11 cities and six for the WAEMU cities).

Two factors are probably at work here, in different proportions for men and women. Men suffer from a lack of wage employment opportunities because of the low level of private and public sector recruitment and their low skill levels. Women are held back by domestic tasks, related in part to the presence of young children, who are cared for exclusively by women in the household.

Figure 7.6 Average Weekly Hours Worked by Men and Women in 11 Cities in Sub-Saharan Africa, by Age

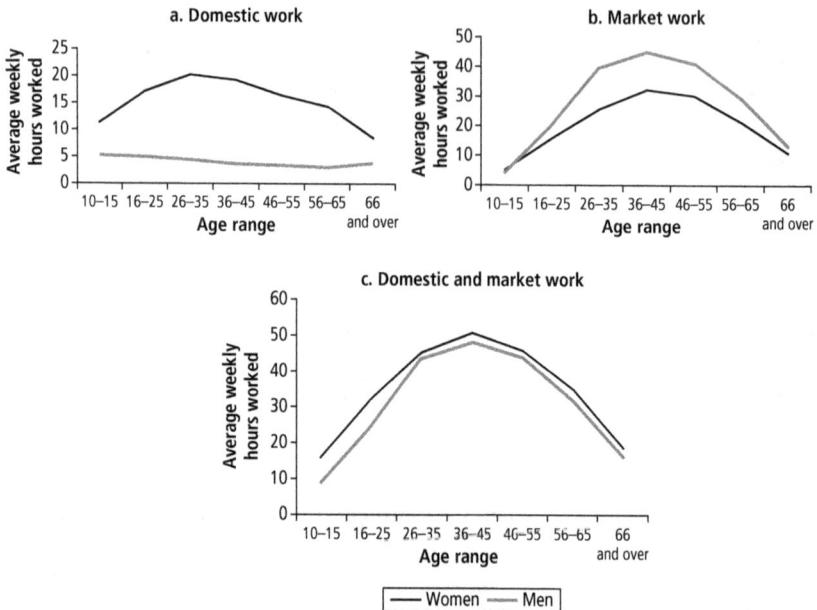

Sources: Based on Phase 1 of the 1-2-3 surveys of selected countries (see table 7.1 for details).

When domestic working time is added to market working time, the inequalities narrow for the population over 25. These figures indicate that women work more than men at all ages.

The position in the household plays a minor role in women's specialization in domestic activities (figure 7.7). Female heads of household, wives, and daughters all spend more of their working time on domestic activities than their male counterparts. Household position comes into play for women only marginally, in the breakdown of domestic and market working time. Other relatives, who are more specialized in domestic work, make significant contributions to the household's market and domestic work. This category may include disguised forms of forced labor, such as foster children acting as servants for the households.

Table 7.7 sums up the differences found in the female participation rate; women's contribution to total working time; and their contribution to household income, with and without the inclusion of domestic work. The first two

Figure 7.7 Household Position and Division of Time between Domestic and Market Work in 11 Cities in Sub-Saharan Africa

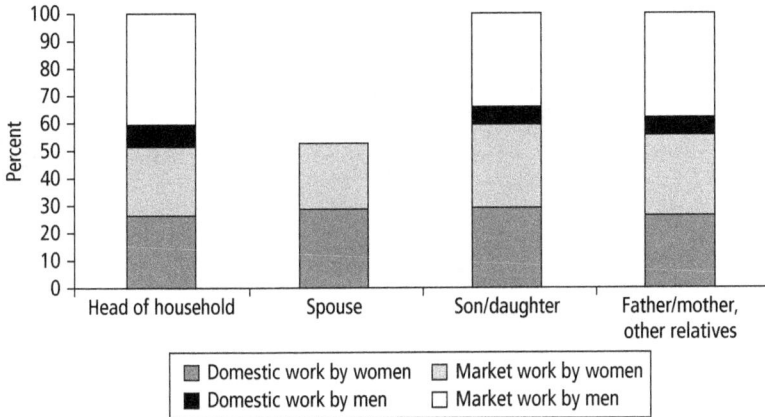

Sources: Based on Phase 1 of the 1-2-3 surveys of selected countries (see table 7.1 for details).

indicators were built using data collected in the 1-2-3 surveys; values had to be imputed for the contribution of domestic work to household incomes. Given the absence of markets for goods and services to substitute for domestic work, we imputed the equivalent of each country's minimum hourly wage for domestic work.

If account were taken of hours worked producing domestic goods and services, the female labor force participation rate would increase 70 percent (from 52 percent to 88 percent) on average, and the wide disparities in female participation rates across cities would narrow considerably. Female participation would be higher than male participation in all 11 cities (13 percent higher in WAEMU cities and 11 percent higher across the full sample). This finding holds when considering women's contribution to total working time. Inclusion of domestic working time in total household working time reveals the predominant contribution of women to working hours in the African cities in the sample.

If total income from the main and second job alone is considered, women account for 28 percent of total household income. Imputing a wage for domestic work (based on the minimum hourly wage) raises women's contribution to 38 percent. Looking at absolute amounts, the potential income from domestic activity is greater than the income from market activity in all WAEMU countries but not in Cameroon and Madagascar.

Table 7.7 Women's Economic Contribution to Economic Activity in 11 Cities in Sub-Saharan Africa
(percent)

City	Labor force participation rate		Total working time of household		Household income	
	Without domestic work	With domestic work	Without domestic work	With domestic work	Without domestic work	With domestic work
Abidjan	62.1	84.4	43.7	53.7	26.7	35.2
Antananarivo	54.5	94.6	44.2	52.3	35.9	41.9
Bamako	49.0	79.7	35.2	51.7	23.0	34.1
Cotonou	61.1	89.4	51.0	59.8	30.9	42.9
Dakar	48.0	82.8	35.5	52.7	26.9	42.6
Douala	57.6	96.2	37.2	49.5	26.7	34.7
Kinshasa	41.0	86.5	43.1	55.9	33.1	45.3
Lomé	69.1	95.3	49.8	59.3	32.1	43.2
Niamey	43.7	83.2	30.1	51.6	22.5	38.1
Ouagadougou	57.2	84.6	37.6	52.8	25.7	42.1
Yaoundé	51.2	95.7	37.2	49.0	30.6	37.1
West African Economic and Monetary Union (WAEMU)	56.4	84.9	41.5	54.4	26.7	38.2
All	51.5	88.0	41.2	53.5	27.9	38.1

Sources: Based on Phase 1 of the 1-2-3 surveys of selected countries (see table 7.1 for details).

Model and Econometric Estimation of Determinants of Allocation of Time

This section examines the breakdown of time spent on domestic and market work. We postulate that the division of labor within the household (domestic work versus market work) is determined more by social standards than economic factors. Economic factors related to human capital play a marginal role because of the very low level of formal education and lack of formal job opportunities.

We adopt the approach proposed by Hersch and Stratton (1994) in their study of working couples in the United States, used by Anxo, Flood, and Koco-glu (2002) in their comparative study of couples in France and Sweden. One important difference between our analysis and these studies is that we focus on the gender-based division of labor of all household members, not just adults, as children in developing countries perform domestic work and sometimes participate in the labor market. The prevalence of extended families (42 percent of households in our sample) and the existence of polygamy (3 percent of households) also justifies considering all members 10 and older in the analysis.[8]

The dependent variable in the first equation is women's relative contribution to domestic (market) work. The dependent variable in the next two equations is total working time for men and working time for women in domestic (market) activities. The values of the dependent variables (relative male/female share and weekly working hours in domestic and market work) are left censored and range from 0 to 100 percent and 0 to 113 hours (leisure time is estimated residually). Hence the ordinary least squares (OLS) procedure produces biased results.[9]

A more suitable approach would therefore appear to be left- and right-censored Tobit estimates. The Tobit model assumes that the same variables determine both the probability of an observation being censored and the values of the noncensored observations. Moreover, the marginal effect of a variable is constrained to the same sign for both types of observations. Given that individuals with a zero value present particular characteristics (their nonparticipation is not random), the estimated coefficients present biases, even when taking account of the censored values.

Heckman's model ("Heckit") relaxes these assumptions by taking account of the possible selection bias (estimating the probability of observing a value different from zero) and the determinants of values above zero. In the model estimated below, the number of young children in the household is negative correlated with participation in market activities (and positively correlated with hours of domestic work); it is not necessarily correlated with the number of hours of market work. The merits of the Heckit model can be appreciated from the value of the Mills ratio coefficient. A value statistically different from zero indicates the presence of a selection bias that invalidates the Tobit estimation.

Three equations are estimated for each work aspect (domestic and market based). In the first equation, the dependent variable is the relative contribution of each woman (man) to domestic work. The other two equations seek to identify the determinants of domestic (market) working time separately for men and women. The first equation hence explains the gender-based division of labor; the other two equations are required to interpret how this division varies depending on the characteristics of individuals and their households. For example, an increase in the contribution to domestic work by the most educated men could reflect a decrease in absolute time spent on domestic work by educated women, without an increase in total domestic working time.

Table 7.8 reports the marginal effects estimated using the Tobit model. Although the residual normality and heteroskedasticity tests reject the residual normality hypothesis, and the Mills ratio coefficients are significant in most cases, our comments concern only the results of the Tobit model, because of problems encountered with the specification of the selection equation and implausible estimated coefficient values. These results should therefore be seen as initial estimations only.

Table 7.8 Determinants of Time Use (Domestic and Market Work) in 10 Cities in Sub-Saharan Africa

Variable	Percentage of women's domestic working hours/total household domestic working hours (1)	Women's domestic working hours (2)	Men's domestic working hours (3)	Percentage of men's market working hours/total household market working hours (4)	Women's market working hours (5)	Men's market working hours (6)
Age (reference = 26–45)						
10–15	−3.92***	−3.27***	1.17***	−21.48***	−19.44***	−28.71***
16–25	6.24***	0.78***	0.94***	−9.16***	−7.71***	−9.01***
46–55	−10.06***	−2.41***	−0.28***	−0.79**	−0.35	−2.56***
56+	−19.33***	−7.12***	−0.11	−12.44***	−9.63***	−18.88***
Relation to head of household (reference = head of household)						
Spouse	6.43***	3.37***	1.86***	−11.41***	−1.99***	−3.39*
Son or daughter	−17.08***	−2.19***	0.16	−15.74***	−5.37***	−11.07***
Father or mother	−15.22***	−5.66***	−1.53**	−16.64***	−8.63***	−17.26***
Other relative	−10.93***	−0.64**	0.45***	−11.97***	−3.07***	−6.96***
Unrelated person	−1.52	1.86***	1.00***	−9.51***	−0.43	−4.16***
Level of education (reference ≥11 years)						
No education	2.42***	3.30***	−0.45***	0.33	3.23***	8.54***
1–5 years	2.08***	2.33***	−0.22***	0.74**	2.64***	8.73***
6–10 years	1.51***	1.53***	−0.15**	−1.16***	0.12	3.36***
Labor market						
Predicted hourly earnings	0.00	0.00	0.00	0.00***	0.00***	0.00***
Employed worker (equations 1–3)	−3.05***	−1.61***	−0.31***	−0.71***	−1.01***	−1.93***
Domestic worker (equations 4–6)						
Religion (reference = other religion)						
Muslim	1.17**	−0.01	−0.70***	−1.40***	−0.76**	1.76***

Catholic	-0.18	-0.03	-0.01	-0.32	-0.25	-0.56
Protestant	-0.27	0.31	0.03	-0.46	-0.44	-0.67
No religion	-1.72	-0.85	-0.02	0.09	0.67	1.55**
Dominant ethnic group	-0.22	-0.19	-0.23***	0.12	0.25	0.39*
Household's demographic structure						
Number of children 0–5	1.03***	0.41***	0.00	-0.29***	-0.39***	0.64***
Number of children 6–9	0.30**	0.15**	-0.02	0.18	0.03	0.07
Number of male children 10–17	-2.09***	0.05	0.03	-0.19*	0.12	-0.30***
Number of female children 10–17	-5.49***	-0.40***	-0.14***	-0.26***	0.31***	-0.03
Number of men 18–25	-0.68***	-0.07	-0.15***	-0.97***	0.06	0.68***
Number of women 18–25	-5.24***	-0.89***	-0.21***	-0.10	0.88***	-0.21*
Number of men 26–55	0.09	0.18**	0.04	-1.90***	-0.30***	-0.32***
Number of women 26–55	-3.70***	-0.62***	-0.22***	-1.31***	-0.03	-0.65***
Number of men 56+	1.01***	0.28*	0.10	1.57***	0.26	1.68***
Number of women 56+	-0.58*	-0.13	-0.10	0.72***	0.20	-1.45***
Household type (reference = couple with children)						
Couple without children	18.19***	-0.63*	-0.04	0.18	-1.32***	0.90*
Nuclear single parent	1.75***	0.27	-0.09	5.91***	0.97**	0.64
Extended single parent	-6.28***	0.18	-0.11	-0.49	0.37	1.08**
Extended couple	-6.63***	-0.15	0.16**	0.55**	1.31***	0.38
Number of spouses in the household	-2.69***	-0.51***	-0.47***	-0.95***	-1.04***	-0.06
With servants	-0.22	-2.25***	-0.65***	1.44***	1.10***	-0.77
Access to public services (reference = has access)						
Electricity	0.08	-0.31**	-0.24***	-1.05***	-1.25***	-0.81***
Water	-0.01	-0.53***	-0.23***	-0.33	-1.13***	-1.53***

(continued next page)

Table 7.8 (continued)

Variable	Percentage of women's domestic working hours/total household domestic working hours (1)	Women's domestic working hours (2)	Men's domestic working hours (3)	Percentage of men's market working hours/total household market working hours (4)	Women's market working hours (5)	Men's market working hours (6)
Electric, gas, or oil stove	0.07	0.09	0.11	-0.34	-0.62***	-0.48*
Number of rooms in dwelling	-0.06	0.01	0.04***	-0.06	-0.16***	-0.13**
Household with car	-0.41	-1.51***	-0.52***	-1.58***	-1.13***	0.65**
Household with bicycle or motorbike	-0.13	0.21	0.09	-0.28	0.92***	1.43***
Household with refrigerator	-0.61*	-0.48***	-0.08	0.41*	0.20	-0.75***
City (reference = Antananarivo)						
Abidjan	5.92***	-3.33***	-4.72***	0.95*	0.20	-3.67***
Bamako	5.61***	-2.73***	-4.80***	-1.25**	-4.30***	-6.08***
Cotonou	5.67***	0.46	-2.01***	2.88***	1.99***	-2.92***
Dakar	2.66***	-0.96***	-4.09***	-3.74***	-6.23***	-2.97***
Douala	1.95***	2.37***	-0.27*	-0.60	-1.05**	0.76
Kinshasa	2.43***	-2.06***	-2.73***	-0.26	-2.25***	-10.66***
Lomé	4.90***	3.98***	-0.79***	2.85***	2.51***	-1.13**
Niamey	3.86***	-0.58*	-3.80***	-5.00***	-8.26***	-5.60***
Ouagadougou	4.22***	-1.60***	-4.54***	-1.79***	-4.72***	-5.62***
Yaoundé	1.89**	1.84***	-0.10	-1.67	-2.51***	-0.44
Number of observations	42,522	45,311	42,980	42,189	45,311	42,980
Number of uncensored observations	28,359	34,247	14,346	15,984	18,323	22,746

Sources: Based on Phase 1 of the 1-2-3 surveys of selected countries (see table 7.1 for details).
Note: Figures show results of right- and left-censored Tobit models (marginal effects evaluated with respect to the average value for the explanatory variables).
* significant at the 10 percent level, ** significant at the 5 percent level, *** significant at the 1 percent level.

Effect on Domestic Labor

Age has a strong impact on the division of domestic labor by gender. Women 16–25 work 0.8 hours a week more than women 26–45, a period during which they have left school, married, and have young children. Women 46–54 reduce the time spent on domestic work slightly (2.4 hours less than women 24–45); women 56 and older spend 7.1 hours less a week than women 26–45. After 55, women are often heads of their household or members of extended households.

The relative contribution of women to domestic work is similar to the absolute number of domestic working hours. Men perform very few hours of domestic work throughout their life cycle. They perform the most domestic work when they are children (10–15). The reverse is true of women, who put in fewer hours of domestic work at each end of their life cycle.

Position in the household also plays a very important role in the division of labor by gender. Women who are married to the household head devote the most time to domestic work; daughters and mothers contribute less time. This pattern would seem to suggest a hierarchy in which domestic working time decreases from the outer rim of the household circle (nonrelatives) inward toward the center (children). Consequently, the daughters and mother of the head of household spend fewer hours on domestic work (2.2 fewer for daughters and 5.7 fewer for mothers) than other female relatives (0.64 hour less) and nonrelatives (1.9 more hours). Sons contribute virtually as much time (0.16 hours) as household heads; other male relatives spend half an hour more on domestic work than the household head (males nonrelatives dedicate one hour more than the household head to domestic work). Qualitative studies are needed to determine whether this work is being performed by foster children or reflects payment for accommodations (see chapter 12).

The type of household also plays an important role in the division of labor within the household. Women make smaller contributions in extended households than in other types of households, probably because domestic work is distributed among a larger number of people and individuals on the outer rim of the household circle make a larger contribution to domestic tasks. Women in polygamous households also make smaller relative and absolute contributions to domestic working time. The presence of servants in the household significantly decreases the number of domestic working hours performed by women (–2.3 hours) and moderately reduces the number worked by men (–0.65 hour). The decrease in women's contribution to domestic work compared with the share of men (–0.22 percentage points) is small and not significant.

Having a larger number of women in the household reduces the contribution of each woman, especially for women 10–25. Having a larger number of children under 10 increases women's contribution to domestic work; it has no effect on the domestic workload of men. The division of domestic labor by gender changes very marginally with the arrival of adult men in the household.

Relative to non-Muslim women, Muslim women account for a larger share of the household's total time spent on domestic activities, because Muslim men spend less time on domestic activities. Islam therefore appears to be one of the channels, albeit a secondary one, through which social standards and practices concerning men's role are crystalized.

Belonging to the dominant ethnic group has no effect on either the division of domestic labor by gender or the time women spend on domestic work. However, it contributes to a modest reduction (0.21 hour) in the time men spend on domestic work. The ethnic group variable could be said to be a proxy for social standards, already partly taken into account by religion. Men in the dominant ethnic group may therefore be thought to have more power in the household, enabling them to reduce the time spent on domestic work.

Contrary to expectations, access to public services has no significant effect on the domestic division of labor by gender. This result can be explained by the fact that access to water and electricity reduces the domestic tasks performed by men and women in similar proportions. Access therefore reduces total domestic working time for the household as a whole rather than redistributing labor by gender.

Household appliances do not change the household's division of labor by gender or affect the absolute working time of men or women. Household wealth, measured by vehicle ownership and the number of rooms in the dwelling, also has no impact on the division of labor. Dwelling size has a positive effect on the time men spend working, as they generally are responsible for house repairs, but no impact on women's working time. However, ownership of a car reduces women's domestic working time by 1.5 hours and men's by 0.5 hour. The effect gives rise to a slightly more female-friendly division of domestic labor (0.4 percentage point reduction in women's share of domestic labor), but the impact is not statistically significant.

Women's education increases equality in the division of domestic work, tipping the balance more than proportionally in women's favor at each level of education. However, as with religion, the reduction in inequalities in the distribution of domestic work comes from adjustment in the hours of domestic work by women only. Women with higher education spend 2.4 hours less on domestic work than women who did not attend school; this reduction narrows to 2.1 hours for women with 1–5 years of education and 1.5 hours for women with 6–10 years of education. The opposite trend is observed for men: the more educated they are, the more they participate in domestic tasks. However, the marginal effects are fairly small: men with no education perform less than half an hour less domestic work a week than men with more than 10 years of education (0.22 hour less for men with primary education and 0.15 hour less for men with secondary education). Education thus makes only a modest contribution to improving equity in the division of labor by gender, and its effect works more by reducing women's working time than by increasing men's working time.

Labor market participation implies a decrease in the share of domestic work performed by women, because of fewer hours of domestic work performed by women (–1.61) and men (–0.31). Households in which women participate in the labor market post lower total domestic working time. The predicted level of hourly earnings has no significant impact on the division of domestic labor by gender or the domestic working time worked by men and women.

Effect on Market Labor

The results on the division of market work are similar to the results for labor. Larger deviations are found for women 10–15 and 56 and older (that is, at the two ends of the life cycle). Spouses of the household head contribute just two hours less than the head of household to market work; nonrelatives come in third place after household heads and spouses, making a valuable contribution to the household's income.

The gradient for the level of education is always negative: the higher the level of education, the fewer hours people work in the market. Men with no education work 3.2 hours more and women work 8.5 hours more than people with 11 years or more of education. The level of education therefore has a strong effect for men and a moderate impact for women. Participation in domestic work reduces the relative participation of women in total market hours worked as well as the absolute number of market hours worked by men and women (–1.0 hour for men and –1.9 hours for women).

Muslim women contribute less than non-Muslim women to the household's market work, both because they work fewer hours than non-Muslims and because Muslim men work more hours. Belonging to the dominant ethnic group has no significant effect on the division of labor.

The household's demographic structure affects the gender-based division of market work. An increase in the number of young dependent household members (children under five) reduces women's relative and absolute contribution to market work. An increase in the number of dependent elderly members (people 56 and over) is associated with an increase in working hours for elderly men and a decrease for elderly women. The number of hours worked in the market decreases for both men and women as the number of male adults in the household increases. The increase in the number of adult women and adolescent girls enables women to increase the number of market hours worked, probably as a result of the lightening of their domestic workload. At the same time, the increase entails a very slight reduction in hours worked in the market for adult men (0.2 hour less for men 18–25 and 0.7 hour less for men 26–55).

Turning to specific geographic effects, Cotonou and Lomé stand out for the much larger contribution of women to market work. Men in these cities work more hours than men in the other cities (except in Cameroon and Madagascar).

Conclusion

On average, domestic work—which remains invisible in national accounts and labor market indicators—represents nearly one-third of total working time in the 11 cities examined. It consumes more time than employment in the formal sector. Large differences are observed across cities in both total working time and the breakdown between domestic and market work. Despite their lower labor market participation rate, women account for 56 percent of household working time (62 percent in WAEMU cities).

Unlike in other regions, women in Sub-Saharan Africa do not "specialize" in domestic activities. Women account for 43 percent of household hours spent working in the labor market (as well as 89 percent of hours spent on domestic work). Women spend 60 percent of their working hours in the labor market and the remaining 40 percent on domestic work.

A number of factors are correlated with gender-based inequalities in the division of labor. Social standards appear to play a decisive role: relative position in the household, age, and Muslim religion all have a significant impact on the gender-based division of both domestic and market-based work. Differences in education are also significant, but their impact is modest and the gradient by level of education is not very steep. Extended households, polygamous households, and households with a large number of adults have a different gender-based division of labor than households made up of couples with young children and monogamous households. Contrary to expectations, access to public services (electricity, water) has no apparent effect on the division of domestic labor by gender. Differences across cities remain significant when account is taken of the observable characteristics of individuals and their households.

The analysis presented in this chapter takes a first step toward including domestic work in GDP estimates and labor market indicators. It sheds light on the question of intrahousehold inequalities, a central aspect in the role and place of women in African societies. Other aspects of intrahousehold inequalities have not yet been explored. Future research could examine time use and other aspects of intrahousehold inequalities, such as gender differences in education and healthcare. It could also take individual heterogeneity into account. Another interesting avenue would be to link the perception of well-being with intrahousehold inequalities in the division of working time, in order to shed light on why such inequalities persist.

Notes

1. The level of household welfare is underestimated when the production of goods and services produced and consumed by the household is not taken into account. As cities and incomes grow, these goods and services are increasingly incorporated into the market sphere, causing gross domestic product (GDP) growth to be overestimated (Stiglitz, Sen, and Fitoussi 2010). In addition to this material welfare dimension, some authors have defined a new form of poverty among households that spend an excessive number of hours working: time poverty (Blackden and Wodon 2006). Although work (market and nonmarket) is the main source of household income and hence welfare, too much time spent working takes away from leisure, rest, family life, and studying and therefore reduces quality of life.

2. The United Nations Statistics Division defines "nonwork" as time spent in "personal care and free time," which includes "bathing, sleeping, eating, time related to personal medical attention, resting, organizational participation, sports and games, socializing and media related activities (reading, television..." UN 1991). All other activities are classified as work. This classification attempts to make visible the economic value of unpaid work in society and to capture the relative work burdens of men and women" (Whitehead 1999, p. 52).

3. The references include administrative reports published by statistics institutes, sometimes jointly with UNDP.

4. Working time is defined here as the counterpart to leisure time. It does not take into account productivity differences, which would have to be considered if the purpose were to study gender-based income disparities. The focus is the distribution of domestic and market time by different household members and its implications for the labor market participation rate.

5. Although Abidjan and Cotonou are not administrative capitals, we refer to them as capitals because they are the most important economic centers in their countries (Cotonou is also the seat of government).

6. This correction affected less than 1 percent of individuals.

7. This term actually covers production for the market and for own consumption (in agricultural produce). It would be more relevant to talk about activities included in the System of National Accounts.

8. Skoufias (1993) also adopts this approach, in a study of the determinants of the division of labor in rural households in India.

9. Nearly half (52 percent) of individuals declare zero market working hours, 44 percent declare zero domestic working hours, and 22 percent declare zero total working hours.

References

Alderman, H., P. A. Chiappori, L. Haddad, J. Hodinott, and R. Kanbur. 1995. "Unitary Versus Collective Models of the Household: Time to Shift the Burden of Proof?" *World Bank Research Observer* 10 (1): 1–19.

Anxo, D., L. Flood, and Y. Kocoglu. 2002. "Offre de travail et répartition des activités domestiques et parentales au sein du couple: une comparaison entre la France et la Suède." *Economie et Statistique* (352–53): 127–50.

Becker, G. S. 1965. "A Theory of Allocation of Time." *Economic Journal* 75: 493–517.

———. 1981. *Treatise on the Family*. Cambridge, MA: Harvard University Press.

Blackden, C. M., and Q. Wodon. 2006. *Gender, Time Use, and Poverty in Sub-Saharan Africa*. Washington, DC: World Bank.

Bourguignon, F., and M. C. Chiuri. 2005. "Labor Market Time and Home Production: A New Test for Collective Models of Intra-Household Allocation." CSEF Working Paper 131, Centre for Studies in Economics and Finance, Naples.

Brown, L., and L. Haddad. 1995. "Time Allocation Patterns and Time Burden: A Gendered Analysis of Seven Countries." International Food Policy Research Institute (IFPRI), Washington, DC.

Browning, M., F. Bourguignon, P. A. Chiappori, and V. Lechene. 1994. "Income and Outcomes: A Structural Model of Intrahousehold Allocation." *Journal of Political Economy* 102 (6): 1067–96.

Browning, M., and P. A. Chiappori. 1998. "Efficient Intra-Household Allocations: A General Characterization and Empirical Tests." *Econometrica* 66 (6): 1241–78.

Canagarajah, S., and H. Coulombe. 1998. "Child Labor and Schooling in Ghana." Policy Research Working Paper 1844, World Bank, Washington, DC.

Fafchamps, M., and A. Quisumbing. 2003. "Social Roles, Human Capital, and the Intrahousehold Division of Labor: Evidence from Pakistan." *Oxford Economic Papers* 55 (1): 36–80.

Gronau, R. 1977. "Leisure, Home Production and Work: The Theory of Time Allocation Revisited." *Journal of Political Economy* 85 (6): 1099–123.

Hersch, J., and L. Stratton. 1994. "Housework, Wages, and the Division of Housework Time for Employed Spouses." *American Economic Review* 84 (2): 120–25.

Ilahi, N. 2000. "The Intra-household Allocation of Time and Tasks: What Have We Learnt from the Empirical Literature?" Policy Research Report on Gender, and Development, Working Paper 13, World Bank, Washington, DC.

———. 2001. "Gender and the Allocation of Adult Time: Evidence from the Peru LSMS Panel Data." Policy Research Report Working Paper 2744, World Bank, Washington, DC.

Kes, A., and D. Swaminathan. 2006. "Gender and Time Poverty in Sub-Saharan Africa." In *Gender, Time Use, and Poverty in Sub-Saharan Africa*, ed. C. M. Blackden and Q. Wodon, 13–32. Washington, DC: World Bank.

Quisumbing, A., and J. Maluccio. 2000. "Intrahousehold Allocation and Gender Relations." FCND Discussion Paper 84, International Food Policy Research Institute, Washington, DC.

Ritchie, A., C. Lloyd, and M. Grant. 2004. "Gender Differences in Time Use Among Adolescents in Developing Countries: Implications of Rising School Enrollment Rates." Working Paper 193, Population Council, Policy Research Division, New York.

Skoufias, E. 1993. "Labor Market Opportunities and Interfamily Time Allocation in Rural Households in South Asia." *Journal of Development Economics* 40 (2): 277–310.

Stiglitz, J. E., A. Sen, and J.-P. Fitoussi. 2010. *Mismeasuring Our Lives: Why GDP Doesn't Add Up*. New York: New Press.

UN (United Nations). 1991. *The World's Women: Trends and Statistics*. New York: Centre for Social Development and Humanitarian Affairs.

Whitehead, A. 1999. "'Lazy Men,' Time Use, and Rural Development in Zambia." *Gender and Development* 7 (3): 49–61.

World Bank. 2006. *Gender, Time Use and Poverty in Sub-Saharan Africa*. Washington, DC: World Bank.

Chapter 8

Reducing Inequality of Opportunities in West African Urban Labor Markets: What Kinds of Policy Matter?

Laure Pasquier-Doumer

African labor markets are compartmentalized into segments with different structures and mechanisms in terms of wages, job prospects, and job security (Brilleau, Roubaud, and Torelli 2005; Kuépié, Nordman, and Roubaud 2009; see chapter 6 of this book). For on understanding of the dynamics of the African labor market, it is therefore vital to understand what determines access to the different segments.

The more labor market positioning depends on social origin, the less the principle of equal opportunities defined by Rawls (1971) is respected. This principle reads as follows: "Assuming there is a distribution of natural assets, those who are at the same level of talent and ability, and have the same willingness to use them, should have the same prospect of success regardless of their initial place in the social system" (p. 104). In addition to meeting a social justice goal, equality of opportunity in the labor market fulfills an economic efficiency function. Indeed, the *World Development Report 2006: Equity and Development* (World Bank 2005) identifies the reduction of unequal opportunities as a core development policy issue. Reducing inequalities of opportunity in the labor market improves the allocation of human capital, directing it to where its returns are highest.

The economic and sociological literature finds a number of mechanisms at work behind the intergenerational transmission of labor market position. Parents' occupational status can directly affect their children's occupational status through the transmission of physical capital, human capital, and social capital.

In a credit-constrained environment, the inheritance of physical capital increases access to socioeconomic groups that require an initial investment (Banerjee and Newman 1993). Human capital can take various forms. One is knowledge of a trade (know-how). Another is information, including knowledge of a professional environment, knowledge of the optimal actions to take within it, and knowledge of one's ability to work in certain occupations. Transmission of this human capital can lead individuals to choose the same occupation as their parents (Galor and Tsiddon 1997; Hassler and Mora 2000; Sjögren 2000). Parents also build social capital in the course of their work, in particular a social network and professional values that they can pass on to their children, making it easier for them to enter the profession in question (Lin, Vaughn, and Ensel 1981).

Parents' occupational status can also indirectly influence their children's position in the labor market by affecting the children's level of education. Many studies show that social origin is decisive in the acquisition of education, particularly as a result of capital market imperfections and the intergenerational transmission of abilities (see Haveman and Wolfe [1995] for a review of the literature on this subject). Parents' occupational status can condition both the resources they have available to educate their children and their children's motivation to study and the returns expected from that education.

The purpose of this chapter is twofold. First, it compares the extent of inequality of labor market opportunities in seven West African commercial capitals: Abidjan, Bamako, Cotonou, Dakar, Lomé, Niamey, and Ouagadougou. The extent of inequality of opportunities is defined here as the net association between individuals' labor market positions and their fathers' positions, irrespective of structural labor market effects. This comparison identifies the characteristics of the cities with the highest levels of inequality of opportunity, providing a basis for assessing theories explaining these differences.

Second, for each city, the chapter estimates the extent to which the effect of fathers' occupational status is direct or indirect (through education). The public policy implications are extremely different in the two cases. In the first case, opportunity leveling policies need to focus directly on the labor market. In the second case, they need to focus upstream, on the education system.

Comparative studies of the inequality of opportunities and social mobility take a quantitative sociology approach, seeking to evaluate which factors explain cross-country differences. Because data are thin on the ground, there are almost no comparative studies of developing countries. Most studies look at developed countries (Erikson and Goldthorpe 1992). Only a few include developing countries in their databases (Grusky and Hauser 1984; Ganzeboom, Luijkx, and Treiman 1989), and the studies that do include them apply the same social stratification used for developed countries. As numerous authors show, this stratification does not consider the particularity of labor markets in developing countries, where the informal sector predominates (Benavides 2002; Pasquier-Doumer 2005). Specific studies of developing countries are therefore needed to take account of the labor market structure in these countries.

Although Africa has the largest income inequalities in the world after Latin America (World Bank 2005), to our knowledge, only three comparative studies of the dynamics of these inequalities have been conducted in Africa (Bossuroy and Cogneau 2008; Cogneau and others 2007; Cogneau and Mesplé-Somps 2008). All draw on the same data, from representative surveys of five African countries: Côte d'Ivoire, Ghana, Guinea, Madagascar, and Uganda. The first two studies look at social mobility; the third focuses on inequality of income opportunity. All run up against a comparability problem, because different surveys use different occupational classifications, forcing the authors to aggregate occupations into just two groups, agricultural and nonagricultural activities. Lack of comparability is a major problem in most comparative studies of this kind, as Björklund and Jäntti (2000) show.

The 1-2-3 survey data (described in box O.1 in the overview) offer both highly detailed information on fathers' occupational status and excellent comparability. They can therefore be used to conduct a detailed analysis of the inequality of opportunities, incorporating a number of labor market aspects, including institutional sector and socioeconomic group.

This chapter is organized as follows. The first section describes the data. The second section compares the degree of inequality of opportunities in access to institutional sectors in seven cities. The third section examines the role of education in inequality of opportunities. The last section draws some conclusions.

The Data

This study examines the commercial capitals of the seven French-speaking countries in the West African Economic and Monetary Union (WAEMU): Benin, Burkina Faso, Côte d'Ivoire, Mali, Niger, Senegal, and Togo. Benin, Côte d'Ivoire, Senegal, and Togo are coastal countries, with a higher level of wealth on the whole than the landlocked countries of Burkina Faso, Mali, and Niger. The human development index draws an even sharper distinction between the two groups of countries (see annex table 8A.1).

The data used for each country are drawn from Phase 1 of the 1-2-3 surveys conducted in the commercial capitals of the WAEMU countries in 2001 and 2002. The surveys indicate the level of education of each respondent's mother and father, along with the father's socioeconomic group, business type, and business sector when the respondent was 15.[1] It is rare to find such detail on the father's occupational status in developing countries. The wording of the questions and the response options are identical in all surveys, making a robust and highly detailed comparison possible. Most studies on unequal opportunities have to make a trade-off between detail and comparability.

The data do not paint a representative picture of the labor market structure for the entire generation of fathers, as they include the occupational status only of fathers whose children were working in one of the seven West African commercial capitals at the time of the survey. Nevertheless, they allow for analysis and cross-country comparison of the professional trends of families currently living in the main urban centers. In particular, they reveal the strength of the association between the labor market situation of these cities' inhabitants and their fathers—the measure of inequality of opportunities used in this study.[2]

Inequality of Opportunities across Cities

This section evaluates the extent to which one's father's institutional sector access conditions one's own access to an institutional sector. The more conditioned the access is, the higher the degree of inequality of opportunities. The section then compares cities on the basis of this criterion, in order to understand what differentiates cities with the least inequality of opportunities from other cities.

The definition of institutional sectors used here is designed to reflect the phenomenon of labor market segmentation (see chapter 6 of this book) in the WAEMU capitals, distinguishing between the formal and informal sector. Individuals are considered part of the informal sector if they work in an unregistered business. We do not know whether the business in which the father worked was registered or not. We therefore consider fathers to have worked in the informal sector if they worked in a very small business, an association or other nonprofit institution, a household, or self-employment. We then separate public and semi-public workers from private sector workers to test the assumption that access to the public sector is more conditioned by social origin than is access to the formal private sector. The three sectors considered are therefore the public and semi-public sector, the formal private sector, and the informal sector.

Inequality of opportunities is defined as the link between the respondent's institutional sector and his or her father's institutional sector, irrespective of the distributions of respondents and fathers. This link captures net social mobility, also known as *social fluidity*. Social fluidity measures the change in the relative chances of individuals from different social origins attaining a given social status. An odds ratios analysis compares cities by level of social fluidity.

Odds ratios reflect the outcome of competition to enter one rather than another sector by individuals whose fathers worked in different institutional sectors. More precisely, they represent the relative inequality between two individuals whose fathers worked in sector i and sector i' in their chances of attaining group j' rather than j. The odds ratio is defined as

$$OR_{\substack{i-i' \\ j-j'}} = \frac{n_{ij}/n_{ij'}}{n_{i'j}/n_{i'j'}} = \frac{n_{ij}n_{i'j'}}{n_{i'j}n_{ij'}}$$

$$(8.1)$$

where n_{ij} is the number of observations in the cell (i, j) of the transition matrix, where row i represents the fathers' three institutional sectors and column j the respondents' institutional sectors. The odds of attaining sector j' rather than j are

$$OR_{\substack{i-i' \\ j-j'}}$$

times higher for an individual whose father worked in sector i' than for an individual whose father worked in sector i. An odds ratio of 1 indicates that having a father in sector i' secures no comparative advantage over having a father in sector i when it comes to entering j'. The further the odds ratio is from 1, the lower the social fluidity between two institutional sectors. The particularity of odds ratios is that they provide a measurement of the statistical association between two variables regardless of the marginal distributions. Figure 8.1 presents the odds ratios for the seven cities.

Comparison of the first three panels of figure 8.1, summarized in the last panel, reveals that in most cities, the transition between the public sector and the informal sector is the least socially fluid: the social distance between these sectors is generally much larger than the social distance between the public sector and the formal private sector or between the formal private sector and the informal sector. In most cities, the social distance between the formal private sector and the public sector is roughly the same as the social distance between the formal private sector and the informal sector. In Bamako, for example, an individual whose father worked in the public sector is about six times more likely to enter the public sector than an individual whose father worked in the informal sector and twice as likely as an individual whose father worked in the formal private sector; an individual whose father worked in the formal private sector is about twice as likely to work in the formal private sector as one whose father worked in the informal sector. The social distances between the formal private sector and the informal sector are not significantly different across cities, with the exception of Ouagadougou, where the social distance is significantly larger than in Abidjan or Dakar.

In terms of social fluidity between the public sector and the formal private sector, two contrasting groups of cities are found: Niamey and Ouagadougou post significantly higher social rigidity than Cotonou, Abidjan, and Dakar. In Niamey, having a father who worked in the public sector increases the chance that an individual works in the public sector by four times as much as having a father in the formal private sector. This ratio is a mere 1.1 in Abidjan, indicating virtual equality of opportunities of entering the formal private sector among individuals of public sector and private sector "origin." Lomé and Bamako stand at the boundary between the two groups.

The same groups are found when looking at fluidity between the public sector and the informal sector, except in Bamako, which joins the group of least fluid cities. In Cotonou, Lomé, and Dakar, the odds ratio averages 2.4; in Niamey, Ouagadougou, and Bamako, it averages 5.3.

Figure 8.1 Odds Ratios for Three Institutional Sectors in Seven West African Cities

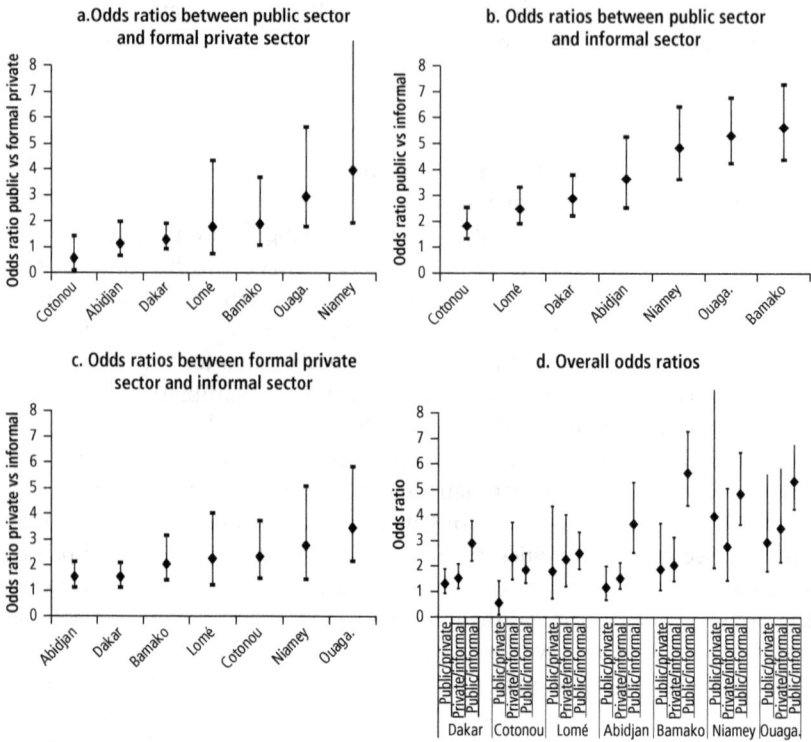

Sources: Based on Phase 1 of the 1-2-3 surveys of selected countries in the West African Economic and Monetary Union (WAEMU) conducted in 2001/02 by the Observatoire économique et statistique d'Afrique Subsaharienne (AFRISTAT); Développement, Institutions et Mondialisation (DIAL); and national statistics institutes.
Note: Figures are for individuals 35 and older. For each city, the median, represented by a diamond, corresponds to the odds ratio. The lower and upper limits, represented by the horizontal bars, correspond to the limits of a 90 percent confidence interval. Ouaga. = Ouagadougou.

Uniform difference log-multiplicative (unidiff) modeling, developed by Erikson and Goldthorpe (1992) and Xie (1992), is used to summarize these findings and propose an ordering of the cities covering all three dimensions. This modeling provides a composite measure of how the association between two qualitative variables—the respondent's sector and the father's sector—differs depending on a third variable, the city, regardless of the categories of the two qualitative variables considered. This composite measure is called the β, or intensity, parameter.[3] The change in the intensity parameter therefore represents the intercity variation in social inequalities in access to an institutional sector.

The parameter value for Dakar is set at 1. A parameter above (below) 1 represents a stronger (weaker) intensity of unequal opportunities. All the odds ratios between Dakar and the other city considered and for the three institutional sectors are assumed to increase with the same intensity β_j. The significance of the differences between each of the parameters was systematically tested and used to define groups of cities.

Inequality of opportunity in access to institutional sectors differs widely across the seven cities (figure 8.2). Two groups of cities emerge. The first is made up of the coastal cities of Abidjan, Cotonou, Dakar, and Lomé. The second comprises Bamako, Niamey, and Ouagadougou.[4] The level of inequality of opportunity in these cities is nearly two-thirds higher than in the cities in the first group. Abidjan and Bamako form a grey area between the two groups.[5]

The cities in the group with the least social fluidity are the capitals of countries that share certain characteristics (see annex table 8A.1). Burkina Faso, Mali, and Niger are landlocked countries. They have the lowest human development index rankings of the seven countries studied, the lowest levels of education and literacy, and the highest rates of mortality and malnutrition. Urbanization is lower in these countries, and their fertility index rankings are at least one point higher than the other four countries.

These findings are consistent with the liberal theory of social mobility, which states that the more industrialized a society, the more meritocratic the labor

Figure 8.2 Parameters of Intensity of Link between Institutional Sector of Individuals and Their Fathers

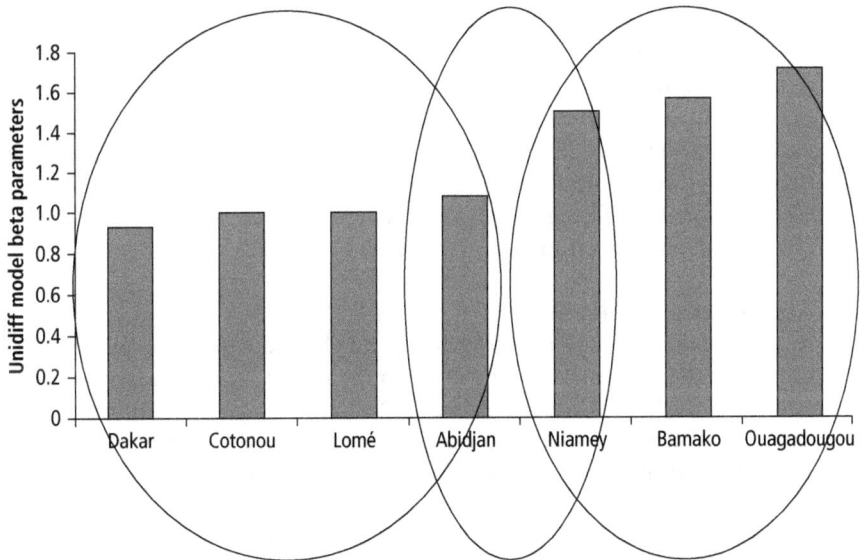

Sources: Based on Phase 1 of the 1-2-3 surveys of selected countries (see table 8.1 for details).
Note: Figures are for individuals 35 and older. The circles aggregate cities' intensity parameters that are not significantly different from one another.

market selection criteria, because the increase in the demand for skilled labor and urbanization prompt geographic mobility and reduce the feeling of community (Parsons 1960; Blau and Duncan 1967; Treiman 1970).

The Role of Education in Inequality of Opportunities

The above analysis provides no information on the causal link between the father's institutional sector and his children's sector. Is the effect direct, or does the father's occupation affect other characteristics, such as the children's level of education, which in turn influences access to an institutional sector?

This section considers a broader definition of social origin that includes place of birth and ethnic group and takes into account the individual's level of education. It seeks to clarify the channel through which social origin affects access to an institutional sector.

We start by estimating a logit model for each city to explain the probability of entering one institutional sector rather than the two others based on four aspects of social origin (father's institutional sector, whether the father went to school, individual's place of birth, and individual's ethnic group) while controlling for gender. Model 1 describes access to the public sector, model 3 access to the formal private sector, and model 5 access to the informal sector. Ethnic group is measured as membership in the city's majority ethnic group, except in Abidjan, where we look at membership in the Akan, Krou, and Southern Manding ethnic groups, in order to test the hypothesis of a social division of labor based on "*ivoirité*" (see chapter 9).[6] We then estimate the same models including the respondents' levels of education (models 2, 4, and 6). If social origin still has a significant effect in these models, we conclude that it has a direct effect on access to the institutional sectors. If the effect is no longer significant, we conclude that the effect of social origin is indirect. Table 8.1 presents the odds ratios obtained from estimation of the 42 (6×7) models.

Access to the Public Sector

In the least fluid cities (Bamako, Niamey, and Ouagadougou), the father's institutional sector has an effect on entry into the public sector, irrespective of its impact on the level of education (model 2). In these cities, other things equal, having a father who worked in the public sector rather than the informal sector increases the chances of working in the public sector by a factor of 2.2 in Bamako, 1.6 in Ouagadougou, and 1.5 in Niamey. In the capitals of the three landlocked countries, the father's occupational status thus has a direct effect on access to the public sector through a mechanism other than education (knowledge of the professional environment, know-how, penchant for the public sector, and so forth).

Table 8.1 Logit Estimation of Effects of Social Origin on Access to Public, Formal Private, and Informal Sectors in Seven Cities in West Africa, 2001/02

Variable/city	Public sector		Formal private sector		Informal private sector	
	Model 1	Model 2	Model 3	Model 4	Model 5	Model 6
Father in public or semi-public sector (reference = informal sector)						
Abidjan	2.5*	1.6	1.0	0.8	0.6*	1.0
Bamako	4.0*	2.2*	1.0	0.8	0.3*	0.6*
Cotonou	1.2	0.8	2.9*	2.5*	0.4*	0.6*
Dakar	2.1*	1.1	1.8*	1.6*	0.4*	0.6*
Lomé	2.3*	1.4	1.8*	1.4	0.4*	0.6*
Niamey	3.0*	1.5*	2.2*	1.5	0.3*	0.5*
Ouagadougou	3.5*	1.6*	1.8*	1.3	0.3*	0.6*
Father in formal private sector (reference = informal sector)						
Abidjan	2.0*	1.8*	0.8	0.7	0.8	1.0
Bamako	2.3*	1.9*	1.0	0.9	0.6*	0.7
Cotonou	0.9	0.6	1.8*	1.4	0.8	1.3
Dakar	1.4*	1.1	1.5*	1.2	0.6*	0.8
Lomé	1.1	0.8	1.7	1.5	0.7	0.9
Niamey	0.8	0.4*	2.8*	2.5*	0.6	1.0
Ouagadougou	1.5	0.6	2.0*	1.5	0.5*	1.2
City of birth						
Abidjan	0.9	0.9	1.3	1.2	0.9	0.9
Bamako	1.0	0.8	1.7*	1.6*	0.8*	0.8
Cotonou	0.5*	0.5*	1.0	1.2	1.6*	1.4*
Dakar	0.9	0.8	1.1	1.0	1.0	1.2
Lomé	0.6*	0.7*	0.9	0.8	1.5*	1.5*
Niamey	0.9	0.7	1.4	1.3	1.0	1.1
Ouagadougou	0.8	0.8	1.1	1.1	1.2	1.1
Member of majority ethnic group						
Abidjan (membership in the Akan, Krou, or Southern Manding ethnic group)	4.4*	2.2*	2.0*	1.4*	0.3*	0.5*
Bamako	1.0	1.2	0.7*	0.7	1.3*	1.1
Cotonou	1.4*	1.3*	0.9	0.9	0.8	0.9
Dakar	0.9	0.9	0.7*	0.7*	1.4*	1.4*
Lomé	0.7*	0.8	1.1	1.1	1.2	1.1
Niamey	1.2	1.4*	0.9	0.9	0.9	0.8*
Ouagadougou	0.5*	1.0	0.5*	0.6*	2.5*	1.5

(continued next page)

Table 8.1 (continued)

Variable/city	Public sector		Formal private sector		Informal private sector	
	Model 1	Model 2	Model 3	Model 4	Model 5	Model 6
Gender (reference = female)						
Abidjan	2.3*	1.2	4.6*	3.6*	0.2*	0.3*
Bamako	1.6*	1.1	6.8*	6.2*	0.3*	0.3*
Cotonou	3.1*	1.6*	4.8*	3.0*	0.2*	0.3*
Dakar	2.0*	1.6*	4.1*	4.2*	0.2*	0.2*
Lomé	3.4*	1.8*	5.8*	4.0*	0.2*	0.3*
Niamey	1.8*	1.3	4.6*	3.8*	0.3*	0.4*
Ouagadougou	2.1*	1.6*	2.9*	2.6*	0.3*	0.4*
Father attended school						
Abidjan	1.2	0.7	2.0*	1.7	0.5*	0.7
Bamako	1.5*	0.9	1.3	1.2	0.6*	0.9
Cotonou	2.1*	1.2	1.2	0.7	0.5*	1.1
Dakar	1.6*	1.4*	1.8*	1.5	0.5*	0.6*
Lomé	1.1	0.6*	1.6*	1.3	0.7*	1.2
Niamey	1.7*	0.9	1.3	1.0	0.5*	1.1
Ouagadougou	1.1	0.7	1.6	1.3	0.7*	1.3
Completed primary school or incomplete lower-secondary school (reference = less than completed primary school)						
Abidjan	—	5.5*	—	2.6	—	0.3*
Bamako	—	3.4*	—	1.4	—	0.5*
Cotonou	—	5.1*	—	2.2	—	0.3*
Dakar	—	5.2*	—	2.0	—	0.3*
Lomé	—	3.4*	—	2.5	—	0.3*
Niamey	—	4.8*	—	2.8	—	0.2*
Ouagadougou	—	6.3*	—	2.7	—	0.2*
Completed lower-secondary school or above (reference = less than completed primary school)						
Abidjan	—	25.0*	—	2.8	—	0.9*
Bamako	—	19.9*	—	2.3	—	0.1*
Cotonou	—	17.2*	—	7.4	—	0.0*
Dakar	—	13.2*	—	2.9	—	0.1*
Lomé	—	13.5*	—	3.4	—	0.1*
Niamey	—	18.1*	—	3.3	—	0.0*
Ouagadougou	—	24.5*	—	3.5	—	0.0*

Sources: Based on Phase 1 of the 1-2-3 surveys of selected countries (see figure 8.1 for details).
Note: Figures are for individuals 35 and older. The interpretation of a cell is the following: In model 1, for Dakar, having a father in the public sector increases the odds of working in the public sector by 2.1 compared with having a father in the informal sector. This means that other things equal, the probability of working in the public sector divided by the probability of not working in the public sector increases by 110 percent when the father worked in the public rather than the informal sector. — = not available.
* significant at the 10 percent level.

In the more fluid cities (Abidjan, Cotonou, Dakar, and Lomé), having a father who worked in the public sector has no direct effect on access to the public sector: once its effect on the level of education has been taken into account, the father's institutional sector is no longer a determinant of entry into the public sector.[7] We can therefore conclude that in Abidjan, Cotonou, Dakar, and Lomé, the father's institutional sector plays an indirect role in providing access to the public sector by determining the level of education. However, other aspects of social origin also come into play.

In Bamako and Niamey, having a father in the formal private sector also has a significant effect on accessing the public sector compared with having a father in the informal sector, but the effect is positive in Bamako and negative in Niamey. These findings reflect the short social distance between the formal private and informal sectors in Niamey and between the public sector and the formal private sector in Bamako (see panel d in figure 8.1). This distance is also apparent when considering other aspects of social origin, level of education, and gender.

In Niamey, inequality of opportunity is exacerbated by the significant role played by ethnicity in access to the public sector. Everything else equal, belonging to the Djerma ethnic group increases the probability of entering the public sector and significantly decreases the probability of entering the informal sector (model 6). Although the Djerma are a minority in Niger, they live in the western part of the country and are consequently the majority ethnic group in Niamey. The Djerma are also the first to have taken up senior positions in the colonial administration and army. Moreover, the leaders of Niger from independence through 1993 came from this ethnic group.

Ethnic group also has a significant effect on access to the public sector in Abidjan: members of the Akan, Krou, and Southern Manding ethnic groups are 2.2 times as likely to work in the public sector as members of the Northern Manding or Voltaic ethnic groups. They are also more likely to work in the formal private sector and less likely to work in the informal sector (models 4 and 6, respectively). These findings are consistent with the theory of a social division of labor based on *ivoirité*, which separates the "native" ethnic groups of the south from the "nonnative" ethnic groups of the north of Côte d'Ivoire.[8]

The public sector in Cotonou and Lomé is more open to migrants (defined here as people born outside the city) than to nonmigrants, other things equal. This finding runs counter to the expectation that being born in the city generates social capital that fosters entry into the public sector. It could be interpreted as favoritism toward people from certain regions. People from Kozah, the home prefecture of presidents Gnassingbé Eyadéma and Faure Gnassingbé (presidents of Togo since 1967), are overrepresented in Togo's public sector, and people from Natitingou, the department where Mathieu Kérékou (president of Benin, 1972–91 and 1996–2006) was born, are overrepresented in the public sector in

Benin. In Cotonou, the inequality of opportunities by region of birth is compounded by a significant ethnic group effect on access to the public sector: other things equal, members of the Fon, the majority ethnic group in Cotonou, are 1.3 times as likely as members of other ethnic groups to work in the public sector.

In four of the seven cities—Cotonou, Dakar, Lomé, and Ouagadougou—women are less likely to work in the public sector than men, other things equal.

Access to the Formal Private Sector

Among the least fluid cities (Bamako, Niamey, and Ouagadougou), only Niamey reveals the direct effect of the father's labor market position on access to the formal private sector: having a father who worked in the formal private sector increases the chances of working in it oneself by a factor of 2.5 (model 4). In Bamako and Ouagadougou, other aspects of social origin condition access to the formal private sector. In Bamako, being born in the city significantly increases access to the formal private sector. One interpretation of this finding is that being born in Bamako—and implicitly having spent most of one's life there—promotes the development of the social network required to enter the formal private sector. In Ouagadougou, everything else equal, the Mossi have less chance of entering the formal private sector than other ethnic groups, and they are overrepresented in the informal sector (model 6).

Among the most fluid cities (Abidjan, Cotonou, Dakar, and Lomé), the father's institutional sector has no direct effect on access to the formal private sector in Abidjan and Lomé. This result does not hold in Cotonou and Dakar: everything else equal, people whose fathers worked in the public sector are 2.5 times more likely to work in the formal private sector in Cotonou and 1.6 times more likely to do so in Dakar. This finding suggests the presence of an intergenerational bridge from the public to the private sector. No significant effect is found for the other aspects of social origin, except in Dakar, where, as in Ouagadougou, belonging to the majority ethnic group reduces the probability of entering the formal private sector and increases the chances of working in the informal sector.

Women in all seven cities are at a disadvantage relative to men when it comes to entering the formal private sector.

Access to the Informal Sector

Irrespective of the level of education, having a father who worked in the informal sector increases the probability of doing so oneself, except in Abidjan, where it has no significant direct effect. The effect of ethnicity differs across countries: it has no effect in Bamako, Cotonou, and Lomé; is significantly positive in Dakar and Ouagadougou; and is significantly negative in Abidjan and Niamey. Being born in the city increases the probability of working in the informal sector in Cotonou and Lomé. This effect is the counterpart of the negative effect of birth in the city on access to the public sector. In all cities, everything else equal, women have a higher probability of working in the informal sector than men.

Conclusion

This study uses perfectly comparable data to show that social origin in the seven West African capitals considered plays a decisive role in determining the sector of the labor market in which individuals work. Not all cities present the same level of inequality of opportunities: cities in the three landlocked countries with the lowest levels of human development and wealth (Bamako, Niamey, and Ouagadougou) have higher levels of inequality of opportunity than the coastal cities (Abidjan, Cotonou, Dakar, and Lomé). On average, the level of inequality of opportunity in access to an institutional sector is nearly two-thirds higher in Bamako, Niamey, and Ouagadougou than in Cotonou, Dakar, Lomé, and Abidjan. This ordering of cities into two groups is robust to the choice of the outcome variable considered (institutional sector, socioeconomic group, and level of education).[9]

For the four coastal cities, the intergenerational channels for the transmission of inequality are mainly indirect. Entering the public or the formal private sector depends crucially on the level of education, which is affected by the fathers' occupational status. In Bamako, Niamey, and Ouagadougou, fathers' occupational status also has a direct effect on the probability of working in the public sector (in Niamey it also affects entry into the formal private sector). This direct intergenerational transmission could reflect the existence of inheritable social or information capital that parents have built up as a result of their position in the labor market. In all cities, the likelihood of working in the informal sector is much greater, other things equal, if one's father worked in the informal sector.

A policy to reduce inequality of educational opportunities in Cotonou, Dakar, Lomé, and Abidjan would greatly reduce the inequality of opportunities in access to different institutional sectors. In Bamako, Niamey, and Ouagadougou, however, such a policy would fall short of the mark if the observed direct effect of the father's position reflects inheritable social or information capital that parents build up as a result of their position in the labor market. In the long run, leveling the educational playing field through extensive changes to society's standards and values could reduce the direct effect of fathers' status on labor market position.

Occupational status is not the only aspect of social origin that affects labor market position. In Abidjan, Dakar, Niamey, and Ouagadougou, ethnicity affects labor market position, even after controlling for migrant status. Belonging to the Djerma group in Niamey and the Akan, Krou, and Southern Manding groups in Abidjan significantly raises the chances of entering the public sector or being a wage earner and reduces the probability of working in the informal sector. In Dakar and Ouagadougou, belonging to the largest ethnic group in the city reduces the chances of entering the formal private sector or being a wage earner and increases the likelihood of working in the informal sector. In Bamako, Cotonou, and Lomé, migrant status affects labor market position. Relative to nonmigrants, migrants are more likely to work in the public sector and wage jobs in Cotonou and Lomé; in Bamako, they are less likely to work in the formal private sector.

Policies in three areas could increase equality of opportunity in the choice of sector: improving the supply of education, increasing demand for education, and developing the labor market. Specific policies are identified below.

Improving the Supply of Education

1. Prioritize the poor in public education spending. Public education spending in Africa does not prioritize the disadvantaged (Boudon 2006). To remedy this situation, some countries, such as Burkina Faso, have defined school catchment areas to identify areas and populations not served by school services and then made more equitable investment choices in terms of new establishments and teacher allocations. This practice is far from widespread, however. Other countries—including many English-speaking countries as well as Benin, Madagascar, and Rwanda—have adopted new methods of allocating educational resources, such as providing subsidies per pupil to cover nonwage expenses. In South Africa, a higher per pupil subsidy is allocated to schools educating poor children or located in poor areas, and the teacher-to-pupil ratio is higher in disadvantaged schools. These measures have helped reduce the huge inequalities that existed under apartheid

2. Make school more affordable by phasing out fees in primary school. One of the first African countries to eliminate primary school fees was Malawi, in 1991. The effects were immediate: school enrollment rose from 1.9 million in 1993/94 to 2.9 million in 1999/2000 (Al-Samarrai and Zaman 2007). Uganda followed suit in 1997, posting a comparable increase in enrollment. Many countries have followed their lead since, including Cameroon in 1999, Tanzania in 2001, Zambia in 2002, Madagascar in 2003, and Burundi in 2005. This reform has increased school enrollment rates in all these countries, particularly among the poorest children and children in rural areas. It has not had a positive impact on pupil retention among the poor, however, mainly because of a sharp downturn in the quality of education (Oketch and Rolleston 2007), highlighting the importance of implementation.

3. Make the education supply more flexible and tailor it to the needs of poor pupils by relaxing regulations that impede enrollment (requirement to present a birth certificate on first registration or to be registered by the parents, exclusion of

pregnant girls and girls who have given birth); changing the school calendar to bring it into line with the agricultural calendar; and developing specific programs for certain disadvantaged groups, including AIDS orphans, child soldiers, disabled children, and others.

4. Ensure access to good education for the most gifted poor children. Some countries encourage the highest-achieving children to enroll in good schools that will prepare them to enter higher education. Many African countries have prestigious establishments for this purpose—boarding schools and selective middle/secondary schools that groom the best pupils for higher education. The fairness of these programs depends on the selection process and whether disadvantaged children and rural children are equitably represented in these establishments. Attempts to introduce quotas (in Tanzania, for example) have rarely been effectively or fairly implemented in the long run. Some countries have introduced measures targeting underrepresented groups. India has set up special boarding schools for underrepresented castes. It also runs free boarding schools for girls in rural areas, to encourage them to graduate to secondary education. Cost considerations keep this type of measure thin on the ground in Africa, but efforts could be made to develop it.

Increasing Demand for Education

1. Reduce the indirect costs of education. A number of programs reduce the indirect costs of education for the poor, in order to stimulate demand for education. Among the most popular are conditional cash transfers and school meal programs. Conditional cash transfers are highly developed in Latin America. They pay a monthly allowance to poor families on the condition that they send their children to school. Impact assessments of these programs generally conclude that they significantly raise school enrollment and retention in the school system among the poor (IEG 2011). Projects of this kind are being pilot tested in some African countries, including Ghana, Kenya, Malawi, Mozambique, Nigeria, South Africa, Tanzania, Yemen, Zambia, and Zimbabwe.

   Numerous African countries operate school meal programs. Many studies have highlighted the positive impact of this type of action on pupil participation and attendance (Kremer 2003). School meals improve the neediest pupils' learning capacities and provide an incentive for families to send and keep their children in school. These programs are especially effective because they are applied early in the course of education and target schools teaching the largest numbers of very poor and vulnerable children.

2. Improve children's educability. The early childhood years are key to the development of the human brain. Poor hygiene, malnutrition, and abuse in

infancy and early childhood can permanently impair physical, mental, cognitive, and emotional development. Programs combining health care, vaccination, nutrition, and stimulation actions for infants and children under three can help reduce inequalities in cognitive development. The earlier these programs begin, the better.

Developing the Labor Market

1. Improve access to information on employment opportunities. Little use is made of formal job-seeking channels in Africa: in the WAEMU capitals, only 10 percent of workers find their jobs through formal job-seeking channels. The rate of job-seeker registration with employment agencies is very low, mainly because of the low profile of such agencies: 65 percent of job-seekers not registered with these agencies are simply unaware of their existence. Making employment agencies more efficient and raising their profile would improve equity of access to the labor market.

2. Help the poor access the credit market. If the direct intergenerational transmission of labor market position works through the transmission of physical capital, improving access to the credit market should make for more equal opportunities on the labor market.

3. Help the poor create social networks that will serve job-seeking. More than 60 percent of workers in the WAEMU capitals used their social network to find their job. A policy to develop the poor's social network would probably reduce the inequality of opportunities in the labor market. One possible course of action would be to develop partnerships between private and public enterprise and the training bodies that cater to the disadvantaged.

Annex: Economic and Social Statistics on Seven Countries in West Africa

Table 8A.1 Economic and Social Statistics on Seven Countries in West Africa

Statistic	Benin	Burkina Faso	Côte d'Ivoire	Mali	Niger	Senegal	Togo
Per capita GDP (constant dollars)	313	230	623	208	153	424	248
Gini coefficent	0.53	0.56	0.58	0.58	0.58	0.54	0.57
Rural population (percentage of total population)	58	83	56	70	79	53	67
Human development indicator (rank)	0.420 (158)	0.325 (169)	0.428 (156)	0.386 (164)	0.277 (172)	0.431 (154)	0.493 (141)
Malnutrition weight for age (percentage of children under 5)	23	34	21	33	40	23	25
Fertility index (births per woman)	6	7	5	7	8	5	6
Mortality rate (per 1,000 inhabitants)	13	18	17	18	22	12	12
Literacy rate (percentage of children 15 and older)	35	22	49	19	29	39	53
Primary completion rate (percent)	53	27	48	27	27	51	78
Gross intake rate (percent)	99	50	78	61	64	85	100

Sources: Data on GDP, rural population, malnutrition, fertility, and mortality are from World Bank 2000. Data on the Gini coefficient are from Amegashie and others 2005. Data on human development indicator are from UNDP 2002. Data on literacy are from World Bank 2004. Data on primary completion and gross intake are from UNESCO/BREDA 2005.
Note: GDP = gross domestic product.

Notes

1. Age 15 was chosen to ensure that all fathers were more or less in the same part of their life cycle, particularly their working life cycle, and that their job was the one they held just before their children entered the labor market. Comparability between individuals' work and their fathers' work is guaranteed when individuals are examined in the same part of their life cycle as their fathers. We therefore removed from the sample all individuals under 35, on the assumption that they had not yet reached the level of professional maturity their fathers had achieved when the individuals were 15. Retaining only the employed workers whose father worked leaves some 1,500 observations per city. The nonresponse rates are presented on the companion site to this book, http://www.dial.ird.fr/publications.

2. It would have been useful to compare women's occupations with their mothers' occupations, as the mother is potentially the main reference for women. However, too many observations are lost because of mothers' low labor force participation. The methodological choice to use fathers as the benchmark consequently underestimates the mobility of women on the whole.

3. More details on this modeling can be found on the book's companion site, http://www.dial.ird.fr/publications.

4. This coastal/landlocked city division is robust to the change in the definition of the informal sector: if we define the informal sector for respondents in the same way it is defined for their fathers (that is, working in a very small business, an association or other nonprofit institution, a household, or self-employment), Bamako, Niamey, and Ouagadougou still reveal high levels of unequal opportunities compared with Cotonou, Dakar, and Lomé, with Abidjan forming a gray area.

5. In the study by Cogneau and others (2007), Côte d'Ivoire, the only country featured in both that study and this one, has a much higher level of inequality than the two English-speaking countries studied (Ghana and Uganda).

6. The Akan are made up mainly of the Baoulé, Agni, and Ebrié. The Krou comprise primarily the Bété, Krou, and Bakoué groups. The Southern Manding comprises the Guro, Dan, and Gagu groups. Other ethnic groups are the Northern Manding groups (Dioula, Malinké, Koro, and others) and the Voltaic ethnic groups (Kulango, Lobi, Birifor, and others).

7. In Cotonou, however, having a father who worked in the private sector reduces the chances of working in the public sector; in Abidjan, it increases the chances compared with individuals whose fathers worked in the informal sector. These findings reflect more than the intergenerational transmission of labor market position, however. They are a sign of the social distance between sectors, especially the short distance between the public and formal private sectors in Cotonou and the long social distance between the public and informal sectors in Abidjan, where the public and formal private sectors are very close (see panel d in figure 8.1).

8. According to Banégas (2007, p. 28), under the first president of Côte d'Ivoire, Felix Houphouët-Boigny, "the economic and social integration of foreigners in urban areas came about relatively easily in the form of a social division of labor, a legacy of the colonial buy-in policy, which could be summed up by the following formula: to the people of Ivoirian 'extraction' (the term in use today to describe the populations

of the South) go the salaried jobs in the administration and the large public and semi-public corporations...; to foreigners and Northerners (especially Dioula) go small trade, transport and casual jobs in the informal sector."

9. These robustness checks are presented on the companion site to this book, http://www.dial.ird.fr/publications.

References

Al-Samarrai, S., and H. Zaman. 2007. "Abolishing School Fees in Malawi: The Impact on Education Access and Equity." *Education Economics* 15 (3): 359–75.

Amegashie, F., A. Brilleau, S. Coulibaly, O. Koriko, E. Ouedraogo, F. Roubaud, and C. Torelli. 2005. "La conception et la mise en oeuvre des enquêtes 1-2-3 en UEMOA. Les enseignements méthodologiques." *Statéco* 99: 21–41.

Banégas, R. 2007. "Ivory Coast: The Young Rise into Men. Anticolonialism and Ultra-nationalism among Patriotic Youth in Abidjan." *Les Études du CERI* 137, Center for International Studies and Research, Paris.

Banerjee, A. V., and A. F. Newman. 1993. "Occupational Choice and the Process of Development." *Journal of Political Economy* 1011 (2): 274–98.

Benavides, M. 2002. "Class Mobility and Equality of Opportunities in the Context of Erratic Modernization: The Peruvian Case." Ph.D. diss., Department of Sociology, Pennsylvania State University, State College, PA.

Björklund, A., and M. Jäntti. 2000. "Intergenerational Mobility of Socio-economic Status in Comparative Perspective." *Nordic Journal of Political Economy* 1: 2–32.

Blau, P., and O. D. Duncan. 1967. *The American Occupational Structure*. New York: Wiley and Sons.

Bossuroy, T., and D. Cogneau. 2008. "Social Mobility and Colonial Legacy in Five African Countries." DIAL Working Paper 2008–10, Développement, Institutions et Mondialisation, Paris.

Brilleau, A., F. Roubaud, and C. Torelli. 2005. "L'emploi, le chômage et les conditions d'activité dans la principale agglomération de sept états de l'UEMOA: premiers résultats de l'enquête emploi 2001–2002." *Statéco* 99: 43–63.

Boudon, J. 2006. "Coût et financement de l'éducation primaire en Afrique subsaharienne." In *Défis du développement en Afrique subsaharienne: l'éducation en jeu*, ed. M. Pilon. Paris: Centre, Population et Développement (CEPED).

Cogneau, D., and S. Mesplé-Somps. 2008. "Inequality of Opportunity for Income in Five Countries of Africa." *Research on Economic in Equality* 16: 99–128.

Cogneau D., L. Pasquier-Doumer, T. Bossuroy, P. De Vreyer, C. Guénard, V. Hiller, P. Leite, S. Mesplé-Somps, and C. Torelli. 2007. "Inequalities, and Equity in Africa." *Note et Documents* 31, Agence Française de Développement, Paris.

Erikson, R., and J. H. Goldthorpe. 1992. *The Constant Flux: A Study of Class Mobility in Industrial Societies*. Oxford: Clarendon Press.

Galor, O., and D. Tsiddon. 1997. "Technological Progress, Mobility, and Economic Growth." *American Economic Review* 87 (3): 363–82.

Ganzeboom, B. G., R. Luijkx, and D. J. Treiman. 1989. "Intergenerational Class Mobility in Comparative Perspective." *Research in Social Stratification, and Mobility* 8. Greenwich, CT: JAI Press.

Grusky, D., and R. Hauser R. 1984. "Comparative Social Mobility Revisited: Models of Convergence and Divergence in 16 Countries." *American Sociological Review* 49: 19–38.

Hassler, J., and J. R. Mora. 2000. "Intelligence, Social Mobility, and Growth." *American Economic Review* 90 (4): 888–908.

Haveman, R., and B. Wolfe. 1995. "The Determinants of Children's Attainments: A Review of Methods, and Findings." *Journal of Economic Literature* 33: 1829–78.

IEG (Independent Evaluation Group). 2011. *Evaluation and Lessons Learned from Impact Evaluations on Social Safety Nets.* Washington, DC: World Bank.

Kremer, M. 2003. "Randomized Evaluations of Educational Programs in Developing Countries: Some Lessons." *American Economic Review* 93 (2): 102–06.

Kuépié, M., C. J. Nordman, and F. Roubaud. 2009. "Education and Earnings in Urban West Africa." *Journal of Comparative Economics* 37: 491–515.

Lin, N., J. C. Vaughn, and W. M. Ensel. 1981. "Social Resources and Occupational Status Attainment." *Social Forces* 59 (4): 1163–81.

Oketch, M., and C. Rolleston. 2007. "Policies on Free Primary and Secondary Education in East Africa: Retrospect and Prospect." *Review of Research in Education* 31: 131–58.

Parsons, T. 1960. *Structure and Process in Modern Societies.* Glencoe, IL: Free Press.

Pasquier-Doumer, L. 2005. "Perception de l'inégalité des chances et mobilités objective et subjective: une analyse à partir d'entretiens qualitatifs auprès de Liméniens." DIAL Working Paper 2005–17, Développement, Institutions et Mondialisation, Paris.

Rawls, J. 1971. *A Theory of Justice.* Cambridge, MA: Harvard University Press.

Sjögren, A. 2000. "Redistribution, Occupational Choice, and Intergenerational Mobility: Does Wage Equality Nail the Cobbler to His Last?" Working Paper 538, Research Institute of Industrial Economics, Stockholm.

Treiman, D. J. 1970. "Industrialization and Social Stratification." *Sociological Inquiry, Special Issue: Stratification Theory and Research* 40: 207–34.

UNDP (United Nations Development Programme). 2002. *Human Development Report.* New York: UNDP.

UNESCO/BREDA (United Nations Education, Scientific and Cultural Organization/Regional Bureau for Education in Africa). 2005. *Paving the Way for Action.* Dakar: UNESCO/BREDA.

World Bank. 2000. *World Development Indicators.* Washington, DC: World Bank.

———. 2004. *World Development Indicators.* Washington, DC: World Bank.

———. 2005. *World Development Report 2006: Equity and Development.* Washington, DC: World Bank.

Xie, Y. 1992. "The Log-Multiplicative Layer Effect Model for Comparing Mobility Tables." *American Sociological Review* 57 (3): 380–95.

Chapter **9**

Decomposing Gender and Ethnic Earnings Gaps in Seven Cities in West Africa

Christophe J. Nordman, Anne-Sophie Robilliard, and François Roubaud

Women and certain ethnic groups often face unequal treatment in labor markets, in both developed and developing countries. Many studies examine ethnic and gender wage gaps in developed countries (Altonji and Blank 1999; Blau and Kahn 2000). In contrast, only 3 percent of the studies on the gender wage gap draw on African data (Weichselbaumer and Winter-Ebmer 2005). As a result, little is known about inequalities in labor market outcomes in Africa.

Enhancing the literature on the gender and ethnic gap in the poorest countries is important for several reasons. First, there are manifest shortcomings of studies on African countries, particularly because of the thinness of the data (Bennell 1996). Second, gender and ethnic inequalities are likely to be greater where markets do not function efficiently and the state lacks the resources to introduce corrective policies. Third, understanding the roots of gender and ethnic inequalities and narrowing these gaps could help policy makers design poverty-reduction policies.

Under the Poverty Reduction Strategy Paper (PRSP) initiative, which concerns more than 60 of the world's poorest countries, policies designed to counter gender discrimination are among the recommended solutions to reduce poverty.[1] Goal 3 of the Millennium Development Goals (MDGs) is specifically aimed at reducing gender inequalities. In order to put this recommendation into practice, policy makers need to understand whether differences in labor outcomes stem from differences in individual characteristics or differences in the returns to these characteristics. Different sets of policies are called for in each case.

The literature on gender gaps confirms the presence of gender inequalities for both wage-earners and self-employed workers. In Guinea, differences in individual characteristics account for only 45 percent of the gender gap in earnings from self-employment and 25 percent of the differences in earnings from public sector employment; in the private sector, women earn more than men (Glick and Sahn 1997). Armitage and Sabot (1991) find gender inequality in the public sector of Tanzania; they find no evidence of gender discrimination in Kenya's labor market. Glewwe (1990) finds no wage discrimination against women in Ghana. On the contrary, women in the public sector seem to earn more than men.[2] Siphambe and Thokweng-Bakwena (2001) show that in the public sector of Botswana, most of the wage gap reflects differences in individual characteristics between men and women rather than discrimination. In contrast, most of the wage gap in the private sector reflects discrimination. Appleton, Hoddinott, and Krishnan (1999) find evidence that the public sector of Côte d'Ivoire and Uganda practices less wage discrimination than the private sector. Nordman and Roubaud (2009) find a similar result for Madagascar, where a gender gap in the public sector favors women.

The magnitude of gender wage gaps in the public and private sectors varies across countries. However, the main reason for this diversity may be in the heterogeneity of the data sources used by different authors (labor force or household surveys undertaken for purposes other than studying the labor market), in the period they consider, and in the methodology they implement.

Concerning the ethnic wage gap, the literature is even scarcer. Barr and Oduro (2000) find that standard observed differences in workers' characteristics explain much of the earnings differentials across ethnic groups in Ghana. The role of ethnolinguistic fractionalization in development has received much more attention. Easterly and Levine (1997) conclude that "Africa's growth tragedy" is in part related to its high level of ethnic diversity, resulting in poor institutional functioning.

This chapter casts light on these issues by using the set of 1-2-3 surveys conducted in the capital cities of the seven French-speaking countries of the West African Economic and Monetary Union (WAEMU) (for a description of these surveys, see box O.1 in the overview). This approach is important for two reasons. First, the data used were collected using the same sampling method and virtually identical questionnaires in each city in the same period of time (2001–02), making for totally comparable results. Second, the chapter analyzes both gender and ethnic gap issues using the same methodological approach for each city.

The chapter is organized as follows. The first section discusses the data, concepts, and econometric methods used. The second section analyzes the results. The last section summarizes the main findings and draws conclusions.

Data, Concepts, and Methodology

This section presents the data and concepts used. It then discusses the methodology of earnings decompositions, an essential aspect of the investigation.

Data and Concepts

The data are taken from Phase 1 of the 1-2-3 surveys conducted in the seven French-speaking capitals of the WAEMU countries. The sample surveyed in Phase 1 included 93,213 individuals (17,841 households). All respondents were asked about their ethnic group. The nonresponse rate was very low, with just 665 respondents failing to identify their ethnic group.

When restricted to working individuals with nonzero earnings, on whom our estimations are based, the sample size is reduced to 20,878 observations (table 9.1), with a minimum of 2,294 observations in Niamey and a maximum of 3,575 observations in Dakar. This sample is still large enough to allow disaggregation of the data by sector (public sector, formal private sector, and informal sector) and gender.

The number of ethnic groups listed in the questionnaire ranged from 9 in Benin and Niger to 40 in Togo. In order to harmonize the data and the number of categories considered, we collapsed the 40 Togolese groups and 18 Ivorian groups into 6 groups.

Wage Gap Decomposition Techniques

Traditional gender earnings decompositions rely on estimations of Mincer-type earnings functions for men and women of the form

$$\ln w_i = \beta \mathbf{x}_i + \varepsilon_i \tag{9.1}$$

where $\ln w_i$ is the natural logarithm of the observed hourly earnings for individual i; $\mathbf{x}_i$ is a vector of observed individual characteristics; β is a vector of coefficients; and ε_i is a disturbance term with an expected value of zero. Earnings

Table 9.1 Number of Working Individuals in Sample with Nonzero Earnings in Seven Cities in West Africa, by Sector and Gender

City	Public sector		Formal private sector		Informal sector	
	Men	Women	Men	Women	Men	Women
Abidjan	221	85	679	177	1,358	1,543
Bamako	336	126	389	71	1,462	1,558
Cotonou	296	115	387	142	1,389	1,881
Dakar	356	147	738	245	1,760	1,815
Lomé	238	78	250	60	1,252	1,727
Niamey	427	174	326	95	1,316	978
Ouagadougou	404	191	260	88	1,534	1,305

Sources: Based on Phase 1 of the 1-2-3 surveys of selected countries in the West African Economic and Monetary Union (WAEMU) conducted in 2001/02 by the Observatoire économique et statistique d'Afrique Subsaharienne (AFRISTAT); Développement, Institutions et Mondialisation (DIAL); and national statistics institutes.

functions are first estimated separately for men and women and for the different sectors.

There is no universally accepted set of conditioning variables that should be included in describing the causes of gender differentials, although the consensus seems to be that controls for productivity-related factors such as education, labor market experience, and marital status should be included. It is debatable whether job characteristics, occupation, and industry should be taken into account: if employers differentiate between men and women by tending to hire into certain occupations, then occupational assignment is an outcome of employer practices rather than an outcome of individual choice or productivity differences.[3]

It was not possible to account for workers' actual experience in the labor market; potential experience, which can be viewed as reflecting the "gross" time individuals have spent while in the labor force (measured as age minus years of schooling minus six, the legal age at school entry), was therefore used. Use of potential rather than actual experience represents a possible limitation of the study, because differences in labor force attachment by gender are important in explaining the size of the gender wage gap. Indeed, measures of women's work experience are particularly prone to errors given the discontinuity of women's labor market participation (women often leave the labor force to bear and raise children, for instance). Using proxy measures such as potential experience may thus overestimate experience for women; it may be a good approximation of experience for men with greater labor force attachment (Nordman and Roubaud 2009).[4]

Concerns arise over possible sample selection biases in the estimations. One source is the fact that earnings are observed only when people work, and not everyone is working. The second source is the selective decision to work in the public sector rather than the private or informal sectors.

We address both issues using Lee's two-stage approach to take account of the possible effect of endogenous paid-work participation and sector allocation on earnings (Lee 1983).[5] In the first stage, multinomial logit models of individual i's participation for pay in sector j are used to compute the correction terms λ_{ij} from the predicted probabilities $\mathbf{P}_{ij}$. The sectors considered in the multinomial logit are the public sector, the formal private sector, and the informal sector. The reference category includes all other working-age individuals (inactive, unemployed, and unpaid workers).

A potential problem is that the multinomial logit may suffer from the independence of irrelevant alternatives (IIA) assumption, which in most cases is questionable. Hausman-type tests (Hausman and McFadden 1984) for each city and sector provide massive evidence that the IIA assumption is not violated, except in the informal sector of Bamako. In Lee's procedure, identification is achieved by including additional individual variables in the first-stage selection equations that are omitted in the second-stage earnings regressions: a set of dummies indicating relationship to the household head, the dependency ratio (number of non-working-age individuals divided by the total number of individuals in the household), and the household size.[6] We assume that these variables do not influence earnings.

Oaxaca and Neumark's traditional earnings decompositions. The most common approach to identifying sources of gender wage gaps is the Oaxaca-Blinder decomposition (based on the seminal work of Oaxaca 1973 and Blinder 1973). In this approach, two separate standard Mincerian log earnings equations are estimated for men and women:

$$\overline{\ln w_m} - \overline{\ln w_f} = \beta_m (\overline{x}_m - \overline{x}_f) + (\beta_m - \beta_f)\overline{x}_f \tag{9.2}$$

where w_m and w_f are the means of earnings by men and by women; x_m and x_f are vectors containing the means of the independent variables for men and women; and β_m and β_f are the estimated coefficients. The first term on the right-hand side captures the earnings differential caused by differences in the individual characteristics of men and women. The second term is the earnings gap attributable to different returns to those characteristics or coefficients.

It can be argued that, under discrimination, men are paid competitive wages and women are underpaid. If this is the case, the coefficients for men should be taken as the nondiscriminatory wage structure, as in equation (9.2). Conversely, if employers pay women competitive wages but pay men more, then the women's coefficients should be used as the nondiscriminatory wage structure. The issue is thus how to determine the wage structure β^* that would prevail in the absence of discrimination. This choice poses the well-known index number problem. A priori neither appears preferable, but the decomposition can be quite sensitive to the selection made. The literature proposes different weighting schemes to deal with the underlying index problem (Neumark 1988). We rely on the general decomposition proposed by Neumark, which can be written as follows:

$$\overline{\ln w_m} - \overline{\ln w_f} = \beta^* (\overline{x}_m - \overline{x}_f) + [(\beta_m - \beta^*)\overline{x}_m + (\beta^* - \beta_f)\overline{x}_f]. \tag{9.3}$$

This decomposition can be reduced to Oaxaca's two special cases if it is assumed that there is no discrimination in the wage structure for men (that is, $\beta^* = \beta_m$) or for women ($\beta^* = \beta_f$). Neumark shows that β^* can be estimated using the weighted average of the wage structures of men and women and advocates using the pooled sample to estimate β^*. The first term is the gender wage gap attributable to differences in individual characteristics. The second and third terms capture the difference between the actual and pooled returns for men and women.

Earnings decompositions with sample selectivity. Neuman and Oaxaca (2004) show that sample selection complicates the interpretation of earnings decompositions. They offer several alternative decompositions, each based on different assumptions and objectives. We use one of them that considers selectivity as a separate component. This technique has the advantage of not calling for any prior hypothesis regarding the links between individual characteristics and selectivity. An additional term in the decomposition measures the contribution of selection effects to the observed gender earnings gap, $\hat{\theta}_m \hat{\lambda}_m - \hat{\theta}_f \hat{\lambda}_f$, where $\hat{\lambda}$ and $\hat{\theta}$ denote the mean correction term (generalized Mills ratio) and its estimated coefficient from each regression by gender. Hence, in the full sectoral decomposition that follows, when trying to account for sample selectivity, we consider the decomposition of offered instead of actual earnings (that is, earnings net of the selection effects $\hat{\theta}\hat{\lambda}$) (see Reimers 1983).

Full sectoral decomposition. Although the improvement proposed by Neumark's decomposition is attractive, it is not immune from criticisms of decomposition methods in general. One of them is that without evidence that employers care only about the proportion of each type of labor employed, it is not clear that the pooled coefficient is a good estimator of the nondiscriminatory wage structure. The full sectoral decomposition of Appleton, Hoddinott, and Krishnan (1999) takes into account differences in sectoral structures by gender by using an approach similar to Neumark's and decomposing the gender earnings gap into three components.

Let $\overline{W}_m$ and $\overline{W}_f$ be the means of the natural logs of men's and women's earnings and $\overline{p}_{mj}$ and $\overline{p}_{fj}$ the sample proportions of men and women in sector j. Earnings can be written as the sum of sectoral earnings weighted by the proportion of workers in each sector:

$$\overline{W}_m = \sum_{j=1}^{3} \overline{W}_{mj} \overline{p}_{mj} \tag{9.4}$$

$$\overline{W}_f = \sum_{j=1}^{3} \overline{W}_{fj} \overline{p}_{fj} \tag{9.5}$$

One can decompose the difference in mean earnings into intrasectoral earnings differences and differences in proportions employed in the different sectors. In order to overcome the index problem, Appleton, Hoddinott, and Krishnan (1999) assume the sectoral structure that would prevail in the absence of gender differences in the impact of individual characteristics on sectoral choice.

Let $\overline{p}_j^*$ be the proportion of workers in sector j under this assumption. Appleton, Hoddinott, and Krishnan decompose the difference in mean earnings as follows:

$$\overline{W}_m - \overline{W}_f = \sum_{j=1}^{3} \overline{p}_j^* (\overline{W}_{mj} - \overline{W}_{fj}) + \sum_{j=1}^{3} \overline{W}_{mj} (\overline{p}_{mj} - \overline{p}_j^*) + \sum_{j=1}^{3} \overline{W}_{fj} (\overline{p}_j^* - \overline{p}_{fj}) \tag{9.6}$$

The first term can be decomposed using the Neumark decomposition presented earlier. The second and third terms can be decomposed further, in order to distinguish differences arising from differences in individual characteristics from differences arising from differences in returns to these characteristics. One can derive the average probability of being employed in a given sector for men and women from the estimation of pooled and separate multinomial logit models for each gender. These mean probabilities are denoted by $\overline{p}_{mj}^*$ and $\overline{p}_{fj}^*$.

Embedding the self-selection process in equation (9.6) allows the full decomposition to be written as follows:

$$\overline{W}_m - \overline{W}_f = \sum_{j=1}^{3} \overline{p}_j^* (\overline{x}_{mj} - \overline{x}_{fj}) \beta_j^* + \sum_{j=1}^{3} \overline{p}_j^* \overline{x}_{mj} (\beta_{mj} - \beta_j^*) + \sum_{j=1}^{3} \overline{p}_j^* \overline{x}_{fj} (\beta_j^* - \beta_{fj})$$

$$+ \sum_{j=1}^{3} \overline{W}_{mj} (\overline{p}_{mj}^* - \overline{p}_j^*) + \sum_{j=1}^{3} \overline{W}_{fj} (\overline{p}_j^* - \overline{p}_{fj}^*) + \sum_{j=1}^{3} \overline{W}_{mj} (\overline{p}_{mj} - \overline{p}_{mj}^*)$$

$$+ \sum_{j=1}^{3} \overline{W}_{fj} (\overline{p}_{fj}^* - \overline{p}_{fj}) \tag{9.7}$$

The first three terms are similar to Neumark's decompositions of within-sector earnings gaps. The fourth and fifth terms measure the difference in earnings caused by differences in the distribution of men and women in different sectors. The last two terms account for differences in earnings resulting from the deviations between predicted and actual sectoral compositions of men and women not accounted for by differences in individual characteristics.

Earnings gap decomposition for ethnic groups. Extending decomposition methods developed and traditionally used to analyze possible discrimination against women to the study of earnings differentials between ethnic groups is not straightforward. One of the main problems is related to the definition and measurement of ethnicity: what defines an ethnic group? In developed countries, there exist conflicting views and different traditions regarding the collection of data on ethnic origin. Anglo-Saxon societies are accustomed to measuring and analyzing data on so-called racial and ethnic groups; many other countries refuse to categorize individuals using ethnic or racial criteria and, as a result, do not collect statistical data on ethnic origin.[7]

In Africa, the notion of ethnicity also raises a number of questions that social scientists have debated extensively (Bayart 1989). Anthropologists have shown that ethnic groups are not characterized by genetic homogeneity. Depending on countries and contexts, the constitution of ethnic groups appears to be more or less recent and their definition malleable. Some groups have their origin in a common myth or ancestor; others share only a language and culture. Some "ethnic groups" have been constructed by other groups, following migration, invasion, or colonization.

These various origins notwithstanding, ethnicity plays an important role in social relations in many African countries. There is, for instance, strong evidence of high levels of endogamy (marriage within a specific group, as required by custom or law), not only in rural areas, where ethnic homogeneity is often observed, but also in urban areas, where different ethnic groups cohabit. In recent years, economists have examined the importance of ethnicity to development and growth. The seminal paper is the study by Easterly and Levine (1997), who conclude that "Africa's growth tragedy" is in part related to its high level of ethnic diversity, which results in poor institutional functioning. This conclusion remains a subject of debate (see Bossuroy 2007 for a discussion).

This chapter focuses on the impact of ethnicity on labor market outcomes measured through earnings. To apply the methods developed for the analysis of the gender earnings gap, one is inclined to construct a dichotomous variable identifying either a possibly favored or discriminated-against ethnic group. Data collection on ethnicity at the household or individual level is common in Africa: most household and employment surveys include a variable indicating ethnic group. However, given the diversity of national contexts, two difficulties arise. The first is related to identifying a priori a discriminated-against ethnic group. Should one consider the majority ethnic group as favored? Or should one consider instead the group to which the head of state belongs? The second difficulty arises because of our comparative framework. How does belonging to different groups compare across countries? For instance, is being a Mossi in Ouagadougou (77 percent of the population) comparable to being a Bambara in Bamako (34 percent of the population). We consider various aspects of possible ethnic discrimination on urban labor markets while keeping in mind the different national contexts.

Results

We now turn to the presentation and analysis of results obtained using the different approaches presented above.

Neumark Decomposition of Gender and Ethnic Earnings Gaps

This section analyzes gender and ethnic earnings gaps using traditional decomposition approaches. We identify the largest ethnic group in each city (table 9.2). These groups represent a majority of the population in three of seven cities (Cotonou, Lomé, and Ouagadougou; see the annex for details).

In six of the seven cities, the largest ethnic group corresponds to the majority group at the national level. The sole exception is Niamey, where the Djerma are the largest ethnic group but the Haoussa represent 54 percent of the population of Niger. Figure 9.1 reports two Herfindhal concentration indices for ethnolinguistic fractionalization (ELF) in each country.[8] The first is computed at the national

Table 9.2 Largest Ethnic Group in Seven Cities in West Africa, 2001/02

City	Ethnic group	Percentage of population
Abidjan	Akan	34.2
Bamako	Bambara	34.4
Cotonou	Fon	60.9
Dakar	Wolof	40.4
Lomé	Ewe-Mina-Wachi	74.2
Niamey	Djerma	49.5
Ouagadougou	Mossi	78.2

Sources: Based on Phase 1 of the 1-2-3 surveys of selected countries (see table 9.1 for details).

Figure 9.1 Herfindhal Concentration Indices of Ethnolinguistic Fractionalization in Seven Countries in West Africa, 2001/02

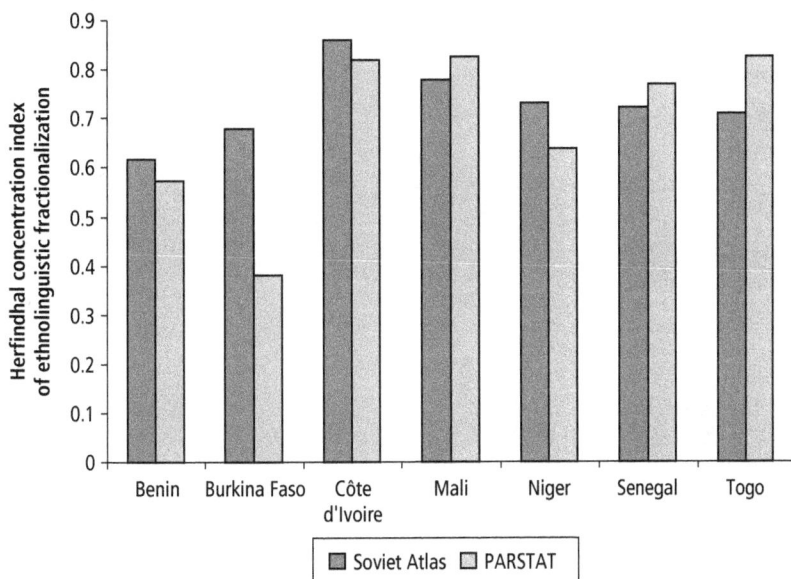

Sources: Soviet Atlas data are from Fearon 2003; survey data are from Phase 1 of the 1-2-3 surveys of selected countries (see table 9.1 for details).
Note: The ELF measure, available for 129 countries, captures the likelihood that two people chosen at random will be from different ethnic groups. It is calculated using a simple Herfindahl concentration index. The Herfindahl concentration formula is $ELF = 1 - \sum_{i=1}^{n} s_i^2$, where s_i is the share of group i ($i = 1, \ldots, n$). The Soviet Atlas data were compiled by Soviet ethnographers in the early 1960s and published in the *Atlas Narodov Mira* in 1964. ELF = ethnolinguistic fractionalization; PARSTAT = Programme d'Appui Régional à la Statistique.

level; the second is computed for the seven cities, using the 1-2-3 survey data. Levels are similar across all countries except Burkina Faso, where the ELF index appears to be much lower in the capital than at the country level. This difference stems from the fact that the ethnic majority group (Mossi) represents 78 percent of the population in Ouagadougou and only 50 percent at the national level.

Table 9.3 reports the decomposition of earnings gaps based on Neumark's approach. A number of results are worth emphasizing. Raw gender earnings gaps are large and significant, and they range widely across cities (from 50.0 in Niamey to 79.2 in Abidjan). These figures indicate that, on average, women's earnings in Abidjan are 20.8 percent of men's earnings. Raw gender earnings gaps are positive by construction, because they are computed as the difference between a "high group" and a "low group." In the sample of countries, women always correspond to the low group. In contrast, the largest ethnic group corresponds to the high group in Abidjan, Dakar, and Niamey and to the low group in Bamako, Cotonou, Lomé, and Ouagadougou.[9]

Table 9.3 Neumark Decompositions of Gender and Ethnic Earnings Gaps in Seven Cities in West Africa, 2001/02

Type of gap/city	Raw earnings gap	Without occupation or sector dummies			With occupation dummies			With occupation and sector dummies		
		Explained	Unexplained	Unexplained (percent)	Explained	Unexplained	Unexplained (percent)	Explained	Unexplained	Unexplained (percent)
Gender earnings gaps										
Abidjan	0.792***	0.337	0.455	57.4	0.396	0.396	50.0	0.420	0.372	47.0
Bamako	0.736***	0.301	0.435	59.2	0.283	0.452	61.5	0.306	0.430	58.4
Cotonou	0.779***	0.339	0.439	56.4	0.355	0.423	54.3	0.361	0.418	53.7
Dakar	0.556***	0.194	0.361	65.0	0.203	0.353	63.5	0.246	0.309	55.7
Lomé	0.787***	0.427	0.360	45.7	0.481	0.306	38.9	0.482	0.305	38.7
Niamey	0.500***	0.196	0.304	60.9	0.197	0.303	60.6	0.195	0.305	61.0
Ouagadougou	0.754***	0.248	0.506	67.1	0.305	0.449	59.5	0.305	0.448	59.5
Ethnic earnings gaps										
Abidjan	0.279***	0.225	0.054	19.4	0.253	0.027	9.5	0.255	0.025	8.8
Bamako	-0.182***	-0.103	-0.079	43.4	-0.109	-0.073	40.1	-0.111	-0.071	39.0
Cotonou	-0.015	0.040	-0.055	369.7	0.048	-0.062	421.5	0.050	-0.065	441.1
Dakar	0.068**	-0.001	0.069	101.9	0.024	0.044	65.2	0.022	0.046	68.1
Lomé	-0.113***	-0.055	-0.059	51.7	-0.066	-0.047	41.3	-0.081	-0.032	28.3
Niamey	0.019	-0.034	0.053	278.8	-0.022	0.041	216.8	-0.024	0.043	226.7
Ouagadougou	-0.537***	-0.430	-0.107	20.0	-0.463	-0.074	13.8	-0.461	-0.076	14.2

Sources: Based on Phase 1 of the 1-2-3 surveys of selected countries (see table 9.1 for details).
* significant at the 10 percent level, ** significant at the 5 percent level, *** significant at the 1 percent level.

Gender differences in the distribution of individual characteristics related to productivity—such as education and experience—explain less than half of the raw gender gap in six of the seven cities. Lomé is an exception, with differences in individual characteristics explaining almost 55 percent of the gap. Including variables related to the type of occupation decreases somewhat the unexplained share of the raw gender gap. This decrease appears to be substantial in Abidjan, Lomé, and Ouagadougou.

Men are systematically favored over women in all cities in the sample. In contrast, the largest ethnic groups do not appear to have a systematically favorable position in the urban labor markets. Only in Abidjan and Dakar is the gap both significant and favorable for the largest ethnic group (in Abidjan, the Akan earn 28 percent more than other ethnic groups; in Dakar, the Wolof earn 7 percent more than other ethnic groups). In Bamako, Lomé, and Ouagadougou, members of the largest ethnic group earn significantly less than members of other ethnic groups. In Ouagadougou, lower average earnings by the Mossi could be related to their spatial distribution: they represent 78 percent of the population of the capital city but just 50 percent of the population of Burkina Faso. It could be that only better-performing non-Mossi migrate to the capital.

The decomposition of ethnic earnings gaps reveals markedly different results across cities. In Abidjan, differences in the distribution of individual characteristics explain more than 85 percent of the gap, leaving little room for discrimination (the unexplained share). In Bamako, the unexplained share of the gap is 43 percent (39 percent once occupational and sector dummies are included in the regressions). In Dakar, 100 percent of the gap is left unexplained until job characteristics related to occupation and sector are introduced. In Ouagadougou, where the majority ethnic group (Mossi) earns less than other groups, the gap is also in large part explained by differences in the distribution of individual characteristics, such as education and experience; just 20 percent of the differential is unexplained.

Full Decomposition of Gender Earnings Gap

There are at least four types of labor markets in most developing countries: rural (or agricultural), public, formal private, and informal. Each of these markets has its own characteristics, such as job seasonality, uncertainty of demand, the nature of contracts, and the structure of wages and earnings. As a result, gender and ethnic labor allocation across these sectors can be expected to contribute to earnings gaps.

Following Appleton, Hoddinott, and Krishnan (1999) and Nordman and Roubaud (2009), we provide comparable estimates of the size and determinants of gender earnings gaps using the full decomposition method described previously. Given that we are analyzing urban labor markets, only three types of labor markets are examined: public, formal private, and informal. The results are reported without (table 9.4) and with (table 9.5) correction for selectivity of participation and sectoral allocation.

Table 9.4 Full Decomposition of Gender Earnings Gap in Seven Cities in West Africa without Correction for Selectivity, 2001/02

Raw earnings gap	Abidjan	Percent	Bamako	Percent	Cotonou	Percent	Dakar	Percent	Lomé	Percent	Niamey	Percent	Ouagadougou	Percent
	0.792***		0.736***		0.779***		0.556***		0.787***		0.500***		0.754***	
Within-sector differences attributable to														
Characteristics	0.099	12.5	0.133	18.1	0.166	21.3	0.043	7.7	0.240	30.5	0.060	12.1	0.092	12.3
Differences in men's returns	0.192	24.3	0.199	27.0	0.238	30.6	0.143	25.8	0.191	24.2	0.110	22.1	0.210	27.9
Differences in women's returns	0.185	23.4	0.209	28.4	0.178	22.9	0.161	28.9	0.122	15.5	0.164	32.7	0.250	33.1
Subtotal	0.476	60.2	0.541	73.5	0.582	74.8	0.347	62.4	0.553	70.2	0.334	66.9	0.552	73.3
Sectoral location differences attributable to														
Characteristics	0.245	30.9	0.165	22.4	0.167	21.4	0.136	24.4	0.182	23.2	0.126	25.1	0.170	22.5
Differences in effect of characteristics on men's location	0.022	2.7	0.009	1.3	0.010	1.3	0.028	5.0	0.018	2.3	0.012	2.5	0.010	1.3
Differences in effect of characteristics on women's location	0.049	6.2	0.021	2.8	0.020	2.5	0.045	8.2	0.033	4.2	0.027	5.5	0.023	3.0
Subtotal	0.316	39.8	0.195	26.5	0.197	25.2	0.209	37.6	0.233	29.7	0.165	33.1	0.203	26.8

Sources: Based on Phase 1 of the 1-2-3 surveys of selected countries (see table 9.1 for details).
Note: The raw earnings gap is defined as log(men's earnings) − log(women's earnings).
* significant at the 10 percent level, ** significant at the 5 percent level, *** significant at the 1 percent level.

Table 9.5 Full Decomposition of Gender Earnings Gap in Seven Cities in West Africa with Correction for Selectivity, 2001/02

Raw earnings gap	Abidjan	Percent	Bamako	Percent	Cotonou	Percent	Dakar	Percent	Lomé	Percent	Niamey	Percent	Ouagadougou	Percent
	0.970***		2.050***		1.060***		1.361***		361***		0.885***		1.237***	
Within-sector differences in earnings attributable to														
Characteristics	0.107	11.1	0.198	9.7	0.205	19.3	0.053	3.9	0.250	29.2	0.074	8.4	0.144	11.7
Differences in men's returns	0.204	21.0	0.729	35.6	0.343	32.3	0.408	30.0	0.163	19.0	0.245	27.6	0.423	34.2
Differences in women's returns	0.235	24.2	0.956	46.6	0.334	31.5	0.547	40.2	0.009	1.0	0.355	40.2	0.490	39.6
Subtotal	0.546	56.3	1.883	91.9	0.882	83.1	1.008	74.1	0.422	49.2	0.674	76.2	1.057	85.5
Differences between sectoral locations attributable to														
Characteristics	0.319	32.9	0.150	7.3	0.154	14.5	0.212	15.6	0.331	38.6	0.162	18.3	0.151	12.2
Differences in effect of characteristics on men's location	0.042	4.4	0.015	0.7	0.012	1.1	0.065	4.8	0.032	3.8	0.013	1.5	0.004	0.3
Differences in effect of characteristics on women's location	0.062	6.4	0.002	0.1	0.013	1.3	0.076	5.6	0.072	8.4	0.036	4.1	0.024	2.0
Subtotal	0.423	43.7	0.167	8.1	0.179	16.9	0.353	26.0	0.435	50.8	0.211	23.9	0.179	14.5

Sources: Based on Phase 1 of the 1-2-3 surveys of selected countries (see table 9.1 for details).

Note: The earnings gap is defined as log(men's earnings) – log(women's earnings). Decomposition is based on observed earnings.
* significant at the 10 percent level, ** significant at the 5 percent level, *** significant at the 1 percent level.

Within-sector differences in earnings account for the largest share of the gender gap, with contributions ranging from 60 percent in Abidjan to 75 percent in Cotonou. The remaining difference can be attributed to gender differences in the proportions of workers in each sector. The positive sum of these three terms for all cities implies that the differences in sectoral locations favor men. For instance, the gender earnings gap would have been 40 percent smaller in Abidjan if men and women had been equally distributed across the three sectors, because fewer women work in the higher-paying sectors.

Differences attributable to individual characteristics account for a relatively small share of within-sector differences in earnings, ranging from 10 percent in Dakar to 41 percent in Lomé (not shown in the table). Differences attributable to individual characteristics account for a very large share of the sectoral location differences between men and women, ranging from 65 percent in Dakar to 85 percent in Bamako and Cotonou.

Differences attributable to differences in the returns of men and women are of the same order of magnitude, indicating that both "discrimination" against women and "nepotism" in favor of men contribute to the gender earnings gap. Both factors also contribute to differences in sectoral location but at a much lower level.

Taking into account selectivity leads to analyzing the decomposition not of actual earnings but of offered earnings, computed using the coefficients of the selection term in the earnings equations. The results in table 9.5 show that offered earnings gaps are much higher in Cotonou, Bamako, and Dakar and lower in the other cities. Higher earnings gaps when sectoral selectivity is accounted for are not systematically associated with a larger contribution of sectoral location differences, however; except in Niamey, within-sector earnings differences remain the main contributor to gender gaps.

Ethnic Earnings Differentials

Concerning ethnic earnings gaps, the results in table 9.6 (without correcting for selectivity) indicate that the contribution of sectoral location to explaining the gap varies markedly between cities. In Abidjan, differences in sectoral location explain 86 percent of the gap, of which 75 percent is accounted for by differences in individual characteristics. In Bamako, within-sector differences in earnings account for 77 percent of the earnings gap, of which 33 percent is attributable to differences in individual characteristics; both nepotism (16 percent) and discrimination (28 percent) significantly contribute to the gap through their contribution to within-sector differences in earnings. In Ouagadougou, the gap can be attributed almost evenly to differences in sectoral location (53 percent) and within-sector earnings (47 percent).

Sectoral location differences are almost entirely explained by differences in individual characteristics. In Lomé, in contrast to Bamako, the deviation in the effect of individual characteristics on location explains a large share of sectoral location differences. In contrast to the results obtained for gender, where

Table 9.6 Full Decomposition of Ethnic Earnings Gap in Seven Cities in West Africa without Correction for Selectivity, 2001/02

Raw earnings gap	Abidjan 0.279***	Percent	Bamako -0.182***	Percent	Cotonou -0.015	Percent	Dakar 0.068**	Percent	Lomé -0.113***	Percent	Niamey 0.019	Percent	Ouagadougou -0.537***	Percent
Within-sector differences in earnings attributable to														
Characteristics	0.004	1.5	-0.061	33.3	0.014	-96.0	0.021	31.6	0.009	-8.0	-0.049	-258.9	-0.156	29.0
Differences in majority group returns	0.011	3.9	-0.029	15.9	-0.039	262.9	0.034	49.9	-0.023	19.9	0.019	102.8	-0.076	14.2
Differences in minority group returns	0.024	8.5	-0.051	28.2	-0.027	179.3	0.051	75.3	-0.009	7.8	0.024	125.1	-0.019	3.5
Subtotal	0.039	13.9	-0.141	77.4	-0.052	346.2	0.106	156.8	-0.023	19.7	-0.006	-31.0	-0.251	46.7
Differences between sectoral location attributable to														
Characteristics	0.181	64.7	-0.050	27.4	0.018	-120.0	-0.009	-13.7	-0.015	13.2	-0.008	-41.8	-0.250	46.5
Differences in effect of characteristics on majority group location	0.017	5.9	0.003	-1.7	0.012	-78.1	-0.012	-17.0	-0.053	47.2	0.017	88.0	-0.028	5.2
Differences in effect of characteristics on minority group location	0.043	15.5	0.006	-3.1	0.007	-48.2	-0.018	-26.0	-0.022	19.8	0.016	84.9	-0.008	1.5
Subtotal	0.241	86.1	-0.041	22.6	0.037	-246.3	-0.039	-56.7	-0.090	80.2	0.025	131.1	-0.286	53.2

Sources: Based on Phase 1 of the 1-2-3 surveys of selected countries (see table 9.1 for details).
Note: The earnings gap is defined as log(majority group earnings) – log(minority group earnings). Decomposition is based on observed earnings.
* significant at the 10 percent level, ** significant at the 5 percent level, *** significant at the 1 percent level.

sectoral location systematically increases the gap in favor of men, in some cities sectoral location plays a compensating role in observed earnings gaps.

Taking selectivity into account changes some measures of the gaps (table 9.7). The gap decreases in Abidjan, Dakar, and Ouagadougou and increases in Bamako. In Lomé, the gap is actually reversed, possibly indicating that on average the offered earnings of the largest ethnic group are higher than they are for other ethnic groups. This puzzling result requires further investigation (for instance, in order to understand the features of earnings negotiations, one would need to know the ethnic group of the employer).

The largest number of ethnic groups is in Bamako and Ouagadougou (10), followed by Dakar (9); Lomé and Niamey (7); and Abidjan and Cotonou (6) (table 9A.2). Table 9.8 reports the coefficients of the dummies indicating each ethnic group in regressions of city-level earnings equations. In the first column, ethnic group dummies are the only regressors. A set of usual controls is introduced in the specification reported in the second column (table 9.9 reports the coefficients for these variables).

Two results are evident from these regressions. First, there is at least one significant coefficient on ethnic dummies in all cities, indicating differences in average earnings of different ethnic groups.[10] Second, most of these differences diminish—and in some cases vanish—once other individual characteristics are controlled for. Overall, dominant ethnic groups do not seem to be favored on the labor market once one controls for productivity-related individual characteristics. On the contrary, in Benin, Burkina Faso, and Mali, some nondominant groups have higher earnings than the dominant group after controlling for other factors. Moreover, none of the favored groups seems to be related to the ethnicity of the head of state at the time of the survey.[11]

Conclusion

The findings in this chapter are important for two main reasons. First, international comparisons of earnings gaps are still rare in Africa. The 1-2-3 surveys used here rely on identical methodologies and virtually identical questionnaires in each city, making for totally comparable results.

Second, we address the issue of sample selectivity associated with endogenous sector choices, because gender and ethnic labor allocation between these sectors can be expected to contribute to earnings gaps. Following Appleton, Hoddinott, and Krishnan (1999), we then provide comparable estimates of the size and determinants of gender and ethnic earnings gaps using decomposition methods that address the sectoral allocation issue.

The results show that gender earnings gaps are large in all seven cities in our sample and that gender differences in the distribution of individual characteristics usually explain less than half of the raw gender gap. In contrast, dominant

Table 9.7 Full Decomposition of Ethnic Earnings Gap in Seven Cities in West Africa with Correction for Selectivity, 2001/02

Raw earnings gap	Abidjan	Percent	Bamako	Percent	Cotonou	Percent	Dakar	Percent	Lomé	Percent	Niamey	Percent	Ouagadougou	Percent
	0.254***		−0.224***		0.021		0.048		0.127***		−0.003		−0.403***	
Within-sector differences in earnings attributable to														
Characteristics	0.020	−7.8	−0.042	18.8	0.013	64.1	0.022	45.9	0.021	16.6	−0.043	1335.8	−0.091	22.7
Differences in majority group returns	0.016	−6.3	−0.042	18.5	−0.036	−169.6	0.020	42.5	0.110	86.9	0.000	14.2	−0.029	7.1
Differences in minority group returns	0.001	−0.4	−0.078	34.6	−0.024	−113.4	0.042	88.3	0.090	70.8	−0.012	376.7	0.021	−5.1
Subtotal	0.037	−14.5	−0.162	71.9	−0.047	−218.9	0.084	176.7	0.221	174.3	−0.055	1726.7	−0.099	24.7
Sectoral location differences attributable to														
Characteristics	0.213	84.2	−0.080	35.8	0.029	140.8	−0.009	−19.0	−0.010	−7.9	−0.016	492.6	−0.266	66.1
Differences in effect of characteristics on majority group location	0.027	10.6	0.004	−2.0	0.023	109.6	−0.007	−15.2	−0.030	−23.5	0.025	−770.0	−0.028	6.9
Differences in effect of characteristics on minority group location	0.050	19.8	0.013	−5.7	0.014	68.6	−0.020	−42.5	−0.055	−42.9	0.043	−1349.2	−0.010	2.4
Subtotal	0.290	114.6	−0.063	28.1	0.066	319.0	−0.036	−76.7	−0.095	−74.3	0.052	−1626.6	−0.304	75.4

Sources: Based on Phase 1 of the 1-2-3 surveys of selected countries (see table 9.1 for details).
Note: The earnings gap is defined as log(majority group earnings) − log(minority group earnings). Decomposition is based on observed earnings.
* significant at the 10 percent level, ** significant at the 5 percent level, *** significant at the 1 percent level.

Table 9.8 Ethnic Earnings Differentials in Seven Cities in West Africa, 2001/02

City/ethnic group	Earnings gaps		Ordinary least squares estimate	
	Raw earnings differential	Standard error	Coefficient	Standard error
Abidjan				
Akan (largest ethnic group)	Reference	n.a.	Reference	n.a.
Krou	0.020	0.061	−0.025	0.045
Mande North	−0.268***	0.054)	−0.013	0.042
Mande South	−0.112	0.090	−0.035	0.067
Native of Burkina Faso	−0.414***	0.045	−0.124***	0.037
Voltaic	−0.300***	0.069	−0.086*	0.052
Missing	−0.333	0.250	0.084	0.186
Bamako				
Arab	0.450***	0.149	0.078	0.122
Bambara (largest ethnic group)	Reference	n.a.	Reference	n.a.
Bobo	0.006	0.107	−0.069	0.087
Dogon	−0.042	0.091	0.009	0.074
Haoussa	0.303***	0.102	0.126	0.083
Malinke	0.057	0.052	0.039	0.043
Peul	0.220***	0.054	0.081*	0.044
Sarakole	0.245***	0.060	0.182***	0.049
Senoufo	0.398***	0.093	0.051	0.077
Songhai	0.436***	0.104	0.110	0.085
Missing	0.109	0.115	0.126	0.094
Cotonou				
Adja	−0.077*	0.039	0.035	0.031
Dendi	0.373***	0.135	0.467***	0.107
Fon (largest ethnic group)	Reference	n.a.	Reference	n.a.
Yoa	−0.498***	0.147	−0.213*	0.116
Yoruba	0.193***	0.051	0.102**	0.040
Other	0.033		0.009	
Dakar				
Diola	−0.088	0.068	−0.103*	0.054
Lebou	0.032	0.063	0.034	0.050
Manding	0.009	0.081	−0.020	0.064
Mandjag	−0.073	0.102	−0.005	0.081
Peul	−0.016	0.044	−0.032	0.035
Sarakole	0.117	0.101	−0.054	0.080
Serere	−0.271***	0.046	−0.190***	0.036
Wolof (largest ethnic group)	Reference	n.a.	Reference	n.a.
Other	0.075	0.065	−0.024	0.052

(continued next page)

Table 9.8 (continued)

City/ethnic group	Earnings gaps		Ordinary least squares estimate	
	Raw earnings differential	Standard error	Coefficient	Standard error
Lomé				
Akposso-Akebou	0.121	0.136	−0.003	0.111
Ana-Ife	0.126	0.107	0.005	0.087
Ewe-Mina-Wachi (largest ethnic group)	Reference	n.a.	Reference	n.a.
Kabye-Tem	0.058	0.055	0.001	0.045
Para-Gourma-Akan	0.068	0.092	0.028	0.075
Other Togolese	−0.042	0.191	0.062	0.156
Other non-Togolese	0.297***	0.081	0.276	0.066
Niamey				
Djerma (largest ethnic group)	Reference	n.a.	Reference	n.a.
Gourma	0.542*	0.285	0.240	0.223
Haoussa	−0.004	0.044	−0.068*	0.035
Peul	0.167**	0.083	0.041	0.065
Touareg	−0.237***	0.089	−0.102	0.070
Other	−0.143*	0.075	−0.046	0.059
Missing	−0.259	0.199	−0.075	0.156
Ouagadougou				
Bissa	0.379***	0.095	0.093	0.070
Bobo	0.561***	0.165	0.168	0.120
Dagari	0.474***	0.155	0.083	0.113
Gourmantche	0.781***	0.178	0.197	0.130
Gurunsi	0.613***	0.099	0.073***	0.099
Mossi (largest ethnic group)	Reference	n.a.	Reference	n.a.
Other Manding	0.555***	0.092	0.136**	0.068
Peul	0.552***	0.137	0.161	0.100
Senoufo	1.335***	0.203	0.370**	0.149
Other	0.498***	0.117	0.109	0.086
Missing	−0.141	0.209	−0.130	0.152

Sources: Based on Phase 1 of the 1-2-3 surveys of selected countries (see table 9.1 for details).
Note: n.a. = Not applicable.
* significant at the 10 percent level, ** significant at the 5 percent level, *** significant at the 1 percent level.

ethnic groups do not appear to have a systematically favorable position in the urban labor markets in our sample, and observed gaps are small relative to gender gaps. Moreover, "favored" minority groups do not seem to be related to the ethnicity of the head of state at the time of the survey.

Whatever the sign of the gap, the contribution of differences in the distribution of individual characteristics varies markedly across cities. Taking into

Table 9.9 Control Variables for Ethnic Earnings Differentials in Seven Cities in West Africa, 2001/02

Variable	Abidjan	Bamako	Cotonou	Dakar	Lomé	Niamey	Ouagadougou
Gender (1 = women)	-0.507	-0.464	-0.495	-0.370	-0.425	-0.314	-0.525
	(0.028)***	(0.030)***	(0.026)***	(0.025)***	(0.033)***	(0.031)***	(0.028)***
Education	0.028	0.045	0.046	0.066	0.030	0.077	0.100
	(0.008)***	(0.009)***	(0.007)***	(0.007)***	(0.010)***	(0.009)***	(0.008)***
Education squared	0.007	0.004	0.004	0.003	0.006	0.004	0.004
	(0.000)***	(0.001)***	(0.000)***	(0.000)***	(0.001)***	(0.001)***	(0.001)***
Potential experience	0.051	0.062	0.038	0.066	0.052	0.052	0.067
	(0.004)***	(0.004)***	(0.004)***	(0.003)***	(0.004)***	(0.004)***	(0.004)***
Potential experience squared	-0.049	-0.065	-0.039	-0.073	-0.057	-0.047	-0.073
	(0.007)***	(0.006)***	(0.006)***	(0.005)***	(0.007)***	(0.005)***	(0.006)***
Marital status (1 = married)	0.120	0.093	0.043	0.059	0.032	0.067	0.160
	(0.029)***	(0.031)***	(0.026)*	(0.028)**	(0.032)	(0.032)**	(0.031)***
Constant	-2.568	-3.013	-2.725	-2.769	-3.311	-3.086	-3.549
	(0.066)***	(0.063)***	(0.060)***	(0.053)***	(0.070)***	(0.069)***	(0.061)***
Number of observations	4,060	3,928	4,209	4,929	3,600	3,295	3,774
R^2	0.47	0.35	0.39	0.37	0.34	0.40	0.50

Sources: Based on Phase 1 of the 1-2-3 surveys of selected countries (see table 9.1 for details).
Note: Figures in parentheses are standard errors.
* significant at the 10 percent level, ** significant at the 5 percent level, *** significant at the 1 percent level.

account differences in sectoral locations in the decomposition of gender earnings gaps provides evidence that within-sector differences in earnings account for the largest share of the gender gap and that differences in sectoral locations are always more favorable to men than to women. In contrast, full decomposition of ethnic earnings gaps indicates that sectoral location sometimes plays a "compensating" role. Looking at finer levels of ethnic disaggregation confirms that ethnic earnings differentials are systematically smaller than gender differentials.

Annex: Ethnicity in Seven West African Countries

Table 9A.1 Ethnolinguistic Fractionalization in Seven Countries in West Africa

Country	Description of largest ethnic group	Ethnolinguistic fractionalization	
		Soviet Atlas	1-2-3 surveys
Benin	The Fon are a major ethnic and linguistic group in Benin and southwest Nigeria, made up of more than 2 million people. Their language, a member of the Gbe language group, is the main language spoken in southern Benin. Closely related cultures include the Ewe, Adja, and Guin. The Fon are said to originate from Tado, a village in southeast Togo, near the border with Benin.	0.6182	0.5742
Burkina Faso	The Mossi live in central Burkina Faso, mostly in the villages of the Volta River Basin. They are the largest ethnic group in Burkina Faso, constituting 40 percent of the population (about 6.2 million people). The other 60 percent of Burkina Faso's population is composed of more than 60 ethnic groups, mainly the Gurunsi, Senufo, Lobi, Bobo, and Fulani. The Mossi speak the More language.	0.6783	0.3814
Côte d'Ivoire	The Akan are a linguistic group in West Africa that includes the Akuapem, Akyem, Ashanti, Baoulé, Anyi, Brong, Fante, and Nzema peoples of Côte d'Ivoire and Ghana.	0.8593	0.8204
Mali	The Bambara (*Bamana* or sometimes *Banmana* in their own language) are a Mande people living in West Africa, primarily in Mali but also in Burkina Faso, Guinea, and Senegal. Among the largest Mande ethnic groups, they are the dominant Mande group in Mali, where 80 percent of the population speaks the Bambara language, regardless of ethnicity.	0.7783	0.8254
Niger	The Djerma (also spelled *Zerma, Zarma, Dyerma,* and *Zaberma*) live in western Niger and adjacent areas of Burkina Faso and Nigeria. Their language is one of the Songhai languages, a branch of the Nilo-Saharan language family. The Djerma are considered to be a branch of the Songhai people.	0.7326	0.6401
Senegal	The Wolof live in The Gambia, Mauritania, and Senegal. In Senegal, they form an ethnic plurality, with about 40 percent of the population self-identifying as Wolof. They are the majority in the region stretching from Saint-Louis in the north, Kaolack in the south, and Dakar to the west.	0.7228	0.7695

(continued next page)

Table 9A.1 (continued)

Country	Description of largest ethnic group	Ethnolinguistic fractionalization	
		Soviet Atlas	1-2-3 surveys
Togo	The Ewe live in southeastern Benin, Ghana, and Togo. They speak the Ewe language and are related to other speakers of Gbe languages, including the Fon and the Adja of Benin and Togo. Their original homeland is Oyo, in western Nigeria.	0.7107	0.8254

Sources: Soviet Atlas data are from Fearon 2003; survey data are from Phase 1 of the 1-2-3 surveys of selected countries (see table 9.1 for details).
Note: The ELF measure, available for 129 countries, captures the likelihood that two people chosen at random will be from different ethnic groups. It is calculated using a simple Herfindahl concentration index. The Herfindahl concentration formula is $ELF = 1 - \sum_{i=1}^{n} s_i^2$, where s_i is the share of group i ($i = 1, \ldots, n$). The Soviet Atlas data were compiled by Soviet ethnographers in the early 1960s and published in the Atlas Narodov Mira in 1964. ELF = ethnolinguistic fractionlization.

Table 9A.2 Ethnic Composition of Sample in Seven Cities in West Africa, 2001/02

City/ethnic group	Sample size	Extrapolated percentage of total
Abidjan		
Akan	1,278	32.4
Krou	444	11.5
Mande North	631	16.3
Mande South	171	4.4
Native of Burkina Faso	1,188	26.9
Voltaic	328	8.2
Missing	20	0.5
Bamako		
Arab	57	1.0
Bambara	1,382	35.7
Bobo	115	3.5
Dogon	163	4.4
Haoussa	128	2.8
Malinke	660	16.9
Peul	602	15.6
Sarakole	445	11.1
Senoufo	155	3.7
Songhai	123	2.9
Missing	98	2.3
Cotonou		
Adja	889	21.5
Dendi	56	1.3
Fon	2,475	60.3
Yoa	47	1.1
Yoruba	447	9.9
Other	295	5.9

(continued next page)

Table 9A.2 (continued)

City/ethnic group	Sample size	Extrapolated percent of total
Dakar		
Diola	278	5.8
Lebou	337	9.1
Manding	191	3.9
Mandjag	115	2.3
Peul	822	16.0
Sarakole	118	2.4
Serere	747	16.0
Wolof	2,008	38.1
Other	313	6.3
Lomé		
Akposso-Akebou	66	1.8
Ana-Ife	109	3.1
Ewe-Mina-Wachi	2,582	71.8
Kabye-Tem	467	13.1
Para-Gourma-Akan	148	4.2
Other Togolese	33	0.8
Other non-Togolese	195	5.2
Niamey		
Djerma	1,542	46.6
Gourma	15	0.5
Haoussa	1,044	32.1
Kanouri	41	1.2
Peul	199	6.1
Touareg	170	5.4
Other	253	7.2
Missing	31	1.0
Ouagadougou		
Bissa	155	4.1
Bobo	50	1.0
Dagari	57	1.4
Gourmantche	43	1.2
Gurunsi	142	4.1
Mossi	2,921	77.2
Other Manding	168	4.2
Peul	73	1.8
Senoufo	33	0.8
Other	101	3.1
Missing	31	1.4

Sources: Based on Phase 1 of the 1-2-3 surveys of selected countries (see table 9.1 for details).

Notes

1. Poverty Reduction Strategy Papers (PRSPs) are documents required before low-income countries can receive aid from most major donors and lenders. The PRSP process encourages countries to develop more poverty-focused policies and to own their own strategies by developing the plan in close consultation with the population.

2. See Siphambe and Thokweng-Bakwena (2001) on Botswana; Lachaud (1997) on Burkina Faso and Cameroon; Appleton, Hoddinott, and Krishnan (1999) on Côte d'Ivoire, Ethiopia, and Uganda; Kolev and Suarez Robles (2007) and Temesgen (2006) on Ethiopia; Glewwe (1990) on Ghana; Glick and Sahn (1997) on Guinea; Kabubo-Mariara (2003), Milne and Neitzert (1994), and Agesa (1999) on Kenya; Armitage and Sabot (1991) on Kenya and Tanzania; Nordman and Roubaud (2009) and Nordman, Rakotomanana, and Robilliard (2010) on Madagascar; Nordman and Wolff (2009b) on Morocco; Nordman and Wolff (2009a) on the formal sectors of Madagascar and Mauritius; Isemonger and Roberts (1999) on South Africa; and Cohen and House (1993) on Sudan.

3. Conversely, one can argue that analyses that omit occupation and industry may underestimate the importance of background and choice-based characteristics on labor market outcomes (Altonji and Blank 1999).

4. Regan and Oaxaca (2006) show that using potential versus actual experience in earnings models is best viewed as a model misspecification problem rather than a classical errors-in-variable framework. Instrumental variable techniques are the traditional approach used to correct classical measurement error. In the absence of actual experience measures, instrumenting potential experience does not solve the model specification problem, as Regan and Oaxaca (2006) emphasize.

5. Following Tunali (1986), an alternative approach would be to employ a sequential selection rule (nested multinomial logit) rather than a combined one. Doing so would mean controlling for self-selection into the paid-work group and then different endogenous choices of the public, formal private, and informal sectors. This technique requires finding at least one variable affecting the decision to enter the paid-work group but not the sector choice in order to achieve identification through the use of exclusion restrictions. It was impossible to find variables that could be used in the first-stage selection equation and arguably excluded from a second selection equation of sector allocation.

6. In the context of a two-step sectoral selection correction, Appleton, Hoddinott, and Krishnan (1999) use the proportion of children in the household as an identifying instrument.

7. In France, the collection of data on ethnic origin is subject to authorization by a government body and is not granted systematically.

8. Easterly and Levine (1997) and Collier and Hoeffler (1998) define ethnolinguistic fractionalization (ELF) as the probability of two randomly drawn individuals from the same country belonging to different ethnic groups.

9. Nordman, Robilliard, and Roubaud (2011) explore the factors likely to explain differences in gender gaps across cities. Their findings suggest that cities with large gender earnings gaps are characterized by high levels of female labor market participation, large gender education gaps, and large shares of self-employment. Gender earnings gaps are particularly large in the informal self-employment sector. The

differences in access to capital and the low productivity of activities engaged in by self-employed women may explain this finding.

10. In some cities, the groups considered represent very small shares of the population (see annex table 9A.2). For this reason, we did not implement decomposition methods at this level of ethnic disaggregation.

11. Data on the ethnicity of the head of state at the time of the survey are provided in the data set put together by Fearon, Kasara, and Laitin (2007).

References

Agesa, R. U. 1999. "The Urban Gender Wage Gap in an African Country: Findings from Kenya." *Canadian Journal of Development Studies* 20 (1): 59–76.

Altonji, J. G., and R. M. Blank. 1999. "Race and Gender in the Labor Market." In *Handbook of Labor Economics*, vol. 3C, ed. O. Ashenfelter and D. Card, 3143–257. Amsterdam: North Holland.

Appleton, S., J. Hoddinott, and P. Krishnan. 1999. "The Gender Wage Gap in Three African Countries." *Economic Development and Cultural Change* 47 (2): 289–312.

Armitage, J., and R. Sabot. 1991. "Discrimination in East African's Urban Labor Market." In *Unfair Advantage: Labor Market Discrimination in Developing Countries*, ed. N. Birdsall and R. Sabot. Washington, DC: World Bank.

Barr, A., and A. Oduro. 2000. "Ethnicity and Wage Determination in Ghana." Policy Research Working Paper 2506, World Bank, Washington, DC.

Bayart, J.-F. 1989. "Le théâtre d'ombres de l'ethnicité." In *L'état en Afrique: la politique du ventre*, 65–86. Paris: Fayard.

Bennell, P. 1996. "Rates of Return on Education: Does the Conventional Pattern Prevail in Sub-Saharan Africa?" *World Development* 24 (1): 183–99.

Blau, F., and L. Kahn. 2000. "Gender Differences in Pay." *Journal of Economic Perspectives* 14 (4): 75–99.

Blinder, A. S. 1973. "Wage Discrimination: Reduced Form and Structural Estimates." *Journal of Human Resources* 8 (4): 436–55.

Bossuroy, T. 2007. "Ethnicity as a Resource in Social Capital." Développement, Institutions et Mondialisation (DIAL), Paris.

Cohen, B., and W. J. House. 1993. "Women's Urban Labour Market Status in Developing Countries: How Well Do They Fare in Khartoum, Sudan?" *Journal of Development Studies* 29 (3): 461–83.

Collier, P., and A. Hoeffler. 1998. "On Economic Causes of Civil War," *Oxford Economic Papers*. 50: 563–73.

Easterly, W., and R. Levine. 1997. "Africa's Growth Tragedy: Policies, and Ethnic Divisions." *Quarterly Journal of Economics* 111 (4): 1203–50.

Fearon, J. D. 2003. "Ethnic and Cultural Diversity by Country." *Journal of Economic Growth* 8 (2): 195–222.

Fearon, J., K. Kasara, and D. Laitin. 2007. "Ethnic Minority Rule and Civil War Onset." *American Political Science Review* 101 (1): 187–93.

Glewwe, P. 1990. "Schooling, Skills, and the Return to Education: An Econometric Exploration Using Data from Ghana." Living Standards Measurement Working Paper 76, World Bank, Washington, DC.

Glick, P., and D. E. Sahn. 1997. "Gender and Education Impacts on Employment and Earnings in West Africa: Evidence from Guinea." *Economic Development and Cultural Change* 45 (4): 793–823.

Hausman, J. A., and D. McFadden. 1984. "Specification Tests for the Multinomial Logit Model." *Econometrica* 52 (5): 1219–40.

Isemonger, A. G., and N. Roberts. 1999. "Post-Entry Gender Discrimination in the South African Labour Market." *Journal for Studies in Economics, and Econometrics* 23 (2): 1–25.

Kabubo-Mariara, J. 2003. "Wage Determination and the Gender Wage Gap in Kenya: Any Evidence of Gender Discrimination?" Research Paper 132, African Economic Research Consortium, Nairobi.

Kolev, A., and P. Suarez Robles. 2007. "Addressing the Gender Pay Gap in Ethiopia: How Crucial Is the Quest for Education Parity?" Agence Française de Développement, Paris, and World Bank, Washington, DC.

Lachaud, J.-P. 1997. *Les femmes et le marché du travail urbain en Afrique subsaharienne.* Paris: Editions l'Harmattan.

Lee, L.-F. 1983. "Generalized Econometric Models with Selectivity." *Econometrica* 51 (2): 507–12.

Milne, W., and M. Neitzert. 1994. "Kenya." In *Labor Markets in an Era of Adjustment,* ed. S. Horton, R. Kanbur, and D. Mazumdar, 405–57. EDI Development Studies. Washington, DC: World Bank.

Neuman, S., and R. Oaxaca. 2004. "Wage Decompositions with Selectivity-Corrected Wage Equations: A Methodological Note." *Journal of Economic Inequality* 2 (1): 3–10.

Neumark, D. 1988. "Employers' Discriminatory Behavior and the Estimation of Wage Discrimination." *Journal of Human Resources* 23 (3): 279–95.

Nordman, C. J., F. Rakotomanana, and A.-S. Robilliard. 2010. "Gender Disparities in the Malagasy Labor Market." In *Gender Disparities in Africa's Labor Markets,* ed. J. S. Arbache, A. Kolev, and E. Filipiak, 87–153. Washington, DC: World Bank.

Nordman, C. J., A.-S. Robilliard, and F. Roubaud. 2011. "Gender and Ethnic Earnings Gaps in Seven West African Cities." *Labour Economics* 18: S132–S145.

Nordman, C. J., and F. Roubaud. 2009. "Reassessing the Gender Wage Gap in Madagascar: Does Labour Force Attachment Really Matter?" *Economic Development and Cultural Change* 57 (4): 785–808.

Nordman, C. J., and F.-C. Wolff. 2009a. "Islands through the Glass Ceiling? Evidence of Gender Wage Gaps in Madagascar, and Mauritius." In *Labor Markets and Economic Development,* ed. R. Kanbur and J. Svejnar, 521–44. London: Routledge.

———. 2009b. "Is There a Glass Ceiling in Morocco? Evidence from Matched Worker-Firm Data." *Journal of African Economies* 18 (4): 592–633.

Oaxaca, R. 1973. "Male-Female Wage Differentials in Urban Labor Markets." *International Economic Review* 14 (3): 693–709.

Regan, T. L., and R. L. Oaxaca. 2006. "Work Experience as a Source of Specification Error in Earnings Models: Implications for Gender Wage Decompositions." IZA Discussion Paper 1920, Institute for the Study of Labor, Bonn, Germany.

Reimers, C. W. 1983. "Labour Market Discrimination against Hispanic and Black Men." *Review of Economics and Statistics* 65 (4): 570–79.

Siphambe, H. K., and M. Thokweng-Bakwena. 2001. "The Wage Gap between Men and Women in Botswana's Formal Labour Market." *Journal of African Economies* 10 (2): 127–42.

Temesgen, T. 2006. "Decomposing Gender Wage Differentials in Urban Ethiopia: Evidence from Linked Employer-Employee (LEE) Manufacturing Survey Data." *Global Economic Review* 35 (1): 43–66.

Tunali, I. 1986. "A General Structure for Models of Double-Selection and an Application to a Joint Migration/Earnings Process with Remigration." In *Research in Labor Economics*, ed. R. G. Ehrenberg, 235–84. Greenwich, CT: JAI Press.

Weichselbaumer, D., and R. Winter-Ebmer. 2005. "A Meta-Analysis of the International Gender Wage Gap." *Journal of Economic Surveys* 19 (3): 479–511.

Part IV

Key Coping Mechanisms and Private Responses

Chapter **10**

Why Do Migrants Migrate? Self-Selection and Returns to Education in West Africa

Philippe De Vreyer, Flore Gubert, and François Roubaud

Migration from and to African countries is extensive, with estimates ranging from about 16 million international African migrants according to the International Organisation for Migration (IOM 2003) to 50 million according to the African Union (African Union 2005). West Africa in particular has a long history of population mobility, both regionally and internationally. Linked to factors as diverse as long-distance trade, plantation agriculture, and urbanization as well as armed conflict, land degradation, and drought, migration in the region played and still plays a major part in shaping settlement patterns. At the political level, several initiatives, including the free movement of people institutionalized by the Economic Community of West African States (ECOWAS), have facilitated labor migration. With this background in mind, this chapter examines the locational choice of a large sample of Africans originating in seven cities in the West African Economic and Monetary Union (WAEMU).[1]

Concern with migration emerged with the work of Sjaastad (1962). In the development literature, however, Todaro (1969) and Harris and Todaro (1970) were the first to present a model in which the decision to migrate results from the rational comparison of the expected costs and benefits of migration. In both models, the difference in average expected earnings between countries or regions of destination and countries or regions of origin plays a key role and is predicted to have a positive effect on migration flows. This kind of model is unable to explain key stylized facts, however, such as migration flows from and to particular regions or countries.

Borjas (1987) and Dahl (2002) adopt a different approach, based on the seminal paper of Roy (1951). In Roy's framework, workers select into income-earning activities on the basis of their comparative advantage. Applied to residential choice, this model explains migration not by average expected earnings differentials but rather by differences in individual expected returns to skills that are either observed or unobserved by the econometrician. As a result, migration flows are not necessarily one-sided. This literature argues that migrants' self-selection should be taken into account when estimating the returns to human capital in countries where the flow of migrants is significant.

Estimation of this kind of model is usually very difficult, however, because of the impossibility of gathering data on origin and destination labor markets at the same time. In this chapter, we take advantage of the fact that the 1-2-3 surveys of the Programme d'Appui Régional à la Statistique (PARSTAT) project were conducted simultaneously, with the same questionnaire, thus providing the data needed to study migration choices in the region (for a description of these surveys, see box O.1 in the overview). Data on the country of birth and the last country of residence allow international migrants to be identified within each national sample.

This chapter is important for three reasons. First, it fills a gap in the knowledge of cross-border migration within Africa. Second, it evaluates the extent of the bias in the estimated returns to education when international migration is not accounted for. Third, it determines whether earnings differentials matter in the choice of the country of residence.

The model assumes that individuals are born randomly in one of the seven countries under review (Benin, Burkina Faso, Côte d'Ivoire, Mali, Niger, Senegal, and Togo) but rationally choose the country in which they reside by comparing the utility associated with each choice. Estimation of this model provides unbiased estimates of the returns to education, together with the effect of expected earnings differentials on the probability of choosing a particular country. Given the data at hand, the universe of destination countries is restricted to countries that are close to one another geographically, legally, culturally, and economically. The seven countries studied share the same language (French), use a common currency (the CFA franc), and, most important, belong to ECOWAS, within which people are free to move and settle.

We cannot account for migration movements outside the WAEMU region. Although this restriction is regrettable and constitutes a clear limitation of our study, it nevertheless makes sense to analyze migrants' choice of destination in West Africa, where there are no legal barriers to migrate and most international migration takes place intraregionally. We find that migration behavior plays an important role in determining earnings differentials between countries and between individuals with different education levels. Our results also suggest that earnings differentials matter in locational choice.

This chapter is organized as follows. The first section presents the data and some descriptive statistics. The second section specifies the model and describes the estimation strategy. The third section discusses the model identification and the choice of variables. The fourth section provides the estimation results. The last section summarizes the chapter's main conclusions.

Data and Descriptive Statistics

Movements of labor are not a new phenomenon in West Africa. For generations, people have migrated in response to demographic, economic, political, and other factors, such as population pressure, environmental disasters, poverty, and conflicts.

Despite their importance, little is known about these migrations. The information provided by census data; immigration and emigration statistics; and a small number of ad hoc surveys on the number, identity, and motivations of both inter- and intracontinental African migrants is spotty and unreliable. Evidence is even scarcer concerning transborder migrations within the West African subregion. How many transborder migrants are there in each West African country? Who are these migrants? What are their main motivations? These are some of the questions this chapter addresses.

The data used are a pooling sample of the seven 1-2-3 surveys of the PARSTAT project. All seven French-speaking members of WAEMU belong to ECOWAS. At the time of its creation, in 1975, one of the key objectives of ECOWAS was to remove obstacles to the free movement of goods, capital, and people in the subregion. In line with this objective, the Protocol on Free Movement of Persons and the Right of Residence and Establishment was signed in May 1979; the right of entry was established in 1980 and the right of residence in 1986. In 2000, members of ECOWAS agreed to introduce a new passport for citizens of the subregion, which will gradually replace national passports. Although much remains to be done to achieve complete liberalization of labor migration within the community, these measures to create a borderless West Africa provide a good opportunity to study the residential choice of people within the community.

We consider as migrants all individuals who meet the following three criteria: they are not citizens of the country they reside in; they were not born in the capital city of the country they reside in; and they have not been residing continuously in the capital city since they were born.[2] Individuals who are not migrants are considered natives. In the empirical analysis that follows, we restrict the sample to all active individuals 15–65 originating in one of the seven countries covered by the 1-2-3 surveys and residing in the capital city of one of these countries, either as natives or immigrants.

As the figures in table 10.1 suggest, a wide variety of migration configurations is evident within WAEMU. Despite the severe sociopolitical crisis that started

Table 10.1 Composition of Samples Used to Analyze Migration in West Africa, 2001/02

City	Number of immigrants from									Total number of immigrants	Total number of natives	Total sample size
	Benin	Burkina Faso	Côte d'Ivoire	Mali	Niger	Senegal	Togo	Other	No data			
Abidjan	53	446		256	90	72	87	310	133	1447	**5,974**	7,416
Of which WAEMU nationals	**52**	**428**		**231**	**85**	**65**	**79**	120	124	1184		
Bamako	8	14	11		8	12	0	62	8	123	**7,148**	7,272
Of which WAEMU nationals	**3**	**13**	**10**		**6**	**11**	**0**	36	6	85		
Cotonou		3	6	15	58	3	102	138	18	343	**6,994**	7,337
Of which WAEMU nationals		**3**	**6**	**15**	**55**	**2**	**100**	38	16	235		
Dakar	11	0	2	9	0		4	130	53	209	**11,773**	11,977
Of which WAEMU nationals	**7**	**0**	**2**	**9**	**0**		**1**	74	35	128		
Lomé	88	9	9	11	50	3		113	23	306	**5,927**	6,254
Of which WAEMU nationals	**87**	**9**	**8**	**11**	**44**	**3**		24	21	207		
Niamey	76	49	4	122		5	59	52	26	393	**7,710**	8,106
Of which WAEMU nationals	**67**	**49**	**4**	**119**		**5**	**48**	27	23	342		
Ouagadougou	11		7	8	2	1	16	18	11	74	**8,198**	8,251
Of which WAEMU nationals	**6**		**7**	**7**	**0**	**1**	**16**	5	7	49		
Total	247	521	39	421	208	96	268	823	272			
Of which WAEMU nationals	222	502	37	392	190	87	244	324	232			

Sources: Based on Phase 1 of the 1-2-3 surveys of selected countries in the West African Economic and Monetary Union (WAEMU) conducted in 2001/02 by the Observatoire économique et statistique d'Afrique Subsaharienne (AFRISTAT); Développement, Institutions et Mondialisation (DIAL); and national statistics institutes.

Note: All individuals 15–65 are considered as natives of country *i* if they always resided in country *i*, whether or not they identify themselves as citizens. Within the sample of immigrants coming from one of the six other WAEMU countries, some are not WAEMU nationals (for example, a French national who spent 10 years in Burkina Faso before moving to Benin is recorded as a migrant coming from Burkina Faso but is not Burkinabe). Groups considered in the analysis are in bold. WAEMU = West African Economic and Monetary Union.

with the military coup of 1999 and resulted in reverse flows of migrants, Côte d'Ivoire is still by far the most important immigration country in the WAEMU region.[3] Although migration flows from Burkina Faso and Mali have been fluctuating since the beginning of the crisis, these two neighboring countries remain the main source of migrants to Côte d'Ivoire. About 15 percent of Abidjan's population between 15 and 65 are immigrants, among which 74 percent are citizens of a WAEMU country (table 10.2).

By contrast, immigrants from bordering WAEMU countries account for only a marginal share of the population in Dakar, the capital of Senegal. Less than 2 percent of Dakar's inhabitants are non-Senegalese, among which a large share comes from Guinea, Guinea-Bissau, The Gambia, Mauritania, or Mali. Expatriates from Mali and Burkina Faso and living in the capital city of a WAEMU country largely outnumber the expatriates from WAEMU countries residing in Bamako or Ouagadougou, suggesting that the two countries remain major labor-exporting countries. By contrast, Benin, Niger, and Togo combine both emigration and immigration.

Table 10.3 reports census statistics on immigrants by country of origin in each of the seven countries studied. Overall, the same general migration patterns emerge: national data confirm the position of Côte d'Ivoire as the main labor-importing country of the region, with most migrants coming from Mali or Burkina Faso. They also confirm the marginal participation of Senegal in intraregional migration flows and the role of Benin, Niger, and Togo as both importers and exporters of labor. The picture for Burkina Faso, however, strongly differs from the one drawn based on data from Ouagadougou only. Rural Burkina Faso is indeed found to host a fairly large number of Malian migrants, who are not accounted for in our urban sample. Our inferences for Burkina Faso using data on Ouagadougou should thus be considered with caution.

Table 10.2 Weighted Shares of Immigrants among Urban Residents in Seven Cities in West Africa, 2001/02
(percent)

Migrant status	Abidjan	Bamako	Cotonou	Dakar	Lomé	Niamey	Ouagadougou
Natives	84.1	98.4	96.4	98.5	95.5	95.6	99.3
Immigrants	15.9	1.6	3.6	1.6	4.5	4.4	0.7
Of which:							
From WAEMU country	73.5	43.8	60.6	13.0	60.7	85.7	70.7
From other developing country	25.2	43.4	36.4	83.9	38.8	12.2	23.9
From developed country	1.3	12.6	3.1	3.1	0.8	2.2	6.2

Sources: Based on Phase 1 of the 1-2-3 surveys of selected countries (see table 10.1 for details).
Note: WAEMU = West African Economic and Monetary Union.

Table 10.3 Composition of Migrant Population in Seven Countries in West Africa, 2000

Country	Percentage of immigrants coming from							Total number of immigrants
	Benin	Burkina Faso	Côte d'Ivoire	Mali	Niger	Senegal	Togo	
Benin		4.7	20.0	5.1	25.3	0.4	44.5	57,971
Burkina Faso	10.2		4.9	61.1	19.3	1.9	2.7	717,271
Côte d'Ivoire	3.7	58.8		29.3	7.8	0.2	0.1	1,661,157
Mali	18.8	49.4	3.2		17.8	4.5	6.3	22,529
Niger	15.9	17.1	7.8	55.3		1.3	2.5	60,922
Senegal	4.8	12.2	1.0	76.1	4.4		1.5	31,077
Togo	77.8	0.8	0.1	2.9	18.1	0.3		92,234
Total number of emigrants	221,362	1,006,194	52,335	987,480	305,471	20,198	50,121	2,643,161

Source: National census data circa 2000.

Representativeness of Sample

It is likely that the migrants' samples from the 1-2-3 surveys are not representative of the whole population of migrants, because they exclude individuals who moved out of their country to settle in a rural area of another WAEMU country. These migrants may strongly differ from the migrants recorded in our samples, especially with regard to their distribution by country of origin.

Another issue possibly affecting the representativeness of our samples relates to the fact that immigrants are a relatively small share of the population and may cluster in some areas. Given the sampling frame of the 1-2-3 surveys, it is possible that such areas were missed when the census sectors were selected in the first stage. This possibility cannot be ruled out in some cities.

We believe our samples are representative in Abidjan, Bamako, and Lomé. In Lomé, where 125 of 129 census sectors were selected, the probability that we missed clusters of migrants is low. In Abidjan and Bamako, our estimates on the immigration rate at the level of the city and on the composition of migrants' stocks by country of origin are very similar to the estimates obtained using census data. In addition, we used our representative samples of census sectors in each city to test the null hypothesis of random allocation of migrants across neighborhoods and rejected it in none of our samples. For other countries, the representativeness of the sample can be questioned.

Migrants' Main Characteristics

Table 10.4 provides descriptive statistics on the main characteristics of natives and immigrants by city of residence. Several findings are worthy of note. First, women are underrepresented in the immigrant populations of Abidjan, Ouagadougou, and Lomé but slightly overrepresented among the

Table 10.4 Mean Characteristics of Natives and Immigrants in Seven Cities in West Africa, 2001/02
(percent, except where otherwise indicated)

Variable	Abidjan Natives	Abidjan Immigrants	Bamako Natives	Bamako Immigrants	Cotonou Natives	Cotonou Immigrants	Dakar Natives	Dakar Immigrants	Lomé Natives	Lomé Immigrants	Niamey Natives	Niamey Immigrants	Ouagadougou Natives	Ouagadougou Immigrants
Men	47.6	61.5**	49.1	51.1	48.2	42.5	47.1	47.4	47.6	56.2**	48.6	43.5	50.7	54.1
Age (years)	29.0	34.6**	31.2	30.4	31.1	30.8	30.9	33.9	30.4	30.9	30.7	33.9**	30.2	30.4
Education and experience														
Years of experience	16.4	26.6**	20.3	18.1	18.5	21.3	19.5	19.4	17.7	20.4**	19.6	25.5**	19.1	18.7
Years of schooling	6.6	2.0**	4.8	5.8	6.6	3.6**	5.3	8.6**	6.6	4.5**	5.1	2.3**	5.1	5.7
No diploma	44.7	83.5**	58.4	55.8	45.8	72.4**	60.2	31.6**	42.8	63.0**	60.9	81.5**	54.3	54.1
Completed primary education	27.6	10.2**	19.2	16.3	26.7	14.9**	18.5	15.8	31.9	24.7**	20.3	11.6**	24.6	13.5
BEPC (*Brevet d'études du premier cycle du second degré*)	10.4	2.7**	8.1	4.7	13.2	6.1**	11.0	21.1	14.7	5.6**	7.2	2.4**	11.3	18.9
Baccalauréat	4.8	0.6**	2.2	7.0**	4.0	3.9	3.8	5.3	3.2	1.2	2.6	0**	1.6	0
Can read and write in French	73.8	28.5**	49.2	51.2	71.6	37.0**	60.4	73.7	73.7	53.7**	56.5	29.8**	59.6	64.9
Can read and write in other language	25.0	10.9**	12.2	34.9**	24.5	26.5	19.3	47.4**	27.1	22.2	21.6	18.2	13.3	24.3**
Religion														
Muslim	31.2	73.3**	97.2	79.1**	9.9	47.0**	93.3	57.9**	9.6	45.7**	98.2	76.4**	55.8	37.8**
Catholic	35.9	17.8**	1.8	18.6**	67.2	31.5**	6.6	42.1**	47.6	24.7**	1.2	19.5**	36.2	18.9**
Protestant	10.7	3.4**	0.5	2.3	5.2	3.9	0.1	0	10.2	0.6	0.4	3.4**	6.5	27.0**
Number of observations	5,974	940	7,148	43	6,994	181	11,773	19	5,927	162	7,710	292	8,198	37

Sources: Based on Phase 1 of the 1-2-3 surveys of selected countries (see table 10.1 for details).
* significant at the 10 percent level, ** significant at the 5 percent level, *** significant at the 1 percent level

immigrant populations of Cotonou and Niamey. Traditional male-dominated short- to long-distance migratory streams in West Africa are thus becoming feminized, suggesting a turnaround in traditional gender roles. Second, immigrants are significantly older than natives in Abidjan, and Niamey but roughly of the same age as natives in the other cities. Third, immigrants appear to be less educated on average than natives in four cities (Abidjan, Cotonou, Lomé, and Niamey). The education gap is particularly large in Abidjan, where immigrants have 2.0 years of schooling on average against 6.6 years for natives.

The statistics for natives were computed using data collected in capital cities only. Some of them are thus likely to be bad proxies for the situation at the national level (mean education levels, for example, are generally much higher in urban areas than in rural ones). It should consequently come as no surprise that immigrants in Abidjan, Cotonou, Lomé, and Niamey (a majority of whom may come from rural areas) are on average less educated than nationals in these cities. The fact that in Bamako, Dakar, and Ouagadougou, immigrants appear to be more educated on average than natives suggests that these cities attract mainly educated people or people from urban areas. Because of the small sample size, however, the figure for Dakar should be taken with caution.

As a complement to table 10.4, table 10.5 provides some descriptive statistics on the main characteristics of natives ("stayers") and emigrants ("movers"), by country of origin. In all countries except Togo and, to a lesser extent, Benin, men are overrepresented in the emigrant population. Intraregional migratory flows from these two countries are motivated mostly by commercial purposes and have traditionally been dominated by women. In terms of education, emigrants appear much less educated than nonmigrant natives in all countries, suggesting that migration flows within the WAEMU region mainly involve low-qualified workers.

Migrants' Employment Status

On average, labor force participation is higher for immigrants than for natives.[4] The difference is particularly large in Abidjan and Niamey, suggesting that migration streams to these cities are motivated mainly by labor market considerations. Given the individual characteristics of immigrants, particularly with respect to their level of education, one would expect their employment situation to be less favorable than that of natives in Abidjan, Cotonou, Lomé, and Niamey and more favorable in Dakar. In developing economies, formal wage workers in the public or private sector are considered to have a favorable employment situation; informal sector workers are considered to have an unfavorable situation.

The figures in table 10.6 indicate that this is indeed the case. The percentage of immigrants working in the informal sector is much higher than the percentage of natives in Abidjan, Bamako, Cotonou, Lomé, and Niamey; it is lower in Dakar and Ouagadougou.

Table 10.5 Mean Characteristics of Natives and Emigrants in Seven Cities in West Africa, 2001/02
(percent, except where otherwise indicated)

Variable	Abidjan Natives	Abidjan Emigrants	Bamako Natives	Bamako Emigrants	Cotonou Natives	Cotonou Emigrants	Dakar Natives	Dakar Emigrants	Lomé Natives	Lomé Emigrants	Niamey Natives	Niamey Emigrants	Ouagadougou Natives	Ouagadougou Emigrants
Men	47.6	54.1	49.1	57.4**	48.2	44.6	47.1	71.2*	47.6	38.5**	48.6	67.9**	50.7	58.4**
Age (years)	29.0	27.9	31.2	34.9**	31.1	32.8**	30.9	37.4**	30.4	30.2	30.7	31.7	30.2	34.7**
Education and experience														
Years of experience	16.4	15.4	20.3	27.7**	18.5	21.5**	19.5	26.9**	17.7	20.0**	19.6	23.4**	19.1	27.0**
Years of schooling	6.6	6.5	4.8	1.2**	6.6	5.3**	5.3	4.1**	6.6	4.2**	5.1	2.3**	5.1	1.8**
No diploma	44.7	43.2	58.4	90.3**	45.8	55.9**	60.2	65.5	42.8	67.2	60.9	81.6**	53.3	86.5**
Completed primary education	27.6	21.6	19.2	6.4**	26.7	23.4	18.5	14.9	31.9	19.3**	20.3	11.6**	24.6	9.0**
BEPC (*Brevet d'études du premier cycle du second degré*)	10.4	8.1	8.1	1.0*	13.2	8.6**	11.0	6.9	14.7	7.0**	7.2	2.6**	11.2	2.2**
Baccalauréat	4.8	8.1	2.2	0.3**	4.0	0.9**	3.8	6.9	3.2	0.8**	2.6	1.1	1.6	0.4**
Can read and write in French	73.8	64.9	49.2	16.1**	71.6	57.2**	60.4	51.7	73.7	48.0**	56.5	27.9**	59.6	27.9**
Can read and write in another language	25.0	37.8**	12.2	13.3	24.5	18.9	19.3	21.8	27.1	18.0**	21.6	31.9**	13.3	8.2**
Religion														
Muslim	31.2	51.4**	97.2	99.2**	9.9	25.2**	93.3	86.2	9.6	24.2**	98.2	96.3	55.8	69.5**
Catholic	35.9	16.2**	1.8	0.3**	67.2	38.7**	6.6	10.3	47.6	44.3	1.2	1.6	36.2	26.1**
Protestant	10.7	2.7	0.5	0.5	5.2	6.8	0.1	1.1**	10.2	12.3	0.4	0.5	6.5	2.2**
Number of observations	5,974	37	7,148	392	6,994	222	11,773	87	5,927	244	7,710	190	8,198	502

Sources: Based on Phase 1 of the 1-2-3 surveys of selected countries (see table 10.1 for details).
* significant at the 10 percent level, ** significant at the 5 percent level, *** significant at the 1 percent level.

Table 10.6 Employment Situation of Natives and Immigrants in Seven Cities in West Africa, 2001/02
(percent except where otherwise indicated)

Variable	Abidjan Natives	Abidjan Immigrants	Bamako Natives	Bamako Immigrants	Cotonou Natives	Cotonou Immigrants	Dakar Natives	Dakar Immigrants	Lomé Natives	Lomé Immigrants	Niamey Natives	Niamey Immigrants	Ouagadougou Natives	Ouagadougou Immigrants
Employment status														
Employed	59.7	77.9	57.5	58.1	68.0	73.1	50.4	57.9	70.6	74.7	47.5	65.7	56.6	56.8
Unemployed	11.4	4.7	4.2	2.3	4.1	2.2	7.5	0.0	6.7	3.7	7.9	3.8	11.0	16.2
Inactive	28.8	17.5	38.4	39.5	27.9	26.5	42.1	42.1	22.6	21.6	44.6	30.5	32.3	27.0
Number of observations	5,974	940	7,148	43	6,994	181	11,773	19	5,927	162	7,710	292	8,198	37
Sector														
Public sector	8.4	1.0	11.5	4.0	8.8	0.0	9.0	0.0	8.1	1.7	17.9	1.0	13.9	9.5
Formal private sector	21.4	12.7	11.7	8.0	11.6	10.9	17.6	36.4	8.2	12.4	13.6	10.4	9.0	19.1
Informal private sector	70.2	86.3	76.8	88.0	79.5	89.1	73.4	63.6	83.8	86.0	68.5	88.6	77.1	71.4
Wage														
Hourly wage (CFA francs, purchasing power parity)	467	276	347	578	255	182	417	754	192	255	337	234	271	240
Number of observations	3,569	732	4,107	25	4,759	129	5,935	11	4,186	121	3,664	192	4,642	21

Sources: Based on Phase 1 of the 1-2-3 surveys of selected countries (see table 10.1 for details).

Average hourly earnings follow roughly the same pattern. Compared with natives, immigrants earn much lower hourly wages in Abidjan (–41 percent), Niamey (–30 percent), and Cotonou (–29 percent); they earn much higher hourly wages in Dakar (91 percent), Bamako (67 percent), and Lomé (33 percent).[5] Lomé is an anomaly: although immigrants are less educated on average and more concentrated in the informal sector, they earn significantly higher hourly wages than natives.

Model Specification and Estimation Strategy

We take advantage of the simultaneity and strict comparability of the 1-2-3 surveys to evaluate the impact of hourly wage differences in the seven cities on individuals' residential choice. The econometric estimation is performed in three steps. First, using the pooled sample of 31,647 individuals observed in the seven cities, we estimate the determinants of individual residential choice, assuming that it reflects comparison of the hourly wage that can be obtained in each destination city, together with other variables. More precisely, we assume that each individual i born in country j and living in city k derives utility from its choice of residence, written as

$$u_i(j, k) = \alpha.\ln y_{ik} + \mathbf{z}_i' \cdot \mathbf{\gamma}_k + v_i(j,k) \qquad (10.1)$$

with $\ln y_{ik}$ the logarithm of individual i hourly earnings in city k, and $\mathbf{z}_i$ a vector of individual characteristics, such as religion. Individual i prefers to live in city k if doing so yields the highest utility:

$$u_i(j, k) - c(j, k) \geq u_i(j, l) - c(j, l) \quad \text{for all } l \qquad (10.2)$$

where $c(j, k)$ is the cost of settling in city k when born in country j.[6] These costs cannot be observed. In the econometric estimation of the model, we use nationality dummies to account for them, assuming that individuals originating from the same country face the same level of costs.

As individual hourly wages are observed only in the city of residence, equation (10.1) is estimated in a reduced form, obtained by replacing the logarithm of wage by a linear combination of its determinants:

$$u_i(j, k) = \alpha \cdot (\mathbf{x}'_{ik} \cdot \mathbf{\beta}_k) + \mathbf{z}_i' \cdot \mathbf{\gamma}_k + \varepsilon_i(j, k) \qquad (10.3)$$

Under appropriate assumptions on the distribution of the error term, this model can be estimated as a multinomial logit. The estimated coefficients can then be used to predict individual probabilities of residing in a given city.

Second, we use the predicted probabilities computed in the first step to correct for the self-selection of migrants in the hourly wage equation:

$$\ln y_{ik} = \mathbf{x}'_{ik \cdot} \beta_k + u_{ik \cdot} \qquad (10.4)$$

Holding account of migrants' self-selection is necessary because migrants could share some unobservable characteristics (such as motivation) that could be correlated with other observable determinants of wages (such as education). Following Dahl (2002), we correct for self-selection by adding to the wage equation a polynomial function of the choice probabilities computed in the first step as a control for unobserved characteristics that would otherwise bias the estimates.

Third, we use hourly wages estimated for each individual in each country to evaluate the impact of expected wage differences on the probabilities of choice (that is, the value of coefficient α in equation [10.1]).

Model Identification and Choice of Variables

In order to be identified, our model relies on various assumptions, which need to be properly tested. In particular, in the second step of our procedure, in which we correct for individuals' self-selection, it is important to include one or more variables that explain locational choice (that is, enter the first-stage equation) but do not influence earnings. In what follows, we use dummies indicating whether the individual's father did not go to school or was absent when the individual was 15, together with dummies for the individual's religion and nationality, as identifying variables. Religion is likely to have an influence on destination choice, given that the dominant religion is different in different cities. Nationality dummies are included to account for macro-level variables, such as average gross domestic product per capita, mortality rates, and the shares of immigrants from ECOWAS countries in the city's population. These variables also capture migration costs between the origin country and destination city.

Any one of these exclusion restrictions could be violated. For example, if there is discrimination against people of a particular nationality or religion in a particular destination city, these variables would influence earnings. If the quality of education is different for people from different countries, nationality could also influence earnings by affecting schooling differences. We believe discrimination on the basis of nationality or religion to be second-order concerns within the cities of our sample, and there is evidence that the quality of schooling does not differ dramatically across countries of origin.[7]

It could also be argued that father's education and father's presence in the household when individuals are 15 are correlated with household wealth, which affects occupational choice and earnings. However, overidentification tests do not reject the null hypothesis of zero correlation between our instruments and the principal equation error terms in five of seven cities.

In the third stage of our procedure, identification of the log-earnings coefficient in the structural model of residential choice depends on the exclusion from equation (10.1) of at least one variable that enters in the log-earnings equation (10.3). We assume that gender, education, and employment sector explain log-hourly earnings but not residential choice, once earnings are accounted for. There are some good reasons why education might determine residential choice, apart from its impact on potential earnings. One possibility is that well-educated individuals prefer cities in which the average level of education is high, not only because their own wages are more likely to be higher but also because they will benefit from positive externalities related to the high average level of education (such as a richer supply of cultural goods). In our sample, however, movers appear much less educated on average than stayers, in both origin countries' capitals and destination cities. We therefore believe this incentive to be low.

It could also be argued that people moving abroad experience a loss in utility because of the remoteness of their home country, extended family, and friends. This loss could induce a direct effect of the gender variable on locational choice, in addition to its indirect effect through earnings, if men (women) experience a greater loss than women (men). However, it is not clear whether the difference between men and women in this utility loss should be large, as both rely on networks of family and friends and may have similar preferences to remain in their home country.

Excluding the employment sector from the locational choice decision does not seem too heroic an assumption given the strong similarities in the structure of urban labor markets (and in the share of public versus private and formal versus informal jobs in particular) in the seven cities.

In the earnings equation, the dependent variable is the logarithm of total hourly earnings in CFA francs. All earnings are expressed in purchasing power parity (PPP). The conversion to PPP CFA francs is necessary in the third step of our estimation, where expected earnings in the seven cities are allowed to influence the probability of choice.[8] Independent variables in the earnings equations are gender, education (as measured by the last diploma obtained), potential labor market experience and its square, the ability to speak French, the ability to speak another foreign language, dummies for the public or private formal sectors, and a series of dummies for the father's activity when the individual was 15. This last set of variables is included both as a determinant of migration behavior and as a proxy for the individual's sector choice, to account for earnings differentials between sectors. The reduced-form multinomial logit model includes these variables, together with dummies for the individual's religion and nationality.

As our estimation strategy is a multistep procedure, we bootstrapped the entire process with 50 replications. Bootstrapped standard errors were used for hypothesis testing.

Estimation Results

We first present the results of the multinomial logit model before turning to the earnings equations and the structural model of residential choice. The section ends with some robustness checks.

Reduced-Form Multinomial Logit of Residential Choice

Tables 10.7–10.9 present the estimation results. Table 10.7 shows the results of the reduced-form multinomial logit estimation. These results are difficult to comment on, because only the differences in the coefficients with respect to the reference city (Dakar) can be identified. Thus, for instance, the positive coefficient of the gender variable in the equation for Cotonou indicates that being

Table 10.7 Reduced-Form Multinomial Logit Estimates of Individual Residential Choice in Seven Cities in West Africa, 2001/02

Variable	Abidjan	Bamako	Cotonou	Lomé	Niamey	Ouagadougou
Gender (1 = male)	1.35***	0.20	0.97***	1.14***	0.34	0.76**
	(0.29)	(0.32)	(0.33)	(0.33)	(0.32)	(0.31)
CEP (*Certificat d'études primaires*)	−0.20	−0.04	−0.67	−0.12	−0.35	0.43
	(0.45)	(0.51)	(0.50)	(0.49)	(0.50)	(0.49)
BEPC (*Brevet d'études du premier cycle du second degré*)	−0.25	0.01	−1.06	−0.49	−0.79	0.87
	(0.58)	(0.71)	(0.65)	(0.65)	(0.67)	(0.67)
CAP (*Certificat d'aptitude professionnelle*)	0.60	1.77	−1.03	−1.04	0.08	1.73
	(1.07)	(1.19)	(1.17)	(1.16)	(1.19)	(1.19)
BEP (*Brevet d'études professionnelles*)	−1.05	0.52	−3.20	−0.24	−0.81	1.09
	(1.95)	(1.91)	(2.06)	(2.00)	(1.99)	(2.09)
Baccalauréat	1.10*	1.35	1.24	1.60**	1.37*	2.32***
	(0.60)	(0.88)	(0.80)	(0.77)	(0.79)	(0.89)
Foundation degree[a]	−0.43	0.21	−2.62	−1.49	−0.86	1.07
	(1.77)	(1.84)	(1.82)	(1.84)	(1.85)	(1.91)
Bachelor's degree	−0.43	0.51	−1.53	−1.20	−0.07	0.84
	(0.92)	(1.00)	(1.00)	(1.00)	(0.99)	(1.03)
Postgraduate degree	−4.88***	−3.85***	−5.51***	−5.45***	−3.99***	−4.01***
	(1.06)	(1.07)	(1.02)	(1.07)	(1.06)	(1.17)

(continued next page)

Table 10.7 (continued)

Variable	Abidjan	Bamako	Cotonou	Lomé	Niamey	Ouagadougou
Marital status (1 = married)	−0.83*** (0.30)	−0.08 (0.33)	−0.34 (0.35)	−0.45 (0.34)	−0.42 (0.34)	−0.65** (0.33)
Speaks French (1 = yes)	−0.29 (0.34)	−0.05 (0.39)	−0.16 (0.40)	0.22 (0.39)	0.22 (0.39)	−0.08 (0.37)
Speaks another language (1 = yes)	0.20 (0.35)	−0.08 (0.39)	1.19*** (0.41)	1.06*** (0.41)	0.23 (0.40)	0.07 (0.41)
Experience (years)	0.16*** (0.04)	−0.04 (0.05)	0.04 (0.04)	0.04 (0.05)	0.08* (0.05)	0.03 (0.05)
Experience squared	−0.002*** (0.00)	0.00 (0.00)	−0.00 (0.00)	−0.00 (0.00)	−0.00 (0.00)	−0.00 (0.00)
Public sector	−1.60*** (0.59)	0.26 (0.63)	−0.18 (0.63)	−0.29 (0.62)	−0.16 (0.62)	0.52 (0.66)
Private sector	−0.17 (0.35)	0.28 (0.39)	0.14 (0.42)	−0.24 (0.41)	0.19 (0.40)	−0.84** (0.38)
Father in agricultural sector	0.72** (0.35)	−0.41 (0.38)	0.12 (0.39)	0.20 (0.39)	−0.02 (0.38)	−0.07 (0.38)
Father in industrial sector	−0.05 (0.52)	−0.52 (0.60)	−0.85 (0.60)	−0.68 (0.60)	−0.40 (0.60)	−0.80 (0.62)
Father in commercial sector	1.38*** (0.35)	0.97** (0.42)	0.81 (0.43)	1.15** (0.43)	0.63 (0.41)	1.20*** (0.41)
Father was senior executive	1.20** (0.59)	1.27* (0.73)	0.34 (0.72)	0.67 (0.72)	1.07 (0.73)	1.99** (0.79)
Father was midlevel executive	0.02 (0.58)	0.61 (0.65)	0.48 (0.64)	−0.08 (0.63)	0.61 (0.64)	0.22 (0.66)
Father was absent at age 15	1.01** (0.48)	0.69 (0.53)	1.47*** (0.54)	1.14** (0.54)	0.63 (0.53)	0.35 (0.53)
Father never went to school	−0.59* (0.34)	−0.69* (0.38)	−0.56 (0.37)	−0.91** (0.37)	0.10 (0.38)	0.31 (0.37)
Father schooling missing	−4.62*** (0.65)	−2.79*** (0.65)	−7.09*** (0.77)	−3.75*** (0.70)	−3.05*** (0.68)	−3.72*** (0.69)
Muslim	−5.74*** (1.78)	−5.72*** (1.84)	−6.00*** (1.80)	−6.88*** (1.79)	−3.18* (1.84)	−5.55*** (1.82)
Catholic	−4.97*** (1.80)	−4.97** (1.88)	−4.15** (1.82)	−5.37*** (1.81)	−3.20* (1.86)	−4.57** (1.84)
Protestant	−1.93 (2.15)	−2.65 (2.25)	−2.47 (2.17)	−3.39 (2.16)	−0.83 (2.22)	−0.92 (2.19)
Intercept	−1.62 (1.94)	−0.92 (2.03)	−3.98*** (2.21)	−2.35*** (2.03)	−6.01*** (2.10)	−4.83** (2.23)
Number of observations	31,647	31,647	31,647	31,647	31,647	31,647

Sources: Based on Phase 1 of the 1-2-3 surveys of selected countries (see table 10.1 for details).
Note: The dependent variable takes the value 1 (Cotonou) to 7 (Lomé), with 6 (Dakar) used as the comparison category. Nationality dummies were included but are not shown. Figures in parentheses are standard errors. University system derives from the French system, in which, until recently, second-year students could receive a diploma. This diploma is referred to here as the foundation degree.
* significant at the 10 percent level, ** significant at the 5 percent level, *** significant at the 1 percent level.

male has a larger effect on the utility resulting from choosing Cotonou than the utility resulting from choosing Dakar. The results suggest that, among the seven cities under review, holding a postgraduate degree or being Muslim or Catholic increases the utility of living in Dakar more than the utility of living in any other city. By contrast, holding a *baccalauréat* degree increases the utility of residing in Abidjan, Niamey, Ouagadougou, or Lomé by much more than that of residing in Dakar. Unsurprisingly, being of Senegalese nationality increases the utility of living in Dakar much more than that of living in any other city except Bamako, where the coefficient is insignificant (results not shown).

Earnings Equation

Following Dahl (2002), we use the estimated coefficients of the reduced-form multinomial logit to compute, for each observation of the sample, a polynomial of choice probabilities that was added to the set of explanatory variables in the earnings equations. Table 10.8 presents the ordinary least squares regression results. As the coefficients of the polynomials of the selection probabilities have no interpretation, we limit the presentation to the coefficients of the variables that have a direct interpretation.

The first column shows the estimated coefficients when no correction for endogenous selection is made. The second column presents the corrected coefficients. The results of a series of Wald tests are shown at the bottom of the table.

We computed several test statistics. First, we tested whether the selection correction terms enter the earnings equation significantly. Second, we tested the hypothesis that the excluded variables (father, religion, and nationality dummies) make no significant contribution to the explanation of the dependent variable.

Tests confirm that the model is correctly identified. With the exception of Bamako and Lomé and the father dummies, the Wald test statistics are insignificant, indicating that the vector of variables used to instrument residential choice does not contribute to the determination of earnings once the correction terms are included. For Bamako and Lomé, including the father dummies as explanatory variables did not change the results significantly.

As for the correction functions, in four cities (Abidjan, Bamako, Cotonou, and Lomé), we can reject the hypothesis that the coefficients of the polynomials included to correct for endogenous selection are all zero, suggesting that holding account of migrants' self-selection affects the estimation of earnings equations in these cities. In no case, however, does adjusting for self-selection change the returns to education enough that the adjusted coefficients lie outside the confidence intervals for the unadjusted estimates. This result suggests either that, given the relatively small number of migrants in our samples, selection

Table 10.8 Ordinary Least Squares Log-Earnings Regressions for Seven Cities in West Africa, 2001/02

Variable	Abidjan		Bamako		Cotonou		Dakar		Lomé		Niamey		Ouagadougou	
Gender (1 = male)	0.40*** (0.05)	0.44*** (0.05)	0.33*** (0.04)	0.30*** (0.06)	0.46*** (0.04)	0.45*** (0.04)	−0.15*** (0.05)	−0.18*** (0.05)	0.31*** (0.05)	0.28*** (0.07)	0.23*** (0.05)	0.28*** (0.07)	0.41*** (0.05)	0.31*** (0.08)
CEP (Certificat d'études primaires)	0.55*** (0.07)	0.55*** (0.08)	0.21*** (0.07)	0.23** (0.10)	0.54*** (0.06)	0.50*** (0.08)	0.36*** (0.07)	0.36*** (0.08)	0.52*** (0.07)	0.52*** (0.08)	0.52*** (0.09)	0.53*** (0.13)	0.44*** (0.08)	0.45*** (0.08)
BEPC (Brevet d'études du premier cycle du second degré)	1.17*** (0.10)	1.19*** (0.08)	0.53*** (0.11)	0.56*** (0.13)	1.00*** (0.09)	0.94*** (0.09)	0.58*** (0.09)	0.57*** (0.09)	1.11*** (0.10)	1.13*** (0.10)	1.07*** (0.14)	1.08*** (0.13)	1.31*** (0.11)	1.30*** (0.12)
CAP (Certificat d'aptitude professionnelle)	1.21*** (0.20)	1.19*** (0.16)	0.48*** (0.12)	0.54*** (0.13)	1.17*** (0.15)	1.07*** (0.16)	0.72*** (0.25)	0.74*** (0.14)	1.10*** (0.23)	1.24*** (0.21)	1.48*** (0.23)	1.42*** (0.18)	1.18*** (0.18)	1.19*** (0.16)
BEP (Brevet d'études profesionnelles)	1.13*** (0.20)	1.03*** (0.14)	0.98*** (0.11)	1.03*** (0.12)	0.95** (0.47)	0.74** (0.35)	0.86*** (0.26)	0.85*** (0.20)	1.31*** (0.18)	1.34*** (0.24)	1.30*** (0.20)	1.22*** (0.20)	1.74*** (0.25)	1.76*** (0.25)
Baccalauréat	1.71*** (0.15)	1.66*** (0.11)	0.81*** (0.20)	0.81*** (0.24)	1.37*** (0.15)	1.35*** (0.14)	0.97*** (0.14)	1.05*** (0.16)	1.63*** (0.16)	1.64*** (0.18)	1.90*** (0.19)	1.90*** (0.19)	1.85*** (0.19)	1.86*** (0.16)
Foundation degree[a]	2.08*** (0.15)	2.08*** (0.12)	1.00*** (0.16)	1.06*** (0.14)	2.14*** (0.20)	1.94*** (0.21)	1.17*** (0.26)	1.14*** (0.22)	2.72*** (0.28)	2.74*** (0.19)	1.90*** (0.25)	1.82*** (0.22)	2.14*** (0.22)	2.10*** (0.24)
Bachelor's degree	2.30*** (0.13)	2.26*** (0.10)	1.42*** (0.12)	1.49*** (0.13)	1.98*** (0.13)	1.89*** (0.13)	1.40*** (0.14)	1.39*** (0.12)	2.53*** (0.16)	2.58*** (0.13)	2.26*** (0.14)	2.16*** (0.11)	2.41*** (0.16)	2.41*** (0.12)
Postgraduate degree	1.81*** (0.21)	1.73*** (0.18)	1.15*** (0.23)	1.14*** (0.22)	1.74*** (0.18)	1.61*** (0.17)	1.39*** (0.18)	1.36*** (0.13)	2.20*** (0.27)	2.27*** (0.21)	1.98*** (0.18)	1.89*** (0.15)	1.62*** (0.23)	1.65*** (0.22)
Marital status (1 = married)	0.28*** (0.05)	0.25*** (0.04)	0.43*** (0.05)	0.47*** (0.06)	0.65*** (0.05)	0.63*** (0.05)	0.38*** (0.06)	0.36*** (0.06)	0.48*** (0.06)	0.49*** (0.06)	0.45*** (0.06)	0.45*** (0.07)	0.36*** (0.06)	0.41*** (0.05)

(continued next page)

Table 10.8 (continued)

Variable	Abidjan		Bamako		Cotonou		Dakar		Lomé		Niamey		Ouagadougou	
Speaks French (1 = yes)	0.06 (0.06)	0.06 (0.07)	0.21*** (0.06)	0.21** (0.08)	0.14** (0.06)	0.15* (0.09)	0.30*** (0.06)	0.32*** (0.07)	0.08 (0.07)	0.07 (0.07)	0.24*** (0.07)	0.24*** (0.08)	0.40*** (0.07)	0.45*** (0.08)
Speaks another language (1 = yes)	0.19** (0.07)	0.17*** (0.06)	0.13** (0.06)	0.08 (0.09)	0.36*** (0.07)	0.41*** (0.07)	0.34*** (0.07)	0.35*** (0.07)	0.04 (0.07)	0.01 (0.08)	0.09 (0.08)	0.17* (0.09)	0.32*** (0.08)	0.34*** (0.09)
Experience (years)	0.12*** (0.01)	0.13*** (0.01)	0.09*** (0.01)	0.08*** (0.01)	0.16*** (0.01)	0.15*** (0.01)	0.14*** (0.01)	0.14*** (0.01)	0.14*** (0.01)	0.15*** (0.01)	0.15*** (0.01)	0.15*** (0.01)	0.16*** (0.01)	0.14*** (0.01)
Experience squared	-0.002*** (0.00)	-0.002*** (0.00)	-0.001*** (0.00)	-0.001* (0.00)	-0.002*** (0.00)	-0.002*** (0.00)	-0.002*** (0.00)	-0.002*** (0.00)	-0.002*** (0.00)	-0.002*** (0.00)	-0.002*** (0.00)	-0.002*** (0.00)	-0.002*** (0.00)	-0.002*** (0.00)
Public sector	0.69*** (0.10)	0.50*** (0.08)	0.33*** (0.07)	0.38*** (0.07)	0.27*** (0.09)	0.32*** (0.06)	0.78*** (0.09)	0.84*** (0.07)	0.64*** (0.10)	0.65*** (0.06)	0.49*** (0.08)	0.46*** (0.08)	0.66*** (0.08)	0.76*** (0.10)
Private sector	0.67*** (0.06)	0.65*** (0.06)	0.17*** (0.06)	0.20*** (0.07)	0.32*** (0.07)	0.34*** (0.07)	0.81*** (0.06)	0.83*** (0.06)	0.33*** (0.09)	0.33*** (0.11)	0.31*** (0.08)	0.30*** (0.09)	0.42*** (0.09)	0.47*** (0.10)
Father in agricultural sector	-0.08 (0.05)	-0.05 (0.06)	-0.11** (0.05)	-0.18*** (0.07)	-0.02 (0.05)	-0.06 (0.06)	0.05 (0.06)	0.01 (0.06)	0.02 (0.06)	0.03 (0.06)	-0.01 (0.06)	-0.02 (0.07)	-0.21*** (0.05)	-0.29*** (0.07)
Father in industrial sector	-0.22** (0.09)	-0.19** (0.10)	-0.06 (0.09)	-0.06 (0.12)	0.15 (0.09)	0.10 (0.12)	-0.11 (0.07)	-0.12 (0.08)	-0.04 (0.10)	-0.02 (0.13)	-0.19 (0.14)	-0.21 (0.21)	-0.32** (0.16)	-0.37* (0.19)
Father in commercial sector	-0.05 (0.07)	-0.02 (0.07)	0.10* (0.05)	0.11* (0.07)	0.06 (0.07)	0.01 (0.08)	0.01 (0.06)	-0.02 (0.07)	0.10 (0.09)	0.08 (0.12)	-0.13 (0.08)	-0.11 (0.12)	0.01 (0.08)	-0.03 (0.11)
Father was senior executive	0.35** (0.14)	0.35*** (0.13)	0.41*** (0.10)	0.43*** (0.11)	0.28** (0.12)	0.19 (0.16)	0.26** (0.13)	0.27** (0.13)	0.17 (0.16)	0.18 (0.18)	-0.20 (0.16)	-0.23 (0.24)	0.24 (0.15)	0.21 (0.16)
Father was midlevel executive	-0.12 (0.09)	-0.18* (0.10)	0.15** (0.07)	0.17*** (0.06)	0.23*** (0.07)	0.25*** (0.07)	0.09 (0.09)	0.10 (0.09)	-0.01 (0.09)	-0.01 (0.11)	-0.05 (0.11)	-0.07 (0.10)	0.09 (0.12)	0.12 (0.13)

Table 10.8 (continued)

Variable	Abidjan		Bamako		Cotonou		Dakar		Lomé		Niamey		Ouagadougou	
Number of observations	4,239	4,239	4,052	4,052	4,736	4,736	5,430	5,430	4,245	4,245	3,701	3,701	4,471	4,471
R-squared	0.41	0.41	0.32	0.32	0.44	0.44	0.34	0.34	0.34	0.35	0.39	0.40	0.39	0.40
Wald test for selection correction terms		10.60*		11.00*		17.30***		5.54		28.00***		6.49		6.02
Overidentification Wald tests														
Father dummies[b]		3.86		8.07**		1.64		1.05		10.10**		2.03		1.63
Religion dummies		3.22		0.33		3.41		0.90		3.44		1.70		0.59
Nationality dummies		5.48		2.45		4.61		0.02		7.17		7.60		7.72

Sources: Based on Phase 1 of the 1-2-3 surveys of selected countries (see table 10.1 for details).

Note: Figures show uncorrected and corrected estimates. Figures in parentheses are standard errors.

a. University system derives from the French system, in which, until recently, second-year students could receive a diploma. This diploma is referred to here as the foundation degree.

b. Father was absent when individual was 15; father had no schooling; father schooling is missing.

* significant at the 10 percent level, ** significant at the 5 percent level, *** significant at the 1 percent level.

319

does not strongly bias the estimated returns to education or that our control functions do not do much to correct for the type of selectivity that matters.

In Abidjan, Cotonou, and Niamey, the corrected coefficients are lower than the uncorrected coefficients, suggesting that migrants to these cities share unobserved characteristics that make their earnings higher than the host city average. The opposite is found in Bamako and Lomé. These results have no implications for migrants' positive or negative selection. Indeed, migrants could have lower than average earnings in their host city but still earn more than they would have in the capital of their country of origin. In order to check whether earnings differentials matter in locational choice, we need to estimate the model in its structural form.

Comparing returns to education shows large differences across cities. In Bamako, and to a lesser extent Dakar, returns to education seem much lower than in the other cities. The increase in returns by grades does not appear very steep either. In Bamako, having completed primary school yields an estimated increase in hourly earnings of only 23 percent over uneducated individuals, a much lower estimate than in Abidjan (about 55 percent). In all cities, the largest returns are for bachelor's degrees. The smallest increase is in Bamako (114 percent over uneducated individuals) and the largest in Lomé (227 percent).

Structural Model of Residential Choice

Do earnings differentials affect locational choice? Table 10.9 presents the results of the conditional logit estimation (equation 10.1). With no correction for endogenous selection, the coefficient is small and weakly significant. Its size more than doubles and becomes very significant when we correct for endogenous selection, bringing support to the idea that individuals tend to locate in countries where their expected earnings are higher.

Table 10.9 Structural Model Estimates of Individual Residential Choice in Seven Cities in West Africa, 2001/02

Model	Estimated value of α
Uncorrected	0.31* (0.16)
Corrected	0.78*** (0.15)

Sources: Based on Phase 1 of the 1-2-3 surveys of selected countries (see table 10.1 for details).
Note: Figures in parentheses are standard errors.
* significant at the 10 percent level, ** significant at the 5 percent level, *** significant at the 1 percent level.

A second assessment of this notion is given by simulations that compare wages between origin and destination countries. We simulated these differences using the following procedure:

- Step 1: For each individual, compute the predicted value of the (log) average hourly income in each city.
- Step 2: For each individual, draw a value in the standard normal distribution.
- Step 3: For each individual i and city k, combine the results of steps 1 and 2 to compute the predicted value of the individual's (log) hourly income in city k, summing the predicted average with the random term multiplied by the estimated standard deviation of (log) wages in that city.
- Step 4: Repeat steps 2 and 3 100 times. For "movers," compute m, the proportion of individuals for whom the predicted hourly income is higher in their current city than in the capital of their country of origin. For "stayers," compute the average value of predicted hourly income in the cities in which they chose not to reside. Then compute s, the proportion of individuals for whom the average value of predicted hourly income is lower in the cities in which they chose not to reside than in their country of origin.

Table 10.10 shows the results of this exercise. For movers (stayers) in each city, it reports the proportion of individuals for whom m (s) exceeds 50 percent. In Bamako, Cotonou, and Ouagadougou, our model does a good job of predicting that movers live in cities in which their hourly income is higher than in their city of origin. In Bamako in particular, income differentials seem to play an important role. The model also does a good job of predicting stayers in Abidjan, Bamako, Dakar, and Niamey. The model fails to predict the destination of movers from Dakar and Lomé and of stayers in Cotonou. The fact that it fails

Table 10.10 Model Simulation Results of Moving and Staying in Seven Cities in West Africa, 2001/02

City	Percentage of movers for whom $m > 50$	Percentage of stayers for whom $s > 50$
Cotonou	85	1
Ouagadougou	90	24
Abidjan	50	59
Bamako	81	63
Niamey	23	83
Dakar	7	68
Lomé	8	31

Sources: Based on Phase 1 of the 1-2-3 surveys of selected countries (see table 10.1 for details).
Note: m = proportion of individuals for whom predicted hourly income is higher in current city than in capital of country of origin. s = proportion of individuals for whom average value of predicted hourly income is lower in cities in which they chose not to reside than in country of origin.

to predict the behavior of workers in some cities should not be surprising, as potential income differentials are not the only motive for migration. Given that income is just one factor among many, the ability of the model to predict workers' choice based on potential income differentials is surprisingly good.

For movers, we computed the difference between the predicted value of hourly earnings in the origin country capital and destination city; for stayers, we computed the difference between the predicted value of hourly earnings in the origin country capital and an average of the predicted value of hourly earnings that could be obtained in the six potential destination cities. We then computed the average value of these differences separately for movers and stayers. The difference is close to zero (–0.36) for stayers, suggesting that for these people there is no real gain of moving abroad. In contrast, movers earned much higher hourly earnings abroad (–3.99) than they would have earned had they stayed in their country of origin.

Robustness Checks

We conducted several robustness checks. First, in the second stage of our estimation procedure, we ran a Heckman selection model using data on labor market participants and nonparticipants instead of an ordinary least squares regression on participants only. In the early estimations, because of the difficulty of controlling for both the endogenous selection of locational choice and labor force participation, we restricted the sample to labor market participants. This limitation is a potential source of bias in our estimates. The identifying variable in the Heckman selection model is whether the individual is married, which is assumed to influence labor market participation but not earnings. Results obtained in the third stage were not affected by this change, suggesting negligible biases. Second, we checked whether self-selected internal migration affected the observed returns to education. We found no evidence of selection bias. Third, as our results might depend on the set of conversion factors used to convert current CFA francs into purchasing power parity values, we reran the model using World Bank (2003) conversion factors. This modification did not change the results significantly.

Conclusion

Our results shed light on migration flows within the WAEMU region. Despite the severe political crisis that began in 1999, Côte d'Ivoire remains the most important destination country in the subregion. Mali and Burkina Faso remain major labor-exporting countries, largely toward Côte d'Ivoire. Benin and Togo combine emigration and immigration.

Migrants tend to be less educated than nonmigrants, in both their origin and destination countries. Cross-border migration within the subregion thus seems to concern mainly people with low levels of education, who are more likely than natives to work in the informal sector and receive lower wages. Not accounting for international migration in estimating returns to education yields upward biased estimates in three of seven countries and downward biased estimates in two others. However, disparities in returns to education between cities do not vanish, suggesting that country-specific amenities and other unobservable nonwage variables play important roles in the locational choice of individuals with different levels of education.

We also find that expected earnings differentials have a very significant effect on choice probabilities: everything else equal, people tend to live in cities in which their expected earnings are higher than elsewhere. Our sample is not a random sample of individuals from the WAEMU region, and we do not include all potential destinations. These caveats notwithstanding, our results on the locational choice of a large sample of West Africans suggest that individuals in developing countries do not always deviate from the predictions of the standard economic model.

Notes

1. WAEMU includes eight countries: the seven under review in this chapter (Benin, Burkina Faso, Côte d'Ivoire, Mali, Niger, Senegal, and Togo) and Cape Verde. ECOWAS is a larger group of countries. It includes all WAEMU countries as well as The Gambia, Ghana, Guinea, Guinea Bissau, Liberia, Nigeria, and Sierra Leone.

2. Although Abidjan and Cotonou are not the administrative capitals of Côte d'Ivoire and Benin, we refer to them as capitals because they are the most important cities in economic terms (Cotonou is also the seat of government).

3. The civil war in Côte d'Ivoire started in September 2002, a few months after completion of the 1-2-3 survey.

4. The unemployment rates reported in tables 10.6 and table 1.6 in chapter 1 differ, for two reasons. First, table 1.6 covers only the active population, whereas table 10.6 includes inactive individuals. Second, table 10.6 is restricted to people 15–65, whereas table 1.6 covers everyone 10 and older.

5. Figures for Bamako and Dakar should be considered with great care given the small sample size.

6. All sampled individuals were born in one of the seven countries under review. We assume that they chose to live in one of the capitals of these countries; the model is built to analyze the determinants of this choice. Throughout the rest of the chapter, we distinguish between countries of origin and cities of destination or residence.

7. Indeed, according to UNESCO's (2005) *Education for All 2005 Monitoring Report*, which provides various indicators of the quality of education, none of the seven countries of concern stands out from the crowd. For instance, Benin ranks first when the quality of education is measured by the probability of being literate after six years of primary school but fourth when quality is measured by test scores and seventh when measured by the average teacher wage.

8. The PPP conversion factors were computed in 1998 by the Agence pour la Sécurité de la Navigation Aérienne en Afrique (ASECNA) and updated through 2001 using national inflation rates.

References

African Union. 2005. "Draft Strategic Framework for a Policy on Migration in Africa." Third Ordinary Session of the Labour and Social Affairs Commission, Pretoria, April 18–23.

Borjas, G. 1987. "Self-Selection and the Earnings of Immigrants." *American Economic Review* 77 (4): 531–53.

Dahl, G. B. 2002. "Mobility and the Return to Education: Testing a Roy Model with Multiple Markets." *Econometrica* 70 (6): 2367–420.

Harris, J., and M. Todaro. 1970. "Migration, Unemployment, and Development: A Two-Sector Analysis." *American Economic Review* 60 (1): 126–42.

IOM (International Organisation for Migration). 2003. *World Migration 2003: Challenges, and Responses for People on the Move.* Geneva: IOM.

Roy, A. 1951. "Some Thoughts on the Distribution of Earnings." *Oxford Economic Papers* 3: 135–46.

Sjaastad, L. A. 1962. "The Costs and Returns of Human Migration." *Journal of Political Economy* 70 (5): 80–93.

Todaro, M. 1969. "A Model of Labor Migration and Urban Unemployment in Less Developed Countries." *American Economic Review* 59: 138–48.

UNESCO (United Nations Educational, Scientific and Cultural Organization). 2005. *Education for All 2005 Monitoring Report.* Paris: UNESCO.

World Bank. 2003. *World Development Indicators* (CD–ROM). Washington, DC.

Chapter 11

Returns to Returning in West Africa

Philippe De Vreyer, Flore Gubert, and Anne-Sophie Robilliard

Although labor migration has attracted much attention among researchers and resulted in a sizable body of literature on the welfare implications of migration and the uses and impact of remittances, the determinants and impacts of return migration have been underresearched. This neglect is surprising, because a large proportion of migrants return home at some point in their life cycle, making many migrations temporary.[1]

In West Africa, subregional, interregional, and international migration is essentially temporary (although tighter immigration policies in Europe have lengthened the duration of migration there) (Adepoju 2005; Ba 2006). According to surveys conducted in 1993 by the Réseau Migrations et Urbanisation en Afrique de l'Ouest (REMUAO) in seven countries, 111,000 people ages 15 and older migrated from REMUAO countries to Europe between 1988 and 1992, and 33,000 migrants returned (Bocquier 1998).[2]

Empirical evidence concerning the relationship between return migration and development is too fragmentary and contradictory to be used to draw clear conclusions or formulate concrete policy measures. The developmental impact of return migration is likely to vary significantly depending on several critical factors, including its book, the characteristics of return migrants, the degree and direction of selectivity, the reasons for return, and the situation prevailing in the home country. For example, even when migrants acquire new skills and experience abroad, they may not be able to apply them back home. Indeed, it is difficult for migrants who have acquired technical or industrial skills to apply them in rural settings, where the infrastructure needed to make effective use of new skills is lacking. In urban areas, where access to jobs is much easier for individuals with dense social or family networks, return migrants may find it difficult to get a job if they failed to maintain strong social ties with their family and friends in the home country while working abroad.

We estimate the impact of return migration at the individual level. Our aim is to shed light on whether the financial capital and new skills acquired abroad are used productively back home. We examine this issue by investigating whether return migrants' experience abroad provides a positive earnings premium for wage-earners, a productivity advantage for business owners, or both, upon returning.

The chapter is organized as follows. We begin by reviewing the empirical literature on the impact of return migration from sending countries' perspective. In the second section, we describe the data and provide descriptive statistics on the characteristics of return migrants, which we compare with statistics on migrants and nonmigrants. In the third section, we analyze the labor market performance of return migrants by estimating earnings functions or production functions. In the last section, we provide concluding remarks and suggest directions for future work.

Review of the Empirical Literature

Empirical studies on the labor market performance of return migrants investigate whether returnees are able to apply at home what they learned abroad by comparing the wages of return migrants with the wages of people who stayed in the home country (see, for example, Kiker and Traynham 1977; Enchautegui 1993; Co, Gang, and Yun 2000; de Coulon and Piracha 2005; Rooth and Saarela 2007). Contrasting results emerge from this literature.

Using data collected in 1980 on a sample of Puerto Rican men who returned from the United States in the 1970s, Enchautegui (1993) finds that experience abroad is neither penalized nor rewarded. The explanation provided by the author is that Puerto Rican migrants in the United States are confined to low-skilled jobs, where little human capital investment takes place.

In contrast, using panel data on a large sample of Hungarian households, Co, Gang, and Yun (2000) find that foreign experience matters and that a wage premium is paid for having gone abroad. Their results also suggest large differences in the returns to foreign experience by gender and host country: foreign experience strongly matters for women but not for men. Women who migrated to countries in the Organisation for Economic Co-operation and Development (OECD) earn a 67 percent premium over women who have not been abroad. In contrast, the premium is insignificant for women who migrated to non-OECD countries.

No such quantitative analysis has been conducted on African return migrants. However, a study of female migrants from Ghana argues that most of them did not learn anything new while working abroad, because they worked only in unskilled jobs (Brydon 1992).

Potential selection biases are an important methodological issue in this strand of literature. In the case of return migration, individuals are self-selected (see, for example, Nakosteen and Zimmer 1980; Borjas 1987; Borjas and Bratsberg 1996). The selective process is said to be positive if individuals who choose to leave a country (and to return to their home country in the case of return migrants) are more able or more motivated than individuals who choose not to migrate. Ignoring self-selection in the process of return migration may result in biased estimates of the wage premium related to experience abroad.

De Coulon and Piracha (2005) find evidence that return migrants in Albania are negatively self-selected (that is, had they chosen not to migrate, their labor market performance would have been worse than that of nonmigrants). Using Hungarian data, Co, Gang, and Yun (2000) address the self-selection issue by estimating two types of earnings equations. They first estimate an earnings equation using a simple ordinary least squares (OLS) regression in which a dummy variable captures whether an individual has foreign experience or not. They then estimate the same earnings equation using maximum likelihood estimation (MLE) techniques to control for self-selection in the migration decision. For men, the MLE coefficient on foreign experience is smaller than the OLS coefficient. This result means that part of the positive effect on earnings of going abroad in the OLS estimate reflects the effect of self-selection: men who migrated would have earned more whether or not they had gone abroad. The reverse holds true for women, who negatively select migration.

A few empirical studies examine the impact of return migration on the development of small businesses in the home country (Ilahi 1999; McCormick and Wahba 2001; Ammassari 2003; Black, King, and Tiemoko 2003; Wahba 2004; Mesnard 2004; Nicholson 2004). Experience abroad may enable migrants to contribute to small business development in two ways. First, savings accumulated abroad may help alleviate domestic capital market imperfections. Second, migrants may develop new skills and form new ideas abroad.

McCormick and Wahba (2001) explore the extent to which Egyptian returnees become entrepreneurs and the influence on this process of overseas savings, overseas work experience, and premigration formal education. Using data from the 1988 Labor Force Sample Survey, they estimate a simple model of the probability that a return migrant is an entrepreneur. Their findings suggest that among literate returnees, total savings accumulated overseas and the length of overseas employment positively and significantly affect the probability of becoming an entrepreneur. Longer periods overseas have no influence on this probability among illiterate returnees. Ilahi (1999) examines similar issues for Pakistan, providing some evidence that return migrants use their savings to invest in self-employment.

A project by the Centre for Migration Research of the University of Sussex explores the relationship between migration, return, and development among both "elite" and less-skilled returnees to Ghana and Côte d'Ivoire (Black, King, and Litchfield 2003). Although the research is mostly qualitative and the small sample sizes caution against generalizations, the authors identify key variables influencing the propensity of returnees to invest in businesses: the skill level of migrants, the length of time they spend abroad, the work experience they gain and working conditions they experience, and the contacts they have with friends and relatives back home.

Data and Descriptive Statistics

The data are taken from phases 1 and 2 of the 1-2-3 surveys conducted in the seven capital cities of the French-speaking countries of the West African Economic and Monetary Union (WAEMU) (see box O.1 in the overview for a description of these surveys).[3] We first use the sample of all individuals 15 and older interviewed in Phase 1 to compare the characteristics of return migrants relative to nonmigrants and immigrants. Nonmigrants are defined as individuals who never left the country in which they were born and interviewed. Immigrants are nonnative residents, defined as individuals who are not citizens of the country they currently reside in. Return migrants are defined as individuals who were born in the country of current residence (or who are citizens of that country) who lived abroad for some time and then came back. Three types of return migrants can be identified: migrants who came back from a WAEMU country, migrants who came back from an OECD country, and migrants who came back from a country outside WAEMU or the OECD. As we show, the three types of return migrants have somewhat different characteristics.

Because the surveys were not designed to investigate migration, they provide very limited information on the migration experience of returnees. The database contains no information on the year of departure; the place of residence at the time of migration; the duration of the stay (that is, whether it was temporary, seasonal, circular, or longer term); family and labor status during migration; or parents' migrant status.

The total sample comprises 58,459 individuals 15 and older (table 11.1). The sample of return migrants includes 3,594 individuals, 88 percent of them returning from non-OECD countries. Return migrants represent a relatively small share of the population living in the seven cities. The average share is 4.8 percent, but it ranges from 1.9 percent in Dakar to 13.3 percent in Lomé.[4] In five out of seven cities, the share of return migrants in the population is actually higher than the share of immigrants. The exceptions are Abidjan, where the share of immigrants in the population is very high (15.4 percent) and the share of return migrants low (2.1 percent), and Niamey, where the shares of both immigrants (4.3 percent) and return migrants (3.2 percent) are relatively small.

Phase 2 of the 1-2-3 survey is restricted to small informal microenterprises whose owners were surveyed during Phase 1. This sample includes

Table 11.1 Descriptive Statistics of Sample of Seven Cities in West Africa, by Migration Status, 2001/02

| Statistic | Nonmigrants | Return migrants from | | | | Immigrants | Total |
		WAEMU country	OECD country	Other country	All countries		
Sample size	52,267	2,162	390	1,042	3,594	2,598	58,459
Share of sample (percent)	88.5	2.8	0.6	1.4	4.8	6.7	100.0
Average age (years)	31.0 (13.7)	34.8 (15.1)	40.3 (14.6)	36.1 (15.8)	35.9 (15.3)	34.1 (12.2)	31.4 (13.7)
Men (percent)	48.1	50.3	62.0	47.3	50.8	58.6	49.0
Married (percent)	42.7	54.4	60.9	55.4	55.5	62.4	44.6
Years of education	5.6 (4.9)	5.6 (5.2)	11.1 (6.7)	5.5 (5.0)	6.3 (5.7)	3.0 (4.6)	5.5 (5.0)

Sources: Based on Phase 1 of the 1-2-3 surveys of selected countries in the West African Economic and Monetary Union (WAEMU) conducted in 2001/02 by the Observatoire économique et statistique d'Afrique Subsaharienne (AFRISTAT); Développement, Institutions et Mondialisation (DIAL); and national statistics institutes.
Note: Figures are for individuals 15 and older. Figures in parentheses are standard deviations. WAEMU = West African Economic and Monetary Union, OECD = Organisation for Economic Co-operation and Development.

6,619 microentreprises. The survey collected detailed information on production and sales, expenses, employee characteristics, and physical capital. It also includes information on the founding of the enterprise and its sources of capital.

Are return migrants different from nonmigrants in terms of their individual characteristics? How do they compare with immigrants? Migration theory suggests that migrants and return migrants choose where to live by comparing the advantages of living in various places. The utility of living abroad or in the home country can depend on observed and unobserved characteristics. If self-selection occurs, one would expect migrants to be different from nonmigrants and, among migrants, return migrants to be different from migrants who stay abroad. In fact, observable differences between nonmigrants, return migrants, and immigrants in the seven cities studied are significant and informative; differences between return migrants from OECD countries and return migrants from non-OECD countries (both WAEMU and non-WAEMU) are also quite important.

We start by examining the distribution of four individual characteristics: age, gender, marital status, and education. Return migrants tend to be older and better educated than nonmigrants, and they are more likely to be men and married (see table 11.1). On average, return migrants are five years older than nonmigrants, and 51 percent are men (compared with 48 percent in the nonmigrant population). Return migrants from OECD countries are on average five years older than return migrants from non-OECD countries, and the proportion of men is much larger (62 percent versus 49 percent). The fact that return migrants are on average older than nonmigrants is not surprising, as future emigrants and future return migrants are included in the population of nonmigrants. The same reasoning can explain why immigrants in WAEMU are on average older than nonmigrants but younger than return migrants from WAEMU.

On average, return migrants are a bit more educated than nonmigrants. Large differences exist between the average level of education of return migrants from OECD countries (more than 11 years) and return migrants from WAEMU (5.6 years) or other developing countries (5.5 years). These differences do not result from the demographic composition of the samples. As shown in table 11.2, differences in education levels between the three groups of returnees remain after controlling for gender, age, and religion.

Two factors may explain the high average level of education of return migrants from OECD countries. First, educated people may find it more profitable to migrate to a developed country, where the returns to their human capital are likely to be higher. Second, people may migrate to obtain an education, in

Table 11.2 Ordinary Least Squares Regressions of Years of Education on Individual Characteristics in Seven Cities in West Africa, 2001/02

Variable	Coefficient	P > |t|
Gender and age		
Male	2.242	0.000***
Age	0.085	0.000***
Age squared	−0.002	0.000***
Religion (reference = Muslim)		
Catholic	2.758	0.000***
Protestant	2.977	0.000***
Other religion	1.151	0.000***
Migration status (reference = nonmigrant)		
WAEMU return migrant	0.555	0.000***
OECD return migrant	5.969	0.000***
Other return migrant	0.020	0.890
Immigrant	−1.995	0.000***
Constant	2.621	0.000***
Number of observations	58,058	
R^2	0.1478	

Sources: Based on Phase 1 of the 1-2-3 surveys of selected countries (see table 11.1 for details).
Note: Figures are for individuals 15 and older. City dummies were included but are now shown.
WAEMU = West African Economic and Monetary Union, OECD = Organisation for Economic Co-operation and Development.
*** significant at the 1 percent level.

which case it is not surprising to observe that return migrants have a higher level of education than nonmigrants.[5] The policy implications of the two explanations are very different. If educated people move to developed countries to benefit from high returns, brain drain will reduce the chance of the home countries to develop (Bhagwati 1972; Bhagwati and Hamada 1974; Usher 1977; Blomqvist 1986; Haque and Kim 1995), unless a large enough portion of migrants with enough experience from abroad returns to compensate for the original loss, or the possibility to migrate increases the number of individuals who decide to get an education, provided that only a smaller number of them succeed in leaving their country (Stark, Helmenstein, and Prskawetz 1997; Beine, Docquier, and Rapoport 2001, 2003).

Labor Market Performance of Return Migrants

The labor market performances of return migrants can be assessed in various ways. In what follows, we start by examining the labor market participation, sectoral allocation, and earnings of return migrants. We then investigate whether return migrants' experience abroad provides an earnings premium for wage-earners, a productivity advantage for business owners, or both.

Employment Situation of Return Migrants
In developing economies, wage-earners in the public or formal private sector and entrepreneurs or business owners in both the formal and informal sectors are considered "favored" over workers in the informal sector.[6] Given the individual characteristics of return migrants, particularly with respect to their level of education, one would expect their employment situation to be more favorable than that of nonmigrants. Descriptive statistics from table 11.3 indicate that this is the case to some extent for all migrants and very much the case for return migrants from OECD countries.

On average, labor force participation is higher for return migrants than for nonmigrants, with large differences across cities. The labor force participation of returnees is much higher than that of nonmigrants in Abidjan, Dakar, and Niamey. It is lower than that of nonmigrants in Ouagadougou and comparable to that of nonmigrants in Bamako, Cotonou, and Lomé. In contrast, among return migrants from OECD countries, labor force participation with respect to nonmigrants is higher in all cities (substantially so in some cities). Labor force participation of return migrants from countries outside WAEMU and OECD is also very high.

Sectoral differences are not significant on average for active nonmigrants and active return migrants. They are striking, however, among migrants returning from OECD countries. For example, the proportion of the labor force working

Table 11.3 Labor Force Participation of Nonmigrants, Return Migrants, and Immigrants in Seven Cities in West Africa, 2001/02
(percent, except where otherwise indicated)

Variable	Nonmigrants	Return migrants from				Immigrants	All
		WAEMU country	OECD country	Other country	All countries		
Labor force participation	57.2	59.3	63.8	68.2	62.4	74.5	58.6
Public sector wage workers	5.4	5.3	18.1	3.4	6.3	0.9	5.1
Private formal sector wage workers	7.8	6.6	16.9	5.1	7.4	8.5	7.8
Business owners	3.1	4.0	11.2	5.7	5.4	8.3	3.6
Informal sector workers	83.7	84.1	53.8	85.8	80.9	82.3	83.5
Earnings of active individuals (1,000 CFAF purchasing power parity)	55.9	54.7	227.1	46.0	73.4	57.6	56.9

Sources: Based on Phase 1 of the 1-2-3 surveys of selected countries (see table 11.1 for details).
Note: Figures are for individuals 15 and older. WAEMU = West African Economic and Monetary Union, OECD = Organisation for Economic Co-operation and Development.

as wage-earners in the public sector is 18.1 percent among migrants returning from OECD countries, 5.4 percent among nonmigrants, and 5.3 percent among migrants returning from WAEMU countries. Similar differences can be observed with regard to the percentage of individuals working as wage-earners in the formal private sector (16.9 percent among migrants returning from OECD countries versus 7.8 percent among nonmigrants) and as entrepreneurs (11.2 percent among migrants returning from OECD countries versus 3.1 percent among nonmigrants). Overall, these figures suggest that individuals returning from OECD countries gain access to more protected jobs and that the labor status of return migrants from other countries resembles that of nonmigrants.

The share of return migrants from OECD countries with formal sector and management jobs is relatively high (and share of informal sector jobs relatively low). The sectoral distribution of returnees from non-OECD countries is similar to that of nonmigrants.

The high participation rate of return migrants from OECD countries in the formal sector can be explained by their high educational level. But it could also indicate that their education, work experience, or both in OECD countries—if any—allowed them to gain specific knowledge that is valued in the formal sector, such as an ability to deal with or knowledge of foreign regulations, which could be valued in export-oriented sectors.

In order to examine more thoroughly this "specific knowledge" argument, we check whether the higher labor participation of return migrants from OECD countries in formal private, public, or management jobs holds after controlling for a number of individual characteristics. We do so by running a multinomial logit regression of labor status on a number of individual characteristics on the pooled sample of all active individuals in the seven cities (table 11.4). The results indicate that when other individual characteristics are controlled for, the probability of working as a wage-earner in the public sector is actually lower for all return migrants. Thus, return migrants from OECD countries appear better able to secure jobs in the public sector because they have, on average,

Table 11.4 Multinomial Logit Regressions of Alternative Labor Statuses in Seven Cities in West Africa (Marginal Effects), 2001/02

Variable	Men		Women	
	Coefficient	P > |t|	Coefficient	P > |t|
Public sector wage-earner				
Years of education	0.021	0.000***	0.006	0.000***
Potential experience	0.011	0.000***	0.002	0.000***
Potential experience squared	0.000	0.000***	0.000	0.000***
Migration status (reference = nonmigrant)				
WAEMU return migrant	−0.041	0.000***	−0.003	0.032**
OECD return migrant	−0.029	0.004***	−0.004	0.147
Other return migrant	−0.044	0.000***	−0.007	0.000***
Immigrant	−0.075	0.000***	−0.011	0.000***
Private formal sector wage-earner				
Years of education	0.025	0.000***	0.011	0.000***
Potential experience	0.014	0.000***	0.002	0.000***
Potential experience squared	0.000	0.000***	0.000	0.000***
Migration status (reference = nonmigrant)				
WAEMU return migrant	0.005	0.784	0.004	0.507
OECD return migrant	−0.007	0.821	0.021	0.236
Other return migrant	−0.045	0.017**	−0.018	0.002***
Immigrant	−0.055	0.000***	−0.005	0.359
Entrepreneur				
Years of education	0.005	0.000***	0.004	0.000***
Potential experience	0.006	0.000***	0.002	0.000***
Potential experience squared	0.000	0.000***	0.000	0.011**

(continued next page)

Table 11.4 (continued)

Variable	Men		Women	
	Coefficient	P > |t|	Coefficient	P > |t|
Migration status (reference = nonmigrant)				
WAEMU return migrant	0.002	0.862	−0.006	0.272
OECD return migrant	0.078	0.010**	0.115	0.007***
Other return migrant	0.009	0.487	0.000	0.977
Immigrant	0.002	0.769	0.016	0.019
Number of observations	18,436		14,806	
Pseudo R^2	0.1823		0.2998	

Sources: Based on Phase 1 of the 1-2-3 surveys of selected countries (see table 11.1 for details).
Note: Figures are for individuals 15 and older. City dummies are included but not shown. Reference status is informal sector worker. WAEMU = West African Economic and Monetary Union, OECD = Organisation for Economic Co-operation and Development..
* significant at the 10 percent level, ** significant at the 5 percent level, *** significant at the 1 percent level.

more education, not because they migrated. The fact that after controlling for education public sector employment is actually lower for return migrants could reflect the loss in social capital that migrants incur while living abroad.

The probability of working as a wage-earner in the private formal sector is also significantly lower for migrants returning from non-WAEMU and non-OECD countries, but except for them, returnees do not appear more or less able to work in the private sector. The probability of being an entrepreneur in the formal or informal sector is significantly higher for migrants returning from OECD countries, even after controlling for a number of individual characteristics. This result could reflect the acquisition of specific knowledge or the fact that their migration spell allowed them to accumulate capital to start up a business. Experience abroad for returnees from elsewhere does not have a significant impact on entrepreneurship.

Because return migrants from OECD countries have more favorable characteristics and positions in the labor market, it is no surprise that their earnings are higher than those of nonmigrants (see table 11.3). Whether this finding holds true after controlling for individual characteristics and selection biases is examined together with the specific knowledge argument in the rest of the chapter.

Do return migrants access their employment through the same channels as nonmigrants? Statistics presented in table 11.5 suggest that they do not. Return migrants appear to rely less on personal relations than nonmigrants do (35 percent versus 42 percent for nonmigrants). The gap is even larger when the sample of returnees is restricted to migrants returning from OECD countries (23 percent versus 42 percent). Whether these differences hold when controlling for their individual characteristics and the types of positions they obtain remains to be investigated.

Table 11.5 Route of Access to Current Employment by Nonmigrants, Return Migrants, and Immigrants in Seven Cities in West Africa, 2001/02
(percent)

Route	Nonmigrants	Return migrants from				Immigrants	All
		WAEMU country	OECD country	Other country	All countries		
Personal relations	42.1	36.2	22.8	37.9	35.0	38.7	41.4
Directly through employer	9.9	9.9	19.0	7.3	10.3	7.2	9.7
National employment agency or announcement	1.3	1.6	6.2	1.4	2.1	0.5	1.3
Competitive examination (*concours*)	13.5	7.9	16.8	7.5	8.9	2.9	12.3
Personal initiative	31.4	42.3	27.9	44.5	41.2	49.7	33.5
Other	1.9	2.1	7.4	1.5	2.6	1.0	1.8

Sources: Based on Phase 1 of the 1-2-3 surveys of selected countries (see table 11.1 for details).
Note: Figures are for individuals 15 and older. WAEMU = West African Economic and Monetary Union, OECD = Organisation for Economic Co-operation and Development.

The data used in this study are a sample of urban residents living in capital cities of WAEMU. As a result, only migrants returning from abroad to live in the seven cities surveyed are observed; this sample is likely not to be representative of the global flow of return migration, introducing at least two biases. First, on average, one would expect migrants returning to live in capital cities to be more educated/skilled than migrants returning to live in other cities or rural areas. Second, one would expect the share of migrants returning from OECD countries to be larger in capital cities.

To be sure, return migrants' choice to live in an urban or rural area upon returning is likely to be correlated with the residence they left when they chose to migrate. It is therefore informative to compare the destination of migrants originating from different locations. That information is available for Senegal (Ba 2006), where migrants originating in Dakar appear to be much more likely to migrate to an OECD country than migrants from elsewhere in Senegal: almost 75 percent of migrants originating from Dakar migrated to Europe, the United States, or Canada versus 55 percent of migrants originating in other cities and only 40 percent of migrants originating in rural areas.

In what follows, we use phases 1 and 2 of the 1-2-3 surveys to examine the labor market performance of return migrants. Using data from Phase 1, we estimate individual earnings functions to measure the impact of return migration on earnings. We then push the analysis further by investigating whether return migrants are more productive microentrepreneurs, using data on the sample of self-employed workers and small firm owners surveyed in Phase 2.[7]

Experience Abroad and Earnings

We consider a semi-log specification for the earnings equation:

$$\ln Y_i = \mathbf{X_i}\boldsymbol{\beta} + RM_i\alpha + e_i \qquad (11.1)$$

where $\ln Y$ is the natural-log of monthly earnings, β and α are coefficient vectors, and e is the stochastic term. Matrix X includes variables on personal characteristics; RM is a dummy variable indicating whether the individual is a return migrant.

We restrict the estimation of equation (11.1) to the sample of workers who are wage-earners. (The impact of being a return migrant on the remuneration of self-employed individuals and business owners is examined later in the chapter.)

In order to properly estimate the impact of return migration on earnings, one needs to control for the selection of return migrants. A treatment effect model in which return migrants constitute the treated population and non-migrants the untreated (or control) population does so. However, the quality of the treatment depends on the migrants' destination. Return migrants are not a homogeneous population; migrants returning from OECD countries differ significantly from other return migrants. As individuals self-select into the treatment they receive, we run separate regressions for each of the three groups (returnees from a WAEMU country, returnees from an OECD country, and returnees from elsewhere). In each regression, the treated sample includes return migrants and the untreated sample includes nonmigrants. Immigrants are excluded from the regressions.

The self-selection of return migrants is only one potentially endogenous selection. Co, Gang, and Yun (2000) control for a double process of self-selection: labor force participation and return migration. They estimate their model using maximum likelihood, allowing for correlation between the earnings equation error term and the migration and participation equations. We would have liked to control for participation and, among participants, the self-selection of wage workers. However, such a model proved impossible to estimate given the data at hand, forcing us to forgo accounting for individuals' self-selection into wage employment.

The treatment effect model we estimate is given by equation (11.1), to which we add a second equation describing the probability of being a return migrant:

$$RM_i^* = \mathbf{Q_i'}\boldsymbol{\xi} + u_i \qquad (11.2)$$

where RM^* is a latent unobservable variable measuring the propensity to be a return migrant. Vector $\mathbf{Q_i}$ includes X_i, together with instrumental variables.

Assuming normality of the error terms, the model can be estimated by maximum likelihood (MLE) or in two steps.

Proper identification of the full structural model requires valid instruments for the migration model. Co, Gang, and Yun (2000) use the locality in which an individual was born to instrument the probability of being a return migrant. De Coulon and Piracha (2005) employ the number of dependents in the household, the population of the town of residence, and religion. The number of dependents in the household can be a good instrument if a tighter budget constraint acts as a push factor of migration and has no direct impact on the earnings equation. Religion and the number of dependents in the household could not be used in this survey. In some countries (such as Senegal), religion does not offer enough variation in the sample, weakening its ability to explain migration. As for the number of dependents, it is observed only at the time of the survey; it could be very different when the migrant left or returned.

The locality in which an individual was born is a good instrument if there are spatial variations in the probability to migrate—as a result, for instance, of variations in the geographical environment or in attitudes toward migration. We cannot employ the locality in which an individual was born, however, because it cannot be precisely observed for all individuals. Instead, we use the proportion of return migrants in the neighborhood, excluding the worker's household, in the computation. This variable should capture the same kind of variations as the locality of birth. Our second instrument is the father's occupation when the worker was 15. Both instruments are expected to explain migration while having no direct impact on the earnings equation.

In order to assess the magnitude and size of the biases resulting from the two selection processes, we also report estimates of the earnings equation using OLS. To validate our choice of instruments statistically, we examine the combined explanatory power of both variables in the instrumental equation and run overidentification tests. We also take advantage of the existence of two alternative estimators (two-step estimator and MLE) to estimate our model. The two estimators should give asymptotically equivalent results, provided the model is correctly specified. We thus consider as valid and reliable those estimates that are found statistically identical using one estimator or the other.

Table 11.6 presents the estimated coefficients of the return migrant variable estimated on the subsample of migrants returning from WAEMU countries, OECD countries, and other countries.

Controlling for self-selection in going abroad dramatically changes the estimations. Whatever the last country of residence or gender of the returnees, the OLS coefficient estimate is systematically lower than the MLE and the two-step estimates, although the difference is not always significant. This result suggests that migrants are negatively selected in their population of origin—in

Table 11.6 Coefficient Estimates for Return Migrants in Seven Cities in West Africa, 2001/02

	Return migrants from								
	WAEMU country			OECD country			Other country		
Gender/coefficient	OLS	MLE	Two-step estimator	OLS	MLE	Two-step estimator	OLS	MLE	Two-step estimator
Men									
Return migrant dummy coefficient	−0.0118 (0.0409)	0.0625 (0.140)	0.185 (0.220)	0.166** (0.0729)	0.384** (0.193)	0.396* (0.205)	−0.0631 (0.0587)	0.0625 (0.140)	0.185 (0.220)
Correlation coefficient		−0.059			−0.190			−0.0590	
Women									
Return migrant dummy coefficient	0.0750 (0.0550)	0.703*** (0.119)	0.244 (0.218)	0.309*** (0.106)	0.907*** (0.175)	0.744*** (0.238)	0.107 (0.0961)	0.0206 (0.414)	0.0783 (0.396)
Correlation coefficient		−0.540***			−0.572***			0.0684	
All									
Return migrant dummy coefficient	0.0359 (0.0332)	0.292** (0.143)	0.367** (0.163)	0.241*** (0.0608)	0.681*** (0.122)	0.751*** (0.161)	−0.00904 (0.0508)	0.0389 (0.150)	0.128 (0.239)
Correlation coefficient		−0.205*			−0.380***			−0.0353	

Sources: Based on Phase 1 of the 1-2-3 surveys of selected countries (see table 11.1 for details).

Note: Figures are for individuals 15 and older. Reference status is nonmigrant. Figures in parentheses are standard errors. WAEMU = West African Economic and Monetary Union, OECD = Organisation for Economic Co-operation and Development, OLS = ordinary least squares, MLE = maximum likelihood estimation.
* significant at the 10 percent level, ** significant at the 5 percent level, *** significant at the 1 percent level.

other words, they share unobserved characteristics that, everything else equal, lead them to earn less than nonmigrants. This interpretation is confirmed by the negative value of the correlation coefficient between the error terms of the earnings and migration equation (–0.38, significant at the 1 percent level in the pooled sample). This result is unexpected, as it is generally assumed that migrants are positively selected. De Coulon and Piracha (2005) find a similar result in their study of Albania. The finding suggests that individuals who have been abroad may lack some desirable unobserved earnings capabilities. However, by going abroad they acquire other characteristics that the labor market rewards in the form of a wage premium.

Results obtained when male and female workers are pooled suggest that migrants returning from OECD and WAEMU countries earn more than nonmigrants. Splitting men and women into separate samples reveals, however, that the results for WAEMU countries are driven exclusively by women. However, as the MLE and the two-step estimates differ substantially, we suspect that our model is misspecified for this sample and choose not to retain this result. Results for migrants returning from OECD countries appear much more robust, as no significant difference is found between the MLE and the two-step estimates. As MLE is a more efficient estimator, we comment only on the results obtained using this method.

When men and women are pooled, the average wage premium for return migrants is estimated to be as high as 68 percent. When the sample is split, however, the premium for women (91 percent) is much higher than the estimate for men (38 percent).

Using the Hungarian Household Panel Survey, Co, Gang, and Yun (2000) obtain a similar result. They find that women returning from OECD countries earn a premium of 67 percent on the Hungarian labor market. According to the authors, skills acquired abroad may explain such a large premium. During their stay abroad, women learn how Western economies operate. This knowledge is particularly valuable in a country undergoing transition toward a market economy, as Hungary was at the time the data were collected.

A similar explanation can be found here. As differences in the level of development of WAEMU and OECD countries are very large, one would expect workers with Western work experience to have acquired skills that are very valuable on African labor markets. This experience could explain the large wage premium received by return migrants.

Why women receive much larger premiums than men is unclear. Measurement errors in the experience variable could be a possible explanation. Measures of women's professional experience are particularly prone to errors because of the discontinuity of their labor market participation. If nonmigrant women have given birth to a larger number of children (and therefore have had more career interruptions) than women who spent some time abroad, potential experience as a proxy for actual experience is likely to be upwardly biased for nonmigrant women. The large size of the return migrant coefficient could partly capture this bias.

All these results are conditioned on the validity of the instruments. In tables 11.7 and 11.8, we present the values of the Chi-square test for the father's activity dummies and the proportion of return migrants in the neighborhood in the migration equation, together with the values of these statistics when these variables are added in the earnings equation. The father's activity variables are highly significant in the migration equation, except for the regression on women migrants returning from OECD countries. For this sample, the model is identified only by the proportion of return migrants in the neighborhood.

Father's activity variables and the proportion of migrants in the neighborhood are never significant when included among the list of regressors in the earnings equation or when men and women are split into separate samples (table 11.8). Using the pooled sample, the father's activity variables are jointly

Table 11.7 Test of Instrumental Variables in Migration Equation

| | Return migrants from | | | | | |
| | WAEMU country | | OECD country | | Other countries | |
Gender/variable	MLE	Two-step estimator	MLE	Two-step estimator	MLE	Two-step estimator
Men						
Father's activity	25.0 (0.0003)	24.8 (0.0004)	26.6 (0.0002)	28.0 (0.0001)	16.7 (0.0103)	16.7 (0.0106)
Percent return migrants in neighborhood	3.15 (0.076)	3.02 (0.0823)	10.3 (0.0013)	9.72 (0.0018)	5.49 (0.0191)	5.62 (0.0178)
Women						
Father's activity	23.4 (0.0007)	26.2 (0.0002)	6.16 (0.4057)	6.96 (0.3246)	14.6 (0.0235)	14.6 (0.0235)
Percent return migrants in neighborhood	14.2 (0.0002)	14.1 (0.0002)	17.3 (0.0000)	11.3 (0.0008)	0.31 (0.5780)	0.42 (0.5185)
Full sample						
Father's activity	54.5 (0.0000)	51.6 (0.0000)	23.8 (0.0006)	24.8 (0.0004)	24.3 (0.0005)	24.3 (0.0005)
Percent return migrants in neighborhood	14.23 (0.0002)	13.1 (0.0003)	23.2 (0.0000)	19.3 (0.0000)	2.68 (0.1017)	2.76 (0.0964)

Sources: Based on Phase 1 of the 1-2-3 surveys of selected countries (see table 11.1 for details).
Note: Figures are Chi-square values for individuals 15 and older. Figures in parentheses are *p*-values. MLE = maximum likelihood estimation. WAEMU = West African Economic and Monetary Union, OECD = Organisation for Economic Co-operation and Development.

Table 11.8 Overidentification Test of Instrumental Variables in Migration Equation

	Return migrants from		
Gender/variable	WAEMU country	OECD country	Other countries
Men			
Father's activity	7.43	8.38	8.37
	(0.2826)	(0.2115)	(0.2125)
Percent return migrants in neighborhood	1.32	0.53	0.52
	(0.2502)	(0.4674)	(0.5692)
Women			
Father's activity	6.82	4.56	6.35
	(0.3376)	(0.6010)	(0.3854)
Percent return migrants in neighborhood	1.23	0.03	0.28
	(0.2666)	(0.8521)	(0.5953)
Full sample			
Father's activity	14.6	15.6	16.8
	(0.0234)	(0.0158)	(0.0102)
Percent return migrants in neighborhood	1.68	0.97	0.51
	(0.1953)	(0.3247)	(0.4747)

Sources: Based on Phase 1 of the 1-2-3 surveys of selected countries (see table 11.1 for details).
Note: Figures are Chi-square values for individuals 15 and older. Figures in parentheses are *p*-values.
WAEMU = West African Economic and Monetary Union, OECD = Organisation for Economic Co-operation and Development.

significant in the earnings equation, but the proportion of return migrants in the neighborhood remains insignificant, meaning the model is still identified. Moreover, the coefficient of the return migrant dummy does not change when the father's variables are added to the earnings regression. We are thus confident that our results do not suffer from omitted variable bias.

Regarding the other coefficient estimates, both the OLS and MLE coefficients of human capital variables in the earnings equations are in line with expectations: language skills, education, and experience all positively contribute to earnings. Men earn 25 percent more than women in the pooled sample. People working in the public sector earn 48 percent and people working in the private formal sector 42 percent more than people working in the informal sector. The returns to language skills and education are much higher for women than for men. This difference could be driven by workers' unobserved heterogeneity. If workers self-select into education and selection occurs on unobserved characteristics, then returns to education estimates could be upwardly biased if unobserved heterogeneity is positively correlated with hourly earnings. As women are less likely than men to obtain a high level of education, then everything else equal, women are more self-selected than men, and larger biases in the returns to education can be expected.

Experience Abroad and Profits

The production technology of a microenterprise is written as $Y = F(K,L)$ where Y is the value added of the firm, K is the capital stock, and L is labor.

Phase 2 of the 1-2-3 survey collects very detailed information on production levels, sales, and purchases of inputs by microenterprises in the past 12 months, as well as information on expenses such as rent for buildings; wages and salaries; water, gas, electricity, and fuel; telephone; traveling expenses and insurance fees; maintenance and general repairs; rent for machinery and equipment; taxes; and interest. The survey records detailed information on the seasonal patterns of activity over a one-year period and on the timing of transactions, in order to account for potential lags between the time inputs are purchased and sold.

Using these data, we compute a measure of value-added that we then regress on capital and labor inputs as well as on a vector of firm owner's characteristics. It is very difficult to obtain accurate data on value-added and profits of microenterprises in developing countries, because most of them do not keep financial records. One has to rely on recall data, which generally lack precision given the fungibility of money and goods between the business and the household. The Phase 2 questionnaire is designed to obtain more precise information, but the gain over less detailed questionnaires has yet to be proved (for a detailed discussion, see De Mel, McKenzie, and Woodruff 2009).

To obtain a reliable estimate of K, we use information provided by firm owners on the replacement cost of the capital equipment used in their business (tools, equipment, vehicles, real estate, and so on). For labor, we use the total number of hours of work performed by the business owner and his or her employees in the past 12 months.[8]

Assuming a Cobb-Douglas production function, the technology of a microenterprise can be written as

$$\log Y = \log A + \alpha \log L + \beta \log K + u_i \qquad (11.3)$$

where A is total factor productivity, α and β are output elasticities with respect to labor and capital, and u is an error term. This equation can be estimated using standard linear regression, using microenterprise data on value-added, defined as the annual value of production minus the cost of all intermediate inputs, capital, and the number of hours of work. In the regressions, additional variables are included to control for the business owner's characteristics (level of education, age, potential experience, and so forth); sector of activity; and macroeconomic environment (through country dummies). A dummy variable indicating whether the firm owner is a return migrant is included to test whether experience abroad makes individuals more productive.

In order to account for the self-selection of return migrants, we simultaneously estimate equation (11.3) with the return migrant equation (11.2) using maximum likelihood on the sample of microenterprises. As for the earnings equation, migration is instrumented by the percentage of households with return migrants in the area of residence. We run regressions for each of the three groups of return migrants (migrants returning from a WAEMU country, migrants returning from an OECD country, and migrants returning from elsewhere).

Table 11.9 displays estimation results using the Cobb-Douglas production function specification defined in equation (11.3) on pooled microenterprise data. The coefficient of the dummy variable indicating whether the firm owner is a return migrant is positive and significantly different from zero in both specifications. This result suggests that experience abroad gives microentrepreneurs a productive advantage. This advantage could stem either from enhanced entrepreneurial skills or from specific knowledge acquired abroad. The OLS coefficient estimate in the earnings equation is strongly biased downward, however, because of a negative correlation between unobserved characteristics in the earnings and migration equations. The elasticity of value-added is 0.17 with respect to capital and 0.47 with respect to labor. The higher the average level of education of employees, the higher the output, all else equal.

Conclusion

What are the consequences of international migration for home countries? This question attracted much interest in the 1970s, when economists such as Jadish Bhagwati viewed the out-migration of educated migrants as a loss of human capital for countries of origin. Even the migration of educated individuals could benefit the origin country, however, if return migrants are sufficiently numerous and bring back enough capital, physical or human, to irrigate the economy. In this context, the characteristics, motivations, and economic impacts of return migrants on their native countries are crucial questions to address.

This chapter examines the urban labor market performance of return migrants in seven French-speaking cities of West Africa. The review of the literature suggests three effects. First, return migrants may have higher levels of human capital, financial capital, or both. Second, the education they received or the work experience they gained in destination countries may have allowed them to gain some specific knowledge that is valued in the labor market of their home country. Third, return migrants could suffer from a loss of social capital while they lived abroad.

Results from our statistical and econometric analyses show that except for age and gender, return migrants from WAEMU countries have individual and labor participation characteristics that are very similar to those of

Table 11.9 Production Function Estimates for Return Migrants in Seven Cities in West Africa, 2001/02

| | Migrants returning from | | | | | | | | |
| | WAEMU country | | | OECD country | | | Other countries | | |
Variable	OLS	MLE	Two-step estimator	OLS	MLE	Two-step estimator	OLS	MLE	Two-step estimator
Log(capital)	0.171	0.172	0.171	0.162	0.162	0.162	0.160	0.161	0.161
	(12.82)***	(12.92)***	(12.91)***	(12.10)***	(12.00)***	(11.98)***	(12.04)***	(12.04)***	(12.04)***
Dummy = 1 if no capital	0.276	0.279	0.278	0.257	0.258	0.257	0.250	0.259	0.259
	(3.85)***	(3.91)***	(3.90)***	(3.57)***	(3.55)***	(3.54)***	(3.51)***	(3.59)***	(3.59)***
Log(labor)	0.407	0.407	0.407	0.418	0.414	0.413	0.409	0.400	0.400
	(20.21)***	(20.26)***	(20.27)***	(20.49)***	(20.20)***	(20.20)***	(20.40)***	(19.88)***	(19.88)***
Return migrant	-0.007	0.136	0.643	0.605	1.094	2.034	0.283	0.293	0.277
	(0.94)	(0.52)	(1.10)	(2.58)**	(2.32)**	(2.22)**	(2.36)**	(0.81)	(0.60)
Percent return migrants in neighborhood	0.292			0.427			0.411		
	(0.88)			(0.93)			(0.93)		
Constant	2.488	1.496	1.469	3.599	1.486	1.497	3.634	1.622	1.622
	(13.21)***	(9.37)***	(9.05)***	(10.36)***	(9.16)***	(9.20)***	(10.15)***	(8.88)***	(8.88)***
Percent return migrants in neighborhood		2.743	2.727		2.656	2.573		3.034	3.034
		(6.18)***	(6.16)***		(2.68)***	(2.61)***		(6.13)***	(6.13)***
Rho		-0.047			-0.155			0.008	
		(0.55)			(1.23)			(0.06)	
Sigma		0.333			0.327			0.329	
		(34.60)***			(33.22)***			(33.97)***	
Mills ratio			-0.309			-0.608			0.018
			(1.11)			(1.64)			(0.08)
Number of observations	5,438	5,438	5,438	5,214	5,214	5,214	5,323	5,323	5,323

Sources: Based on Phase 1 of the 1-2-3 surveys of selected countries (see table 11.1 for details).
Note: Figures are for individuals 15 and older. Figures in parentheses are p-values. WAEMU = West African Economic and Monetary Union. OECD = Organisation for Economic Co-operation and Development. OLS = ordinary least squares. MLE = maximum likelihood estimation.

nonmigrants. In contrast, return migrants from OECD countries are significantly better educated, more likely to be active in the labor force, and wealthier than nonmigrants. The participation of return migrants from OECD countries in the formal sector (both public and private) is much higher than that of nonmigrants. However, after controlling for education, the advantage of return migrants vanishes, actually becoming negative in some countries. Experience abroad results in a substantial wage premium on average, but the level of the premium ranges widely across cities (it is high in Cotonou and Lomé and low in Bamako). Experience abroad is also associated with a productive advantage for entrepreneurs.

International migration experience can have important consequences for labor market performance upon return to the origin country, particularly if the host country belongs to the OECD. These potential benefits notwithstanding, the small share of return migrants in WAEMU countries suggests that return migration is likely to have only a moderate effect on development, especially as local economic conditions and investment opportunities remain weak.

Notes

1. For instance, labor migration from Southern to Central Europe in the 1950s and 1970s was predominantly temporary, as suggested by Böhning (1984), who estimates that "more than two thirds of the foreign workers admitted in Germany and more than four fifths in the case of Switzerland have returned" (quoted by Dustmann 2000, p. 2). Glytsos (1988) reports that of the 1 million Greeks who migrated to the Federal Republic of Germany between 1960 and 1984, 85 percent returned home. Dustmann and Weiss (2007) find that only about 68 percent of females and 60 percent of males admitted into Britain between 1992 and 1994 were still in the country five years later. For the United States, Jasso and Rosenzweig (1982) report that of the 15.7 million people who immigrated between 1908 and 1957, about 4.8 million returned home.
2. The REMUAO countries are Burkina Faso, Côte d'Ivoire, Guinea, Mali, Mauritania, Niger, and Senegal.
3. Although Abidjan and Cotonou are not administrative capitals, we refer to them as capitals because they are the most important economic centers in their countries (Cotonou is also the seat of government).
4. For disaggregated descriptive statistics by city, see De Vreyer, Gubert, and Robilliard (2009).
5. Unfortunately, the surveys do not provide information on age at the time of migration. It is thus impossible to favor one explanation or the other.
6. Entrepreneurs are people who declare that they hire employees, paid or unpaid. This category does not include self-employed workers without employees.
7. Phase 2 of the 1-2-3 surveys covers only microenterprises in the informal sector. Formal sector microenterprises (that is, microenterprises with a registration number or bookkeeping) are excluded from the sample.

8. The Phase 2 survey provides data on the number of workers employed by each firm; the total number of hours worked by each worker during the month preceding the interview; and worker characteristics, including gender, age, education, relationship to the business owner, and remuneration.

References

Adepoju, A. 2005. "Migration in West Africa." Paper prepared for the Policy Analysis and Research Programme of the Global Commission on International Migration, Geneva.

Ammassari, S. 2003. "From Nation-Building to Entrepreneurship: The Impact of Elite Return Migrants in Côte d'Ivoire and Ghana." Sussex Centre for Migration Research, University of Sussex, Brighton, United Kingdom.

Ba, H. 2006. "Les statistiques des travailleurs migrants en Afrique de l'Ouest." *Cahier des Migrations Internationales* 79F, International Labour Office, Geneva.

Beine, M., F. Docquier, and H. Rapoport. 2001. "Brain Drain and Economic Growth: Theory and Evidence." *Journal of Development Economics* 64 (1): 275–89.

———. 2003. "Brain Drain and Growth in LDCs: Winners, and Losers." IZA Discussion Paper 819, Institute for the Study of Labor, Bonn, Germany.

Bhagwati, J. N. 1972. "The United States in the Nixon Era: The End of Innocence." *Daedalus* 101 (4): 25–47.

Bhagwati, J. N., and K. Hamada. 1974. "The Brain Drain, International Integration of Markets for Professionals, and Unemployment: A Theoretical Analysis." *Journal of Development Economics* 1 (1): 19–42.

Black, R., R. King, and J. Litchfield. 2003. *Transnational Migration, Return and Development in West Africa.* Sussex Centre for Migration Research, University of Sussex, Brighton, United Kingdom. http://www.sussex.ac.uk/migration/research/completed/transrede.

Black, R., R. King, and R. Tiemoko 2003. "Migration, Return, and Small Enterprise Development in Ghana: A Route Out of Poverty?" Sussex Migration Working Paper 9, Sussex Centre for Migration Research, University of Sussex, Brighton, United Kingdom.

Blomqvist, A. G. 1986. "International Migration of Educated Manpower and Social Rates of Return to Education in LDCs." *International Economic Review* 27 (1): 165–74.

Bocquier, P. 1998. "L'immigration ouest-africaine en Europe: une dimension politique sans rapport avec son importance démographique." *La chronique du CEPED* 30 (Juillet–Septembre).

Böhning, W. 1984. *Studies in International Migration.* New York: St. Martin's Press.

Borjas, G. 1987. "Self-Selection and the Earnings of Immigrants." *American Economic Review* 77 (4): 531–53.

Borjas, G., and B. Bratsberg. 1996. "Who Leaves? The Out-Migration of the Foreign-Born." *Review of Economics and Statistics* 78 (1): 165–76.

Brydon, L. 1992. "Ghanaian Women in the Process of Migration." In *Gender and Migration in Developing Countries*, ed. S. Chant, 73–90. London: Belhaven Press.

Co, C. Y., I. N. Gang, and M.-S. Yun. 2000. "Returns to Returning." *Journal of Population Economics* 13: 57–79.

de Coulon, A., and M. Piracha. 2005. "Self-Selection and the Performance of Return Migrants: The Source Country Perspective." *Journal of Population Economics* 18 (4): 779–807.

De Mel S., D. McKenzie, and C. Woodruff. 2009. "Measuring Microenterprise Profits: Must We Ask How the Sausage Is Made?" *Journal of Development Economics* 88 (1): 19–31.

De Vreyer, P., F. Gubert, and A.-S. Robilliard. 2009. "Return Migrants in Western Africa: Characteristics, and Labour Market Performance." DIAL Working Paper 2009–06, Développement, Institutions et Mondialisation, Paris.

Dustmann, C. 2000. "Why Go Back? Return Motives of Migrant Workers." Department of Economics, University College London.

Dustmann, C., and Y. Weiss. 2007. "Return Migration: Theory, and Empirical Evidence." Discussion Paper 02/07, Centre for Research and Analysis of Migration (CREAM), London.

Enchautegui, M. E. 1993. "The Value of U.S. Labor Market Experience in the Home Country: The Case of Puerto Rican Return Migrants." *Economic Development and Cultural Change* 42 (1): 169–91.

Glytsos, N. P. 1988. "Remittances and Temporary Migration: A Theoretical Model and Its Testing in the Greek-German Experience." *Weltwirtschaftliches Archiv* 124: 524–49.

Haque, N. U., and S. J. Kim. 1995. "Human Capital Flight: Impact of Migration on Income and Growth." *IMF Staff Papers* 3 (2): 170–86.

Ilahi, N. 1999. "Return Migration and Occupational Change." *Review of Development Economics* 3: 170–86.

Jasso, G., and M. R. Rosenzweig. 1982. "Estimating the Emigration Rates of Legal Immigrants Using Administrative and Survey Data: The 1971 Cohort of Immigrants to the United States." *Demography* 19: 279–90.

Kiker, B. F., and E. C. Traynham. 1977. "Earnings Differentials among Nonmigrants, Return Migrants, and Nonreturn Migrants." *Growth and Change* 8 (2): 2–7.

McCormick, B., and J. Wahba. 2001. "Overseas Work Experience, Savings, and Entrepreneurship amongst Return Migrants to LDCs." *Scottish Journal of Political Economy* 48 (2): 164–78.

Mesnard, A. 2004. "Temporary Migration and Capital Market Imperfections." *Oxford Economic Papers* 56: 242–62.

Nakosteen, R., and M. Zimmer. 1980. "Migration and Income: The Question of Self-Selection." *Southern Economic Journal* 46 (3): 840–51.

Nicholson, B. 2004. "Migrants as Agents of Development: Albanian Return Migrants and Micro-Enterprise." In *New Patterns of Labour Migration in Central and Eastern Europe*, ed. D. Pop, 94–110. Cluj Napoca, Romania: AMM Editura.

Rooth, D., and J. Saarela. 2007. "Selection in Migration and Return Migration: Evidence from Micro Data." *Economics Letters* 94: 90–95.

Stark, O., C. Helmenstein, and A. Prskawetz. 1997. "A Brain Gain with a Brain Drain." *Economics Letters* 55: 227–34.

Usher, D. 1977. "Public Property and the Effect of Migration upon Other Residents of the Migrants' Countries of Origin and Destination." *Journal of Political Economy* 85 (5): 1001–20.

Wahba, J. 2004. "Does International Migration Matter? A Study of Egyptian Return Migrants." In *Arab Migration in a Globalised World*. Geneva: International Organisation for Migration.

Chapter **12**

The Work-School Trade-Off among Children in West Africa: Are Household Tasks More Compatible with School Than Economic Activities?

Philippe De Vreyer, Flore Gubert, and Nelly Rakoto-Tiana

Theoretical and empirical studies of time allocation decisions for children in developing countries point to a number of determinants of the demand for education and the supply of child labor. These studies can be grouped into two main schools of thought. The first is in the vein of the theory of the demand for education, introduced by Becker (1964). Becker posited that parents' decisions about whether to send their children to school are the result of a trade-off between the expected returns to and the cost of education. This cost includes school-related monetary expenditures and the opportunity cost of forgone wages or other remuneration. If the returns to education are too low compared with its cost, parents will choose not to send the children to school and will have them work instead. Child labor can also be considered as the best option when specific know-how and skills learned on the job are more profitable than education (Rosenzweig and Wolpin 1985; De Vreyer, Lambert, and Magnac 1999).

The second school of thought focuses on the impact of various constraints affecting the supply of child labor, the demand for education, or both. A first set of constraints stems from imperfections in the markets for labor and land (Bhalotra and Heady 2003). When a household does not have enough labor to work all the land it owns, it has two options: hire external labor (farm workers) or rent out or sharecrop part of its land. If external labor is not available—because of labor market imperfections (frequent in rural areas) or a weak or nonexistent land market—the household may put its children to work. Any factor that raises the opportunity cost of children's time tends to increase their labor participation and reduce their attendance at school. Poverty-related constraints (Basu and Van 1998) and credit market imperfections (Jacoby and Skoufias 1997; Ranjan 1999; Baland and Robinson 2000; Skoufias and Parker 2002) may also explain the emergence of child labor and the concomitant fall-off in school attendance.

Many empirical studies set out to identify the factors involved in the work-school trade-off. Many are based on the joint estimation of school attendance and labor participation equations using bivariate or sequential probit models. The definition of child labor differs somewhat across studies. Some studies—including research by the International Labour Organization (ILO)—define child labor as "any economic activity conducted by a child"; children whose only work is performing household tasks within the family sphere are considered economically inactive.[1] Other studies adopt a broader definition, considering participation in household tasks to be a form of child labor. Although this more inclusive definition may seem preferable, grouping domestic and economic activities in the same category amounts to making the strong implicit assumption that the same factors determine both. Analysis of the factors involved in the work-school trade-off would probably be enriched if domestic and economic activities were considered as two distinct alternatives.

On the basis of this principle, we conduct a joint analysis of the determinants of school and work among children 10–14, separating out activities conducted in the household from economic activities. Using the approach adopted by Kis-Katos (2012), we estimate a trivariate probit model using simulated maximum likelihood in which participation in school, household tasks, and economic activities is explained by a vector of variables including the child's characteristics (age, gender, relationship to household head, birth rank, religion, and so forth) and the characteristics of the child's household (wealth, size, composition, activities, and so forth). The data used are drawn from Phase 1 of the 1-2-3 surveys conducted simultaneously in seven West African cities (for a description of these surveys, see box O.1 in the overview).

The findings show that the determinants of participation in the two types of activity are significantly different. For example, having a household head who is a self-employed entrepreneur increases the participation of children in economic activities in five of the seven cities (all except Bamako and Ouagadougou) but has no effect on their participation in domestic activities. Boys participate considerably less in domestic activities than girls, but they have a greater probability than girls of participating in economic activities in two of the seven cities (Dakar and Niamey). There seems to be much more competition in the allocation of time between economic activity and school than between domestic activity and school.

This chapter is structured as follows. The first section presents descriptive statistics drawn from the 1-2-3 survey data on schooling and child labor. The second section presents the empirical strategy for modeling the work-school trade-off. The third section presents and comments on the results of the estimations. The last section summarizes the main conclusions and draws some policy implications.

Work and School among Children in West Africa

Phase 1 of the 1-2-3 surveys is an employment survey providing detailed information on economic and domestic activities (taking care of children, the elderly, and infirm; fetching water and wood; and so forth) of all individuals 10 and older. The following discussion concentrates on children 10–14.[2]

Table 12.1, which presents the work participation and school enrollment rates in each city, reveals wide disparities across cities. The percentage of

Table 12.1 Work Participation and School Enrollment Rates for Children 10–14 in Seven Cities in West Africa, by Gender, 2001/02
(percent)

City	Performs domestic activities	Performs economic activities	Performs domestic or economic activities	Attends school	Inactive	Number of (weighted) observations
Abidjan						
Girls	51.6	20.2	58.0	57.5	5.7	177,888
Boys	17.6	8.9	24.3	80.7	7.7	142,312
All	36.5	15.2	43.0	67.8	6.6	320,200
Bamako						
Girls	51.8	11.5	54.8	71.9	9.0	74,237
Boys	14.6	9.8	22.6	81.3	12.6	73,964
All	33.2	10.7	38.7	76.6	10.8	148,202
Cotonou						
Girls	77.6	19.4	79.3	67.4	1.4	53,254
Boys	61.3	8.0	65.4	87.7	2.5	49,440
All	69.8	13.9	72.6	77.2	1.9	102,694
Dakar						
Girls	58.8	6.8	61.7	65.9	7.9	124,088
Boys	19.5	10.8	27.9	72.5	15.3	117,458
All	39.7	8.7	45.3	69.1	11.5	241,546
Lomé						
Girls	92.0	22.0	92.1	77.7	0.5	48,467
Boys	77.5	9.6	78.6	94.4	0.5	42,780
All	85.2	16.2	85.8	85.5	0.5	91,247

(continued next page)

Table 12.1 (continued)

City	Performs domestic activities	Performs economic activities	Performs domestic or economic activities	Attends school	Inactive	Number of (weighted) observations
Niamey						
Girls	64.4	10.3	66.3	71.3	5.5	45,831
Boys	23.8	14.3	32.5	74.4	13.3	40,660
All	45.3	12.1	50.4	72.8	9.2	86,491
Ouagadougou						
Girls	60.6	9.0	63.5	74.1	4.8	58,187
Boys	21.0	6.8	26.2	85.0	8.4	54,889
All	41.4	7.9	45.4	79.4	6.5	113,076

Sources: Based on Phase 1 of the 1-2-3 surveys of selected countries in the West African Economic and Monetary Union (WAEMU) conducted in 2001/02 by the Observatoire économique et statistique d'Afrique Subsaharienne (AFRISTAT); Développement, Institutions et Mondialisation (DIAL); and national statistics institutes.
Note: Sample weights were used to obtain representative results for the underlying population. Percentages sum to more than 100 percent because children may both engage in economic or domestic activities and attend school.

children 10–14 attending school is higher in Lomé (86 percent), Ouagadougou (79 percent), and Cotonou (77 percent) than in the richer cities of Abidjan (68 percent) and Dakar (69 percent). In Abidjan, this situation reflects discrimination against girls: the Gender Parity Index (GPI) (the ratio of girls' enrollment to boys' enrollment) is 71 percent in Abidjan and more than 85 percent in the other cities (except Cotonou, where it is 77 percent).

Lomé and Cotonou also have the highest rates of children 10–14 working and attending school (72 percent in Lomé, 52 percent in Cotonou) (table 12.2). These figures are much higher than in Niamey (32 percent), Ouagadougou (31 percent), Bamako and Dakar (26 percent), and Abidjan (17 percent). The rate of participation in domestic activities varies widely across cities. In contrast, participation in economic activities is low in all seven cities (9–16 percent). Girls participate much more than boys in domestic and economic activities and attend school less than their male counterparts.

Table 12.3 provides information on the average number of hours worked by working children per week. Not surprisingly, children who work without going to school work longer hours on average than children who combine work and school. However, the observed differences are much larger for the number of hours spent on economic activities, suggesting that it is possible to combine domestic activities and school, at least up to a certain point. The number of hours spent on domestic activities is higher among girls not attending school than for girls attending school (this result does not hold for boys), Table 12.3 also reveals that whether or not they are enrolled in school, girls spend much more time than boys on domestic activities.

Table 12.2 Work-School Trade-Off for Children 10–14 in Seven Cities in West Africa, by Gender, 2001/02

City	Working only	Attending school only	Working and attending school	Inactive	Number of (weighted) observations
Abidjan					
Girls	36.8	36.4	21.2	5.7	177,888
Boys	11.6	68.0	12.7	7.7	142,312
All	25.6	50.4	17.4	6.6	320,200
Bamako					
Girls	19.1	36.2	35.7	9.0	74,237
Boys	6.1	64.8	16.5	12.6	73,964
All	12.6	50.5	26.1	10.8	148,202
Cotonou					
Girls	31.2	19.3	48.1	1.4	53,254
Boys	9.9	32.2	55.5	2.5	49,440
All	20.9	25.5	51.7	1.9	102,694
Dakar					
Girls	26.2	30.4	35.5	7.9	124,088
Boys	12.2	56.8	15.7	15.3	117,458
All	19.4	43.2	25.9	11.5	241,546
Lomé					
Girls	21.8	7.3	70.4	0.5	48,467
Boys	5.1	20.9	73.5	0.5	42,780
All	14.0	13.7	71.8	0.5	91,247
Niamey					
Girls	23.2	28.2	43.1	5.5	45,831
Boys	12.3	54.2	20.2	13.3	40,660
All	18.1	40.4	32.4	9.2	86,491
Ouagadougou					
Girls	21.2	31.7	42.3	4.8	58,187
Boys	6.7	65.5	19.5	8.4	54,889
All	14.1	48.1	31.3	6.5	113,076

Sources: Based on Phase 1 of the 1-2-3 surveys of selected countries (see table 12.1 for details).

Tables 12.4 and 12.5 show the nature of the work children perform and the type of remuneration they receive. Table 12.4 displays a wide range of activities across cities. Family worker status is dominant in six of the seven cities.[3] Wide gender differences are apparent. Family worker is the dominant category for girls in all cities. Among boys, family worker is the dominant category only in Lomé and Niamey. In the other cities, more than 70 percent of boys who work are apprentices in Abidjan, Cotonou, and Dakar, and about 50 percent are apprentices in Bamako and Ouagadougou.

Table 12.3 Average Weekly Hours Worked by Children 10–14 in Seven Cities in West Africa, by Gender, 2001/02

City	Children who work and attend school		Children who work and do not attend school		All children who work	
	Time spent on economic activities	Time spent on domestic activities	Time spent on economic activities	Time spent on domestic activities	Time spent on economic activities	Time spent on domestic activities
Abidjan						
Girls	1.9	6.8	24.3	17.2	16.1	13.4
Boys	1.5	4.7	38.6	3.1	19.2	3.9
All	1.7	6.1	27.2	14.4	16.9	11.0
Bamako						
Girls	5.4	17.4	14.4	22.0	8.5	19.0
Boys	13.1	9.2	36.4	7.3	19.4	8.6
All	7.8	14.8	19.8	18.4	11.7	16.0
Cotonou						
Girls	0.4	11.0	28.0	22.0	11.3	15.3
Boys	0.2	8.8	42.8	6.9	6.6	8.5
All	0.3	9.8	31.4	18.6	9.3	12.4
Dakar						
Girls	1.5	15.0	8.4	19.9	4.4	17.1
Boys	5.5	8.0	33.4	5.2	17.7	6.8
All	2.7	12.9	16.0	15.4	8.4	14.0
Lomé						
Girls	5.0	18.3	29.9	27.1	10.9	20.4
Boys	3.2	11.6	27.7	14.5	4.7	11.8
All	4.1	15.1	29.5	25.0	8.3	16.7
Niamey						
Girls	2.8	16.7	9.7	21.0	5.2	18.2
Boys	12.8	10.2	28.6	8.4	18.7	9.5
All	5.7	14.8	15.7	17.0	9.3	15.6
Ouagadougou						
Girls	1.6	15.6	17.1	24.9	6.7	18.7
Boys	3.8	8.0	37.8	4.2	12.4	7.0
All	2.2	13.3	21.8	20.1	8.3	15.4

Sources: Based on Phase 1 of the 1-2-3 surveys of selected countries (see table 12.1 for details).

Gender differences are also apparent in the breakdown between unskilled and apprentice activities. Except in Lomé, girls have a much lower probability of being apprentices and are much more likely to be unskilled workers than boys. On the whole, these findings suggest that when girls do not go to school, their

Table 12.4 Nature of Work Performed by Children 10–14 in Seven Cities in West Africa, by Gender, 2001/02

City	Unskilled worker	Apprentice	Family worker[a]	Other[b]	Number of observations
Abidjan					
Girls	35.4	7.6	55.4	1.5	34,921
Boys	11.4	73.9	14.7	0.0	12,669
All	29.0	25.3	44.6	1.1	47,590
Bamako					
Girls	24.1	2.7	70.2	3.0	8,257
Boys	7.4	48.0	44.7	0.0	7,022
All	16.4	23.5	58.5	1.6	15,279
Cotonou					
Girls	22.9	11.3	65.9	0.0	10,332
Boys	4.6	81.1	14.4	0.0	3,928
All	17.8	30.5	51.7	0.0	14,260
Dakar					
Girls	35.9	13.9	42.5	7.7	8,352
Boys	7.3	76.4	15.5	0.8	12,675
All	18.7	51.6	26.2	3.6	21,027
Lomé					
Girls	11.3	3.9	84.1	0.7	10,710
Boys	30.5	21.2	48.3	0.0	4,123
All	16.7	8.7	74.1	0.5	14,834
Niamey					
Girls	12.9	7.8	76.9	2.4	4,656
Boys	6.5	21.7	69.5	2.3	5,763
All	9.4	15.5	72.8	2.3	10,419
Ouagadougou					
Girls	18.5	9.4	72.1	0.0	5,194
Boys	9.6	48.3	41.1	1.0	3,738
All	14.8	25.7	59.1	0.4	8,933

Sources: Based on Phase 1 of the 1-2-3 surveys of selected countries (see table 12.1 for details).
a. Includes mostly servants, maids, and vendors.
b. Includes mostly servants and maids who report being paid wages in semi-qualified work.

labor is used to provide the household with income or to perform domestic tasks. In contrast, boys continue to accumulate human capital. Their apprenticeships do not raise the household's income, but they give boys the skills to increase their resources in adulthood. Gender inequality in access to education may therefore be coupled with inequality in access to vocational training. This conclusion is underpinned by the data in table 12.5, which show that girls in all

Table 12.5 Type of Remuneration Working Children 10–14 Receive in Seven Cities in West Africa, 2001/02

City	Fixed wage	Daily or hourly pay	Piece-rate	Commission	Profits	In kind	No remuneration	No answer given	Number of observations
Abidjan									
Girls	16.0	4.3	4.3	12.2	13.6	18.1	30.9	0.7	34,921
Boys	2.5	4.9	0.0	7.1	1.5	1.5	82.4	0.0	12,669
All	12.5	4.4	3.2	10.9	10.4	13.8	44.3	0.5	47,590
Bamako									
Girls	25.4	0.0	0.7	0.0	39.0	9.1	21.6	4.3	8,257
Boys	0.3	9.8	8.6	1.2	35.6	16.7	25.2	2.6	7,022
All	13.8	4.5	4.4	0.5	37.4	12.6	23.3	3.5	15,279
Cotonou									
Girls	15.5	0.0	0.0	0.2	1.7	11.8	70.7	0.0	10,332
Boys	1.6	1.6	0.0	0.0	0.0	7.3	89.4	0.0	3,928
All	11.6	0.4	0.0	0.2	1.3	10.6	75.9	0.0	14,260
Dakar									
Girls	44.6	0.0	2.6	4.9	8.9	4.2	31.3	3.5	8,352
Boys	7.1	3.5	10.6	10.9	5.5	2.0	58.9	1.6	12,675
All	22.1	2.1	7.4	8.5	6.9	2.9	47.9	2.3	21,027
Lomé									
Girls	13.0	2.2	0.8	1.5	26.0	13.6	42.1	0.7	10,710
Boys	5.1	11.6	16.1	2.1	19.9	8.0	37.4	0.0	4,123
All	10.8	4.9	5.1	1.7	24.3	12.0	40.8	0.5	14,834
Niamey									
Girls	16.4	0.0	1.8	0.0	13.5	1.3	63.6	3.4	4,656
Boys	2.3	6.6	18.1	2.2	14.6	2.7	50.8	2.8	5,763
All	8.6	3.6	10.8	1.2	14.1	2.1	56.5	3.1	10,419
Ouagadougou									
Girls	21.9	1.1	2.1	0.0	15.8	20.3	38.3	0.4	5,194
Boys	7.4	9.8	11.4	0.0	26.3	17.9	27.2	0.0	3,738
All	15.9	4.7	6.0	0.0	20.1	19.3	33.7	0.2	8,933

Sources: Based on Phase 1 of the 1-2-3 surveys of selected countries (see table 12.1 for details).

cities have a greater probability than boys of being paid a fixed wage; boys have a higher probability of receiving no remuneration in four of the seven cities (Abidjan, Bamako, Cotonou, and Dakar).

Modeling the Trade-Off between Work and School

Becker's (1964) human capital model considers education as an investment made by autonomous individuals on the basis of their preferences and characteristics (time preference, life expectancy, cognitive skills, and so forth) on the one hand, and the returns to education on the other. Individuals may be more or less constrained in their choices, depending on their capacity to borrow and to make a living while investing in education. In each period, individuals decide whether they continue to invest in education or enter the labor market to get a job based on their qualifications. The optimal level of investment in education is reached when the marginal cost of one additional year of schooling equals the marginal return to the additional year of schooling. This model has been extended to take the trade-off between education and fertility into account (Becker and Lewis 1973), as well as the trade-off in allocating investment in human capital among children within a household (Behrman, Pollak, and Taubman 1982).

This theoretical framework can be used to interpret some of the statistical and econometric results on the determinants of the demand for schooling and child labor. In this setting, it is assumed that the household head allocates the child's time (excluding leisure). Time may be allocated to schooling, domestic tasks, and market work based on the household's preferences, the immediate and future returns to each activity, and various constraints the household faces. Acquisition of specific skills while working may raise future returns on the labor market more than skills acquired at school. Parents may thus decide not to educate their child or to reduce the time they spend at school (De Vreyer, Lambert, and Magnac 1999). Poverty may be one of the constraints to schooling, whatever the household's preferences and the size of the returns to education. All these factors are closely intertwined and determine, to varying degrees, the parents' decision to send their children to school, make them work, or make them participate in domestic tasks. Our empirical strategy deals with this interdependence.

We model children's allocation of time among economic (market) activities, domestic activities, and school, considering these choices to be interdependent and simultaneous. We do not observe the number of hours spent in each activity, but we know whether each child participates in each. We estimate a trivariate probit model in which three latent variables—participation in economic activities, L^*; participation in domestic activities, D^*; and school attendance,

S^*—depend on a vector of explanatory variables $\mathbf{X}$; a vector of parameters β_L, β_D, and β_S; and error terms ε_L, ε_D, and ε_S, which are jointly normally distributed. Formally, we estimate the following system of equations (written for child i):

$$L_i = \begin{cases} 1 \text{ if } L_i^* = \mathbf{X}_i'\beta_L + \varepsilon_L > 0 \\ 0 \text{ if not} \end{cases}$$

$$D_i = \begin{cases} 1 \text{ if } D_i^* = \mathbf{X}_i'\beta_D + \varepsilon_D > 0 \\ 0 \text{ if not} \end{cases}$$

$$S_i = \begin{cases} 1 \text{ if } S_i^* = \mathbf{X}_i'\beta_S + \varepsilon_S > 0 \\ 0 \text{ if not} \end{cases}$$

$$(12.1)$$

$$\text{where } \begin{pmatrix} \varepsilon_{iL} \\ \varepsilon_{iD} \\ \varepsilon_{iS} \end{pmatrix} \rightarrow N(0,\Sigma) \text{ with } \Sigma = \begin{pmatrix} 1 & \rho_{LD} & \rho_{LS} \\ \rho_{LD} & 1 & \rho_{DS} \\ \rho_{LS} & \rho_{DS} & 1 \end{pmatrix}.$$

Coefficients ρ_{jk} (with $j \neq k$) reflect the correlation that can exist between the errors of the three choice equations. Depending on whether the choices are independent or not, these coefficients are zero or significantly different from zero. This model is estimated by simulated maximum likelihood using the GHK (Geweke-Hajivassiliou-Keane) method (Terracol 2002; Greene 2003).

The vector of variables $\mathbf{X}$ includes individual characteristic variables (child's age, gender, migratory status, status in relation to household head, and religion) and household characteristic variables (the household head's gender, the presence or absence of a spouse, the level of education of the household head and his or her spouse, the employment status of the household head, the household size, the number of children, and the level of wealth). Child's age is included to capture the fact that the probability of being in school between the ages of 10 and 14 decreases with age, even in countries (such as Burkina Faso, Côte d'Ivoire, Mali, and Togo) where the age limit for compulsory attendance is higher than 14, the probability declines even more in countries where it is lower than 14 (such as Benin, Niger, and Senegal) (see note 2).

Child's gender is also included among the regressors. As suggested by the descriptive statistics, the allocation of time is likely to differ for girls and boys, with girls having lower levels of schooling on average and being more involved in domestic and market work (except in Dakar and Niamey).

Relationship to the household head is measured by a dummy variable taking the value 1 if the child is the son or daughter of the head (and 0 otherwise). It is included to capture the fact that household heads may be more likely to invest in the education of their biological children, either for altruistic reasons or because they expect to receive greater support from them in the future. (In the absence of well-functioning insurance markets and retirement schemes, education may be part of an implicit contractual arrangement between parents and their children whereby parents invest in their children's education in order to receive support from their children when they are too old to work.)

The child's migratory status (measured by a dummy taking the value 1 if the child originates from a rural area) is included to control for the impact of the child's background on his or her allocation of time. Many children reside in households headed by adults who are not their biological parents, even if their parents reside in these households (the 1-2-3 surveys do not record such detailed information). Children born outside the capital city are likely to be foster children.[4] Time allocation of these children depends partly on the reasons why they are in foster care.

Variables for the gender and education of the household head and spouse are introduced to capture household preferences for sending children to school or work. The education variable also controls for the fact that highly educated adults may offer better learning conditions to children, choose better schools, and facilitate their insertion into the labor market. An increase in the level of education of the household head and his or her spouse is thus expected to result in a decrease in children's participation in economic activity and an increase in their schooling.

The household head's self-employment status is included to control for the opportunity cost of attending school. Because children in households with self-employed members can be easily employed in the family businesses, they bear a higher opportunity cost of attending school, which may negatively affect their schooling investment and increase their participation in market work.

Household size and the number of children in the household may also affect a child's time allocation. The presence of more children in the household may negatively affect schooling and increase participation in domestic tasks if older children take care of younger ones. By contrast, more adults in the household may allow a better allocation of tasks and relax the time constraint, which may positively affect schooling and reduce the likelihood of market work.

The expected sign of the variable measuring household wealth is undetermined a priori. On the one hand, richer households are less likely to be budget constrained, which should positively affect schooling and reduce child labor. On the other hand, richer households are more likely to possess productive assets. By increasing the returns to labor, those assets may increase child labor. As we control for the head's self-employment status, this last effect should already be captured, so that the positive impact of wealth should dominate.

Household wealth is measured by a composite standard-of-living indicator, built using the data on household assets and the characteristics of the dwelling.

This indicator provides a less cyclical measure of the household standard of living than income or per capita consumption. It is built from a principal component analysis, which summarizes the information in 16 variables: (ownership or nonownership of a car, motorbike, bicycle, radio, television, hi-fi, refrigerator, and sewing machine; number of rooms in the dwelling; whether the dwelling is a private house; connection of the dwelling to the electricity grid; type of water supply (tap or standpipe); and type of toilet (private flush lavatory, shared flush lavatory, or latrine) (table 12.6).

The first principal component accounts for 22–30 percent of the total variance. It is significantly and positively correlated with most of the variables

Table 12.6 Weights of Variables in the First Principal Component

Variable	Abidjan	Bamako	Cotonou	Dakar	Lomé	Niamey	Ouagadougou
Assets owned							
Car (yes = 1; no = 0)	0.26	0.36	0.32	0.25	0.32	0.33	0.32
Motorbike (yes = 1; no = 0)	0.00	0.13	0.17	0.10	0.13	0.09	0.22
Bicycle (yes = 1; no = 0)	0.01	0.14	0.14	0.10	0.08	0.16	0.03
Radio (yes = 1; no = 0)	0.17	0.13	0.15	0.15	0.16	0.19	0.10
Television (yes = 1; no = 0)	0.27	0.33	0.31	0.33	0.33	0.34	0.33
Hi-fi (yes = 1; no = 0)	0.25	0.30	0.27	0.24	0.28	0.23	0.28
Refrigerator (yes = 1; no = 0)	0.25	0.37	0.31	0.20	0.33	0.29	0.32
Sewing machine (yes = 1; no = 0)	0.10	0.18	0.10	0.17	0.13	0.15	0.13
Dwelling characteristics							
Number of rooms	0.34	0.22	0.26	0.25	0.25	0.23	0.15
Connected to the electricity grid (yes = 1; no = 0)	0.11	0.32	0.24	0.26	0.29	0.30	0.32
Private house (yes = 1; no = 0)	0.25	0.24	0.27	0.26	0.32	0.31	0.31
Connected to running water (yes = 1; no = 0)	0.37	0.31	0.30	0.39	0.30	0.36	0.34
Water access via a standpipe (yes = 1; no = 0)	−0.35	−0.19	−0.28	−0.37	−0.22	−0.31	−0.32
Private lavatory (yes = 1; no = 0)	0.40	0.30	0.36	0.33	0.34	0.28	0.31
Shared lavatory (yes = 1; no = 0)	−0.20	−0.02	−0.20	−0.21	−0.03	−0.01	−0.02
Latrine (yes = 1; no = 0)	−0.22	−0.14	−0.03	−0.15	−0.16	−0.04	0.04
Percentage of total inertia explained by first principal component	0.27	0.23	0.26	0.22	0.26	0.28	0.29

Sources: Based on Phase 1 of the 1-2-3 surveys of selected countries (see box O.1 and table 12.1 for details).

concerned and can be interpreted as an indicator of the households' standard of living or wealth.

Some variables (such as child's migration status and the household wealth index) are likely to be correlated with unobserved heterogeneity terms that affect the probability of going to school, performing domestic activities, or working. Children that migrated, either on their own or to follow their parents, may adopt different behavior with respect to working or going to school not because they migrated but because migration was a precondition for them to get involved in these activities (an example is children who are being fostered so that they can attend school in the capital). The wealth index might be positively correlated with the probability of going to school without having any causal relation to it (if, for instance, the wealthiest households have a higher preference for education). Control variables, such as the education of the household head and spouse, are included in the list of explanatory variables in order to reduce this source of bias, but we cannot guarantee that we eliminated it completely. Without any credible instrument that would allow the use of two-stage least squares to solve the problem, we have no choice but to recognize possible sources of bias when commenting on the regression results in the next section.

Econometric Results

Table 12.7 presents the results of the estimations. Given that the standard deviations of the estimated coefficients are potentially biased by error term correlations for children from the same household, the error terms have been corrected.

The residual correlation coefficients indicate that the unobservable variables have opposite effects on school attendance and work (either domestic or market work). This finding suggests that a form of competition exists between school and work. Competition between school and economic activity (P_{LS}) appears to be much stronger than competition between school and domestic activity (P_{DS}). The value of the correlation coefficient P_{DS} is low and not significantly different from zero for four of the seven cities (Bamako, Cotonou, Lomé, and Ouagadougou), whereas the value of P_{LS} is significant and high for all cities. This finding is similar to that obtained by Dumas (2004) for Brazil and Kis-Katos (2012) for two northern Indian provinces.

For individual characteristics, the results show that older children have a lower probability of going to school and a higher probability of participating in both market activities and domestic tasks. This result is robust to the sample and the specification. In many cities, boys have a higher probability of going to school than girls and a systematically lower probability of participating in household tasks. The findings on participation in economic activities are more

Table 12.7 Results of Trivariate Probit Model of Allocation of Time of Children 10–14 in Seven Cities in West Africa, 2001/02

Variable	Abidjan	Bamako	Cotonou	Dakar	Lomé	Niamey	Ouagadougou
Attends school							
Age	-0.131**	-0.0685**	-0.183**	-0.126**	-0.0926*	-0.141**	-0.165**
	(0.0309)	(0.0262)	(0.0324)	(0.0208)	(0.0377)	(0.0245)	(0.0267)
Boy (dummy)	0.670**	0.206*	0.215	0.188*	0.779**	0.0227	-0.0186
	(0.191)	(0.101)	(0.158)	(0.0770)	(0.195)	(0.0822)	(0.155)
Child of household head (dummy)	0.601**	0.363*	1.174**	0.0859	0.624**	0.310**	0.636**
	(0.125)	(0.143)	(0.124)	(0.0820)	(0.174)	(0.113)	(0.127)
Muslim (dummy)	-0.134		-0.273		-0.0550		-0.483**
	(0.129)		(0.177)		(0.193)		(0.105)
Muslim × child of household head (dummy)	-0.299		0.237		-0.494		0.185
	(0.201)		(0.301)		(0.303)		(0.167)
Male-headed household (dummy)	0.0240	0.232	-0.0859	-0.206	-0.251	0.0579	0.832**
	(0.179)	(0.346)	(0.231)	(0.182)	(0.231)	(0.296)	(0.216)
Single-headed household (dummy)	0.238	0.381	0.370	0.162	0.0763	0.0840	0.702**
	(0.156)	(0.338)	(0.228)	(0.187)	(0.230)	(0.298)	(0.215)
Education of household head	0.0208	0.0466**	0.00895	0.0476**	0.0309	0.0518**	0.0280*
	(0.0143)	(0.0132)	(0.0139)	(0.0103)	(0.0168)	(0.0116)	(0.0139)
Education of spouse of household head	0.0274	0.0149	0.0156	0.0483**	0.0279	0.0199	-0.0106
	(0.0191)	(0.0162)	(0.0162)	(0.0140)	(0.0233)	(0.0142)	(0.0157)
Education of household head × boy	0.0481*	0.0272	0.0441*	0.00471	0.00380	0.00191	0.0515*
	(0.0245)	(0.0200)	(0.0217)	(0.0136)	(0.0318)	(0.0160)	(0.0232)
Education of spouse × boy	-0.0624*	0.00379	0.0349	-0.0153	0.0315	0.0336	0.0178
	(0.0311)	(0.0259)	(0.0307)	(0.0193)	(0.0479)	(0.0218)	(0.0258)
Self-employment of household head (dummy)	-0.190	-0.244*	-0.232*	-0.298**	-0.287*	-0.213**	-0.0322
	(0.102)	(0.0974)	(0.106)	(0.0720)	(0.119)	(0.0816)	(0.0873)

(continued next page)

Number of adults in household	0.0344 (0.0197)	0.0610** (0.0194)	−0.0152 (0.0260)	−0.00742 (0.0110)	0.0528 (0.0283)	−0.00297 (0.0147)	0.0184 (0.0200)
Number of children in household	0.0283 (0.0274)	−0.0545* (0.0218)	−0.0142 (0.0259)	−0.0242 (0.0141)	−0.0133 (0.0385)	−0.0136 (0.0156)	−0.0382 (0.0203)
Internal migrant (dummy)	−0.787** (0.137)	−0.831** (0.185)	−0.809** (0.150)	−0.638** (0.143)	−0.590** (0.176)	−0.675** (0.196)	−0.314* (0.158)
Migrant × child of household head	0.746** (0.203)	0.469* (0.235)	0.566** (0.210)	0.537** (0.207)	0.736** (0.244)	0.568* (0.228)	0.699** (0.212)
Wealth index	0.155** (0.0285)	0.0241 (0.0320)	0.0972** (0.0302)	0.114** (0.0195)	−0.00642 (0.0327)	0.0820* (0.0328)	0.0316 (0.0255)
Intercept	1.295** (0.431)	0.894 (0.536)	2.238** (0.515)	2.070** (0.324)	1.638** (0.582)	1.999** (0.449)	1.718** (0.447)
Participates in domestic tasks							
Age	0.0989** (0.0284)	0.0848** (0.0237)	0.0811** (0.0257)	0.137** (0.0197)	−0.0312 (0.0325)	0.0545* (0.0218)	0.0801** (0.0225)
Boy (dummy)	−0.762** (0.186)	−1.106** (0.101)	−0.598** (0.138)	−1.266** (0.0802)	−0.852** (0.194)	−1.065** (0.0839)	−0.949** (0.125)
Child of household head (dummy)	−0.392** (0.126)	−0.171 (0.136)	−0.219 (0.126)	−0.150 (0.0789)	−0.144 (0.153)	−0.0561 (0.117)	−0.144 (0.123)
Muslim (dummy)	0.155 (0.140)		−0.577** (0.164)		0.0817 (0.298)		0.0747 (0.0953)
Muslim × child of household head (dummy)	−0.617** (0.205)		0.609** (0.228)		−0.0829 (0.368)		−0.153 (0.139)
Male-headed household (dummy)	−0.218 (0.175)	0.105 (0.317)	0.125 (0.172)	−0.0600 (0.138)	−0.0243 (0.226)	0.374 (0.253)	0.370 (0.219)
Single-headed household (dummy)	−0.268 (0.162)	−0.110 (0.309)	−0.117 (0.173)	−0.126 (0.138)	−0.276 (0.233)	0.302 (0.250)	0.241 (0.219)

Table 12.7 (continued)

Variable	Abidjan	Bamako	Cotonou	Dakar	Lomé	Niamey	Ouagadougou
Education of household head	-0.0190 (0.0147)	0.0123 (0.0110)	-0.0112 (0.0138)	-0.0105 (0.00972)	-0.0325 (0.0193)	-0.00486 (0.0109)	-0.0171 (0.0128)
Education of spouse of household head	-0.0242 (0.0196)	-0.0328* (0.0143)	-0.0134 (0.0156)	-0.0197 (0.0129)	-0.0511* (0.0260)	-0.0117 (0.0139)	0.00592 (0.0148)
Education of household head × boy	-0.00487 (0.0209)	-0.0152 (0.0152)	-0.00234 (0.0166)	0.0208 (0.0131)	0.0275 (0.0244)	0.0110 (0.0152)	0.0235 (0.0157)
Education of spouse × boy	0.0297 (0.0268)	0.0371 (0.0197)	0.0302 (0.0209)	0.0364* (0.0180)	0.0266 (0.0313)	-0.0201 (0.0225)	-0.0278 (0.0199)
Self-employment of household head (dummy)	-0.132 (0.115)	-0.131 (0.0897)	0.172 (0.0986)	0.152* (0.0747)	0.0550 (0.117)	0.132 (0.0814)	0.00493 (0.0836)
Number of adults in household	-0.0327 (0.0223)	-0.0367* (0.0156)	-0.0586* (0.0238)	-0.0227* (0.0110)	-0.0115 (0.0260)	-0.0152 (0.0156)	-0.0107 (0.0174)
Number of children in household	-0.0613 (0.0327)	0.0286 (0.0193)	-0.0389 (0.0256)	-0.00119 (0.0136)	0.0205 (0.0334)	0.00199 (0.0177)	-0.0516** (0.0199)
Internal migrant (dummy)	0.251 (0.141)	0.0961 (0.176)	0.133 (0.168)	-0.00141 (0.149)	0.508* (0.199)	0.300 (0.193)	0.389* (0.160)
Migrant × child of household head	-0.309 (0.194)	-0.105 (0.220)	-0.0390 (0.209)	0.0579 (0.204)	-0.0568 (0.235)	-0.130 (0.225)	-0.198 (0.191)
Wealth index	-0.0748* (0.0311)	-0.0346 (0.0277)	-0.0313 (0.0287)	-0.0249 (0.0204)	0.00148 (0.0344)	-0.0493 (0.0296)	-0.0309 (0.0232)
Intercept	-0.185 (0.441)	-0.743 (0.483)	0.307 (0.412)	-1.104** (0.295)	2.156** (0.567)	-0.610 (0.396)	-0.810* (0.408)
Participates in market activities							
Age	0.126** (0.0399)	0.199** (0.0356)	0.208** (0.0348)	0.247** (0.0307)	0.0917** (0.0341)	0.0848** (0.0269)	0.174** (0.0317)
Boy (dummy)	-0.364 (0.218)	0.213 (0.112)	-0.0358 (0.175)	0.369** (0.110)	-0.451** (0.170)	0.237* (0.0972)	0.0394 (0.203)

	(1)	(2)	(3)	(4)	(5)	(6)	(7)
Child of household head (dummy)	-0.348* (0.165)	-0.0442 (0.153)	-1.145** (0.133)	0.000821 (0.110)	-0.327* (0.160)	-0.216 (0.143)	-0.612** (0.146)
Muslim (dummy)	-0.0873 (0.153)		0.270 (0.175)		-0.305 (0.200)		0.382* (0.152)
Muslim × child of household head (dummy)	0.320 (0.239)		-0.399 (0.353)		0.126 (0.294)		-0.0761 (0.215)
Male-headed household (dummy)	-0.166 (0.196)	-0.236 (0.406)	0.263 (0.231)	0.260 (0.172)	0.356 (0.202)	0.157 (0.269)	-0.416 (0.301)
Single-headed household (dummy)	-0.201 (0.173)	0.0699 (0.400)	-0.169 (0.247)	-0.00493 (0.176)	0.239 (0.209)	0.238 (0.259)	-0.190 (0.293)
Education of household head	-0.0257 (0.0181)	-0.00460 (0.0134)	-0.0128 (0.0152)	-0.0200 (0.0144)	-0.0188 (0.0162)	0.00319 (0.0154)	-0.0295 (0.0192)
Education of spouse of household head	0.0125 (0.0200)	0.00876 (0.0170)	-0.0285 (0.0186)	-0.0423* (0.0214)	-0.00510 (0.0242)	-0.0433* (0.0183)	0.0262 (0.0216)
Education of household head × boy	-0.0498 (0.0277)	-0.0316 (0.0171)	-0.0760** (0.0276)	-0.0361 (0.0202)	0.00239 (0.0252)	-0.0389 (0.0199)	-0.00870 (0.0256)
Education of spouse × boy	0.0320 (0.0301)	-0.0415 (0.0223)	-0.00248 (0.0389)	0.0358 (0.0276)	-0.00833 (0.0339)	0.0510* (0.0236)	-0.0205 (0.0285)
Self-employment of household head (dummy)	0.322* (0.130)	0.171 (0.110)	0.284* (0.117)	0.237* (0.0934)	0.279* (0.112)	0.330** (0.0996)	0.0803 (0.111)
Number of adults in household	-0.0522 (0.0308)	-0.0185 (0.0196)	0.0172 (0.0264)	0.00425 (0.0150)	0.0406 (0.0237)	-0.0249 (0.0189)	-0.0456 (0.0236)
Number of children in household	-0.0126 (0.0353)	0.0183 (0.0216)	0.0202 (0.0300)	0.0176 (0.0168)	-0.0304 (0.0332)	-0.00986 (0.0230)	0.0560 (0.0319)
Internal migrant (dummy)	0.635** (0.171)	0.626** (0.185)	0.588** (0.149)	0.703** (0.173)	0.556** (0.173)	0.577** (0.210)	-0.0511 (0.180)
Migrant × child of household head	-0.718** (0.256)	-0.507* (0.250)	-0.562* (0.220)	-0.738** (0.266)	-0.476* (0.218)	-0.291 (0.255)	-0.465 (0.269)

(continued next page)

Table 12.7 (continued)

Variable	Abidjan	Bamako	Cotonou	Dakar	Lomé	Niamey	Ouagadougou
Wealth index	0.00113	−0.0128	−0.0389	−0.0866**	−0.0767*	−0.0394	−0.0324
	(0.0354)	(0.0329)	(0.0314)	(0.0269)	(0.0342)	(0.0395)	(0.0328)
Intercept	−1.959**	−3.558**	−3.173**	−4.964**	−2.313**	−2.315**	−2.875**
	(0.604)	(0.671)	(0.567)	(0.454)	(0.524)	(0.459)	(0.543)
ρ_{DS}	−0.389**	−0.0749	−0.0618	−0.0968*	−0.165	−0.156**	−0.0934
	(0.0636)	(0.0535)	(0.0630)	(0.0417)	(0.0932)	(0.0482)	(0.0506)
ρ_{LS}	−1.189**	−0.389**	−1.866**	−0.671**	−0.766**	−0.411**	−0.759**
	(0.108)	(0.0650)	(0.148)	(0.0646)	(0.0850)	(0.0655)	(0.0789)
ρ_{LD}	0.0746	0.231**	0.101	−0.0293	0.362**	0.222**	0.0524
	(0.0744)	(0.0612)	(0.0696)	(0.0563)	(0.0774)	(0.0479)	(0.0506)
Number of observations	1,168	1,526	1,327	2,367	1,130	1,820	1,744

Sources: Based on Phase 1 of the 1-2-3 surveys of selected WAEMU countries 2001/02.
Note: Figures in parentheses are robust standard errors.
* significant at the 10 percent level, ** significant at the 5 percent level, *** significant at the 1 percent level.

varied: boys are less likely to engage in an activity outside the home environment in Lomé but more likely to do so in Dakar and Niamey. The nature of the child's relationship to the household head is an important determinant of allocation of time between work and school. Biological children of the household head have a higher probability of going to school and a lower probability of working (at home or in the market) than other children.[5] Children who were not born in the capital have a significantly lower probability of going to school and a higher probability of working in all cities except Ouagadougou.[6] This result is true only for children who do not reside with their biological parents, however, as the migratory status variable's interaction with the children of household head dummy is always significantly positive. This finding suggests that children who migrated to the capital and whose biological parents are likely to live elsewhere are more likely to work than to go to school.

One possible explanation of these results is that migration status may affect the probability of working or attending school because migration and the choice of activity are part of the same project. Children who migrated with their parents may be more likely to go to school because one of the reasons for migrating was to enhance the possibilities of getting the children educated.[7] Children who migrated without their parents may have moved in order to find work.

Many nonbiological children, particularly children born outside the capital, are likely to have been fostered to an adult member of the household. In Senegal, for instance, about 12 percent of children 15 and younger are fostered, and 32 percent of households host or send one or more fostered children (Beck and others 2011). The fact that these children have a lower probability of going to school than the biological children of their hosting household is consistent with the hypothesis, popular among some international organizations and supported by some academic works, that fostering may have a negative impact on children's well-being (Kielland 1999; UNICEF 1999; Case, Lin, and McLanahan 2000; Case, Paxson, and Ableidinger 2004; Bishai and others 2003). Early studies on child fostering, such as the study by Ainsworth (1996), find evidence that does not contradict this hypothesis, but these studies are limited by the nature of the data, which do not allow comparison of fostered children with children in their household of origin.

Using data that match the origin and hosting households of fostered children in Burkina Faso, Akresh (2008) shows that fostered children do not have a lower probability of going to school than the biological children of their hosting household and that this probability is significantly higher than that of their nonfostered siblings. Using 2006/07 data from Senegal, Coppoletta and others (2011) show that adults who were fostered when young have slightly higher levels of education and better positions in their households than adults who had not been fostered. Hence, in the absence of other evidence, we cannot interpret our results as firm evidence that fostered children are disadvantaged compared with their biological siblings.

A number of household characteristics also influence the time allocation decisions made for children. Having an educated head of household—and, to a lesser extent, spouse—raises the probability of a child going to school in most cities and reduces the probability of the child working. This finding is consistent with what is generally found in the literature: the presence of educated adults in a household raises children's returns to education by providing fertile ground for learning and encouraging them to spend more time in school and less time working. The impact of the level of education of the household head is particularly strong among boys in Abidjan, Cotonou, and Ouagadougou.

The level of education of the spouse of the household head is less significant, because it encompasses two opposite effects. On the one hand, an educated woman has more employment opportunities and is therefore more likely to delegate domestic work to children in her household, which reduces their chances of going to school (however, results from chapter 7 show that the number of hours of domestic work does not decline when women work for income). On the other hand, an educated women is in a better position to support the children in her household in their school education and therefore to send them to school rather than work.

The effect of the number of adults in the household on children's schedules is significant in only a few cities. In Bamako and, to a lesser extent, Abidjan and Lomé, the presence of more adults increases the probability of going to school; it reduces participation in domestic activities in most cities. These results suggest a distribution of tasks among different household members. Children in the same household appear to compete with one another to go to school, as an increase in the number of children tends to reduce school attendance. However, the impact is not statistically strong or significant, except in Bamako.

Self-employment by the head of household and the household wealth indicator have strong effects on children's allocation of time. Living in a household whose head is a self-employed entrepreneur significantly raises children's participation in economic activities in five of the seven cities (all except Bamako and Ouagadougou), at the expense of schooling. One could argue that the decision of the household to start a business depends on whether there are young children able to help out. If this is the case, entrepreneurship is jointly determined with child work.

This finding can be interpreted in two other ways. First, labor market imperfections may make it difficult to hire external labor. A household head could consequently be driven to rely on family members, especially children. This interpretation mirrors in an urban setting the finding of Bhalotra and Heady (2003) in rural Ghana and Pakistan.

Second, work experience gained by children in the family business could enhance their employability, encouraging them to opt out of school. Household heads using the labor of their children (or other children in the household) could well be equipping them with skills or specific human capital they can then sell on the labor market. This interpretation echoes the hypothesis that children's professional experience gained in the first period raises their labor productivity in the second period.

As many empirical studies show (see, in particular, Psacharopoulos 1997; Ray 1999, 2000; Lachaud 2004), household wealth is an important determinant of the time allocation decisions made for children. It has a positive and significant effect on school attendance among children in four of the seven cities (Abidjan, Cotonou, Dakar, and Niamey), where it reduces their participation in work (economic or domestic) activities. This effect is to be expected where access to the financial market depends on the level of household wealth. Higher wealth allows households to relax the budgetary constraint, favoring school enrollment. Given that the wealth variable is not instrumented, one cannot exclude the risk of an upward bias for the wealth coefficient estimate in the schooling equation and downward bias in the labor market participation equation. However, given that the education levels of the household head and spouse are included in the equations and qualitatively identical results were obtained in five of seven cities (all but Bamako and Ouagadougou), a true wealth effect appears to be at work, at least in some cities.

Conclusion

The chapter examines some of the factors influencing the allocation of children's time in seven West African cities. It finds that both domestic and economic activities compete with school, but many children combine school with domestic activities. Marked differences are evident between boys and girls, biological and nonbiological children, and migrant and nonmigrant children, with boys, biological children, and nonmigrant children having a higher propensity for going to school and a lower propensity for participating in domestic tasks and (for all groups but boys) economic activities. The propensity to attend school (work) is generally significantly higher (lower) in more educated and wealthier households and households in which the household head is not a self-employed entrepreneur.

This last finding points to a potential drawback of the standard recommendation of providing credit and other asset-building mechanisms to poor households. To the extent that these mechanisms allow parents to operate their own business, they could actually increase child labor (Del Carpio and Loayza 2012 for Nicaragua and Hazarika and Sarandi 2008 for rural Malawi find results that confirm this intuition). This negative impact on school attendance may be miti-gated if children learn specific skills that allow them to increase their resources in adulthood by more than the forgone earnings attributable to reduced school-ing. The data suggest that boys seem to have privileged access to this alternative way of accumulating human capital. If further investigations confirm this result, it would mean that gender inequality in access to education is coupled with inequality in access to on-the-job training in West African countries.

Notes

1. The ILO definition of child labor is rather restrictive. It includes work that is "men-tally, physically, socially or morally dangerous and harmful to children; and inter-feres with their schooling by: depriving them of the opportunity to attend school; obliging them to leave school prematurely; or requiring them to attempt to combine school attendance with excessively long and heavy work" (ILO 2012). According to this definition, a child who is prevented from attending school because of involve-ment in family activities is not considered at work as long as these activities are not dangerous or harmful.

2. The age of the end of compulsory schooling varies across countries (11 in Benin; 12 in Niger and Senegal; 15 in Côte d'Ivoire, Mali, and Togo; 16 in Burkina Faso). It is not clear whether this age is relevant, however, as it is not rigorously enforced. As is usual in the literature, we thus chose to focus on children ages 10–14.

3. Dakar, where 52 percent of working children are apprentices, is the exception. Apprentices are also important in Cotonou (32 percent), Ouagadougou (26 percent), Abidjan (25 percent), and Bamako (24 percent). Apprentices are generally not paid, but they learn to become welders, mechanics, tailors, blacksmiths, tinsmiths, and restaurant servers.

4. Although Abidjan and Cotonou are not administrative capitals, we refer to them as capitals because they are the most important economic centers in their countries (Cotonou is also the seat of government).

5. Children with the status of domestic staff were excluded from the sample to avoid biasing the results.

6. A large proportion of children in some cities (37 percent in Lomé, 31 percent in Abidjan, 27 percent in Cotonou, and 23 percent in Ouagadougou) were born outside the capital. This proportion is lower in Bamako (17 percent), Niamey (15 percent), and Dakar (9 percent).

7. It could also be the case that these children share with their parents common unob-served characteristics that increase both the probability of migration and the prob-ability of attending school. Our data do not allow us to test this possibility.

References

Ainsworth, M. 1996. "Economic Aspects of Child Fostering in Cote d'Ivoire." In *Research in Population Economics,* vol. 8, ed. T. P. Schultz, 25–62. Greenwich, CT: JAI Press.

Akresh, R. 2008 "School Enrollment Impacts of Non-traditional Household Structure." BREAD Working Paper 89, Bureau for Research and Economic Analysis of Develop-ment, Durham, NC.

Baland, J. M., and J. A. Robinson. 2000. "Is Child Labor Efficient?" *Journal of Political Economy* 108 (4): 663–79.

Basu, K., and P. Van. 1998. "The Economics of Child Labor." *American Economic Review* 88 (3): 412–27.

Beck, S., P. De Vreyer, S. Lambert, K. Marazyan, and A. Safir. 2011. "Child Fostering in Senegal." Paris School of Economics. http://www.parisschoolofeconomics.eu/docs/lambert-sylvie/confiage7-1.pdf.

Becker, G. S. 1964. *Human Capital*. New York: Columbia University Press for the National Bureau of Economic Research.

Becker, G. S., and H. Lewis. 1973. "On the Interaction between the Quantity and Quality of Children." *Journal of Political Economy* 81 (2): S279–88.

Behrman, J. R, R. Pollak, and P. Taubman. 1982. "Parental Preferences and Provision for Progeny." *Journal of Political Economy* 90 (1): 52–73.

Bhalotra, S., and C. Heady. 2003. "Child Farm Labor: The Wealth Paradox." *World Bank Economic Review* 17 (2): 197–227.

Bishai, D., E. D. Suliman, H. Brahmbhatt, F. Wabwire-Mangen, G. Kigozi, N. Sewankambo, D. Serwadda, M. Wawer, and R. Gray. 2003. "Does Biological Relatedness Affect Survival?" *Demographic Research* 8 (9): 262–77.

Case, A., I.-F. Lin, and S. McLanahan 2000. "How Hungry Is the Selfish Gene?" *Economic Journal* 10 (466): 781–804.

Case, A., C. Paxson, and J. Ableidinger. 2004. "Orphans in Africa: Parental Death, Poverty, and School Enrollment." *Demography* 41 (3): 483–508.

Coppoletta, R., P. De Vreyer, S. Lambert, and A. Safir. 2011. "The Long Term Impact of Child Fostering in Senegal: Adults Fostered in their Childhood." Paris School of Economics. http://www.parisschoolofeconomics.eu/docs/lambert-sylvie/lotif_ver22.pdf.

De Vreyer, P., S. Lambert, and T. Magnac. 1999. "Educating Children: A Look at Household Behaviour in Côte d'Ivoire." Document de travail, Centre d'Etude des Politiques Economiques de l'Université d'Evry (EPEE) 99-13, Evry, France.

Del Carpio, X. V., and N. V. Loayza. 2012. "The Impact of Wealth on the Amount and Quality of Child Labor." Policy Research Working Paper 5959, World Bank, Washington, DC.

Dumas, C. 2004. "Impact de la structure familiale sur les décisions parentales de mise au travail des enfants: le cas du Brésil." *Revue d'Economie du Développement* 18 (1): 71–99.

Greene, W. H. 2003. *Econometric Analysis*, 5th ed. New York: Prentice Hall.

Hazarika, G., and S. Sarangi. 2008. "Household Access to Microcredit and Child Work in Rural Malawi." *World Development* 36 (5): 843–59.

ILO (International Labour Organization). 2012. "What Is Child Labour?" http://www.ilo.org/ipec/facts/lang--en/index.htm.

Jacoby, H., and E. Skoufias. 1997. "Risk, Financial Markets and Human Capital in a Developing Country." *Review of Economic Studies* 64: 311–35.

Kielland, A. 1999. "Children's Work in Benin: Estimating the Magnitude of Exploitative Child Placement." World Bank, Social Protection Sector, Washington, DC.

Kis-Katos, K. 2012. "Gender Differences in Work-Schooling Decisions in Rural North India." *Review of Economics of the Household*. doi:10.1007/s11150–012–9153–x.

Lachaud, J.-P. 2004. "Le travail des enfants et la pauvreté en Afrique: un réexamen appliqué au Burkina Faso." Working Paper 96, Centre d'Economie du Développement, Université Montesquieu Bordeaux IV.

Psacharopoulos, G. 1997. "Child Labour Versus Educational Attainment: Some Evidence from Latin America." *Journal of Population Economics* 10 (4): 377–86.

Ranjan, P. 1999. "An Economic Analysis of Child Labor." *Economics Letters* 64 (1): 99–105.

Ray, R. 1999. "The Determinants of Child Labor and Child Schooling in Ghana." *Journal of African Economies* 11 (4): 561–90.

———. 2000. "Child Labor, Child Schooling, and Their Interaction with Adult Labor: Empirical Evidence for Peru and Pakistan." *World Bank Economic Review* 14 (2): 347–67.

Rosenzweig, M., and K. Wolpin. 1985. "Specific Experience, Household Structure, and Intergenerational Transfers: Farm Family Land and Labor Arrangements in Developing Countries." *Quarterly Journal of Economics* 100 (5): 961–87.

Skoufias, E., and S. Parker. 2002. "A Cost-Effectiveness Analysis of Demand and Supply-Side Education Interventions." FNCD Discussion Paper 227, International Food Policy Research Institute, Washington, DC.

Terracol, A. 2002. "Triprobit and the GHK Simulator: A Short Note." Appendix to the Stata Triprobit command. http://fmwww.bc.edu/repec/bocode/g/GHK_note.pdf.

UNICEF (United Nations Children's Fund). 1999. "Child Domestic Work." Innocenti Digest No. 5, International Child Development Center, Florence, Italy.

Chapter **13**

Working in West Africa after Retirement Age

Philippe Antoine

Until recently, the retirement age in most French-speaking capitals in West Africa was 55. However, only people who work for the government or private firms in the formal sector of the economy pay contributions and are therefore entitled to pensions. The majority of workers work in the informal sector and do not receive pensions.

There is very little interest in seniors (defined here as people 55 and older) in the labor market, mainly because they represent just 5 percent of the population. Yet there are at least two good reasons for looking into their situation. The first has to do with the sharp upturn in their numbers, which will grow more rapidly in Africa than any other continent (Velkoff and Kowal 2007). The second concerns the participation of seniors in the labor force at relatively later ages.[1]

Who works after 55 and in what lines of business? What are the proportions of older men and women in the labor market? Do some people see retirement as a time to retrain and change occupation? Is the prolonged activity of old workers a potential source of conflict between generations?

To answer these questions, this chapter analyzes data from the 1-2-3 surveys coordinated by the Observatoire économique et statistique d'Afrique Subsaharienne (AFRISTAT) and Développement, Institutions et Mondialisation (DIAL) in seven capitals in the West African Economic and Monetary Union (WAEMU).[2] This secondary analysis of a survey designed mainly to study the labor market identifies the position of seniors on the labor market in each of the capitals studied, differentiating between informal sector workers and pension recipients. Most of these people still have children to support and therefore need to work.

Data and Variables Used

The data used come from the 1-2-3 surveys conducted in the seven French-speaking West African Economic and Monetary Union capitals in 2001/02. The

373

analysis covers 4,955 individuals 55 and older who were interviewed in Phase 1 of the surveys (table 13.1).

The main variables covered by Phase 1 of the surveys are the characteristics of the household and each of its members. The Phase 1 augmented labor force survey concerns all individuals 10 and older. The questionnaire covers current employment, main job and any second job held, job-seeking, unemployment, father's job, previous employment, and unearned income. Most of the respondents are employed workers, but information from the surveys also sheds light on individuals 55 and older.

Sociodemographic Characteristics

One-third of WAEMU's population live in towns and cities. A large proportion of this urban population is concentrated in the country's economic capital, which generally attracts most investment. Some cities, such as Abidjan (population 3 million) and Dakar (population 2 million), are large.

The population is young: people 55 and older account for a very small proportion of the capital's population, ranging from 3.2 percent in Abidjan to 6.8 percent in Dakar. A large share of the capital's population are migrants from the country's interior, many of whom arrived in the 1970s and are now reaching retirement age.

A substantial proportion of the population in each of the capitals has no schooling; this share is particularly high among people 55 and older. Although illiteracy is being pushed back among the younger generations, many people lack postprimary education. Work still needs to be done in this area, particularly in Dakar, Niamey, and Bamako.

Table 13.1 Number of People Interviewed in Phase 1 of the 1-2-3 Surveys in Seven Cities in West Africa, 2001/02

City	Number of households	Number of individuals	Number of seniors	Seniors as percent of sample
Abidjan	2,494	11,257	360	3.2
Bamako	2,409	12,760	707	5.5
Cotonou	3,001	11,535	761	6.6
Dakar	2,479	18,700	1,272	6.8
Lomé	2,500	9,676	457	4.7
Niamey	2,500	14,342	683	4.8
Ouagadougou	2,458	13,513	715	5.3
Total	17,841	91,783	4,955	5.4

Sources: Based on Phase 1 of the 1-2-3 surveys of selected WAEMU countries conducted in 2001/02 by the Observatoire économique et statistique d'Afrique Subsaharienne (AFRISTAT); Développement, Institutions et Mondialisation (DIAL); and national statistics institutes.

Importance of the Informal Sector

Labor force participation rates for men range from 59 percent in Cotonou to 70 percent in Abidjan (table 13.2). For women, there are sharp differences between the capitals of the Gulf of Guinea countries (Benin, Côte d'Ivoire, and Togo), where just over 60 percent of women 10 and older participate in the labor force, and the capitals of the Sahelian countries (Burkina Faso, Mali, Niger, and Senegal), where 35–50 percent of women do so. These figures reflect differences in the status of women in the two regions (Adjamagbo and others 2005).

The survey divides the sample into five institutional sectors: public administration, public sector corporations, the formal private sector, the informal sector, and nonprofit organizations (Brilleau, Roubaud, and Torelli 2005). The informal sector accounts for 76 percent of employed workers across all seven capitals. There is little difference across cities (table 13.3). The formal private sector is in second place (except in Niamey), accounting for an average of 14 percent of jobs, ranging from about 10 percent in Cotonou to about 18 percent in Abidjan. Except in Niamey, relatively few people are employed in the public sector, which accounts for just 8.4 percent of employed workers (6.6 percent in the administration and 1.8 percent in public and semi-public corporations).

Even in the formal private sector, most workers (71–92 percent) do not pay pension contributions) (table 13.4). The majority of workers thus work in a sector that provides no social security.

Table 13.2 Sociodemographic Characteristics of the Sample in Seven Cities in West Africa, 2001/02
(percent, except where otherwise indicated)

Statistic	Abidjan	Bamako	Cotonou	Dakar	Lomé	Niamey	Ouagadougou
Population (thousands)	3,046	1,143	809	1,906	784	675	856
Structure by age							
0–14	34.1	44.0	36.4	34.6	35.0	43.0	37.6
15–54	62.9	50.8	58.3	58.9	60.4	52.4	56.9
55+	3.0	5.2	5.3	6.5	4.6	4.6	5.5
Male labor force participation rate among population 10 and older	70.1	59.3	58.8	62.1	68.9	63.5	66.3
Female labor force participation rate among population 10 and older	60.3	45.6	60.9	41.1	66.9	35.2	49.6
Net primary school enrollment rate	73.2	70.7	81.2	65.9	83.2	70.5	79.7

Sources: Population and labor force participation statistics are from Brilleau, Roubaud, and Torelli 2005; structure of the population by age statistics are from Phase 1 of the 1-2-3 surveys of selected countries (see table 13.1 for details).

Table 13.3 Distribution of Employment by Institutional Sector in Seven Cities in West Africa, 2001/02
(percent)

Institutional sector	Abidjan	Bamako	Cotonou	Dakar	Lomé	Niamey	Ouagadougou	All
Public administration	5.5	7.5	6.3	5.7	5.2	13.5	10.4	6.6
Public sector corporation	1.1	2.5	2.2	1.8	2.3	1.8	2.3	1.8
Formal private sector	17.6	11.4	9.9	15.0	10.5	11.8	11.8	14.2
Informal sector	74.7	77.5	80.3	76.4	81.0	71.1	73.4	76.2
Nonprofit organization	1.1	1.1	1.3	1.1	1.0	1.8	2.1	1.2
Total	100	100	100	100	100	100	100	100

Source: Brilleau, Roubaud, and Torelli 2005.

Table 13.4 Proportion of Workers in Private Formal Sector Paying Pension Contributions in Seven Cities in West Africa, 2001/02
(percent)

Sector	Abidjan	Bamako	Cotonou	Dakar	Lomé	Niamey	Ouagadougou	All
Formal private	10	19	12	13	8	15	17	12
Nonprofit organization	0	26	5	7	5	17	16	8

Sources: Based on Phase 1 of the 1-2-3 surveys of selected countries (see table 13.1 for details).

In the seven cities studied here, as in many other low- and middle-income countries, the social security system covers only a tiny minority of the population (mainly civil servants and formal sector workers). Informal sector workers—the vast majority of the population—have no welfare protection and are therefore particularly vulnerable when they can no longer work (Apt 2002). Improving these workers' lives, especially in terms of health and pensions, requires giving them the option of joining the state social security systems (Kannan 2007). Setting up a real welfare safety net is an effective way of protecting the poor against the risk of destitution (for a discussion of these issues, see James 1999; Gillion et al. 2000; Kakwani and Subbarao 2005; Scodellaro 2010; Willmore 2000).

The Importance of Seniors

The demographic weight of seniors in Sub-Saharan Africa is still small. In 2006, about 7.2 percent of the population was older than 55. Aging-related problems are not expected to emerge until 2030 (United Nations 2003; Velkoff and Kowal 2007). It would be a mistake to underestimate the demographic, social, and economic importance of seniors because their numbers are small, however; although their authority is gradually being challenged, elders continue to play an important economic role (Antoine 2007).

By the time they are 55, most men are heads of household (or at least say they are), except in Dakar, where men become household heads later than in other cities and not all men become heads of household (figure 13.1).[3]

The proportion of female heads of household is high in Abidjan, Lomé, Cotonou, and, to a lesser extent, Dakar and Niamey. The proportions are much lower in Bamako and Ouagadougou. The large proportion of older female heads of household mainly reflects women who are widowed and do not remarry (Adjamagbo and Antoine 2009).

Although people 55 and older account for a very small share of the population, they make up a significant share of heads of household, ranging from 10 percent in Abidjan to 32 percent in Dakar. Nearly one in four people lives in a household whose head is 55 or older; these figures range from 16 percent of the population in Abidjan to more than 40 percent in Dakar (table 13.5).

Pensions in Africa

The term *pensioner* is sometimes used incorrectly in Africa, as not all "pensioners" receive pensions. The 1-2-3 survey defines as pensioners all people who report drawing a pension. All seven countries have similar pension schemes: a contributory pension scheme for the economy's formal private sector and a system for civil servants, whose pensions are budgeted for in the national budget and paid out based on the number of years spent in the civil service.

Case Study of Senegal

State pensions in Senegal are managed by two institutions, the Senegal Pension Insurance Institution (IPRES) for the private sector and the National Pension Fund (FNR) for the public sector. Pursuant to the labor code in force since 1952, in 1958 an agreement between management and labor unions set up the West African Welfare Institute (IPRAO) for private sector employees. Following the break-up of the French West Africa federation and the independence of its member states, many of these states withdrew from IPRAO. In Senegal, IPRAO became IPRES in 1978. In 1975, it became a legal obligation for all salaried employees and employers to join this pension scheme (Diop 2003).

The IPRES pension system is a contributory scheme, which pays out to pensioners part of the contributions paid by contributors (employers and employees) after deductions for administrative expenses. The pensions for a given period are financed by the same period's levy on earnings, giving rise to a relationship between the number of contributors and the number of pensioners.

Figure 13.1 Age Distribution of Heads of Household in Seven Cities in West Africa, 2001/02

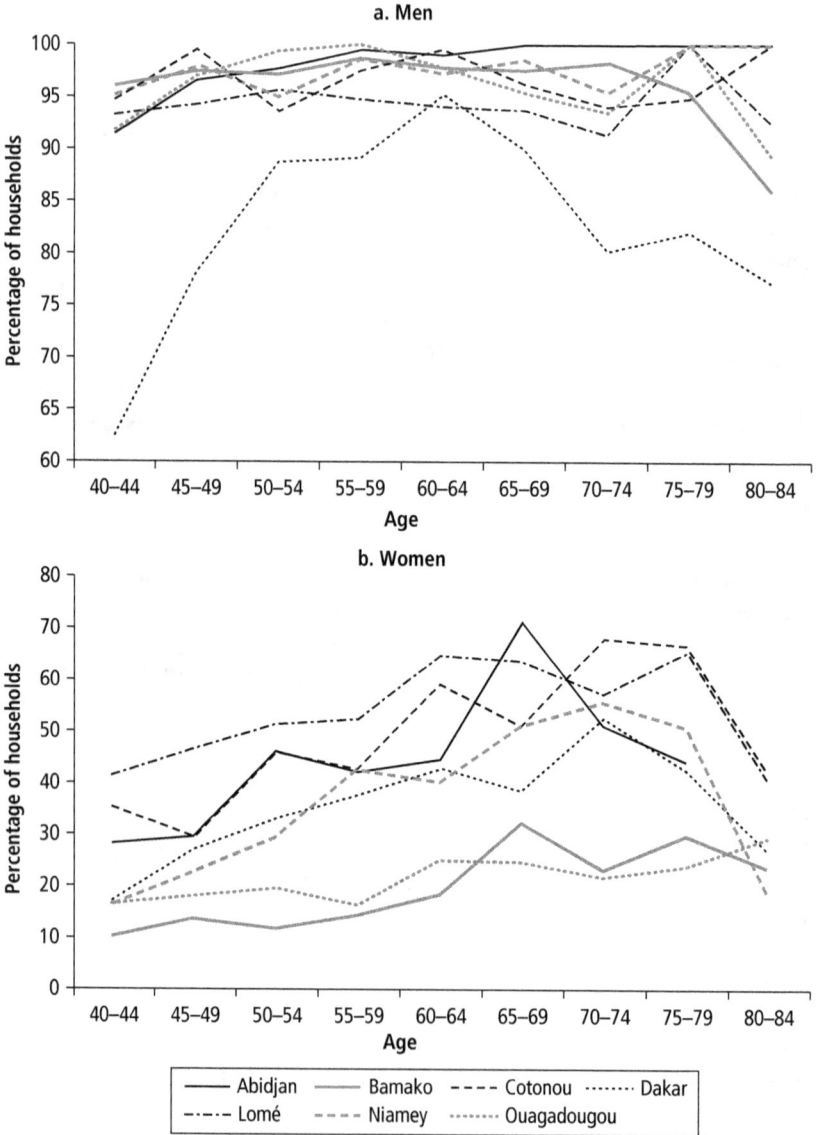

a. Men

b. Women

Sources: Based on Phase 1 of the 1-2-3 surveys of selected countries (see table 13.1 for details).

Table 13.5 Importance of People 55 and Older in Seven Cities in West Africa, 2001/02

Item	Abidjan	Bamako	Cotonou	Dakar	Lomé	Niamey	Ouagadougou
Heads of household 55 and older as percentage of all heads of household							
Male	9	20	16	30	10	19	18
Female	16	26	24	36	19	31	23
All	10	20	18	32	13	21	19
Proportion of individuals living in household headed by person 55 or older							
Percent	16	26	20	41	18	28	25

Sources: Based on Phase 1 of the 1-2-3 surveys of selected countries (see table 13.1 for details).

The FNR is a special Treasury account. It handles the pension scheme for civil servants (government employees in stable employment governed by service regulations). The scheme is a contributory system. Pensioners enjoy the same health care and treatment advantages on the same terms as working civil servants in state hospitals and health care structures. Until 2005, the retirement age was also 55, except for certain groups of employees. Since then, it was raised to 60.

There are some 118,000 pensioners in Senegal across both public and private sectors. Because of financial problems in the system, they are no longer sure of collecting their pensions. The FNR has a deficit of CFAF 6 billion. IPRES is also struggling to meet its obligations. With just over 100,000 contributors, it was expected to pay pensions to nearly 60,000 pensioners, 35,000 widows, and 2,370 orphans in 2003. In 2003, IPRES paid out a quarterly average of CFAF 71,408 to pensioners, CFAF 28,666 to widows, and CFAF 15,789 to orphans (CFAF 793 a day to pensioners, CFAF 319 to widows, and CFAF 175 to orphans).

The extremely low level of pensions means that retirement forces changes in pensioners' economic situation. The substantial drop in income can disrupt the running of the household, as explained by a recent retiree interviewed in Dakar: "The family head who earns CFAF 100,000 to feed his family when he is working gets CFAF 60,000 a quarter when he retires. It's very tough. It's not enough to support a household." This respondent noted that the cut in resources makes retirement a time of insecurity. "You can't put your feet up when you retire, because the money you get is useless. So you're retired, but you're scrabbling about for money to survive," he observed. For people receiving IPRES pensions, the fact that payments are made quarterly adds to their problems. Another person interviewed observed that retirement was an unpleasant surprise because of the unexpectedly low pension. "I was disappointed when I retired. I worked for companies that didn't make the contributions for me. I worked for 45 years and now I get a pension of CFAF 22,000 every three months. What can you buy with that?"

Other Countries in the Region

The situation is similar in the other West African capitals. In most countries, the retirement age is 55, except in certain civil service corps. An exception is Niamey, where the retirement age is 60 for men and 55 for women. In 1998, the government of Niger responded to pressure from the Bretton Woods institutions and to the need to curb its expenditure by introducing a number of unpopular measures, among which was retirement at 55 or following 30 years of service. In May 2006, the government reinstated the retirement age of 60 for civil servants.

In most of the countries in our study, the pensioner-contributor ratio is increasing, putting a heavy strain on cash flows. This erosion partly reflects the fact that younger cohorts are increasingly working in insecure jobs with no social security coverage (Antoine, Razafindrakoto, and Roubaud 2001; Diagne 2006).

Everywhere, the same union cry has gone up: raise the retirement age, mainly to increase the low level of most pensions. In Burkina Faso, for example, these demands were voiced in January 2004, when the government decided to increase the retirement age for all workers. In the civil service, the retirement age now ranges from 55 to 63, depending on occupational category. In November 2004, the statutory retirement age for private and semi–public sector workers was set at 56 for manual and equivalent workers; 58 for nonmanual and equivalent workers; 60 for supervisors, managers, and equivalent; and 63 for doctors and professors working in the private sector (*Le Pays*, December 31, 2004). In Senegal, the retirement age for civil servants was raised to 60 in 2005; a management-labor agreement provides, in principle, for a gradual transition to 60 in the private sector. Implementation of this agreement has been slow; in June 2006, bank workers in Dakar donned red armbands to lobby for increasing the retirement age to 60 (*Wal Fadjri*, June 12, 2006).

Workers' concerns are matched by experts' fears about the viability of a pension system inherited from the colonial period. They believe that the pension system is oversubsidized and balanced only by making the entire population pay. "These systems can impose unfair burdens on the less well-off outside the formal economy, while providing them no systematic support in their old age," notes Holzmann (2000, p. 18). Pension expenditure accounts for about 1.5 percent of gross domestic product, but the sums paid out are often paltry. In 2004, Robert Palacios, a senior pension economist at the World Bank, advocated for reforms in Senegal to increase the retirement age, raise the contribution base, reduce benefits, and improve management to cut costs. He raised questions about the long-term viability of the system and stressed the need to raise contributions to keep the schemes in the black (Palacios 2004).

Seniors Who Work

The productivity of seniors generally decreases with age, either because they are physically diminished or because they find it hard to learn new techniques. The proportion of workers falls at retirement age for both men and women. There is a clear drop in the share of workers between 50–54 and 55–59 in all capitals except Niamey, where the retirement age is higher (figure 13.2). This sudden decline at 55 is surprising, given that most people work in the informal sector and are not covered by pension systems. Some male respondents mention health and disability problems; the share of the population citing these factors rises with age (4 percent at 55–59, 8 percent at 60–64, and up to 20 percent after 70). Large percentages of older men continue to work very late in life, however, with more than 45 percent in Bamako and more than 30 percent in Niamey and Ouagadougou still working at 70–74.

Women are also well represented in the labor market after age 55, especially in Lomé, Cotonou, and Niamey (figure 13.2, panel b). Older women have sometimes gone back to paid work very late in life, after bringing up their children. This is the case in particular in Dakar (Adjamagbo and Antoine 2009). Higher percentages of women than men cite health problems: 11 percent at 55–59, 16 percent at 60–64, and 32 percent at 70–74.

When it comes to work by seniors, the cities can be divided into two groups. In the first group, the proportion of working women is higher than the proportion of working men. Cotonou, Lomé, and, to a lesser extent, Abidjan are in this group. Women in these cities have more independence than women in the Sahelian countries, which leads them to continue to work longer than men (figure 13.3). In the second group, men work more in old age than women. The Sahelian countries, especially Mali and Burkina Faso, are in this group. This pattern reflects a certain level of continuing dependence among women.

Rates of employment among older men vary widely in Western countries (table 13.6). In some countries, the majority of men still work at 60–64 (65 percent in Japan, 55 percent in the United States). Rates are very low in other countries, such as Belgium (21 percent) and France (15 percent). These differences reflect countries' welfare policies and the ages at which retirement is actually taken (the average retirement age is often three to five years lower than the official age).

West African workers do not enjoy the same welfare protection as Western workers. Their employment rate at 60–64 is high, although the official retirement age is lower than in Western countries. Their life expectancy at 55 is also much shorter than in the developed countries. Working late into life therefore leaves them fewer years of retirement.

The already dominant share of informal sector jobs in West Africa is even larger for older workers. There is a clear swing to the informal sector between

Figure 13.2 Proportion of Employed Workers in Seven Cities in West Africa, by Age Bracket, 2001/02

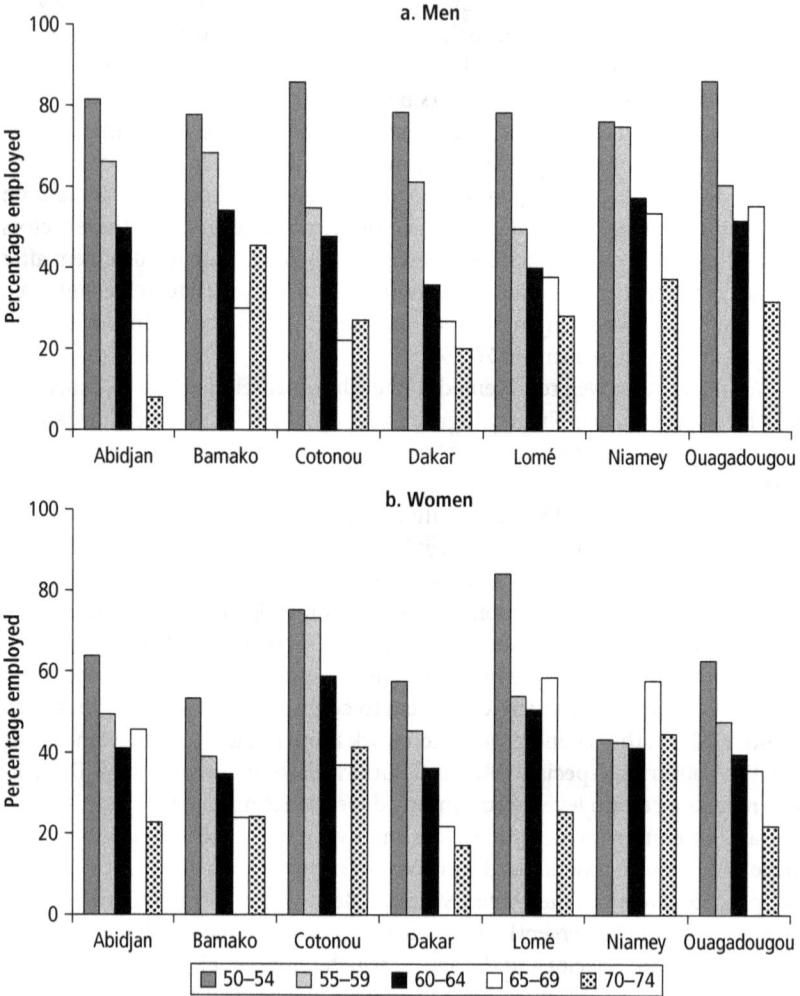

Sources: Based on Phase 1 of the 1-2-3 surveys of selected countries (see table 13.1 for details).

the 50–54 and 55–59 age brackets in all seven capitals. The proportion of men working in the informal sector in Abidjan increases from 37 percent at 50–54 (before retirement) to 61 percent at 55–59 (after retirement) (figure 13.4). The picture is the same in Bamako (where 44 percent of people 50–54 and 75 percent of people 55–59 work in the informal sector) and Cotonou (where 42 percent of people 50–54 and 62 percent of people 55–59 work in the informal sector).

Figure 13.3 Male-Female Differences in Proportion of Employed Workers in Seven Cities in West Africa, by Age Bracket, 2001/02

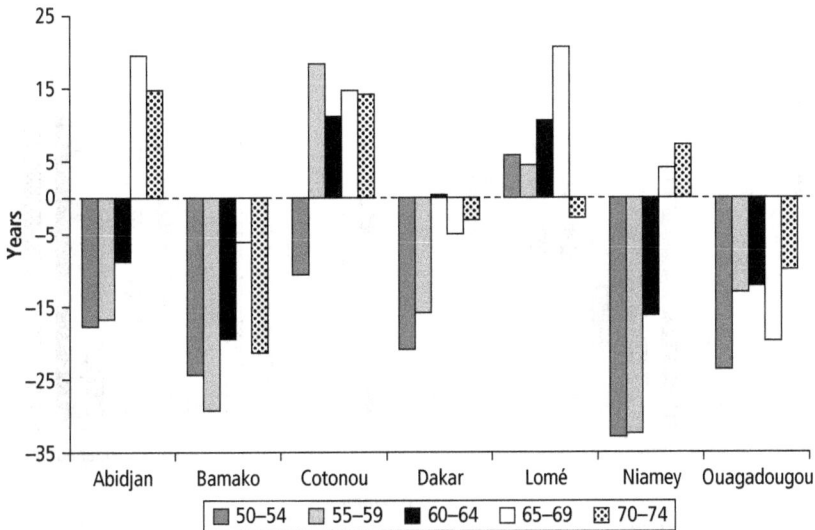

Sources: Based on Phase 1 of the 1-2-3 surveys of selected countries (see table 13.1 for details).

Table 13.6 Proportion of Men in Selected Countries Who Are Working, by Age Bracket, 2001/02

Country or city	25–49	50–54	55–59	60–64
Developed countries				
Belgium	85.7	77.1	52.3	21.3
France	87.5	84.0	60.2	14.5
Japan	92.0	92.1	88.8	64.7
United States	86.5	92.3	74.2	54.5
Africa				
Dakar	77.7	80.2	61.3	35.9
Niamey	80.5	75.7	75.0	57.5
Average for seven commercial capitals in West African Economic and Monetary Union	82.2	81.7	63.2	47.0

Sources: Data for Western countries are from d'Autume, Betbèze, and Hairault 2005. Data on Africa are from Phase 1 of the 1-2-3 surveys of selected countries (see table 13.1 for details).

Three causes underlie this transition. Individuals reaching retirement age today were massively recruited into the formal sector in the 1960s and early 1970s. They represent a larger proportion of formal sector workers than subsequent generations (people in their 40s and younger). On retirement, some of the people who worked in the formal sector switched to the informal sector.

Figure 13.4 Proportion of Employed Workers in Seven Cities in West Africa Working in the Informal Sector, by Gender and Age Bracket, 2001/02

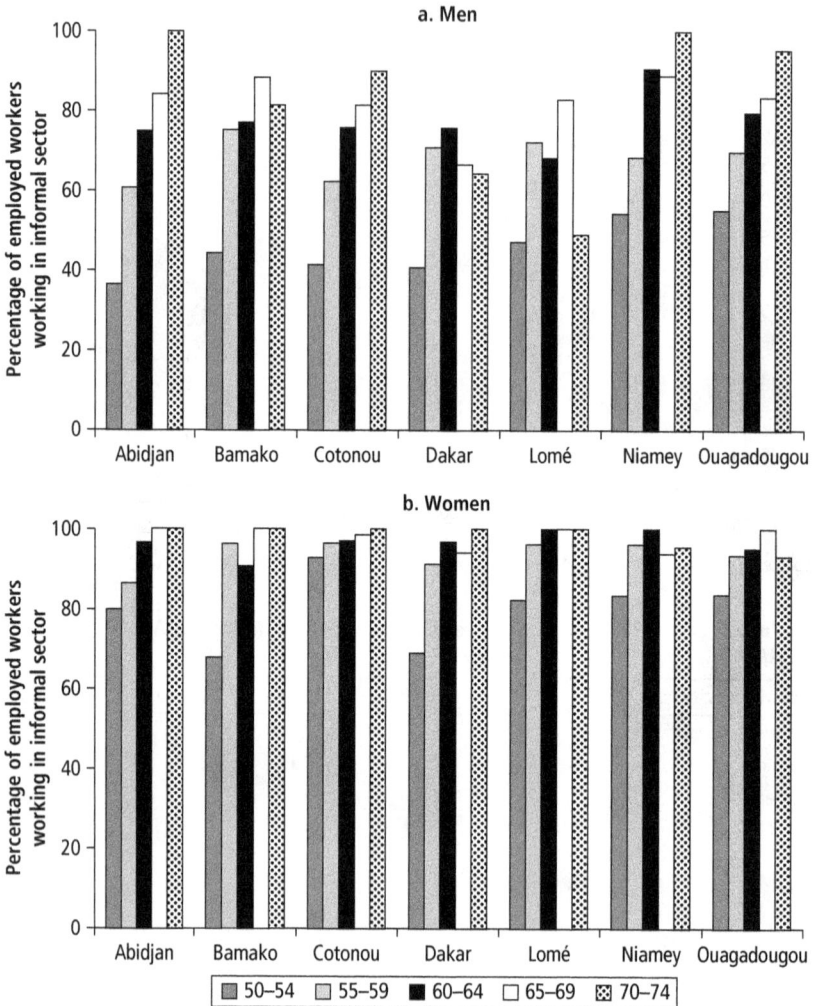

Sources: Based on Phase 1 of the 1-2-3 surveys of selected countries (see table 13.1 for details).

Other formal sector workers withdrew from the labor market. Informal sector workers continue to work longer than formal sector workers. Together, these factors mean that after 55, the older individuals get, the more likely they are to work in the informal sector if they continue to work. This tendency is even more pronounced among women. In Abidjan, for example, the share of active women in the informal sector is 85 percent at 55–59 work, 95 percent at 60–64, and 100 percent at 65 and older. Similar patterns are found in other cities.

The change in socioeconomic group on retirement could be studied only for a small number of individuals, because this information is available only for people who receive a pension and are still working. In the absence of sufficient numbers for each city, the calculations were made for all seven cities.

A large proportion of managers (74 percent) become self-employed or set up a small business. Half of all nonmanual and skilled manual workers (53 percent) and a majority of unskilled workers (67 percent) do likewise (table 13.7).

The switch from formal to informal sector is therefore the dominant swing among formal sector workers who continue working after retirement age. Only a minority continue to work in the formal sector, either because their status allows them to do so (as is the case with certain civil service management positions) or because they secure new contracts. The small share of workers who were employers or self-employed obviously remain in their original sectors.

Not all workers have the experience they need to succeed in a new job that is sometimes very different from their previous job. Unions and pensioner associations are nevertheless pushing for working retirement by fostering access to loans and means of production. One of the motions tabled by the Eighth Congress of the National Association of Civilian and Military Retirees of Senegal (ANRCM) was that the government and private business should promote third-age access to new information and communication technologies in order to help reintegrate seniors into production. It would be useful to take a closer look at this transition, to determine how many retirees attempt to switch sectors and how many are successful in doing so.

Table 13.7 Previous and Current Jobs of 55- to 64-Year-Old Working Retirees with Pensions in Seven Cities in West Africa, 2001/02
(percent)

Previous socioeconomic group	Current socioeconomic group				
	Manager	Nonmanual/skilled manual worker	Unskilled worker	Employer	Self-employed
Manager	23	2	0	37	37
Nonmanual/skilled manual worker	6	30	11	4	49
Unskilled worker	0	0	33	0	67
Employer	0	0	0	0	100
Self-employed	0	0	0	21	79

Sources: Based on Phase 1 of the 1-2-3 surveys of selected countries (see table 13.1 for details).

A Range of Situations among Seniors

We combine labor status with pension status to gain a clearer picture of the diversity of situations among people 55 and older. Figure 13.5 shows the share of the population in each of the following five groups:

- Nonworking pensioners (people who receive pensions and no longer work)
- Nonworking nonpensioners (people who do not work and do not receive pensions)
- Working pensioners (people who work and receive pensions)
- Working nonpensioners (people who work and do not receive pensions)
- Deferred retirees (people who continue to work in the same job in the formal sector).[4]

The majority of men (63 percent) still work at 55–59, with a minority (less than 5 percent) combining work with a pension.[5] The majority of pensioners in this age bracket have stopped working (18 percent); 43 percent of men 55–59 who work have no pension. About 15 percent of the men in this age bracket have not yet claimed their pension and continue to work in the same formal sector firm or administration. The older they get, the fewer male seniors work: by 60–64, 53 percent have stopped working. Nevertheless, nearly one-quarter of men 70–74 still work, with one-fifth of them also drawing pensions.

The situation differs across cities. Lomé (10.5 percent) and Cotonou (7.5 percent) have the highest proportion of pensioners who switched to a new job (table 13.8). Between 5.4 percent (Lomé) and 11.9 percent (Abidjan) of men 55–74 continue to work in the same business. The relatively high proportion of seniors in Niamey who have not retired reflects the higher legal retirement age (60).

The major differences across cities are in the proportion of seniors without pensions who continue to work. Their numbers are much lower in Cotonou, Dakar, and Lomé than in Niamey and Ouagadougou. It is hard to explain these differences, which could reflect particularities of the labor market in each city or structural age bracket issues. In some capitals, in particular in the coastal countries (Benin, Côte d'Ivoire, and Togo), retirement could mark the age when individuals leave the capital and move back to their home regions. Beauchemin (2000) addresses this question using data from a 1993 Ivorian survey on emigration and urbanization.[6] He finds that emigrants from urban areas are five times less likely to be retirees than nonmigrants, implying that return migration from retirees is marginal. Beauchemin suggests that pensioners are probably people whose urbanization is most complete. In the absence of a more detailed analysis of this phenomenon of older people migrating from the capital to the hinterland, the question remains open.

Figure 13.5 Work and Pension Status of Men and Women Past Retirement Age in Seven Cities in West Africa, by Age Bracket, 2001/02

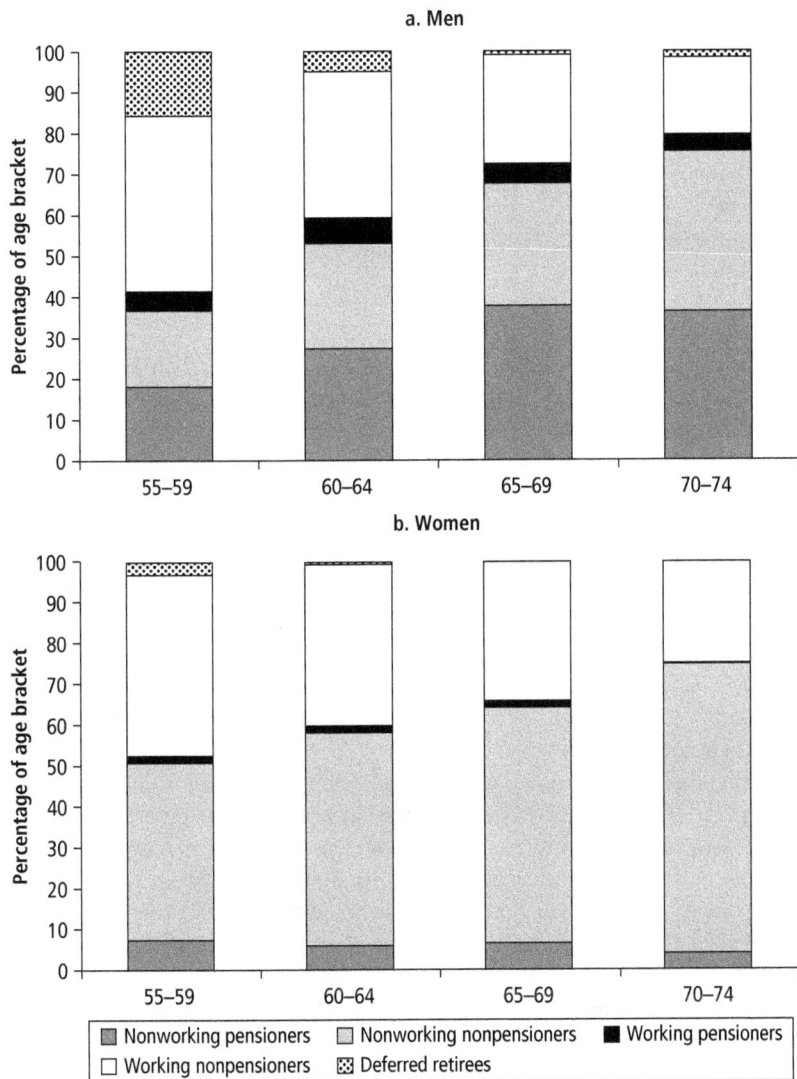

a. Men

b. Women

Legend: Nonworking pensioners · Nonworking nonpensioners · Working pensioners · Working nonpensioners · Deferred retirees

Sources: Based on Phase 1 of the 1-2-3 surveys of selected countries (see table 13.1 for details).

Table 13.8 Working and Pension Status of Men 55–74 in Seven Cities in West Africa, 2001/02
(percent)

Status	Abidjan	Bamako	Cotonou	Dakar	Lomé	Niamey	Ouagadougou	All
Nonworking pensioner	30.7	17.9	36.4	31.5	32.4	11.7	19.7	27.6
Nonworking nonpensioner	20.9	30.1	20.6	27.7	25.4	26.4	27.1	25.4
Working pensioner	1.9	4.3	7.5	6.1	10.5	4.1	6.3	5.4
Working nonpensioner	34.6	39.7	29.4	28.6	26.3	47.9	41.3	33.8
Deferred retiree	11.9	8.0	6.1	6.1	5.4	9.9	5.6	7.7

Sources: Based on Phase 1 of the 1-2-3 surveys of selected countries (see table 13.1 for details).

A slightly different picture emerges for women. Far fewer women draw pensions.[7] Most women who draw pensions no longer work, and most women who still work do not receive pensions. Nearly half (49 percent) of all women still work at 55–59, a much smaller proportion than among men (63 percent). Among women 70–74, 26 percent work (the figure for men is 23 percent). Half of these women are widowed heads of household. The others are married and take the place of their husbands, who are generally much older, to find the resources the household needs to survive. Most of these women sell food.

Workers with pensions, workers without pensions, and deferred retirees work in different occupations (table 13.9). Most active men without pensions are heads of small businesses or self-employed, mainly in informal trade (82 percent). A minority of pensionless workers (18 percent) are wage earners, generally in low-skilled or unskilled jobs.

A much broader range of situations is evident among pensioners who are still working. The majority (62 percent) turn to self-employment or set up small businesses; a substantial proportion of the men in this category remain employees, some as managers, others in skilled jobs. People who stay at work past 55 often work in management positions and skilled jobs; half of them are in the civil service. The self-employed tend to be traders in the formal sector, who are generally in relatively well-paid positions.

Regardless of whether they draw a pension, the majority of women are self-employed in the informal trade sector. The small minority of older women who have not yet retired work mostly in the civil service, mainly as teachers.

Responsibilities of Older Heads of Household

Employment among seniors is far from negligible. Most men 55–74 are heads of household with a large number of dependents. What percentage of the

Table 13.9 Job Type and Pension Status of Men and Women 55–74 in Seven Cities in West Africa, 2001/02

(percent)

Type of position	Men			Women		
	Without pension	Pension	Deferred retirement	Without pension	Pension	Deferred retirement
Senior manager	1.6	7.7	18.7	0.1	4.0	5.8
Middle manager	1.5	3.8	18.6	0.1	5.8	30.4
Skilled manual/nonmanual	3.6	12.9	21.5	0.3	1.3	9.6
Semi-skilled manual/nonmanual	4.4	2.9	10.8	0.6	0.0	26.9
Unskilled	6.7	10.7	14.1	1.8	0.0	20.7
Employer/proprietor	12.8	23.0	10.1	6.5	0.0	2.2
Self-employed	69.4	39.0	6.2	90.7	88.9	4.4

Sources: Based on Phase 1 of the 1-2-3 surveys of selected countries (see table 13.1 for details).

household's resources do the head's earnings represent? We consider three sources of income for the household:

- Income from the head of household's employment
- Other sources of income of the head of household (pension, real property income, remittances, and so forth)
- Income from other household members (earned income, property income, remittances, and other sources).

The combination of these sources yields eight possibilities:

- No income from the household itself
- Income solely from household members
- Unearned income from head of household
- All income from other household members and unearned income from head of household
- Earned income from head of household only
- All income from other household members and earned income from head of household
- Head of household's earned income and other income sources
- All income from head of household and other household members.

The male head of household's earned income is the sole source of income in a minority of households, ranging from 14 percent in Lomé to 31 percent in Niamey (figure 13.6). His earned income contributes to the household budget in about half of all households (in Niamey, the percentage is 62 percent).

Figure 13.6 Sources of Income of Households Headed by Men and Women 55–74 in Seven Cities in West Africa, 2001/02

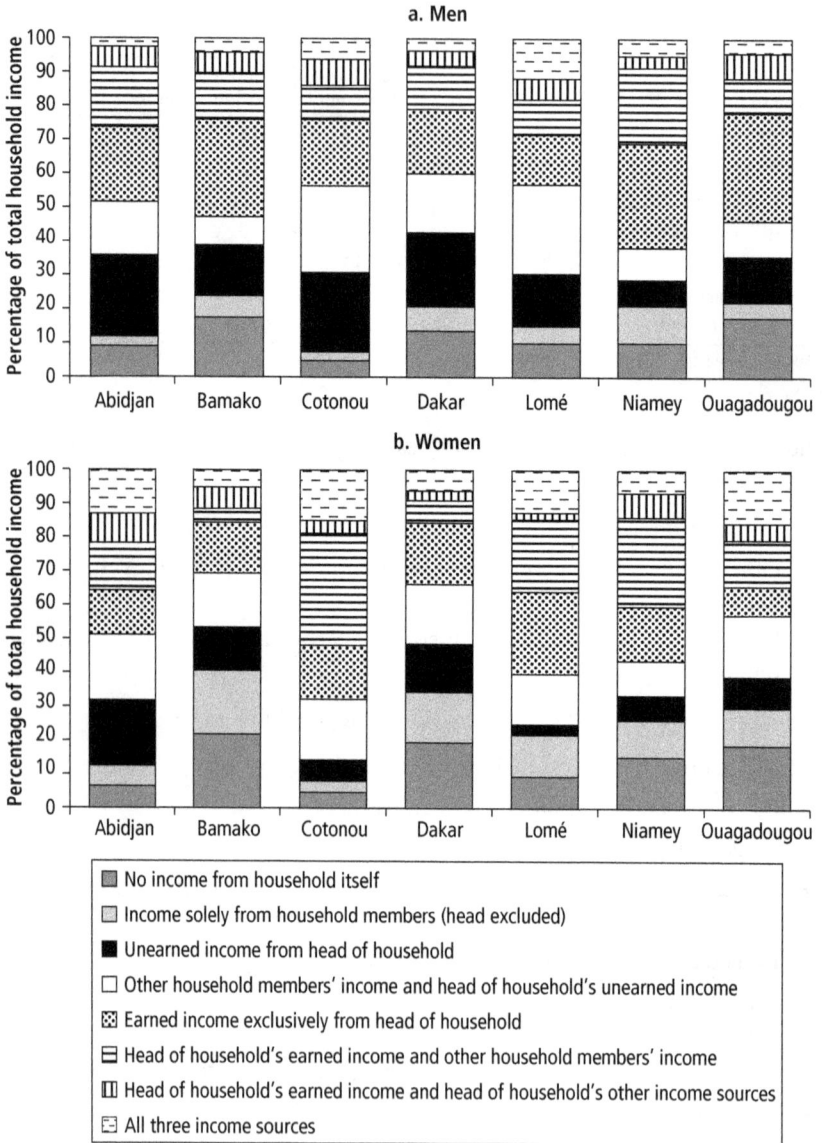

a. Men

b. Women

■ No income from household itself

☐ Income solely from household members (head excluded)

■ Unearned income from head of household

☐ Other household members' income and head of household's unearned income

⊠ Earned income exclusively from head of household

⊟ Head of household's earned income and other household members' income

Ⅲ Head of household's earned income and head of household's other income sources

⊡ All three income sources

Sources: Based on Phase 1 of the 1-2-3 surveys of selected countries (see table 13.1 for details).

Including other sources of income, mainly pensions and rental housing income, about 80 percent of the households live totally or partially off the head of household's resources. Differences across cities partly reflect the fact that the proportion of households in which no member declared any income ranges widely, from 4.8 percent in Cotonou and 8.8 percent in Abidjan to about 17.5 percent in Bamako and Ouagadougou. In the Sahelian cities (Bamako, Niamey, and Ouagadougou), seniors remain the head of the family compound; in some cases, children living elsewhere finance the compound's expenditure. However, only about 5 percent of households live solely off the resources of other household members (11 percent in Niamey). These findings reinforce the idea that older heads of household have more than just an age-related position of prestige. They also fulfill an economic function linked to their income, whatever its origin.

The household head's earned income is the only source of income for 16.5 percent of households headed by women. The proportion is particularly high in Lomé (24 percent), with its massive contingent of dynamic women on the labor market. At the other end of the scale is Ouagadougou, where the proportion is relatively low (8 percent). About half of households draw on income from their female head's employment. This figure is the same as for male heads, but the disparities across cities are greater. Most households headed by women in Cotonou (68 percent) and Lomé (60 percent) draw on the household head's earned income. In contrast, just one-third of households in Bamako and Dakar do so. This Sahelian–coastal city split partly reflects differences in the status of and roles conferred on women. As with men, only a small proportion of households (about 10 percent) live solely off income from other household members (generally children or close family members). Exceptions are Bamako (19 percent) and Dakar (15 percent).

Older male heads of household generally still have dependent children. Late fatherhood is common, and very large age differences are often found between the oldest and the youngest child. We take a single indicator to illustrate this situation: the proportion of households headed by men with at least one child still at school (table 13.10). This indicator is imperfect, because not all children go to school in these capitals. However, it provides a rough measure of the share of households headed by men over 55 with dependent children.

Across all work and pension statuses, a large proportion of male heads of household (72 percent on average) still have dependent children at 55–59. This proportion decreases with age but remains high even among men 70–74 (almost 40 percent). It is lowest among households headed by working non-pensioners. A large share of men in this category (informal sector workers) have no schooling, and some of them do not send their children to school. This indicator therefore underestimates the proportion of still-dependent children in these households. It reveals the extent of family responsibilities weighing on

Table 13.10 Proportion of Households Headed by Men 55–74 with at Least One Child Still in School, in Seven Cities in West Africa, 2001/02
(percent)

Status	55–59	60–64	65–69	70–74	Proportion of heads of household with no schooling
Nonworking pensioner	84	66	56	48	30
Nonworking nonpensioner	74	65	58	32	61
Working pensioner	78	78	70	36	28
Working nonpensioner	62	63	68	37	70
Deferred retirement	83	66	66	48	32
All	72	66	60	39	52

Sources: Based on Phase 1 of the 1-2-3 surveys of selected countries (see table 13.1 for details).

older male heads of household, who often have to cope with the problems of aging while raising and supporting young children.

Conclusion

A relatively large share of men in West Africa continue to work after reaching retirement age (more than 60 percent of men 55–59). The proportion of workers decreases with age but still stands at more than 50 percent among men 65–69 in Ouagadougou and Niamey and at about 30 percent in the five other cities studied. The situation is more varied among women. They are still very much on the labor market at 55–59, especially in Cotonou (nearly 75 percent) and Lomé (55 percent), and they continue to work as they age, working longer than men in Cotonou and Lomé. With age, workers are increasingly confined to the informal sector.

Pensions in West Africa are very low, especially outside the public sector, suggesting that they act more like minimum survival income than replacement income. Retirees struggle to make their meager incomes meet family outlays. People 55 and older still make substantial contributions to the economic life of their households; few seniors depend exclusively on their family's help (women appear more dependent on family support than men). In fact, most household heads still have young children to support. Elderly heads of household often support adult children who have not yet entered the labor market. Understanding of these issues remains weak; more research on them is called for.

Throughout the WAEMU region, countries are gradually raising the retirement age in the formal sector to 60. Later retirement provides a short-term individual solution for formal sector workers; it does nothing for the already shaky pension scheme balance. In addition, it restricts the younger generation's access to jobs in the formal sector and the informal sector, the main sector in which seniors continue to work, exacerbating the already difficult youth employment situation (DIAL 2007). The debate on raising the retirement age is thus really a generational debate. The effect of a higher retirement age is currently marginal, as only a minority of the West African population draw pensions. It will take on growing importance as the number of seniors rises and their needs have to be met.

Later entry into the labor market may make retirement even more difficult for future generations than it is for today's retirees. It is not uncommon in West Africa to start a career in the formal sector at 30–35. Even with the retirement age at 60, this late start makes for a very short contribution period. Moreover, the majority of workers are still excluded from pension systems, although some trade associations have started to provide benefits. Extension of social security to all remains a major challenge.

Notes

1. The issue of seniors continuing to work late in life is high on the West African social agenda; unions in the region are calling for the retirement age to be raised to 60, because of the very low level of most pensions. Most countries in the West African Economic and Monetary Union (WAEMU) negotiated public sector solutions in 2004/05; talks are still under way in the formal private sector in several countries.
2. The cities are Abidjan, Bamako, Cotonou, Dakar, Lomé, Niamey, and Ouagadougou. Although Abidjan and Cotonou are not administrative capitals, we refer to them as capitals because they are the most important economic centers in their countries (Cotonou is also the seat of government). For a description of the 1-2-3 surveys, see box O.1 in the overview.
3. The relatively high cost of housing in Dakar doubtless prevents some men from establishing an independent home for their families; some couples and their children continue to live with another family member. It is difficult for a man who lives with his father to declare himself the household head, even if he is the main income provider.
4. The 1-2-3 surveys were not designed to study retirees; they therefore lack specific questions on their situation. In the absence of information on individual transitions to retirement, we draw on a number of variables to identify formal sector workers who continue to work in the same business after 55 and do not yet claim their pension.
5. It may be that more former formal sector workers attempt to make the switch to the informal sector. The survey does not provide information on this point.
6. This survey defines retirees as people who draw pensions. It therefore underestimates the number of people who leave Abidjan when they feel they have come to the end of their working lives.
7. The questionnaire is not clear about how widows' survivor's pensions are classified: we assume that they are classified as "other pensions"; only the pension paid to female employees is classified as a work pension.

References

Adjamagbo, A., and P. Antoine. 2009. "Être femme 'autonome' dans les capitales africaines: les cas de Dakar et Lomé." In *Du genre et de l'Afrique: hommage à Thérèse Locoh*, ed. J. Vallin, 281–94. Paris: Ined.

Adjamagbo, A., P. Antoine, D. Béguy, and F. B. Dial. 2005. "Comment les femmes concilient-elles mariage et travail à Dakar et à Lomé." Sixièmes journées scientifiques du réseau démographie de l'Agence Universitaire de la Francophonie (AUF), "Ville du sud: dynamiques, diversités et enjeux démographiques et sociaux," Cotonou, November 21–24.

Antoine, P., ed. 2007. *Les relations intergénérationnelles en Afrique: approche plurielle.* Paris: CEPED, Collection Rencontres.

Antoine, P., M. Razafindrakoto, and F. Roubaud. 2001. "Contraints de rester jeune? Evolution de l'insertion dans trois capitales africaines: Dakar, Yaoundé, Antananarivo." *Autrepart* 18: 17–36.

Apt, N. A. 2002. "Ageing and the Changing Role of the Family and the Community: An African Perspective." *International Social Security Review* 55 (1): 43–53.

Beauchemin, C. 2000. *Le temps du retour: l'émigration urbaine en Côte d'Ivoire, une étude géographique.* PhD diss., Institut Français d'Urbanisme, Université Paris VIII.

Brilleau, A., F. Roubaud, and C. Torelli. 2005. "L'emploi, le chômage et les conditions d'activité dans la principale agglomération de sept états de l'UEMOA: premiers résultats de l'enquête emploi 2001–2002." *Statéco* 99: 43–63. http://www.dial.prd.fr/dial_publications/PDF/Doc_travail/2004-06.pdf.

D'Autume, A., J. P. Betbèze, and J. O. Hairault. 2005. *Les seniors et l'emploi en France.* Paris: La Documentation Française.

Diagne A. 2006. *L'entrée en vie adulte à Dakar.* PhD diss., Institut de Démographie, Université Paris I.

DIAL (Développement, Institutions et Mondialisation). 2007. "Youth and Labour Markets in Africa: A Literature Review." Working Paper 49, Département de la Recherche, Agence Française de Développement.

Diop, A. Y. 2003. "Gouvernance des régimes de sécurité sociale: tendances au Senegal." *Revue Internationale de Sécurité Sociale* 56 (3–4): 21–28.

Gillion, C., J. C. Turner, C. Bailey, and D. Latulippe. 2000. "Africa in Social Security Pensions: Development and Reform." *Social Security Pensions: Development and Reform*, 515–31. Geneva: International Labour Organization.

Holzmann, R. 2000. "The World Bank Approach to Pension Reform." *International Social Security Review* 53 (1): 13–42.

James, E. 1999. "Coverage under Old-Age Security Programs and Protection for the Uninsured. What Are the Issues?" Policy Research Working Paper 2163, World Bank, Washington, DC.

Kakwani, N., and K. Subbarao. 2005. *Ageing and Poverty in Africa and the Role of Social Pensions.* Working Paper 8, United Nations Development Programme, International Poverty Center, New York.

Kannan, K. P. 2007. "Social Security in a Globalizing World." *International Social Security Review* 60 (2–3): 21–41.

Palacios, R. 2004. *La politique des pensions en Afrique.* World Bank Institute, Human Development Group, Pension Reform Social Protection Unit, Washington, DC. http://info.worldbank.org/etools/docs/library/77113/june2004/ppt/palacios.pdf.

Scodellaro, C. 2010. "Les articulations entre solidarités publiques et solidarités privées en Afrique du Sud: les pensions de vieillesse et leurs effets." *Autrepart* 53: 57–74.

UN (United Nations). 2003. *Living Arrangements of Older Persons around the World.* New York: UN.

Velkoff, V. A., and P. R. Kowal. 2007. *Population Aging in Sub-Saharan Africa: Demographic Dimensions 2006.* Washington, DC: U.S. Census Bureau, National Institute on Aging.

Willmore, L. 2000. "Three Pillars of Pensions? A Proposal to End Mandatory Contributions." DESA Discussion Paper 13, Department of Economic and Social Affairs, United Nations, New York.

Part V

Moving Forward

Chapter **14**

Challenges and Directions for Future Research

Philippe De Vreyer and François Roubaud

The 1-2-3 surveys provide a wealth of information and analysis on labor markets in Sub-Saharan Africa. To build on and expand on the knowledge they yield, researchers could follow several paths.

Three chapters that were supposed to have been included in this book were ultimately left out, because the research was not completed in time. The first deals with spatial inequalities and African labor markets. It explores two types of questions: spatial polarization and ghettoization phenomena and agglomeration and social interaction effects. The originality of the idea lies in exploiting the area frame for primary sampling units (enumeration areas) of the 1-2-3 survey sampling method in order to study neighborhoods, based on recent research (Ioannides 2002; Goux and Maurin 2007). The second considers within-firm training. It quantifies this phenomenon and measure its returns in terms of human capital accumulation, by applying matching techniques to estimate the effects of training. The third tackles regulation and employment in Sub-Saharan Africa. At its heart lies the issue of potential labor market rigidities and their possible consequences on labor and income. Through a political economy perspective, this research examines the following questions: Did structural adjustment programs lead to liberalization of labor legislation in Sub-Saharan Africa? Are African countries (in particular French-speaking countries) more rigid than other developing countries? To what extent is labor legislation actually applied? What is the impact of the highlighted rigidities (on unemployment, the size of the informal sector, and so forth)?

All these issues are still relevant. We strongly encourage their authors to continue and finalize their research, even if recent studies (as well as older ones; see the overview to this book) suggest that labor regulations are not major binding constraints in Sub-Saharan Africa (AfDB and others 2012). For instance, according to the enterprise surveys conducted by the World Bank (2011), only 0.9 percent of African firms blame labor legislation as the greatest obstacle to doing business on the continent, the second lowest (with courts) of 15 potential obstacles proposed (access to finance and electricity were the most cited obstacles by entrepreneurs, with about 20 percent of respondents citing each). This figure appears at odds with the conclusion drawn from the same surveys that labor regulations in Sub-Saharan Africa are the most rigid in the world. The apparent paradox can easily be explained by the huge gap between de jure and de facto regulation: although the restrictions stipulated in national laws are unfavorable on paper, they are not effectively applied, because of weak enforcement capacity. Lack of enforcement does not mean that labor market regulation issues should not be addressed, particularly given the fact that regulations are tighter in richer African countries (South Africa and the countries of North Africa) and will likely increase in poorer countries as they continue to develop.

The survey data can also be used to investigate other issues (some of which have already been explored), including the role of trade unions, social networks and information, and efficiency wages; the integration of young people (Antoine, Razafindrakoto, and Roubaud 2001; DIAL 2007); the modeling of unemployment or multiactivity (holding more than one job at the same time); and the characteristics of employment in the public sector (Razafindrakoto and Roubaud 2001) and in international firms and export processing zones (Glick and Roubaud 2006; Cling, Razafindrakoto, and Roubaud 2005, 2009). In terms of methodology, it is necessary to depart from reliance on the earnings equation, which, despite the intrinsic fragility of income measures (see the overview), is overused.

Three areas are at the top of the list for further exploration: employment and the informal sector, especially in relation to poverty; the microeconomic and macroeconomic dynamics of the labor market; and the impact of public policies. The three sets of issues are closely interconnected.

Employment, the Informal Sector, and Poverty

Using the definitions proposed by the International Labour Organization (ILO) and the official statistics community (labor statisticians and national accountants), the chapters in this book show that the concepts of the informal sector and its extension (informal employment) could pay off analytically, provided they are handled with a rigor; given their importance in labor markets in the region, understanding informality is critical. Alternative concepts (such as *vulnerable employment*, defined below) are more problematic.

Given that the 1-2-3 survey was designed precisely to understand the informal sector and informal employment, use of survey phases 2 and 3 should generate significant knowledge about the informal economy, especially in Africa. The completed project "Unlocking Potential: Tackling Economic, Institutional and Social Constraints of Informal Entrepreneurship in Sub-Saharan Africa" (2009–11) has already provided decisive additional results (Grimm, van der Hoeven, and Lay 2011; Grimm and others 2012). Among the issues it addresses are the returns to physical and human capital (economic constraints), the costs of legalization and corruption (institutional constraints), and the weight of redistributive pressure and the role of social networks in informal sector performances (social constraints). Combining the three phases of the 1-2-3 survey also yields a tool that is well suited to measuring and analyzing the working poor (as defined by the ILO).

Microeconomic and Macroeconomic Labor Market Dynamics

The only dynamic aspect addressed in this book is intergenerational mobility. Expanding research on this issue requires cross-sectional, multiround surveys or panel data. Both types of 1-2-3 surveys have been conducted in African countries such as Madagascar, where a 15-year series (1995–2012) is available.

Comprehensive development of all the issues that could be studied is outside the scope of this chapter (a research program conducted by Développement, Institutions et Mondialisation [DIAL] on macro and micro labor market dynamics that addresses them is in progress). It should be possible to gain insight into the cyclical or countercyclical nature of the informal sector from cross-sectional or pseudo-panel data; panel data could be used to study job transitions between the formal and informal sectors to gain a better understanding of labor market segmentation. Independent of their time properties, panel data form an invaluable source of information with which to enrich analysis, as they can be used to control for "unobservables" assumed to be constant over time. As a result, information can be gathered on questions as simple and crucial as the largely unknown impact of international financial crises on labor markets in Sub-Saharan Africa.

Impact of Public Policies

Africa is rife with programs that directly or indirectly target the labor market, including education, vocational training, and on-the-job training; support to job seekers, young entrants, and staff of privatized public enterprises; programs that seek to increase market access and access to information; microcredit programs; social security schemes; and other policies. These programs are rarely rigorously evaluated. All of the policy evaluation examples that appear in the latest ILO report on youth employment trends (2010) and the report on growth, employment, and social cohesion by the ILO and the International Monetary Fund (2010) concern developed countries.

Many African governments want to extend existing protection schemes in order to reduce poverty and increase social cohesion and political stability, with the aim of achieving universal coverage. Many policy makers want to reform these programs, which many believe are dysfunctional. Before embarking on a new agenda of reforms—such as decoupling social protection from employment status, creating individual unemployment saving accounts, or more broadly liberalizing African labor markets (by, for example, eliminating severance pay)— existing and planned mechanisms should be carefully and rigorously assessed.

The recent, well-founded interest in ex post public policy evaluation evidently applies, and these approaches warrant development. The 1-2-3 surveys, rounded out by ad hoc protocols, could serve as a suitable medium for analysis (see, for example, Gubert and Roubaud 2006 for an impact study on a microfinance institution in Madagascar). Researchers also need to study the impact of further-reaching macroeconomic policies (such as the effect of international openness on the informal economy) and shocks such as the international financial crisis, inflation created by the food crisis, and the rise in commodity prices and deregulation policies (minimum wage, labor code liberalization, and so forth).

The Data Challenge

The glaring lack of data has led the ILO to develop macroeconometric models to estimate and forecast employment and unemployment worldwide (the TRENDS model provided by KILM [Key Indicators of the Labor Market] databases). Given the rather crude assumptions they use, these models are no substitute for survey data. More surveys—that are comparable over time—are needed in Sub-Saharan Africa.

The paucity and low quality of national labor force surveys has forced researchers to use other sources of data. The chapter on youth employment in Africa in the study by the AfDB and others (2012) draws heavily on the Gallup World Poll labor market module. The main arguments for using these data are broader coverage (39 African countries covered between 2008 and 2010 versus only 16 labor force surveys conducted between 2002 and 2007); the fact that the data are more recent; the greater comparability across countries, thanks to the use of identical questionnaires; and the inclusion of valuable opinion questions dealing with key issues such as subjective well-being and perceptions of obstacles and opportunities, job search, and business success.

Using the Gallup World Poll data rather than national labor force surveys also has some drawbacks (AfDB and others 2012). Some labor market concepts are not aligned with ILO standards, and the sample sizes are limited (about 1,000 respondents, compared with the 20,000 or more usually included in labor force surveys). These issues are not the main source of concern about use of these data, however. Delegating the collection of information on labor markets to private polling represents the de facto privatization of the national statistical system. As a public good, labor market indicators should be delivered by public statistics authorities, in Sub-Saharan Africa as elsewhere in the world.

For two decades, we have been calling for the generalization of labor force surveys in Sub-Saharan Africa (Roubaud 1992), until recently without much effect. As stressed in the overview of this book, the ideal tool should be an extended labor force survey designed not primarily to measure unemployment but instead to capture the fundamental labor market specificities in developing countries, particularly the informal sector and informal employment. Adapted indicators should also be developed. The conventional split into primary, secondary, and tertiary sectors to proxy productive versus unproductive jobs is not useful in Sub-Saharan Africa. Using such an aggregate divide to assess modernization and structural change theory in developing countries is deeply misleading where the informal sector colonized manufacturing, construction, and services and coexists with the formal sector (see overview).

Not all recent efforts to expand labor market indicators are useful. For example, the concept of *vulnerable employment* (defined as self-employment and contributing family jobs) proposed by the ILO seems much less relevant than the NEET (not in education, employment, or training) ratio or the over- and undereducation ratios developed in this book. The concept of vulnerable employment is consistent with the conventional view of duality and informality, which implies that all wage jobs are good jobs and all self-employed jobs are bad jobs. The recent literature clearly shows that the picture is mixed. Once all dimensions of jobs quality and individual preferences are taken into account, self-employed workers in the informal sector may be better off than wage workers in the formal sector (see Roubaud 1994; Maloney 2004; Bargain and Kwenda 2011; Falco and others 2011; Nordman, Rakotomanana, and Roubaud 2012; Nguyen, Nordman, and Roubaud 2011; Razafindrakoto, Roubaud, and Wachsberger 2012; and chapter 6 of this book). The vulnerability intensity indicator developed in chapter 4 seems much more convincing in this respect.

The NEET indicator is much more useful than the youth unemployment rate, because it reincorporates the massive component of discouraged workers excluded by the usual measures of underemployment, providing a much better indicator of the true extent of the potential lack of jobs. Incorporating subjective dimensions (such as job satisfaction and happiness, and opinion questions) into labor force survey questionnaires is also needed (see chapter 3).

To incorporate these dimensions, the 1-2-3 surveys should be developed further, building on the work by DIAL and others in recent years. A new generation of surveys incorporating some methodological innovations is already planned in Sub-Saharan Africa. The new surveys will address two pending measurement issues. First, they will broaden geographical coverage at the national level to capture informality, farming, and off-farm activities in rural areas. Second, the Phase 1 questionnaire has been adapted and a new module developed in a participatory manner to fit with the Decent Work agenda (Herrera and others 2012). Expanding the focus in Sub-Saharan Africa beyond the French-speaking countries would add a wealth of information. More broadly, official socioeconomic household surveys in Sub-Saharan Africa should rely on generic surveys: augmented labor force surveys (such as 1-2-3 surveys) to assess the labor market and the informal economy, and living conditions surveys to assess poverty and livelihoods (Razafindrakoto and Roubaud 2007).

This data collection work will not yield results without associated programs in which researchers from developing countries, especially Africa, participate. On this continent where poverty and the informal economy are at their most intense and where research activities are the least developed, we need to work to gradually bring the information and research on labor markets into step with the wealth of information and research found in this area in Latin America (where the many panel surveys have made for substantial progress with our understanding of the mechanisms at work) and, to a lesser extent, in Asia.

"Good Jobs" and "Bad Jobs"

All of the issues raised above share a common denominator: the "good jobs" versus "bad jobs" dilemma, described in the *World Development Report 2013* (World Bank 2012). Beyond the imperative to create jobs to tackle the paradox of "jobless growth," the nature of the jobs provided is at the core of the development agenda. Identifying and promoting good jobs is far from trivial. Doing so depends on the objective sought: increasing short-term or long-term employment, improving individual or collective welfare, raising living standards, increasing productivity, enhancing social cohesion. For example, some jobs may enhance the monetary outcomes and well-being of the people who hold them but hurt long-term development (rent-based jobs). Similarly, good jobs in one country may be bad jobs in another (low-technology jobs). Trade-offs are involved. Creating (some) jobs at any cost is not the best solution.

The frontier between good jobs and bad jobs is fuzzy, and the priority in terms of policy promotion is not straightforward. Some authors claim that creating good jobs may have an eviction effect on global job creation, a point put in a provocative way by Teal (2012) in his blog post "Why We Need More Bad Jobs (and Fewer Good Ones)." Teal argues that the creation of protected jobs with better pay increases poverty, because it requires a lot of capital. The choice is simple: "You either use that capital to benefit the lucky (well-educated) few who get these good jobs or you use it to create more 'bad' jobs for the many."

Even if one can see in this extreme view the classical argument of the rhetoric of reaction developed by A. Hirschman in his seminal book (1991), it warrants attention. Is the lack of capital responsible for labor underemployment in Africa (DIAL 2007)? It is tempting to accept this explanation. Between 1960 and 1994, when average annual investment outside Africa was 15.6 percent of gross domestic product, Africa invested just 9.6 percent (Hoeffler 2002). The result was a lower stock of capital per worker than in other continents. Some authors have suggested that this lack of investment is the main source of underdevelopment in Africa (Barro and Lee 1994; Collier and Gunning 1999). However, investment is endogenous. Several recent studies suggest that when its endogeneity is taken into account and the effect of other parameters, such as quality of governance, is controlled for, the long-term effect of investment on growth tends to disappear in Africa. An increase in investment flows would therefore probably not be sufficient to increase the growth rate and reduce underemployment (Hoeffler 2002; Devarajan, Easterly, and Pack 2003).

Whatever the cause of underemployment in Sub-Saharan Africa, informal sector jobs are at the core of this discussion. In Sub-Saharan Africa—and low-income countries in general—the informal sector is a key part of structural transformation. Lewis's (1954) dualistic view of the job market does not accurately describe how modernization will occur. There will be no shortcut between agricultural jobs and formal sector jobs: modernization will occur through an increase in informal sector jobs in most countries, spurred by demographic, urban, and off-farm transitions. This transformation is also an opportunity, because informal sector jobs are more productive, pay higher wages, and yield higher job satisfaction than smallholder farm jobs (Haggblade, Hazell, and Reardon 2010; Fox and Pimhidzai 2011), including in high-growth economies where agriculture is exceptionally dynamic, such as Vietnam (Cling and others 2010; Razafindrakoto, Roubaud, and Wachsberger 2012). Even compared with formal sector jobs, informal sector jobs cannot always be considered "bad jobs." The question is thus not quantity versus quality or formal versus informal sector jobs. A multipronged strategy should be promoted by facilitating transitions from both agriculture to off-farm jobs and from informal sector jobs to formal sector jobs. At the same time, increasing productivity and protection for informal sector (and agricultural) workers is imperative.

How best to improve productivity and working conditions remains unclear. What is certain is that employment policy should broaden its focus beyond the formal sector.

References

AfDB (African Development Bank), ECA (Economic Commission for Africa), OECD (Organisation for Economic Co-operation and Development), and UNDP (United Nations Development Progamme). 2012. "Promoting Youth Employment." In *African Economic Outlook 2012*, 99–176. Paris: OECD Publishing.

Antoine, P., M. Razafindrakoto, and R. Roubaud. 2001. "Contraints de rester jeune? Evolution de l'insertion dans trois capitales africaines: Dakar, Yaoundé, Antananarivo." *Autrepart* 18: 17–36.

Bargain, O., and P. Kwenda. 2011. "Earnings Structures, Informal Employment, and Self-Employment: New Evidence from Brazil, Mexico and South Africa." *Review of Income and Wealth* 57 (May): 100–22.

Barro, R., and J. W. Lee. 1994. "Losers and Winners in Economic Growth." In *Proceedings of the Annual World Bank Conference on Development Economics 1993*, ed. M. Bruno, 267–314. Washington, DC: World Bank.

Cling, J.-P., Thç Thu Huyçn Nguyçn, Hçu Chí Nguyçn, Ngçc Trâm Phan, M. Razafindrakoto, and F. Roubaud. 2010. *The Informal Sector in Vietnam: A Focus on Hanoi and Ho Chi Minh City*. Hanoi: Gioi Edition.

Cling J.-P., M. Razafindrakoto, and F. Roubaud. 2005. "Export Processing Zones in Madagascar: A Success Story under Threat?" *World Development* 33 (5): 785–803.

———. 2009. "Export Processing Zones in Madagascar: The Impact of Dismantling of Clothing Quotas on Employment and Labor Standards." In *Globalization, Wages, and the Quality of Jobs*, ed. R. Robertson, D. Brown, G. Pierre, and M. L. Sanchez-Puerta, 237–64. Washington, DC: World Bank.

Collier, P., and J. W. Gunning. 1999. "Explaining African Economic Performance." *Journal of Economic Literature* 7 (1): 64–111.

Devarajan, S., W. Easterly, and H. Pack. 2003. "Low Investment Is Not the Constraint on African Development." *Economic Development and Cultural Change* 51 (3): 547–71.

DIAL (Développement, Institutions et Mondialisation). 2007. "Youth and Labour Markets in Africa: A Literature Review." Working Paper 49, Département de la Recherche, Agence Française de Développement, Paris.

Falco, P., A. Kerr, N. Rankin, J. Sandefur, and F. Teal. 2011. "The Returns to Formality and Informality in Urban Africa." *Labour Economics* 18(Supplement 1): S23–S31.

Fox, L., and O. Pimhidzai. 2011. "Is Informality Welfare-Enhancing Structural Transformation? Evidence from Uganda." Policy Research Working Paper 5866, World Bank, Washington, DC.

Glick, P., and F. Roubaud. 2006. "Export Processing Zone Expansion in Madagascar: What Are the Labor Market and Gender Impacts?" *Journal of African Economies* 15 (4): 722–56.

Goux, D., and E. Maurin. 2007. "Close Neighbours Matter: Neighbourhood Effects on Early Performance at School." *Economic Journal* 117 (523): 1193–215.

Grimm, M., R. van der Hoeven, and J. Lay. 2011. *Unlocking Potential: Tackling Economic, Institutional and Social Constraints of Informal Entrepreneurship in Sub-Saharan Africa: Main Findings and Policy Conclusions.* International Institute of Social Science (ISS), The Hague. http://www.iss.nl/research/research_programmes/informality/publications/.

Grimm, M., R. van der Hoeven, J. Lay, and F. Roubaud. 2012. *Neubewertung des informellen Sektors und Unternehmertums in Sub-Sahara Africa.* DIW Vierteljahreshefte zur Wirtschaftsforschung, German Institute for Economic Research, Berlin.

Gubert, F., and F. Roubaud. 2006. "Le financement de très petites entreprises urbaines: étude d'impact de microfinance à Antananarivo (Madagascar)." In *Le développement face à la pauvreté*, ed. B. Decaluwe, F. Mourji, and P. Plane, 167–89. Paris: AUF/Economica/CRDI.

Haggblade, S., P. Hazell, and T. Reardon. 2010. "The Rural Non-Farm Economy: Prospects for Growth and Poverty Reduction." *World Development* 38 (11): 1429–41.

Herrera, J., C. J. Nordman, X. Oudin, and J.-M. Wachsberger. 2012. "Révision des questionnaires des enquêtes-emploi en vue de mieux enregistrer les différentes dimensions du travail décent." An output of the EC-funded RECAP project implemented by the International Training Centre of the International Labour Organization, Turin.

Hirschman, A. O. 1991. *The Rhetoric of Reaction: Perversity, Futility, Jeopardy.* Cambridge, MA: Belknap Press.

Hoeffler, A. 2002. "The Augmented Solow Model and the African Growth Debate." *Oxford Bulletin of Economics and Statistics* 64 (2): 135–58.

ILO (International Labour Organization). 2010. *Global Employment Trends for Youth.* Geneva: ILO.

ILO (International Labour Organization) and IMF (International Monetary Fund). 2010. "Challenges of Growth, Employment and Social Cohesion." Discussion Document, Joint ILO–IMF conference in cooperation with the Office of the Prime Minister of Norway, Geneva.

Ioannides, Y. M. 2002. "Residential Neighborhood Effects." *Regional Science and Urban Economics* 32 (2): 145–65.

Lewis, W. A. 1954. "Economic Development with Unlimited Supplies of Labour." *Manchester School of Economics and Social Studies* 22 (May): 139–91.

Maloney, W. 2004. "Informality Revisited." *World Development* 32 (7): 1159–78.

Nguyen, H. C., C. J. Nordman, and F. Roubaud. 2011. "Who Suffers the Penalty? A Panel Data Analysis of Earnings Gaps in Vietnam." DIAL Working Paper 2011–14, Développement, Institutions et Mondialisation, Paris.

Nordman, C. J., F. Rakotomanana, and F. Roubaud. 2012. "Informal versus Formal: A Panel Data Analysis of Earnings Gaps in Madagascar." DIAL Working Paper 2012–12, Développement, Institutions et Mondialisation, Paris.

Razafindrakoto, M., and F. Roubaud. 2001. "Vingt ans de réforme de la fonction publique à Madagascar." *Autrepart* 20: 43–60.

———. 2007. "Towards a Better Monitoring of the Labor Market." In *Vietnam Development Report 2008: Social Protection.* Hanoi: World Bank.

Razafindrakoto, M., F. Roubaud, and J. M. Wachsberger. 2012. "Travailler dans le secteur informel: choix ou contrainte? Une analyse de la satisfaction dans l'emploi au Vietnam." In *L'économie informelle dans les pays en développement*, ed. J.-P. Cling, S. Lagrée, M. Razafindrakoto, and F. Roubaud, 47–66. Paris: Edition de l'AFD.

Roubaud, F. 1992. "Proposals for Incorporating the Informal Sector into National Accounts." *Interstat* 6: 5–26.

———. 1994. *L'économie informelle au Mexique: de la sphère domestique à la dynamique macro-économique*. Paris: Karthala/Orstom [Spanish version: *La economía informal en México: de la esfera doméstica a la dinámica macroeconómica*. Mexico City: Fondo de Cultura Económica.]

Teal, F. 2012. "Policies for Jobs in Africa: Why We Need More Bad Jobs (and Fewer Good Ones)." CSAE Blog, March 1, Centre for the Study of African Economies, Department of Economics, Oxford University. http://blogs.csae.ox.ac.uk/2012/03/policies-for-jobs-in-africa-why-we-need-more-bad-jobs-and-fewer-good-ones/.

World Bank. 2011. *Doing Business 2012: Doing Business in a More Transparent World*. Washington, DC: World Bank.

———. 2012. *World Development Report 2013: Jobs*. Washington, DC: World Bank.

Index

Page numbers with the italicized letter *b, f, m, n,* or *t* refer to boxes, figures, maps, notes, tables, respectively.

1-2-3 surveys, 2–5, *4t, 6t,* 9–11, *9b,* 12*m,* 30*n5,* 399–402, 404. *See also* Sub-Saharan Africa and studies

A

Abidjan, Côte d'Ivoire
  1-2-3 surveys in, 11
  earnings and, 63, 70, 279, 281, 284–86
  education and, 168–69, 171, 182, 189
  employment and, 42–44, 43–44, 49
  heterogeneity of labor markets and, 17
  homogeneity of labor markets and, 17
  household composition and, 40
  inequalities and, 252, 257, 262, 263, 268*n4,* 268*n7*
  informal employment and, 61
  informal sector and, 60
  job prospects and, 76
  job satisfaction and, 113, 116, 120, 126–29
  job structure and, 55–57
  migration and, 305–11, 306, 316–20
  return migration and, 328, 333
  returns to qualifications and, 187
  segmentation and, 195, 209, 214–15, 215–16
  seniors in labor force and, 374, 375–77, 381–84, 386

  sociodemographic characteristics and, 39–40, 391, 393*n6*
  unemployment and, 52
  vulnerability in employment and, 138, 154, 155, 156*n5*
  work-school trade-off among children and, 331, 352, 357, 368–69, 370*n3,* 370*n6*
AfDB (African Development Bank), 402
Africa. *See specific cities and countries*
African Development Bank (AfDB), 402
AFRISTAT (Observatoire économique et statistique d'Afrique Subsaharienne), 373
age bracket, and composition of working labor force, 62–63, 62*f*
Agence pour la Sécurité de la Navigation Aérienne en Afrique (ASECNA), 324*n8*
Akresh, R., 367
Alderman, H., 196
Antananarivo, Madagascar
  1-2-3 surveys in, 11, 130*n4*
  domestic work and, 224, 229
  earnings and, 54–55, 63, 66
  education and, 40
  employment and, 44
  heterogeneity of labor markets and, 17
  informal employment and, 61